ONE STEP BEYOND

CHRIS MOON

ONE STEP BEYOND

PAN BOOKS

First published 1999 by Macmillan

This edition published 2000 by Pan Books
an imprint of Macmillan Publishers Ltd
25 Eccleston Place, London SW1W 9NF
Basingstoke and Oxford
Associated companies throughout the world
www.macmillan.co.uk

ISBN 0 330 37155 X

Grateful acknowledgement is made to William Heinemann,
an imprint of Random House UK Limited, for permission to reprint
excerpts from *To Kill a Mockingbird* by Harper Lee.

1 3 5 7 9 8 6 4 2

A CIP catalogue record for this book is available from
the British Library.

Typeset by SetSystems Ltd, Saffron Walden, Essex
Printed and bound in Great Britain by
Mackays of Chatham plc, Chatham, Kent

It is not the critic who counts
Nor the man who points out how
the strong man stumbles
Or where the doer of deeds
Could have done better.
The credit belongs to the man
Who is actually in the arena;
Whose face is marred by dust
And sweat and blood;
Who knows great enthusiasm,
Great devotion and the triumph
of achievement.
And who, at the worst, if he fails
At least fails while daring greatly –
So that his place shall never be
With those odd and timid souls
Who know neither victory nor defeat.
You've never lived until you've almost died.
For those who have had to fight for it
Life has truly a flavour
The protected shall never know.

THEODORE ROOSEVELT
'Citizenship in a Republic',
23 April 1910, the Sorbonne, Paris

CONTENTS

ACKNOWLEDGEMENTS

I must thank my literary agent Mark Lucas for his good advice and friendship.

Thanks also to Mr Livingstone, Dr Gill and my lecturers at Leicester University, Gordon Stevens (writer) and Simon Ashenden (primary school friend and English teacher) for their consistent encouragement.

The events described in this book are, to the best of my recollection, as they happened. In a few cases I have changed names to respect the privacy of my friends.

Owing to constraints of time and space it has not been possible to cover everything. Many horrific and wonderful moments remain unreported, but I must state my admiration for those who work in every field to alleviate suffering.

Thanks to everyone at Macmillan, who've been wonderful, even though I can't type as fast as everyone else. (I now have a high-tech adaptation to speed things up – a piece of Blu-Tack on the end of my hook.)

I've always noticed authors frequently thank their wives. Now I know why. Thank you to my wife, Alison, and of course my family and friends.

FOREWORD

There have been many tragedies in my country. During the Pol Pot period I saw unspeakable horrors, many of my friends and family were killed. Life has been hard, but I was lucky that I was able to teach myself English and find work to support my family. Many Cambodian people struggle to get enough rice to survive, and there is still much suffering and poverty, but our country and its people are beautiful. I am nearly forty years old, I have a wife and two wonderful children and I am Cambodian. I am proud of this and the work that I do with my colleagues from the HALO Trust, clearing mines.

When I first met Chris Moon I saw a strong, determined man who worked tirelessly to clear mines, ensure the safety of his staff and help the Cambodian people. He was very fit and went running every day. He had very high standards, rigidly followed procedures and never asked anyone to do anything he would not do himself, always leading by example. He quickly earned the respect, loyalty and affection of his staff. He has a great sense of humour, a strong sense of right and wrong, and a deep concern for the disadvantaged and disabled that is exceptional.

In spite of many requests to clear the village, and guarantees of security from all factions, the Khmer Rouge kidnapped us. Everyone was surprised. The local people were told we would be interrogated and killed in the forest. As we ate with the Khmer Rouge I thought it would be our last meal. Chris did not give up; he stayed calm and tried to understand them. By the grace of God, against all odds, we negotiated our release. Throughout that period we understood the true nature of loneliness, friendship and trust, and now we have the bond of brothers.

I do not know why bad things happen to good people, but I do know that good people can change things and by their example inspire us. As Chris says, 'We can all make a difference and help someone.'

When I first heard he had been blown up, I did not believe it; he is one of the most careful people I know. I knew he would never suffer from self-pity and that he would fight to overcome his injuries. His story is one of courage, compassion and the triumph of the human spirit over adversity. Step by step he fought to regain his health, and then to raise funds for mine clearance and for those injured by mines. I asked him to tell people about our work and he has.

In Cambodia it is possible for us to clear the mines that are ruining lives, but we need help to be able to do this. If you would like to support our work we would be most grateful. Thank you very much.

HOUN SAMRIN

HALO
PO Box 7712
London, SW1V 3ZA

1

PROLOGUE

We arrive at the site at dusk. I want to talk to the team leader alone. I have asked the operations officer to interview the deminers and section commanders. From the tented camp we walk through the growing darkness into the town. The glow of oil lamps shows through glassless windows of the shabby grey bungalows.

We occupy a table in front of the small stall that sells tinned sardines and Coca-Cola and sit by the flickering orange light of an oil lamp. Apart from the sound of the night insects and the presence of the mute stallholder we are completely alone.

'Saul, please tell me exactly what happened.'

Saul comes from Southern Mozambique. He was recruited from the Mozambican army and is Sandhurst trained. He lifts his head back slightly and I can see from his wide, white staring eyes that he is reliving the nightmare of the day.

'Oh, Sir,' he breathes, 'it was very terrible.'

He shakes his head as if trying to dislodge the images from his mind. He opens his mouth then pauses before speaking. His teeth look almost fluorescent in the darkness that surrounds us, but there is no trace of a smile.

'Señor Orlando he was working well. He always work well. In the morning he found three PMNs [old-style Russian mines] in his lane and I destroyed them, no problem. Then he call back to the number two that he had found another PMN and that he was going to prod to the side of it.'

Saul sits silently as he tries to work his way through the sequence of events. The PMN is brown with a black top, the size of a small tin of sweets. It's as if he is coming to terms with the brutal, destructive power of the simple device for the first time. 'Then a second later there was a flash and a very large explosion. He was blown backwards. Me, the section commander and the medics were there very quickly. He was very badly injured.'

Saul shudders and leans forward. He narrows his eyes as if in deep thought and says, 'When he was hurt he mumbled. It could have been about something by the side of it. Another mine, a booby trap.'

I make a few notes, then I sit up and gaze out into the African night. The heat is intolerable. They say there will be a storm soon.

'Saul, you know I'm not interested in blaming anybody. I just have to find out exactly what happened. If there was an error of drill we can correct it. If it was a booby trap we must develop a new technique. Is there anything else you can tell me?'

He shakes his head. 'The bottom of that lane is a very bad place, Sir. A very bad place.' As he speaks I see his eyes are full of fear.

I nod. 'Tomorrow morning, when we have established communication with Quelimaine, I will investigate the bottom of the safety lane before we allow any of the deminers back to work.'

As we walk back to the camp in the darkness we stamp our feet heavily. Saul tells me that the vibrations will scare the snakes away. At night they come to the side of the road to prey on the rats and mice that live here. The people in the town say there are a lot around here. I find it hard to believe Saul's repeated assurances that the snakes are more afraid of me than I am of them.

*

The call had come through that afternoon.

The woman pointed at the map board and paused. Above me the electric ceiling fan rotated methodically, but did little to reduce the overbearing East African heat. The low concrete building felt like an oven. Sam, the operations officer, and the other three Mozambicans worked silently at their desks. A trickle of sweat made its way down the side of my face. I waited for her to speak again but she was haunted by memories.

'The fighting in this area was bad, very bad. The soldiers put many mines down to protect the town, but RENAMO still took it. The villages here, here and here were destroyed. Many people were mutilated and killed.'

She fell silent again; lost in the unspeakable horror of a two-decade civil war.

The radio crackled into life, an urgent voice. One of our guys had been injured on operations. I excused myself as politely as I could and went to stand behind the radio operator. This hadn't happened in the eighteen months the project had been running, but everyone knew what they had to do. The CASEVAC aircraft and the hospital were being contacted. People were moving fast.

The loudspeaker rattled as the team leader sent his report. I had to give the man on the ground time to do his job. I'd just got back from a recce in the northernmost province and on my return journey I'd had a feeling that something was wrong.

After a while I took the mike from the operator and clarified a few details. It was important to stay calm, in control. I tried to make things as easy as possible. I knew how the team leader felt. He was fighting chaos, panic and perhaps even his own fear while trying to restore order. He was struggling to do his best among the blood and blasted flesh, aware that he would be judged later by those who were not there.

Outside the gate I saw townspeople go about their business like drowsy soldier ants in the heat of the day. I could feel their sadness.

I got my colleague Rupert, an ex-Para and qualified medic, to take care of the casualty and find Marjolaine, one of the aid agency doctors. Rupert's good when the shit hits the fan. Once that was done my job was to work out what had gone wrong.

As we drove through the outskirts of town the Land Rover lurched and bumped across the large sandy potholes in the asphalt road. Soon there were more potholes than asphalt and then the little that was left merged into the sand. My nostrils twitched at the smell of the rotting rubbish under the nearby trees.

*

The sun is high in the sky and it's hot.

I've quartered the area with the operations officer, team leader and section commanders. Most of the minefield has been cleared. Neatly-painted white sticks starkly mark the safety lanes. The vegetation is cut as short as possible to allow metal detectors to sweep close to the ground. The mined sector is obvious because of the scrub, low bushes and long thick grass.

I'm standing in the control point, about 250 metres from the road. There are four large mango trees that provide welcome shade for the first-aid point, the radio vehicle and the explosive and equipment stores. I lift my rucksack easily off my shoulders with one hand and let it drop back into the Land Rover. I feel good. Most evenings I run for at least an hour, despite the heat. I've found my niche. I never have to ask the blokes to do anything I wouldn't do myself.

I ease my head through the two elastic straps that hold the blue canvas covered kevlar apron in place and fasten the Velcro belt. I pull down the groin protector flap on the front of the apron and pick up the metal detector in my right hand. As I do I look around me. Eight villagers have died slow, dirty deaths in this place. I remember the look in Saul's eyes.

I move forward into the safety lane. Eight hundred metres away I can see the wrecked buildings that edge the airfield. Their skeletal roofs and shabby grey concrete walls show through the trees, decaying remains of a shattered Portuguese colonial dream. I lower my visor.

I sweep the metal detector over the parched, red-brown earth. At the bottom of the lane I examine the seat of Orlando's explosion. The hole in the ground is about thirty-five centimetres deep and the blast has cleared everything for about a metre around it. I pass the detector carefully around the edge of the crater, prod gently and sift through the soil.

These mines were laid by FRELIMO (government) soldiers to protect them from the RENAMO rebels. They mainly used Russian PMNs with 240 grams of TNT, enough to blow off one lower leg completely and often damage the other enough to necessitate amputation – if you're lucky. In remote places like this people normally die before they get to hospital.

I continue the process, prodding gently and sifting, prodding and sifting. The other mine found here is the Portuguese 969, a toe blower. Eighty grams of cast trialene explosive designed to mangle a foot, virtually guaranteeing below knee amputation. The sun's high. I feel sweat prickle on my cheeks and in my armpits.

It takes nearly all morning to do the investigation. I have found fragments of the PMN that Orlando reported finding.

They are clearly identifiable. I have also found a few tiny fragments of green plastic. I place them carefully in a polythene bag and put them in my right pocket.

There could have been two mines here. Orlando located the first and as he was prodding to uncover it he must have initiated the second. It would explain the detonation and the severity of his injuries. A large blast. Two mines. I believe I have the answer, but I still feel uneasy. I think of Saul's description of blood and blasted limbs and something doesn't feel right.

As I take a step forward I see the fragments of casing with unnatural clarity and remember the smell of amputation from the hospital in Cambodia. My heart beats a little faster. It's time to take a break.

As I stand up my senses heighten. I turn around and step carefully along the safety lane. I look around and strain my ears as I walk back a few paces to the hopelessly inadequate shade of a palm tree. There is no escape from the searing sun. I take off my visor and wipe the sweat off my forehead with the already soaked sleeve of my cotton boiler suit.

Near my feet I see a crusty brown patch on the soil that is covered in flies. It must be Orlando's blood. I think of his agony in the confusion of blasted limbs as he felt his blood trickle from his body into the dirt. Base told me on the radio that he died a few hours ago. I am surprised he was able to hold on to life for so long.

About five metres in front of me a small whirlwind turns through the minefield. It's a twister. They're quite common in hot climates. As the small spiral of wind twists its demented circular jig it lifts bits of dead grass and leaves. I remember seeing them in the dry season in Cambodia. It has unpleasant associations. The last time I saw something like this was on the edge of a remote road near the Thai border.

I had arrived just after a road worker was killed. He was clearing a ditch by the side of the road. The local people didn't think there were any mines there. They were wrong and a mine he struck with his shovel melted the metal into his face.

I turn to go and then I feel it. I don't believe it. I actually feel cold. In the middle of the heat of the African day how can I feel cold? A shiver runs down my spine and the hairs on the back of my neck rise. Suddenly, I'm frightened.

Ahead of me at the bottom of the lane there is something vile and evil moving towards me. I have felt this before. I can only describe it as obscene and utter blackness. I must have had too much sun. I'm dehydrated. Be reasonable.

I know I must not stay here. I am starting to feel sick. My guts ache. I turn quickly and start to walk back down the safety lane.

I take three paces and hear the loudest bang I've ever heard.

*

The noise of the explosion is ringing in my ears.

Everything is calm. It's strange how the silence is so loud after an explosion. I'm lying on my chest. I feel fine. No pain.

It was very close. My mind races. I know that nobody else is carrying out demolitions here so it must be mortar fire from the Khmer Rouge. Wow, that one was a bit close, I think I'll take Pol Pot off my Christmas card list again.

As I look up I can see the closely cropped grass. There is something wrong. This is bush grass, African grass. I am not in Cambodia. I raise my hand. It's bleeding. I can't move it. Cautiously I start to raise myself. I know the body produces endorphins in time of traumatic injury. I won't have pain for a minute or so.

I must follow the correct SOP.

Prepare yourself.

It must have been a mine.

I turn over carefully and sit up. My hand is mangled and bleeding like a squashed strawberry.

I look down at my right leg.

The air is sharp with the smell of the explosion and my burnt and blasted flesh.

I stare.

My lower leg has completely gone. The foot has vanished. There is just a finger of splintered yellow bone surrounded by ragged pink flesh.

I am surprised that my bone is so yellow. I always thought it was white.

2

REMEMBRANCE

I am kneeling in a fire position behind a pile of grey concrete blocks. They are stacked two deep near the doorway of the partly constructed building. The walls are nearly complete and the shell of the outhouse gives good cover. I have a perfect line of sight to the area around the tree. I strain my eyes and try to keep perfectly still. My rifle is pulled tightly into my shoulder and I'm ready to shoot.

It seems strange to think I've been practising so long for this moment and now I start to wonder whether or not I'm doing the right thing. I strain my ears. Can I hear movement? My heartbeat sounds like a drum pounding inside my head. I know that nobody else can hear it and I try to breathe quietly. I just hope the others remain silent.

I try to control my breathing. I pull the rifle tighter with my left hand. My right hand is relaxed and my forefinger rests lightly on the trigger guard. The safety catch is off and the realization I might have to shoot makes my heart beat faster and the adrenalin flow.

The jagged edges of the concrete blocks are digging into my arm and leg, but it doesn't matter. I'm covered in cement dust from the newly-laid concrete floor. I had to crawl through it to get here. It came from an open bag of cement just inside the doorway that's spread across the floor. I can see it out of the corner of my eye.

The warm May breeze swirls into and around the building and I squint to try to keep the dust out of my eyes.

In the distance I can hear a car. It's a long way off and I know I can't be seen. I hope it doesn't scare them away. Now things are so close I cannot bear the thought of failure. My stomach is full of butterflies and I take a deep breath.

I can hear birdsong. I look down the sights expectantly and wait. I struggle to control my breathing and try to allow the rifle to point naturally in the area of the target, just as I have always been told.

Sparrows chirrup in a nearby bush and I'm pleased. If the birds are singing and moving around me then I'm unlikely to be noticed. I watch and wait; the warm May sun on my face. I see a slight movement in the fir tree, or am I imagining it? I strain my eyes and put my finger on the trigger ready to squeeze.

I pause.

I'm ready to shoot.

More cement dust blows into my eyes and I have to squint again. The branch moves. My heart misses a beat and I just start to squeeze the trigger. Then I release it because I can see it's only the wind.

I'm starting to get pins and needles in my right leg and my right foot's going to sleep. I try to wiggle my toes. I decide to adjust my position, slowly take my right hand off the weapon and gently raise my right knee. I brush my hand under my knee and flick out the small stone that was digging in. As I look down the sights of the rifle I wonder how much longer I'm going to have to wait.

Then I see the branch move again. Everything is calm and there's a lull in the wind. My finger tightens on the trigger and I watch like a hawk.

An eye stares at me from among the leaves. I take aim just above the eye. I control my breathing and when I have perfect aim I squeeze the trigger gently. It is all happening much more slowly than I thought it would. My ears register the crack of the rifle and my shoulder absorbs the recoil.

I wait for a short while. I watch, in limbo. There's no movement. I think fast. I've been watching all the time. Ever since I squeezed the trigger I tried to keep my eyes open.

I look around and decide to move. I clutch the rifle and start running across the rough ground. As I get closer I see the lifeless body beneath the tree and feel exhilaration.

Then I pause, realizing what I've done. The body feels soft and warm.

He made me do it. I tried everything. Warnings, scare tactics, bits of tin foil on string, but he and the others kept on going. This was the only way to stop the pigeons eating the newly planted greens. I'm ten and I'm proud of my vegetable garden. I'm the only one at school who has his own garden.

I've killed the pigeon with one well-aimed shot. Now I'm a man. I can show my Dad. This is first blood. As I pick up the limp, soft body and try not to retch I wonder exactly what kind of man does this sort of thing and if I really want to be like him?

We live a long way off the road and our house is in the country. We're really lucky because we have a large garden and a small paddock. A large field separates us from our nearest neighbours. Dad tied a large rope to the tree. It's nearly thirty feet high. I can climb all the way to the top. My sister, Kate, can't.

I'm only allowed to use the air rifle in this part of the garden, among the trees. I usually shoot targets. We made a small wooden stand for them at the bottom of the hill. I always have to fire into the hillside and think about where the pellet will land.

I keep the weapon locked in a cupboard. I'm allowed to keep the key. I always hide it in the same place on the window-sill behind the curtain. Dad suggested I keep it there so I don't lose it.

A few months ago he gave me the gun. It belonged to Granddad, who used it to shoot pests in his garden. I always shot targets under Dad's supervision. One day he said the rifle was mine as long as I followed the rules. I have to keep it clean, locked in the cupboard when I'm not using it and I'm not allowed to leave it lying about or use it irresponsibly.

When I asked him what I was allowed to shoot he said, 'Anything at all, as long as there's a good reason and you can explain it.'

I don't want to shoot sparrows. They're too small, you can't eat them and they don't do any harm. Shooting songbirds would be wrong because we like them. I can never get close enough to the rabbits to be in range and when they come in the garden to eat the vegetables they run off before I can lift the rifle.

It looks like it's got to be the pigeons, because around here they're pests. Besides that, the gits have got it coming to them for eating my cabbage plants.

I always try to stick to the rules. But, once I did something very stupid. A friend from school came over. He wanted to see how powerful the gun was. He suggested I shoot it into the side of the old green plastic watering can behind the garage. I did and the pellet broke the brittle plastic. One day Dad found it and summoned me.

He pointed and asked, 'Why?'

I couldn't give him a reason. He didn't hit me hard. He just tapped my shoulder and told me off. He took the rifle away for two weeks. I remember large hot salty tears running down the side of my face. What hurt was the realization of my own stupidity. I'd let Dad down and I'd let myself down too.

*

Captain Wiltshire was killed in action while serving with the Seventh Mounted Infantry near Lindley. I picture him as a dashing hero in crisp khaki uniform and highly-polished brown boots who left this quiet village for war with dreams of adventure and glory.

He was a bell ringer. His family must have been wealthy. The others from our village who didn't come home from the World Wars are remembered on the timeless stone memorial at the church gate. It wasn't so long ago. Most of the people here remember it.

The plaque is fixed to the white, eastern wall of the church, a silent tribute to the captain's courage and his family's grief. On the bottom of the shiny brass plate it says *It is sweet and glorious to die for one's country.* He would have been one of the first and best to go. I often hear the old soldiers say, 'It was the best who went first.'

It is Remembrance Sunday and because I'm in the choir I sit in the front pew. I enjoy singing and although I'm ten everyone here treats me like a grown-up. After church I'll have to take off my cassock and surplice quickly so I can look at the retired soldiers' medals before we go home.

Colonel Brown seems to have the most. A long line are pinned to his jacket. They overlap from his lapel to his armpit. Some have startlingly beautiful ribbons of shiny silk, all the colours of the rainbow. A few of them on the left-hand side of the long row are in the shape of a cross, but most of them are round. The one on the end is a silver cross with a white and purple ribbon.

He's a hero; wounded in action in the Second World War. He's enormously tall and always wears tweed suits and his regimental tie. He was in the infantry, involved in heavy fighting in Europe. He left the army a long time ago and has just retired from his job because he had a stroke. Sometimes his face looks a bit droopy. He tells people he got his medals

for being in the right place at the right time and doesn't like
to talk about it.

He walks with great difficulty using a stick because his leg
doesn't work properly. We often see him walking between here
and the next village. He does it every day to try to make his
leg work again. He always smiles and cheerfully says hello.

I think he's great, he must have been really tough when he
was a soldier. The fighting must have been exciting. Sometimes
when he talks to me we discuss tree climbing and the brown
trout in the stream. I've met his grandchildren, because they
come and stay with him sometimes. They're older than me,
but they're not snobby and always say hello.

When he meets ladies in the village he stops and raises his
hat. His wife is usually on his arm. She helps him discreetly to
walk. Everyone thinks Mrs Brown is marvellous because she
looks after him and is always cheerful and happy. They're a
good team.

One of the best things about being in the choir is that I get
to sit next to Anne. She's the prettiest girl in school and even
though she's a year older we sometimes go to youth club
together. The people in the choir are nice. I've been here for
two years. I can remember a lot of the words to the hymns so
I don't need to read them. Sometimes I get it wrong, but
nobody seems to notice.

The village church is made from stone, flint and oak. The
walls are really thick. In some places they're wider than I am
tall. The outside is hard flint to protect it from the weather,
but inside the wall between the stone buttresses is a mixture of
chalk and stone, an early form of concrete. The church was
built in Norman times and modified in the fifteenth century
when high, elegant arches were added and the roof extended.
The dark strong oak cross-supports offer a home to three bats.
I'm in the front pew and the angle is just right for me to see

them, but I don't think anyone else can. They look small and furry like mice and have wings like leather.

My Dad says they hang upside down and I wonder what happens if they get diarrhoea? I've seen them just as it gets dark flying around the garden. They're strange animals, I don't think they'd make good pets. Sometimes we can see their droppings on the yellow aisle carpet.

The church roof is covered with lead. The gypsies sometimes steal it to sell for scrap. When it happens everyone gets excited, the police come to the village, talk to people and look up at the church roof. Now they've put a special slippery grey paint that doesn't wash off on the drainpipes to stop them getting up there.

The church is built in the shape of a cross. On the western side, a square stone tower houses a spooky stone spiral staircase with thin arrow slits instead of windows. It leads to four enormous dirty bronze bells mounted on rock-solid oak beams. The top of the tower houses a flagpole that proudly sports the Union flag. My friend Simon's dad is an architect who does church repairs. He took us up there once when he was doing a survey to check the lead hadn't been stolen.

At the eastern end there is a stained-glass window. The morning sunshine makes the figures come alive. Jesus is in a red robe holding a round golden ball with a cross on top, like the Queen has. He's surrounded by a selection of saints and disciples who must have been good because they've got haloes and wings.

The rest of the church is full of shiny, hard, dark oak pews. The whole place is enormous and bright. The walls are whitewashed, but the solid stone arches and cornerstones are natural grey white limestone.

When I sit in the end of the pew against the stone buttress I'm next to the hole in the wall. During the sermon the temptation to put my finger in between the two stone blocks and scrape out the soft powdery cement is too great. It's like chalk dust. When you scrape it out it leaves a dusty mark on your black cassock that doesn't easily brush off, so it's best to catch it in your surplice then tip it on the floor. Even when grown-ups sit there they do it too.

A few feet to the right of our front pew the large wooden panels and sky-blue painted pipes of the organ reach almost to the roof. As we kneel in prayer I get a chance to have a good look at it. It must be really hard to play. It has two keyboards, foot pedals and all those knobs and levers on the side. It's not surprising the organist is always nervous.

Suddenly a loud blast of wrong notes interrupts the vicar's prayer. I kneel up with a jolt and Hilary, the girl on my right, is so startled she knocks her books off the ledge. As the organist turned round to see if it was time for the silence she put her elbow on the keyboard and then, in fright, both feet on the pedals. I bet it woke up the old lady at the back. I turn my head to see if I can see her. I look quickly to the front. The organist looks like a cat on hot bricks. Glancing at the vicar she whispers, 'Sorry.'

As usual the vicar ignores her and carries on as if nothing has happened. He must be really deaf. I look at Hilary scrabbling around trying to pick up her books and begin to laugh. She looks at me and starts giggling. I turn to Anne on my left and see that she's put her hand over her mouth to hide it, but her eyes shine with laughter. Colonel Brown is smiling at us. When he sees me looking at him he winks.

The organist was turning round to face the same way as the congregation for the two-minute silence. This week we're all wearing a red poppy made from paper to show we remember those killed and wounded in wars. The Royal British Legion collects money to help ex-servicemen and women. Poppies are used because they were the only flowers that grew in the fields of Flanders where the worst of the First World War battles took place. If everyone was fighting I don't suppose anyone had time to grow flowers.

Now it's time to remember.

Every year I'm surprised how long two minutes is.

We all stand. The vicar says, 'We will remember,' and we repeat it.

This is serious. I mustn't laugh. I should be trying to remember; not just people from our country, but all the soldiers and civilians who were killed in bombing, shelling or extermination camps. It's hard to believe there were places like that.

There is silence.

I look back at the memorial plaque and wonder what it was like for Captain Wiltshire at Lindley. I've seen war on television and can imagine the boom of artillery shells, the rattle of machine-gun fire and men shouting. In the old days they did some terrible things. They made horses fight.

Perhaps things would fall silent as they waited to go over the top. God was on their side and although a few might be nervous, I expect most would have been looking forward to doing their duty. They had to do it to protect their families and villages like ours. There would have been a whistle blast, panic, excitement and confusion. I can imagine the captain calmly drawing his revolver and shouting the order to charge.

I expect he bought his officer's revolver from Whaley and Co, which is on the corner of the market square in Salisbury, five miles from the village. My Dad lived in Salisbury when he was a boy and can remember it. He says the wooden shop front of the Military Tailor and Gentlemen's Outfitter has been repainted a few times, but it's still like it was in the First World War. It has large plate glass-windows with tweed jackets, regimental ties, riding stuff and brown trilbys on display.

At the outbreak of the First World War Granddad was

working in Canada. He'd been in the cavalry, but left because he could see no need to stay a soldier. The Boer War was forgotten and Europe was enjoying a brief period of peace. He read of the outbreak of war, immediately settled his affairs and set sail for England. He returned briefly to the family farm, left his sister to look after their parents and rejoined the army, taking his younger brother with him. They soon obtained field commissions and Granddad was transferred to the navy. He was posted to the Hood Battalion. The Royal Navy fought on the land as well.

My grandfather saw a lot of action and was lucky to survive. He got an MC and so did his brother for taking ammunition and food to soldiers in the front line while they were under heavy shelling. Apparently it was very muddy and very bloody. Granddad never talked about it.

When Granddad died Dad went through the attic. He found an enormous Webley .45 revolver from the Great War, a big Colt .45 from his days as a cowboy and a fearsome Mauser pistol that a German had surrendered to him. I wanted to keep them, but Dad never let me near them. He said they were very dangerous and Granddad only kept them for old times' sake, so we took them to a police station and handed them back with the certificate. The policeman was rather surprised. He got a big magnifying glass to check the numbers on the bottom of the bullets and filled out lots of forms and said thank you.

Dad doesn't talk about the war either. He was too young to join until it was almost over. Then he was an army commando for two years and says all he did was a lot of cross-country running.

Two minutes is a long time to be silent.

I glance behind me to see Dad standing upright and strong. I try to stand like him.

I look to the left and see Miss Willingford. She shares a

house with Miss Moore. They're spinsters. The men they were going to marry were killed in the Second World War. I heard my Mum talking to her friend about it. Miss Willingford was going to marry a Spitfire pilot, but he was shot down and killed in the Battle of Britain. It made her whole life sad. I can see a tear rolling down the side of her face. She wipes it away with her small white lace handkerchief which she holds in front of her nose.

I look around. I don't understand what's going on and I don't know what I'm supposed to do. I mustn't move or I might knock my books off. I feel a fluttering in my stomach. I turn round slightly so I can see Colonel Brown. His head is bowed and he's looking down. That's unusual because he normally looks straight ahead, noticing everything. Maybe I should bow my head and look down too, perhaps that's what you're supposed to do. I look again at Colonel Brown to get a few tips on looking down and I see a tear run down the side of his face.

It can only be his eye watering because of his illness and his droopy face. A man like Colonel Brown wouldn't cry.

The vicar breaks the silence and I'm able to breathe again. The service is nearly over and during the processional hymn I watch the vicar's every move. My heart beats a little faster. I carry the cross and lead the choir so I have to get it right or they'll all be messed up, including the vicar. The first verse starts.

'Dear Lord and father of mankind forgive our foolish ways . . .'

I know the words off by heart but I don't know if it means the people we fought in the wars were foolish and we're forgiving them or if we're all foolish. I glance at the list of the Ten Commandments above the pulpit. *Thou shalt not kill* catches my eye. War is different though. It's very confusing. I'm going to have to ask somebody to explain it.

At the beginning of the third verse the vicar nods. I feel the adrenalin rise and I walk at a measured pace towards the cross. It's in a holder against the wall and I flick the catch back and simultaneously lift it out with my right hand. Holding it up I turn around and walk forward. The vicar follows me back down the aisle. He stops, allows the choir to walk in front and then we process slowly down the aisle.

I have to get the pace right to get the vicar in to the vestry and with enough time to turn round and face the congregation for the last line of the hymn. We cram into the vestry like sardines, observing a strict code of silence until the final blessing is given and the organist plays the loud going home music. Remembrance Sunday is different because the hymn is sung at the end. Everyone sings loudly, as if the burden of silence and remembrance has been too much to bear and we're glad to escape. I sing the loudest and clearest I can.

I put the cross quickly in its holder and take off my cassock and surplus. I only need to undo the top five buttons and then I can step out of it. I put it on a coat hanger, grab my coat and squeeze past the girls who are all talking. The vicar stands in the doorway talking to Westley the lay reader. He's a cheerful and friendly farmer who milks cows and keeps pigs. Sometimes when he's busy he comes to church smelling of the farmyard. He's a popular and colourful character in the village. As he sees me approach, he smiles and says, 'Morning, how did you find the service today?'

I pause, unsure of whether or not I should admit my confusion about how you relate *'Thou shalt not kill'* to a congregation of ex-soldiers and my recent discovery that we were the first to drop the atomic bomb. On the other hand you can't just ask evil people to stop doing bad things; you have to be strong enough to stop them. Going to a foreign place, blowing it up and killing bad people to protect the innocent all sound a great idea. On that note I decide to look at the retired soldiers' medals. I reply quickly, 'Very good thank you,' and try to smile angelically.

He knows I'm in a hurry, I hope he doesn't think I'm rude. I squeeze past the groups of people chatting in the aisle to the front of the church. Two nice ladies from the Women's Institute are chatting to the retired Brigadier. I wish they'd get out of the way so I can see his medals.

In the unspoken hierarchy of the village the retired Brigadier is important. Immaculate in grey suit, white shirt and striped tie he commands respect naturally and seems to be in charge. He doesn't shout or upset people, he just gets things done, such as distributing the parish magazine or helping with the nativity play. People say he's very approachable. I don't want to interrupt so I look at the memorial to Captain Wiltshire again. When he sees me he says, 'Good morning, thank you for coming. It's good to see young people here on Remembrance Sunday.'

He excuses himself from the group. As if he can read my mind he says, '"It is sweet and glorious to die for one's country." That can be very confusing. Some think it's a lie. I've always taken it to mean not the country, but the principles of freedom, democracy and justice that we stand for; the greater good of humanity.'

He pauses to allow me to think about what he has said, then continues, 'We have to be strong to defend ourselves and to stand up to evil. The natural state of things is usually chaos. As human beings we have to try to rise above and control our instincts. I believe in peace through strength. There is an old saying, "If you want peace prepare for war." If we have good defences then nobody will be able to attack us. People will do the most evil things if they can't be held accountable.'

He gives me more time.

I think it through. After a few minutes I say, 'Thank you for explaining that. I think I understand.'

I turn slightly to the left to look at the list of the Ten Commandments. He follows my glance and says. 'There is a debate on the translation of "*Thou shalt not kill*". It's thought the original was "*Thou shalt not commit murder*". If you ever want to talk, I'll be delighted to discuss it. Different people have different views. We have to answer to our conscience.'

I say, 'Thank you very much. That's given me a lot to think about.'

I'm still thinking about it.

*

In my Uncle Gordon's garden the smell of freshly mown grass mingles with the scent of the roses in the balmy summer sunshine. I step carefully across the huge flowerbed to finish trimming the hedge. I tense my shoulder muscles as I open and close the shears rapidly, using the whole strength of my arms like I've been shown. As the last few stems fall I grab them and step back satisfied to admire my handiwork.

The cylinder mower has rolled the lawn into light and dark green stripes. The long herbaceous border blazes with the colours of the rainbow and the bed of brilliant-white and blood-red roses is framed perfectly by the neatly trimmed hedge and immaculately groomed lawn. I inhale the fragrances of paradise.

I stride quickly to the red-brick compost heap and throw in the cuttings. I rearrange them neatly with the fork. The smooth polished wooden handle slides through my hands. It belonged to Uncle Gordon's father. The metal prongs have been worn down by a century of use and are now only six inches long, but it's still a useful tool. It reminds me of an age when horses worked the land.

I run to the fruit cage and undo the clips on the netting. I step in and fasten it back to keep the birds out. I walk carefully past the two rows of brilliant-scarlet strawberries. They nestle on golden straw. The deep green leaves are like umbrellas.

Dad and Uncle Gordon are picking raspberries. Clusters of dark red fruit hang heavily from thin stems. I pick up the bowl and hold it in my left hand. With my right I squeeze the fruit gently between thumb and forefinger. If they're ripe they fall away. If they don't they should be left for tomorrow. I can tell by looking which is ready and which isn't. Ripe raspberry red is like no other colour. We soon finish and it's time for a swim. I change and then sprint barefoot up the lawn.

Uncle Gordon started with one milk float just after the First World War and ended up with his own company. By anybody's definition he's very successful. He's not really my uncle, he's married to my Mum's cousin and they've always been close, so we see a lot of them. He does a lot to support various charities and is a great believer in hard work and common sense. He's not cash rich, but he's invested in his house and garden.

Dad wants a swimming pool. They're very expensive and we can't afford one. He won't be beaten so he's bought a kit and a set of plans and is going to build it himself. The drawings look like the instructions for a giant Airfix model. It's an enormous undertaking, possibly many years' work and he only has holidays and weekends to do it. I'm twelve now and I told him I wanted to help. He says I can if I want to.

It's hot. I estimate the angle and alter my approach slightly. I don't need to worry about slipping because the board's not wet. I jump on to the end. It gives and then I feel it rebound, driving me into the air. I keep my hands straight above my head. For an instant I'm flying, then I hit the water. It's beautifully cool. I keep my arms outstretched and wriggle my fingers to feel the water. I pull them down to my sides and my body is driven forward. I open my eyes to look at the blueness as I glide towards the steps.

3

ROOTS

[BORN 5] MAY 1962

Netherhampton is a small village a few miles from the spire-dominated city of Salisbury in south Wiltshire. On one side of the village the small church, stone farm buildings and a handful of houses meet the chalk hills, which roll upwards to the woods and Salisbury racecourse. On the other is the river and the water meadows, a labyrinth of overgrown ditches and decaying sluice gates which used to be worked by the 'drowners'. They flooded the meadows to produce an early bite of grass for the dairy cows. The introduction of nitrogenous fertilizer rendered them redundant long before my time.

I was born at home. Mum tells me it was very quick. Dad rushed back from work in time to see Mum and the midwife having a cup of tea, with a neatly-wrapped baby nearby. When relatives talk of it they say it's typical of her, she doesn't hang about.

The stone farmhouse has a slate roof and large windows with white-painted frames. To the rear, by the cellar entrance, the large kitchen overlooks a courtyard, which leads to the drive and a line of big fir trees. Either side of the yard, stone buildings extend from the house. The heavy wooden doors and window frames are painted the same dark green as the cast-iron guttering and down pipes.

The front lawn stretches for miles and has huge flowerbeds.

Mum and Dad enjoy gardening. A chalk wall, topped with a thatch roof to protect it from the rain, surrounds the enormous vegetable garden.

It's Saturday and we always work in the garden. At seven I get up and go into Salisbury with Dad. It's my favourite day of the week because I can go everywhere with him. He buys me a comic when he gets the newspaper and sometimes we pick up Dad's friend Mr Tutt. He's a mechanic and is helping do up the Land Rover. It was clapped-out when he bought it, so they repainted it and rebuilt the engine. Now they're working on a little grey Ferguson T20 tractor. When it's cold and I insist on staying out with them, Dad gets me to run to the bottom of the garden and back so that I stay warm. When Dad's working in the garden I run to the shed to get tools for him. I love running. At lunchtime and teatime he races me to the back door. He always slows down to make sure it's a tie.

Dad works for a company advising and supplying agricultural seeds and fertilizers. Mum runs the Girl Guides and works as a secretary and accounts clerk. She's shorter than Dad who is tall and strong. When something is broken Dad can always mend it, and he knows everything about farm animals, cats and dogs.

Mum and Dad are kind. We go into Salisbury to see several old ladies who are friends of the family. They help them in the house and in their gardens and drive them to places they want to visit. Dad says they're on their own now because their husbands are dead and if we can help people we should. One old lady has a hairy chin and always gives me a big wet kiss from her dribbly old pink mouth. When we're going home in the car I tell Dad it was horrible. He says I should take it like a man and be thankful she didn't use her tongue.

This morning we've come to the church hall in Salisbury because it's the summer fête. Dad's running the air-rifle range and Mum is doing the cake stall. The Girl Guides all came to our house last night to bake. They were in pairs around the large old kitchen table, stirring things into mixing bowls. My sister Kate was able to help, but I'm too young so I walked around trying all the mixtures until I felt sick.

We've been told to wait in the Land Rover because we're going home soon. It might also be because I was running up and down the church hall as fast as I could and stopping by skidding into the wall. It was fun. Mum's gone to get the cake tins. I think there's just time.

The Land Rover is painted green and it has a canvas roof. In the winter it's cold so we all wear thick coats. I turn the steering wheel, fiddle with the gear stick and make loud engine noises. Little blobs of saliva land on the round horn button in the middle of the gigantic black wheel with shiny metal spokes. I rub them off with my sleeve because I'm not supposed to sit in the driving seat and Mum will see them. When I do something wrong Mum usually finds out and then I'm in trouble. I can move fast, so when I start to see the hall door open I'll slide back into my seat.

'I'm going to drive the Land Rover,' I say as I try to put my feet on the pedals. I reach down and press the yellow diff-lock handle and rattle the gear lever like I've seen Dad do. Kate is sitting behind me. She prods me in the back and says, 'You have to push that silver button in, lift up the handbrake lever and let it go down slightly. Then we'll go forward a bit. To stop it you have to pull it up again. Go on I dare you.'

My sister is seven, which is two years older than me. She knows a lot and she's a lot more clever than me. She got a *Blue Peter* badge for doing a picture for their competition. She's good at drawing, but she can't drive the Land Rover or the tractor, that's a boy thing.

I look around. No one's looking. The tarmac car park is empty.

I pull up the hand brake lever with both hands. I push in

the silver button and let the lever go down a little. Nothing happens.

We're facing downhill and we haven't moved. I must have to do something else. 'I think I should move the gear stick.' I slide forward and try to put my feet on the pedals.

'Stop it. You'll get in trouble,' Kate says.

'No I won't. You don't know anything because you're a girl.'

I slip forward in the seat and get one foot on a pedal. I press it down and fiddle with the gear lever. Suddenly we're surging forward. We're going faster and we're out of control. That was a big mistake. I wish I hadn't done it. 'Help! Help!'

There's a bang and we stop.

Everyone heard. Mum and other people are around us. I'm in big trouble now. Crying is definitely the best option.

'Are you all right?' she says.

Somebody behind my mother laughs and says, 'No harm done.'

Someone else says, 'They only went a few feet before they hit the wall and there's no damage to the Land Rover.'

At home I still believe the world is going to end and I sit silently as Mum and Dad talk. When she tells him at first it looks like he's going to laugh. Then he bites his lip. I do that sometimes before I cry. He must be really upset. I've never seen Dad cry. I'm confused. He looks concerned, puts his hand on her shoulder and says, 'It's just one of those things. Boys will be boys. You only left them for a minute or so. It wasn't your fault.'

They decide that we're never going to be left alone in the vehicles again, especially on hills, until we're older. Dad beckons me and tells me not to do it again, then says I can go out in the garden with him.

When we get outside he goes into the shed to get the hoe and a fork to dig the new potatoes. As we walk to the garden I struggle to keep up. He waits for me and says, 'Look son, whatever happens in life, no matter how bad things get, don't stick your bottom lip out like that. Life's all about learning and today you've learnt not to try to drive until you can have proper lessons.'

Then he makes me promise I won't drive until he says I can.

As I run down the garden path I feel a surge of relief. The world hasn't ended.

Mrs Jay is a small grey-haired lady, shorter than my mother. She helps sometimes and looks after Kate and me when Mum has to work. She comes two days a week. It's now late on Monday morning and she's mopping the kitchen floor. I'm not supposed to ask how old grown-ups are, especially women, but I don't think she'll mind. She's my friend. I say, 'Mrs Jay how old are you?'

'Very old. Nearly sixty, my dear.'

'Is that why you've got grey hair?'

Our conversation is cut short when Mum and Dad come home for lunch. Dad works from home. He has an office with a big roll-top desk and a large black telephone. Kate and I stay away from there when he has to work because he needs peace and quiet.

As my parents and Mrs Jay talk in the kitchen I stay by the back door to watch the dogs. I've never seen dogs at the bottom of our garden before. I wonder whose they are? We don't have a dog because we've got two cats. I like dogs.

When we go to see Roger I always stroke his dog while he and Dad talk. He's a brown and white retired cow dog called Fred. He's old and smelly now, but I still like him even though he bit me. Dad says dogs bite so you have to be careful, but Fred doesn't bite hard, he just nips, then wags his tail.

I can see three dogs at the bottom of the garden. They're brown and white and they're running towards me. Wow! Now

I can see hundreds of them, and they're all running towards me, barking. I stare at them and freeze. They're chasing our cats. As the pack of yelping hounds gets nearer I know I have to do something. I turn and run into the kitchen.

The two cats bolt past me and run up the curtains. They balance precariously on the pelmet and make hissing noises. Suddenly the kitchen is a sea of barking hounds with big floppy ears and large paws and tails that hurt when they hit you.

Some of them are barking. One comes towards me. I reach out to stroke it. It has huge brown eyes. It stops and looks at me then barks. It smells a lot worse than Fred. I don't like this. I think it might try to eat me. I try to get up, then I hear Mrs Jay shouting, 'Get out of here you mutts.'

The bad dog yelps as Mrs Jay wallops it on the head with the long-handled broom. She says, 'Come on my dear,' and helps me up with one hand while swinging the broom with the other.

Mum goes to ring the kennels and Dad grabs the dogs in the courtyard and puts them in the tool shed so the kennel man can come and retrieve them. I watch from a safe distance behind Mrs Jay's skirts as Dad catches the hounds and Mum opens the door so he can put them in the shed. They're a good team.

Eventually the man comes with a large green horsebox to take the hounds back. He's very apologetic and says that the hunt will pay for any damage. The house is cleaned up and the broken windows mended.

Soon afterwards I start school. I've been looking forward to it. My sister has been going for two years.

After a few months the village school shuts because it's too small. We go instead to Lower Bemerton a few miles away, which is a huge place with nearly a hundred children. Mum takes us there in the Land Rover. I let her do the driving.

When I'm six everything changes. We move house. Mum

and Dad have bought a house in the nearby village of Coombe Bissett. We live on the side of a hill and every morning before I go to school I watch the farmer next door feed the cattle.

I look forward to the holidays when I visit my uncle's farm. My cousins are much older than me and take me with them to feed the pigs and the calves. In the summer I stay and help with the straw bales.

Schooldays drift by and I dream of the day when I'll be on the farm all the time. When I tell people they say, 'Your schooldays are the best of your life.'

I worry and think, Is this as good as it gets?

At Bishop Wordsworth's Grammar School I start to think about what's going on in the world and what I want to do. I try to remember the words of the deputy head Jo Newman. 'Don't be old before your time. Try to read a paper or two a day. Be enthusiastic, try to see other perspectives and understand something new.'

In the summer holidays, aged fourteen, I find my niche. I cycle the eight miles to my Dad's friend Roger's farm and back. He grows a lot of seed corn and the rogue plants, which are a different species that might contaminate the next generation, have to be removed by hand.

We walk the fields, pull out the rogue plants by their roots and put them into bags, which are later burnt. During harvest I man the grain-cleaning equipment and then help to stack the straw bales. I work as hard as I can. I can't wait to leave school to work on a farm.

WINTER 1983

The ringing wakes me suddenly. I sit up and grab the alarm clock. In one fluid movement I switch it off and bang it back on the bedside cabinet. It's 4.15 a.m. I leap out of bed, throw off my pyjamas and snatch my clothes. I kick my feet into my slippers and fumble on the chair for my watch.

The outline of light around the door tells me that as usual Roger's up first. As I charge out, he passes me on the landing putting on his watch. My head hit the pillow at ten thirty. I blinked, then the alarm went. I say, 'Morning. Sleep well?'

He says, 'I woke up too early as usual, so I just dozed.'

The wiry old farmer is as hard as nails. He left school at fifteen with a few pounds saved. By the time he was thirty he'd grafted to earn enough to farm his own land. He has a reputation for doing the work of two men and for being a smart and honest businessman. He's an old family friend. Dad knew I loved being on farms, so as soon as I was old enough he arranged for me to work on Roger's farm in the school holidays. I was probably a nuisance; now I'm twenty-one I like to think I'm more useful. Roger sold his farm near Salisbury last year and moved here to North Devon.

I run downstairs after him. Jumping the last four I leap into the large lounge with its ancient stone fireplace and thick walls. Charlie bolts on to the chair, meows, rolls on his back and sticks his paws in the air. I stroke him quickly as I stride past into the kitchen.

I stick the kettle on, get out the mugs, put in a spoon of coffee and add a slosh of milk from the jug, walk to the back door, put my overalls on and get back just as the kettle clicks off. I pour in the boiling water, leaving space for a few inches of cold from the tap. Unlike Roger I don't have asbestos lips and innards. I chuck the warm coffee down my neck, rinse the mug and head for the door. Roger gets there before me. Around here you have to be fast or you're last.

I pull my boots on as the cat squawks round my feet. Striding down the path I take a good look at the sky. It's clear and full of stars. Good. The prevailing wind is from the south-west. I check that direction and it's clear. Excellent, we should be able to finish the fencing today.

Looking across the valley I can see the single light of the neighbour's sheep shed. His land is north-facing, so their grass is much later than ours. Behind the farmhouse there are no lights, just Exmoor with its wild open moorland and mysterious mists.

The chill of the sharp frost bites into my bones. I pull down the black woollen 'Benny' hat over my ears to cover the peeling chilblains and scan the path and yard for patches of ice. We don't wear gloves outside because we're always moving too fast for our hands to get cold. When I was younger the cold made me feel sick. I remember it was difficult doing anything, but I persevered and got used to it.

We don't need to speak. The routine is well established. Roger goes to start the milking and my first stop is the loose box. I know the heifer hasn't calved. We would have heard her. I take a quick look. No, she hasn't started to lift her tail much, maybe this afternoon.

I walk rapidly round the machinery-shed to the top end of the feeding yard and slip between the fence rails. The sweet smell of silage and cattle greets me. I say, 'G'won. G'won,' which in cow speak means please proceed to the milking yard. Cows are gentle creatures of habit. They shouldn't be stressed. It's usually the same old girls at the back. Some of them still munch the last of the hay from the central feeder. I gently pat their flanks and have my usual early morning conversations.

I check the silage face to make sure there's enough for them to eat after milking. I pull a handful of chopped fermented grass from the ten-foot-high stack that spans the width and breadth of the barn and sniff it and squeeze it as I walk the cows back down the yard. It's light brown and there's hardly any moisture or smell. This is good-quality stuff.

The silage is contained by thick reinforced concrete walls and covered in a black plastic sheet. Summer grass is mown and left to wilt for a day to reduce the moisture. A forage harvester picks it up, chops it finely and throws it into a trailer with high metal or mesh sides. These are towed to the silage clamp. The grass is tipped out and piled up by a tractor with a large push-off buckrake. The tractor rolls the grass repeatedly to force the air out. It's important to prevent it being contaminated with soil or muck, which causes it to rot rather than ferment. Just a small amount of muck can do a lot of damage. When sealed, natural bacteria in the grass ferment. In anaerobic conditions the by-product of the process is lactic acid. This natural preservative pickles the grass. It's the ideal way to provide winter fodder for cattle and it's all down to the genius of nature.

We've studied the process at college. The rumour going around this week is that one day Seale Hayne will merge into Plymouth University because the number of people employed in farming is dropping all the time and it's becoming an increasingly technical business.

I drive the cows gently down the yard and continue thinking.

I blink slightly as I follow the old girls into the cubicle house. The few fluorescent lights in the barn are brighter than the semi-dark yard. This is the cows' rest area, where they chew the cud, and do whatever cows do. Individual spaces are bedded with straw and divided by metal pipes. Each cow has its own personal space. When they're loose bedded in straw it's much harder for them to stay clean and free from infection.

Sometimes udders are trodden on and the weaker animals bullied. In addition, a lot more straw is needed.

The soft high-pitched whirr of the vacuum pump and the rhythmic hiss of the machinery signal the start of milking. I close the gates dividing the yard and rush back to the small barn where I grab the strings of a straw bale in each hand and carry them back into the cubicle house. Then I take the pitchfork and walk down the rows of cubicles, scraping any muck into the passage. Next I take out my knife, cut the orange bale-string by the knots, pull it out, bundle it up and stuff it my pocket. I dash up and down the passage shaking fresh straw in the cubicles.

The top metal gate feels cold. I run to the tractor. The seat's freezing, so is the steering wheel. I reach down, take off the foot brake and stick my foot on the clutch. The tractor rolls forward. I let in the clutch and the old red David Brown roars into life. I wrench the steering wheel round. The tractor's too old to have powered steering. I'm fit and strong and doing something I love. Life's great.

With a scrapper mounted on the hydraulics I push the slurry to the ramp and into the muck-spreader below. I finish the corners with a hand-held C-shaped scraper and park the tractor. I run to the dairy and hose my boots carefully. I wash my hands and put on my thick plastic milking apron and gloves and go down the steps into the milking parlour. It's slightly warmer in here, because the temperature needs to be above freezing for the milking machinery to work. It always smells clean with the background smells of sterile detergent and fresh milk. The white liquid pulses rhythmically into the ten-gallon glass jars. Six cows stand obediently each side of the herringbone parlour. Hygiene is everything.

I pull the handle to operate the cattle-cake feeder and stroke a cow's leg to let her know I'm going to touch her udder. I wash the teats with the warm-water hose and dry them with a paper towel. I guide the cups on and move to Lanky. She's a long-legged heifer with a kick like a mule. I stroke her leg, speak gently and get as close as I can.

The closer you are to a kick the better. There's less room for a cow to get any power behind it. Lanky's got small warts on her teats, so she sometimes kicks. Just as I put the last cup on I can feel her start to move. I lean into it and press my left forearm against her leg as firmly as I can. She tries to kick so I lean harder.

This is a game we've played before. Finally she decides against kicking and instead flicks her shitty tail in my face. Then she cranes her head round to see if she's got me. She realizes she has and settles down. Fortunately, I know when to keep my mouth shut. I wash my face with the hose while Roger is doubled over with laughter.

I watch the flow of milk into the jars. The third cow is finished. I bend the pipes to release the vacuum and gently pull off the unit. I switch the lever to send the milk from the jar to the bulk tank and carefully apply the sterile lanolin-based dip to the teats.

We're finished by seven. The last job is to change the filter on the pipe into the milk tank and check it's cooled to the correct temperature. We wash down the parlour meticulously and clean up the yards, then it's into the house for loads of pinhead oatmeal porridge and toast. Breakfast is always the best meal of the day.

We listen to the news on Radio 4. This morning they're covering Cambodia, Russian spies, The Cold War and, most frightening of all, the Common Agricultural Policy.

I saw the film *The Killing Fields* last week. It was about Cambodia. I think meeting the Khmer Rouge would be any-one's worst nightmare, but Roger says we Europeans have no reason to be high and mighty. The worst wars in history have taken place right on our doorstep.

It's nearly seven thirty. Time to get on. I pull my boots on as Roger finishes feeding the cats. This is one of the rare occasions when I get out of the door before he does. I breathe the crisp morning air and run to get the tractor to scrape the top yards. As I work I think a lot about the economics of farming. Roger has always taught me to look beyond the end of my own nose.

And there in the cold winter dawn I realize that I've never thought of doing anything other than farming, but over-production, the cost/price squeeze and my lack of capital and experience stand against me. I think of the plaque on the church wall. I thought about joining the army last year during the Falklands War. Maybe I should think about it again.

SPRING 1986

The colonel looks about fifty. He studies the form, stares at me over the top of his glasses and glances down again. The office is how I imagined it would be. Clean, sparse and efficient with army-issue furniture. He smiles reassuringly and says, 'What's your favourite book?'

I didn't expect that. I reply instantly, '*For Whom The Bell Tolls* by Ernest Hemingway', because it was the last book I read.

He smiles again and sits forward. 'Yes, excellent, definitely my favourite. I've read it many times.'

I think, oh shit.

'Why do you want to join the army?' he asks.

I remember the conversation I had with the Brigadier on Remembrance Sunday. 'I come from a farming background. I never thought of doing anything else, but now I'm finishing college I want to do something that has more to do with people. I was brought up to respect the tradition of service, and think that freedom is worth defending.'

I wonder if I'm sounding a little too pompous, but I've obviously done something right because a few months later I receive joining instructions for the Royal Military Academy, Sandhurst.

*

I keep jabbing the spade into the frozen ground. The shock rebounds and tingles through my arms and hands. The sandy soil comes away in little chips. It's like digging up concrete. I grab the pickaxe, lift it high above my head and drive it down. I lever it back to lift a lump of frozen earth the size of a fist. Fine icy chips of snow are driven by a bitter wind, which sting as they sandblast my face. I keep my head down to protect my eyes.

First thing this morning there was an hour of sunshine; then without warning the arctic weather moved in. To start with it was like a fine frozen mist. After ten or fifteen minutes it could just be seen lying on the frozen ground; then a series of fierce blizzards smothered the landscape.

The wind bites into my bones but I force myself to dig and squint through the driving snow towards the long stripwood. I can just make out the trees. I drive in the pick again and again. The frost is nearly six inches deep. It's good to keep working. That way I'll stay warm.

I've already dug one trench. This is my second. I grab the shovel and scoop the rocky frosted fragments to the side. A few more frantic minutes with the pickaxe and I've gone through the frost. As I shovel up the lumps I can feel the edge of the spade bite into the soft soil. It would be nice to stop, but I know I have to keep on.

Leaping across to the rolled back grass I jab with the spade and cut deeper into the turf. I grip the thick, long tangle of leaf and stalks and tear it back to reveal the frozen soil. Jumping back over the trench I grab my webbing and rifle and drag them closer. 'The weapon should always be within arm's reach.' I remember the words of the Skill at Arms Instructor.

I lift the SLR by the pistol grip, tap the base of the magazine to make sure it's correctly housed and check the safety catch is on. It's possible we'll get bumped and I don't want to have to shout 'bang' at the enemy instead of shooting them. As our platoon commander says, 'One feels such a fool when one can't return the enemy's fire.'

We're digging in as the forward platoon in a company defensive position. Company headquarters is located behind us in the wood. The spade bites into the sandy soil and I dig rhythmically. I'm warm now. In no time the trench is as deep as my waist.

'Eddie's freezing and I've never been so cold. We're going to have people go down,' Lloyd shouts from the nearest trench. He's an experienced soldier. He's done this before. He continues, 'I spoke to a bloke in the QM's department; says he can't believe it. They've got all the arctic kit, mittens, parkas everything. But they're not allowed to issue it.'

I can only just hear him above the freezing, howling wind. 'Why not?' I shout. I want to learn, which means I have to risk asking stupid questions.

Lloyd explains patiently, 'Because we're not in the Arctic. We're in a temperate winter zone.'

'Of course,' I say. Regulations. Arctic kit can only be issued in Arctic winter zones. We've been issued with temperate winter kit. I think I'm beginning to understand the army.

I carry on digging.

He asks, 'How's the trench?'

'Nearly three feet.' I lever out a large stone.

'Good. I'll send Eddie back to help you, then I can finish ours.' He drags Eddie up, puts on his webbing and gives him his SLR, then points in my direction. 'Get in that trench.'

Eddie ambles over unsteadily. His short, thin build make him a soft target for the biting wind and driving snow. He's wearing just about every item of clothing he's been issued, but he's still shivering and his teeth are chattering. He comes from Belize and this is the first time he's ever seen snow. His black skin has developed a grey-blue tinge. We're worried about him. We keep trying to explain that if he digs he'll warm up, but he's finding it hard.

The Sandhurst directing staff monitor our performance with their clipboards. They're now just as cold as we are, and coming around more frequently to check people aren't going down with exposure. We've studied hypothermia in first aid. It's mainly common sense. Thin, small people are more susceptible to the cold than large well-built people who have a smaller surface area relative to their body mass. Several layers of clothing providing insulation are better than one great thick sweater, but they should be removed if you're active to avoid sweating. The heat loss is far worse when people are wet. It's important to eat and to maintain energy levels. Most heat is lost through the head.

Casualties suffering from exposure may be delirious and unreasonable. The quickest way to warm them up is to take off their outer clothing and put them in a sleeping bag with a warm person who can pass on body heat. I suggested that the chaps who'd recently left boarding school should have it explained they aren't supposed to try and bump-start the casualty. I'm still hoping it doesn't reach the ears of our DS; particularly the one who went to boarding school.

'When will you finish?' Bruce asks as he runs over and squats, panting by the trench. He cradles his SLR with both hands. He's a small well-spoken man. His command appointment today is platoon sergeant. It's going to be a real tester for him in this weather.

Seeing him on my first day at Sandhurst was a surprise. I recognized him immediately – we went to the same college. He studied rural resources and management. He was in his third year when I started my first.

We are a few years older than the other twenty-four officer cadets and share the handicap of no previous military experience. We're the only ones doing everything for the first time, with many skills to learn and we're still getting into the military mindset. We both ask too many questions. The colour sergeant explained that once we get out of the factory we'll find things easier and our other experiences will be useful, but as he rightly pointed out the important thing now is to focus on the factory.

'We've got to finish digging in before last light,' says Bruce.

'I've finished ours. I'm helping Eddie,' I reply.

I find trench digging easy. In fact I enjoy it. This is where my peasant background is paying dividends, but John the Para is the real expert; he's had a lot of practice.

I think everyone worries about passing out more than they let on. I'm used to quietly getting on with things and find coping with bullshit difficult, but I'm sure they're right when they say, 'You must remember attention to detail.' I'm not good when I think I'm being watched or assessed, but I just have to get my brain round it. My biggest problem is that I think things are more difficult than they are. I need to be more confident.

'Ash is coming.' The lads pass the word up the trench line. He's our Sandhurst platoon commander, an Irish Guards captain who has the unenviable task of training us. He's ably assisted by a Scots Guards colour sergeant whom we've imaginatively nicknamed 'JJ' because they're his initials. We call the company sergeant major the CSM, very much on the same basis. I'll never forget his opening words at our first morning parade. 'Good morning gentlemen, I am the company sergeant major. I am a warrant officer, which means you call me *Sir*. You are officer cadets, which means that I call you *Sir*. The only difference is that you mean it.'

They've taught us a lot. The military discipline instilled into us makes most of us more nervous than we need be, but that's good, it keeps us on our toes.

Ash is walking along the trenches. He speaks to everyone as he passes. I recognize his voice. 'How are you Ogaldez?'

Eddie looks up and with enormous effort levers himself out of the trench. In the cold his lips have split and are bleeding slightly. He grabs the green army shovel with both hands, lifts it high above his head and throws it down as hard as he can into the snow. Helmeted heads turn and stare in shock as Eddie shouts, 'Fucking hell man! I'm freezing cold and I've had enough of dis white shit. I want to go home to Belize where de sun shine.'

There is a stunned silence. I bite my lip and try not to laugh. Then I think. Does he realize what he's done? He could be on the next plane home.

The captain doesn't flinch, but I think I see him stifle a grin. 'I can understand how you might find it chilly. We're discussing bringing the foreign students into a command post if it gets any colder, but for the time being you have to try to cope. It's character building.'

The wind howls and the hard snow rattles off our clothing.

'Okay, Sir,' Eddie says finally. He's happier now he's let us know what's on his mind. He gets back in the trench and starts digging.

'You've all done first aid. Look out for signs of exposure, particularly in the foreign students. Any problems send a radio NODUF message to company HQ immediately.'

'Yes, Sir,' we reply in unison.

After a period of furtive digging Eddie looks around him.

Then he grins, revealing brilliant white teeth. 'Everyone here all right? Nobody got exposure?'

As the light begins to fail the call 'stand to' echoes quietly around the trenches. We mustn't give our position away; that means no lights, no smoking and no noise. I pull on my webbing and fumble with the buckle. I should get one of those quick-release belts like John the Para. With the SLR in one hand I jump in the trench and take up a fire position, covering my arcs. We're in Nuclear Biological and Chemical (NBC) state High, which is good news; the protective suits are another layer of clothing.

About an hour ago the foreign students and those who were looking unhealthily cold were withdrawn to a command-post exercise in double layered tents with gas heaters. It's a fair one. Most of them have never seen snow and we've heard every army exercise in the UK has been stopped due to the extreme cold. Every one, that is, except ours. It's minus twenty at night. Somebody in the QM's department said all this was on the news, so it must be true.

'All right Harv?' Neil shouts from the next trench. They call me Harv because there was a TV series called *Shine On Harvey Moon*. It's all quite logical. He's not been out of school long, but Neil is already an old soldier. He's well-acquainted with military terms, such as 'ducking and diving', 'gonk bag' and 'stand down'. Neil is about my height and is well built. His hair is dark brown and cut to the regulation sandpaper effect on the back and sides. To begin with I had to learn a new language, but thanks to Neil's patience I'm now fluent. He also gave a few useful tips on map reading. His old man's a Commando so he grew up with it.

I reply quietly, wishing he hadn't started talking in case the DS catch us. 'Fine thanks. When's scoff?'

'Seven thirty. They'll take us into camp at midnight. They'll have to, because it's so fucking cold. I've got a real sad on. My fingers have been numb all day. This whole situation is a complete horse's arse.'

'Quiet,' Phil says. He's a pay corps staff sergeant who's being commissioned because he's brilliant. He's very sensible and extremely good at everything. To make matters worse, he's a decent and likeable bloke. His only flaw is a shortage of hair, for which he is mercilessly castigated.

'Sorry. It must be really cold for you, chrome dome,' Neil says. 'I can understand why Harv's going to be a monkey. It'll be warmer swinging through the trees than sitting in trenches.'

Monkey is army slang for military police. It's a small organization within the army and apart from policing, its main role is to ensure the effectiveness of main supply routes to front-line troops.

Without the law and the ability to enforce it, there's chaos. People must be held accountable. Particularly in a time of war. Because I believe these things fervently, and because the retired officer advising on army careers only had the RMP address available, I have applied to join them.

At the end of the first term I go on an adventure training course in Wales. It's raining and I'm standing at the bottom of a cliff face and I'm just wondering if I should have heeded the saying, 'Never volunteer for anything'. But I have and it's too late. The instructor clips a rope on to my harness, checks it and says, 'Well done. Off you go.'

I glance back at Bruce. He smiles and gives me a thumbs up. I suspect he and the rest of the class are as apprehensive as I am.

I walk along the small ledge to the rock face. It's a long way down. I do the checks, look up at the instructor with the safety line and say, 'Climbing now.'

I remember to keep three points of contact and start to make my way slowly up the cliff. The only sound is the gust of the biting wind and my hands are so cold they're numb. I keep looking up for the next hold. Now for the difficult bit. I have to step around a small outcrop to put my foot on a ledge. I can't see it from here, but I know that it's there.

I try to move, but I can't. My body has frozen. I look at my feet. A long way below I can see the tops of trees and rocky outcrops. I cling to the rock and try to move. I can't. I *have* to do this. I lift up my shaking leg and hope no one can see how it's wobbling. I push it against the rock and force it around the corner. Ever so gently I lower it. I can feel the ledge. Cautiously I put my weight on it and step on to the ledge. The rest of the climb is easy in comparison.

After passing out of Sandhurst I arrive at the Royal Military Police Training Centre with my new uniforms in neat suit covers, and with expectations of adventure. In the centre of the barracks there is a large sports field bordered by trees. The late spring sunshine makes their emerging leaves almost fluorescent-green. A groundsman rolls the cricket square religiously.

Another fresh subaltern and I are welcomed at the guard-room by a staff sergeant with a red sash and mirror-shiny boots. He winks at me as he says, 'A bit of advice, Sir. The adjutant is a strict disciplinarian who expects young officers to wear service dress for tea.'

Tea in the mess isn't a relaxing affair. The tall, dark, sinisterly moustached adjutant explains immediately that sub-alterns must wear brown trilby hats at all times with their civilian suits or sports jackets.

A nervous young duty officer in immaculate service dress with super-shiny brown shoes, marches in as the adjutant explains the punishing timetable for learning the entire *Manual of Military Law*. 'Excuse me, Sir.'

The adjutant picks up a napkin and dabs a crumb from his moustache. 'Yes, what is it?'

The subaltern flushes bright red and stammers, 'Shall I mount the guard tonight, Sir?'

His superior finishes a mouthful of crumpet, dabs at another crumb and says, 'If you do I'll have to charge you with buggery!'

The adjutant's made a joke. Everyone laughs raucously.

He silences us by raising his hand. 'As you know, Archibald, I like to keep an informal mess. But when you're on duty you should brace up smarter than that. Your tie's not straight and your shoes are not polished to the standard I would expect from one of my officers. Finally, the instructions for mounting the guard are in the duty officer's folder, which you should have read. All things considered I think you could do with a bit more practice. Don't you?'

'Yes, Sir.'

'Good, see the RSM first parade tomorrow and volunteer for thirty-one extra duties.'

Archibald bites his lip and quivers slightly. 'Thank you, Sir.' Then he turns to the right and marches disconsolately away.

The adjutant puts down his plate, grooms his moustache and says, 'Not at all. I'm always keen to help. Now I must go and fight the paper war. I'll see you all at dinner, 19.00 hours sharp.' He gets up and bounds out of the room.

An embarrassed silence follows as we listen to Archibald sobbing loudly outside the anteroom. He is consoled by Ken the mess waiter. 'Don't cry, Sir. Look on the bright side. At least the adjutant has had to stop making you do boxing training after Lieutenant Carter was in a coma for a week.'

At dinner I am appointed mess gardens member because of my agricultural background. As the adjutant is giving me instructions for the procurement of farmyard manure, Ken the waiter bursts through the swing door to the kitchen and shouts, 'Hands up who wants soup.'

Slowly we raise our hands. 'Yes please.'

During the main course an officer pulls a pile of cabbage off his pork chop and says, 'Good God, my chop's nearly raw!'

The adjutant takes control immediately and summons Ken. 'There is a problem with this officer's chop. Please sort it out.'

Ken shrinks visibly and is full of apologies, but rather spoils the effect when he takes the plate back into the kitchen, closes the door, and shouts, 'Hey chef, the fussy bastard doesn't want your sodding dinner.'

After dinner we withdraw to a storming night in the mess, during which I overhear Ken, now performing the duties of barman, trying to sell his sister's sexual favours to my fellow new arrival. I decide to give him a wide berth, but fail when he takes me round the garden to look at the roses and discuss possible dumping sites for the manure.

The next morning, nursing sore heads we attend our initial interview with the commanding officer. As we enter the adjutant's office I'm greeted by 'Ken the mess waiter', who is sitting smiling in uniform at the adjutant's desk.

The Provost Officers Course covers everything from convoy movement and reporting, to dealing with refugees, military and civil law, police studies, the Police and Criminal Evidence Act (PACE) and the Geneva Convention. We are disappointed to find we don't do much on how to run firing squads or break up bar brawls with long-handled batons.

My first posting is an infantry attachment in Northern Ireland.

The blokes have all been here eighteen months and I'm an inexperienced new boy, but I'm doing the best I can to learn fast. My platoon sergeant was posted to the UN just before I arrived and the senior corporal is doing his Brecon course, so I'm introduced to the concept of the steep learning curve. After a few months, and with a lot of help, I settle in.

My radio earpiece crackles static as the team commander says, 'Charlie Three Two will be in position north of VCP One in figures three.' I glance down the road to the gentle bend. It's the site of our first vehicle checkpoint. As we walk down the link road of the housing estate I look around me. The gardens are overgrown and littered with rubbish. Even though the houses are recently refurbished and double-glazed they already show signs of vandalism.

I turn round and walk backwards for a few paces. 'They've just given us figures three, so we'll go firm to give them time to get there.'

We stop and take positions for a short while. The idea is not to stay in the open, but if you have to, then always to keep moving. I squat by a walled front garden and watch the other lads take cover.

The front door of the house is ajar and a boy of three or four stands in a dirty white T-shirt, holding a ragged teddy bear. I feel the chill of the late-January wind. It's a grey, cold day. The child must be freezing.

I scan the road both ways before I turn back to him. He looks at me and says, 'Hello.'

I smile. 'Hello, what's your bear called?'

The front door opens and a pasty-faced woman peers out. I don't want to startle her so I stand up and say, 'Good morning, madam.'

She says, 'Fuck off.' She walks over to her son, hits him, drags him into the house by the arm and says, 'Don't speak to them.' The little boy sobs.

I look around. There's no one in sight. Sometimes, under cover of darkness, people say they're glad we're here.

I check my watch and move on to the VCP. The other two teams radio to say they're in position. I check my team's all right, step into the road and stop a red Fiat saloon. 'Good morning, sir. Can I see your driving licence please?'

He laughs and picks a plastic wallet off the dashboard. I look into his vehicle, then glance around the houses and check the positions of my team before I take the licence. 'May I ask what's funny, sir?' I'm sounding like *Dixon of Dock Green*.

He smiles. 'The last roadblock I came through they weren't as polite.'

I search his car before thanking him for his patience and moving on to the next vehicle. I think how easy it would have been to speak to him the same way the woman had spoken to me. The CQMS was right when he said 'fair, firm and friendly' is the only way to behave.

I enjoy the army and get to meet some great people, but as I watch the Berlin Wall come down, relations with the Soviet Bloc improve and hear talk of massive manpower cuts I begin to wonder if I have a long-term future in the service. Reluctantly, I decide to leave.

I get a job with a large financial institution, but one day, as I look at the coffee-stained carpet, I realize I still long for a real challenge. The only time I feel really happy in this world is on the days when I do enough work to escape for a quick run at lunchtime. I'm beginning to think I should chuck it all in and do some sort of charity work. My tree-hugging and basket-weaving tendencies are surfacing again. I blame my parents.

4

CAMBODIA

EARLY 1993

I check the road's clear and sprint across. I glance at my watch. I've got three minutes. There was a pile-up on the M1, two sets of road works along Edgware Road and a standstill around Hyde Park. I've used up the extra hour I'd allowed for delays. I ask for directions at Reception and dash across the courtyard to the lift. I straighten my tie, comb my hair and wipe my brow to check I'm not sweating. I press the doorbell and check my watch. Amazingly, I'm spot on time. This is meant to be.

The colonel greets me with a firm handshake and ushers me in. He's dressed in a blazer, flannels and plain brown tie. He introduces me to Guy, the field director. The small flat is immaculate. There's an extensive collection of military biographies and memorabilia, and an air of neat efficiency.

Lt Colonel Colin Mitchell became famous in the late 1960s as commanding officer of the Argyle and Sutherland Highlanders. He set up a mine-clearance charity after visiting Afghanistan, where he saw farmers unable to work their land, refugees who couldn't go home and a Red Cross hospital full of amputees.

'HALO stands for the Hazardous Area Life Support Organization. It is totally operationally focused, and is all about getting mines out of the ground. I like to think of deminers as rather like the Knights Templar, keeping the roads open to Jerusalem so the pilgrims could pass safely.'

After briefing me he asks a few questions about my background then leaves Guy to discuss fieldwork and training. 'We currently need people in Cambodia. Mike, the operations officer responsible for training, is a bomb disposal officer who served in the Gulf.'

He shows me photographs of their current sites. 'This is a school we cleared. They found it was mined when three children were blown up. We train and employ demobilized soldiers. They work in metre wide lanes. The process involves feeling for trip wires, carefully cutting the vegetation, removing it, passing the metal detector over the ground and prodding and digging to investigate any metal read-outs. When mines are found they're blown up in situ. As you can see it's not a black art. Maintaining equipment and good political, military and aid agency relationships is vital.'

I don't have any questions. I've already done my research and spoken to people who've worked in the field. It'll take me a few weeks to settle my affairs.

Those who work for Colin Mitchell revere him. He's incredibly efficient and possesses amazing foresight, but he is also remarkably tolerant of human frailty. From their flat in London, he and his wife administer an organization bigger than a battalion, working in four countries. I'm proud to have the opportunity to work for them.

*

We arrived in Bangkok at about five this morning and waited about four hours for our flight to Phnom Penh. Now, an hour and a half later, we land at an airport with white-painted UN helicopters and aircraft parked along the massive runway. Jim points to a lonely corner where a few old silver MIGs have been shoved in ramshackle hangers. One building had collapsed on to its jet.

Four of us are travelling together. Richard, Nigel and I are new recruits and Jim is an old hand returning from leave. Jim is about five feet eight. He's well built and fair-skinned with a shock of sandy hair and a pleasant gentle manner. He's given us a good brief during the journey.

Both Richard and Nigel have recently left the army. Nigel is a tall fair-haired man with a pleasant and affable manner. I sat next to him on the flight and enjoyed talking to him. We have a similar attitude to life. Richard is a forthright and confident character with a great sense of fun. He's about the same height and build as me.

Jim says the Americans built the runway at Pochentong in the 1960s, which is why it's so vast. The UN refurbished it and put up a new control tower to fly in their staff and equipment. UNTAC consists of military observers (UNMOs), operational forces, police (CIVPOL), human rights workers, election supervisors and administrators and a large number of volunteers (UNVs) with skills as varied as accounting and building.

I walk down the aircraft steps into a wall of heat. The sunlight is so bright I have to squint. The low concrete building has the appearance and buzz of a military terminal. Cambodian immigration officers sit sullenly behind desks in ill-fitting Russian-style police uniforms. The sultry heat makes the atmosphere heavy and tense. Baggage reclaim is from a handcart by the runway door.

Soldiers and policemen of all nationalities with UN armbands and berets mill around purposefully in their smart uniforms, presumably looking for each other or their transport. Khmer taxi drivers and porters in stained grubby-white shirts clamour and frantically shout 'My friend' at foreigners and try to carry their bags.

We emerge from the building into the intense midday heat. The air-conditioning in the old Toyota blows dust in our faces as we bounce over the potholed roads into Phnom Penh. We pass UN Movement Control (MOVCON) and other well-constructed and wired complexes. The UN communication centre is full of radio masts and antennae freshly painted red and white. We pass a compound full of empty UN vehicles.

The streets are full of bicycle rickshaws and small motor-bikes carrying people and goods. There are markets offering fruit and vegetables and small stalls by the road sell fuel in lemonade bottles. I watch a rider sit and smoke as a child fills the tank. Closer into town sliding grey metal shutters are pushed to one side to reveal shop fronts in large shabby white concrete buildings.

When we arrive at the house we're shown to our rooms. They've just been able to fit us all in. We're all relieved to have the chance to get a few hours' sleep.

I sit up and rub my hands through my hair. It's soaking. I'm drenched in sweat and all I'm doing is lying on the bed in thin cotton shorts. The room has wooden walls and a window with metal bars and closed French wooden shutters. I stare at the stationary ceiling fan. It's useless because the electricity only comes on for a few hours in the evening and the small generator just runs a few lights, the computer and the radio.

I pull the mosquito net aside and walk across the floor-boards to the balcony. Beyond the high fence topped with barbed wire, dirty children in rags play in a heap of sand under a palm tree. Chicken scratch around them and nearby a black pig roots through the rubbish at the side of the road. The side streets in this part of Phnom Penh are just sand.

Directly opposite they're building a four-storey house. The main structure is reinforced concrete. I watch the lean work-men carrying bricks and cement up the makeshift wooden scaffold. It's lashed together with thick brown string. I'm told they start at first light and finish at last light. In this heat, that's a long, tough day.

Either side of the building site ramshackle huts of wood, corrugated iron and plastic sheet lean precariously in all directions. Rickshaw drivers pedal their passengers over the bumpy ground and motos churn dust as they brake sharply at the crossroads. I glance at my watch. I've got fifteen minutes before I meet Lawrence, the programme manager, for my initial interview. I have a quick shower and put on a clean shirt and trousers.

At exactly three p.m. Lawrence joins me on the balcony.

We sit in the two heavy wooden seats. The polished brown hardwood with black graining is so beautiful you want to stroke it. Lawrence says, 'These are typical Cambodian chairs. They're great for meetings, they're too uncomfortable to sit in for long!'

Lawrence is a former Guard's officer with an impressive résumé. An Oxbridge sporting blue who gained a first-class degree with honours and then served in the army with distinction and decoration. He's someone who can get things done. Blessed with film-star looks he comes across as being a glamorous good egg. I'm reliably informed when he goes out, girls fall over themselves to talk to him. He does, however, have a slightly crooked nose. Conversation reveals it was broken during a rugby game. He has a good sense of humour so I make a mental note to call him 'big nose' on appropriate occasions.

There are two demining locations, one in the centre of the north-west and the other near the Thai border. Tomorrow, Nigel, Richard and I, the three new boys, will travel up country with Jim.

We talk for a while. I ask him what I should know that isn't in the books and if he has any general advice. He pauses, takes a sip of water and says, 'The operations officer is a former bomb disposal officer. He's been here nearly two years and is responsible for all technical training, so that's taken care of. I know you've done all the background reading. The thing I'd stress is the importance of flexibility, keeping an open mind. This is an entirely different culture. I grew up in Africa, so I'm not easily shocked, but there are things here that will shock you. The people smile a lot, but you have to try and work out what's behind the smile. Also, do something such as reading or listening to music for an hour a day to take your mind off the frustrations.'

'Is it safe to run around the towns where the demining operations are based?'

'Yes, no problem as long as you stay on the roads and footpaths within ten kilometres of the town boundaries. Several of us run.'

'What's it like around Phnom Penh?' I'm curious to find out more about the place and aware that I've been sitting on a plane for twenty-four hours.

'Hot and full of exhaust fumes. If you'd like to we can jog a bit later. Speak to Suthy and ask him to drop us on the road to the Killing Fields. We can run back in through the country then along the side streets to avoid the smog. It'll do him good to drive alone, I've just taught him.'

I jump at the chance. My personal interview is over. I feel my way down the dark concrete staircase to the office to look for Suthy. He's the administrator and is a Cambodian of average height in his mid-twenties. He seems diligent and responsible and comes across as one of the good guys.

He's happy to drop us on the outskirts of town. Earlier today they met us at the airport, found our luggage and got us through immigration like greased lightning. I've arranged the run and got permission to read through the files to get a feel for what's going on. I take the black operations folder and sit down in a quiet corner. Now I can relax and think.

In medieval times the Khmer Empire was a feared regional power and rich rice-growing nation. In this period the Angkor Wat temple complex was built. They have elaborate Asian stone carvings of heads, mystical figures and the dancing apsara, a beautiful young woman dancing with a long garland around her neck. I'm told there's a problem with the carvings being stolen and sold.

French colonial rule was established in 1863. The strong French influence can be seen in the architecture, large UNTAC contingent and Khmer people over the age of forty who speak French – a fact they kept secret from the Khmer Rouge, which is why they weren't executed along with all the others who spoke a foreign language.

Cambodia gained independence in 1953 and in 1967 the Khmer Rouge took up arms to support peasants against a rice tax. An American-backed coup ousted King Sihanouk in 1970 and there followed a five-year civil war with the Khmer Rouge who aimed to establish a communist rice-growing dynasty, a combination of Maoism and ancient xenophobic nationalism. Several of the revolution's leaders were educated in France in the 1950s. In the 1970s, Cambodian society was riddled with corruption and nepotism. The US bombed areas heavily near the Vietnam border and well inside Cambodia thought to be part of the Ho Chi Minh Trail. Therefore to a certain extent the emergence of the Khmer Rouge is understandable; but this is definitely one plan that should never have been allowed out of the office, or more precisely the jungle.

In 1975 the Khmer Rouge defeated the American-backed leader Lon Nol after a period of bloody insurgency. Anybody connected to the previous regime was killed. The city dwellers were classed 'new people' and the rural peasants who joined the revolution in the early stages were 'old people'. The cities were emptied and the population put into forced labour growing rice and digging irrigation canals. The entire country was turned into a concentration camp. Nearly two million people died from disease, starvation, torture and execution. The population is now approximately ten million.

In late 1978, in response to repeated border attacks, Vietnam invaded and liberated Cambodia. The current head of the government, Mr Hun Sen, defected from the Khmer Rouge to Vietnam in 1977 when his regiment was being purged and ordered to attack Vietnam. He's now head of the Cambodian People's Party (CPP).

A bloody civil war raged between the Vietnamese-backed government and the non-Communist forces that immediately wanted to reliberate Cambodia from the Vietnamese. A small enclave of 'Free Cambodia' was established in the north-west near the Thai border. The Khmer Rouge continued their battle with the Vietnamese and the CPP. As in many civil wars the alliances were confusing and sometimes clandestine. Hundreds of thousands of refugees had fled into Thailand to escape the Khmer Rouge and the fighting.

The Paris Peace Accord of October 1991 resulted in a ceasefire and the UN mission to Cambodia. The peace is fragile and there are many reports of attacks and skirmishes. The aim of the United Nations Transitional Authority Cambodia (UNTAC) is to establish and monitor free and fair elections, establish democracy in Cambodia and leave the people to live happily ever after.

Many non-government organizations (NGOs) work in Cambodia. These aid and development agencies assist in areas such as medical assistance, agriculture, education and, in our case, clearing landmines and the debris of war.

During the civil war mines were laid indiscriminately. Vast areas of productive land are unusable, and refugees returning from the border camps are unable to go home to their villages or farm their land. It is estimated mines injure 300 people a month. Half die before they get to hospital. In remote areas nobody has any idea how many people are injured because there are no organizations there to keep the statistics.

I read the pamphlet on Warsaw Pact mines and how they function once more before I get changed and join Lawrence and Suthy by the old Toyota.

The air is full of hooting and two-stroke fumes from the motos. Phnom Penh is heaving and this is rush hour. There are no rules of the road except might is right, pull out if you think you can get away with it and look out for the lunatics of whom there seem to be plenty. There are some guidelines: foreigners, or *joo-un bor-ra-dtagh* as the Khmers call us, should avoid those keen to smash into you to claim dollars and try not to get involved with the police because it can be very expensive.

'This is the road to the Killing Fields,' Lawrence says as he folds a red-spotted handkerchief to make a headband. 'Many of the people killed there were Khmer Rouge, their families accused of being foreign spies or disloyal to Pol Pot. They were taken there from Toul Sleng, a torture and interrogation centre. Confessions were extracted and then they were executed. There was no question of guilt or innocence. It was a one-way trip. Each area had its own secret prison and each village its killing field.'

The hustle and bustle of the city gives way to the country. Palm trees and wooden houses with deep ponds dug in the hard clay soil, line the sides of the road. I thank Suthy, shut the door and start jogging. We've agreed to keep the pace slow since I'm not used to the heat.

Within a few minutes sweat stings my eyes. I can see why Lawrence wears a headband. I struggle to keep up. Last year he broke his ankle. He's completely recovered now and it hasn't slowed him down.

The people laugh at us as we run by and a few children

wave and practise their two-word English vocabulary: 'Hello'
and 'Okay'. We wave back and I get my first Khmer lesson.
'Hello' is '*soo-a s'day*'.

The sun turns fiery red and silhouettes the palm trees.
People pull buckets of greeny-brown water from the pools
using ropes. Then they tip the water over their heads to wash
away the dirt of their day's labour. Refuse litters the sides of
the road. People walk by, oblivious to the plastic bags, bottles,
wrappers and heaps of rotting detritus. I'm surprised the locals
don't all get together and clear it up, but I'm told things don't
work like that here. Family is sacred but there's no sense of
community.

On the outskirts of Phnom Penh we cut down a dirty side
street crammed with rickety huts. Mangy dogs rush out and
bark ferociously at me. They know I'm the new kid in town. I
slow and watch them to make sure they don't try and bite. The
medical information says there's rabies here and I'd prefer to
avoid the stomach inoculations.

Lawrence says, 'The best thing is to pretend to throw a
stone. They understand it.'

I bend down, grab a stone and make like I'm going to
chuck it at a yelping grey dog. It turns and runs back under
the hut where it came from. It's a good lesson. Sometimes it
takes force to make unreasonable beings behave reasonably.

I gallop down the road with new found confidence and
arrive at the house just behind Lawrence. The Guard opens the
noisy tin-clad gate to let me in. It scrapes on the concrete. As
we arrive Richard accuses me of being mad, but promises to
join me tomorrow.

It's nearly dark now. Duncan hands us each a bottle of
water. 'The problem when you do any exercise here is that it
takes fifteen or twenty minutes to stop sweating.'

He's right. I'm drenched and slightly dizzy. It's sweltering.
Even though I've showered and changed I'm still perspiring.

'This is the last time for six months you'll be able to have Western food, so we'll eat out tonight,' Duncan says. 'I know a great place.'

He negotiates the bumpy rubbish-strewn streets and shows us the independence monument. There are fewer motos and cyclos around, but the night streets are alive with UN vehicles. He tells us most of the ordinary Khmer people stay in when it's dark because they're afraid of robbery. The night is a dangerous time, although foreigners who were here before the UN arrived en masse say there's less shooting now.

Our first stop is a small bar called the Gecko. They say a lot of journalists use it. There are very few Khmers. For most locals, even those lucky enough to get well-paid jobs with the UN, the prices, which are very low by London standards, are well out of reach. There's a friendly, open atmosphere. Most people say hello as they arrive. It's still early, apparently the place is heaving later on.

We're told that down the road there's a parlour where happy pizzas with special ingredients are available. A man I've been chatting to at the table next to us lets me in on the secret. He's a German doctor working with the UN and he thinks they just use ordinary herbs, but they act like a placebo; everyone thinks it will have that effect so it does. We're told however, it's the best and only place in town to get a pizza. We unanimously decide we'd prefer to have fish and chips. Outside several moto riders sit waiting for their next fare. They shout, 'My friend! My friend! I take you. I wait for you.'

We walk past a few unhappy-looking children begging. A small boy shouts, 'Mr you give me one dollar I look after your car!'

Duncan negotiates and gives him 500 Riel. Nigel and I hand a small amount to two thin children and are immediately surrounded by a screaming horde of others. We escape into the Jeep. Nigel says, 'How many of these kids are orphans? Do you have any advice on dealing with them?'

'It's hard to know,' Duncan replies. 'There are two schools of thought. Number one, you tell them all to get lost so they stop begging and find another way to survive. Number two, you give what you can to the deserving cases, but God knows how you work out which they are. Some are starving, some are thieves.' He wrestles his arm away from two children trying to pull it through the window. 'And some are just bloody irritating.'

He continues. 'Sometimes if you don't pay them to look after the vehicle they might vandalize it, but it's rare. Like a lot of things here; there are no easy answers.'

The street is a dual carriageway separated by a wide, tree-lined mid-section. There are also trees either side of the road in front of the buildings. I look forward to seeing it in daylight. Their trunks are painted white, to stop people walking into them at night. There are no street lights here. We're parked on the central avenue under the trees.

As we walk back Duncan suddenly stops and shines his torch into an open drain about a metre wide and deep. 'There are lots of these here. You need to be careful in the dark. It is easy to break a leg.'

Motos and cyclos without lights meander down the road. Wooden stalls by the roadside sell cigarettes, iced fruit drinks, cooked chicken and moto fuel. A few hours after dark they disappear. Above us I see a myriad stars. This is unlike any other city I've seen.

The restaurant is a majestic three-storey building. A vast orange generator illuminates and cools it. The cement walls are painted ochre and the French shutters green. It has a black and white tiled floor and large tropical plants in massive clay pots line the balcony and interior.

We sit in a quiet corner. It's still early. Several people

Duncan knows come over to chat. The expatriate world seems rife with rumour and gossip. People start to crowd in. It looks like every night is party night. I understand why when I'm told the UN local living allowance is over a hundred dollars a day. Some revel to relieve the pressures of their work and separation from their families and some do it just because they can. Possibly large numbers of the UN don't go out, but you wouldn't know that because you never see them.

Jim tells us Cambodian food is fine, as long as you like rice. We're all tired and once back at the house find our way through the total darkness using torches. We all need a good night's sleep; we're heading up country first thing tomorrow morning.

*

The smell of rotting fish and sewage is overpowering. I can see large ships moored in the reddy-brown waters of the Mekong. A small oil tanker makes the tiny fishermen's boats look like flies. 'On the left is the Olympic Arena.' I turn my head quickly, thinking he's joking, and am surprised to see a concrete stadium and a huge Olympic symbol. They're shabby and tarnished. It must have been hot training.

Jim continues his tour. 'On the right is the bridge to nowhere. It's more of a pier really. It was never finished because the Khmer Rouge took power. They say when the UN first arrived, someone drove off it into the Mekong.'

We stop at a jammed roundabout. The general flow of traffic seems to go to the right; but motos and cyclos head in the opposite direction, apparently at will. There is much hooting and stamping of brakes. The concrete bridge rises the other side and stops in mid-air. It was an understandable mistake, particularly in the dark. I make a mental note of the roundabout and stadium and ask, 'Are there many bridges like this in Phnom Penh?'

'No, just that one. It's also the only uphill road, so it's easy to remember. And it's not always the most dangerous. Bridges and culverts outside Phnom Penh are frequently attacked by the Khmer Rouge. There are government soldiers guarding them all, as you'll see.'

There is a huge UN fuel storage-depot on the left and rusty barges litter the banks. There are people everywhere. Electric-blue sparks fly as a man welds a plate on to a rusty barge by the side of the road. I turn my head quickly, but it's too late to see properly. I don't think he was wearing goggles to protect his eyes.

There are large warehouses on the right and tall palm trees line the road, making it cooler. We pass an overloaded Russian lorry belching black fumes and narrowly avoid taking out a moto whose driver insists on riding in the middle of the road. At the last minute he veers into the side. Some time after we go over a mini-flyover there's a huge timber yard on the right. I could smell the wood a long time before we saw it.

We stop to buy soft drinks in a small town with a Y-junction. I wonder where the other road leads? We continue, then the vehicle lurches. Nigel and I are suddenly thrown off the side seats on to the luggage and end up in a tangle of arms and legs. Half the road has been worn away and the tarmac ends abruptly with a six-inch drop.

Nearby there's a small petrol station that used to be painted white. The ancient pumps are broken. Diesel and petrol are sold by the can and taken from a large metal storage-tank. The enamelled Esso sign would be a perfect museum piece if it hadn't been used for target practice.

As we emerge into the countryside the road is built up above the paddy fields. They look barren and dusty. A canal has been dug either side of the road and the soil thrown in the middle to raise it. Presumably stones were then dumped on top and covered with asphalt.

The wet season is due to start soon. I watch fascinated as we pass a wooden ox cart loaded with terracotta pots and packed with straw. The tarmac road disappears into a bumpy, stony track. Children and old people with small hoes stand and beg with their straw hats by holes they've just filled in. We pass through an area where it looks like the only local industry.

Jim slows down. 'One of the UNMOs told me a few months ago a UN vehicle had an accident here. A child walked in front of it and was killed. They stopped to help, but it was too late. The driver ran away and the mob hacked the UN man to death. It's the way they do things here.' I look around. The road is sandy and seems to stretch ahead forever. The flat rice paddies and occasional trees merge into dark forest on the horizon. There's no other traffic.

We stop in Kompong Chnang for lunch. There's a Red Cross hospital near the centre of town. We sit briefly in front of the restaurant. The sandy ground is covered with rubbish and the table is dirty. Nobody really wants to eat. At the next table two UN soldiers have a Coke and politely say good morning before they leave.

Thirst quenched we continue. The tarmac runs out again and we bump once more over a rocky road. Jim says, 'This was latterite when I first arrived, the locally quarried gravel. In the last seven months it's been completely worn away.'

We have to slow down to a snail's pace as we pass through a village. By the roadside two men kneel over a large grey pig. Its trotters are trussed up with rope. Women and children stand and watch. One of the men has a knife in his hand, the other tightens the ropes. The pig gives a shrill, piercing squeal. A little girl has realized something nasty is going to be done to the family pet. She can't understand. Her face shows confusion and horror of innocence betrayed. As we drive away the screams fade.

In the distance there are two men standing in the road with

guns. We approach a bridge manned by soldiers in faded khaki uniforms. There are four of them. Two are in hammocks. They have long matted hair and several wear a piece of cloth wrapped around their waist like a skirt. Jim calls it a *kramar*. It's cotton and patterned with small coloured squares, usually red and white. In the distance there are two more soldiers standing on the road. As we get closer I see one has an M16 and the other an AK 47. Two rocket launchers lean against trees by the hammocks. They move to the side and gawp at us as we pass. We wave and they wave back without altering their wild stares.

'The late afternoon is a bad time to travel. By then they're usually drunk on palm wine. There are soldiers on every bridge between here and Battambang. They collect taxes from locals using the roads. Most NGOs and the UN don't get stopped. *Joo-un bor-ra-dtagh* are treated with respect and they want the aid agencies to work here, so it's probably too much trouble for them to stop us. The provincial authorities sometimes sort out checkpoints that get out of hand. Our policy is to give nothing at roadblocks. The soldiers are often not paid and when they are it's only about ten or fifteen dollars a month, but in some places the commanders get their men to collect the money and become very rich. Nobody travels outside the towns after dark. There are bandits and the Khmer Rouge frequently cross this road under cover of darkness. There's often fighting around here.'

For hours we clatter and jolt along the dusty red highway. Nigel and I are in the back. Every now and then we laugh and grimace when we take off and land on the hard side seats as the Land Rover negotiates rocks. Nigel's travelling light, with one small bag. We've run out of bumpy road jokes but the countryside is fascinating. We pass wooden houses surrounded by trees, sometimes mango and palm and sometimes lone remnants of the forest, left for shade. Once outside the towns there's little sign of the vast UN peace mission. I wonder how much difference it will make to the lives of the people struggling to survive here? There are so many things to try and understand about this curious place.

We're suddenly back on tarmac. We enjoy the speed and luxury of a flat road. 'How did the road get that bad?' Nigel says. 'Did the Khmer Rouge dig it up?'

'I used to think they must have,' Jim replies, 'but it's just decades of disrepair and overloaded vehicles. In the wet season the rain's so heavy the roads get washed away. You see that new wooden building with the beer signs up ahead? That's the latest dancing restaurant. I think one of the local generals built it. Trouble is, nobody goes there. It's on the edge of town and people are afraid the Khmer Rouge will creep across the paddy fields under cover of darkness and attack them. Then they'll vanish into the forest before the army and police can react.' I've read that Cambodian mythology is full of stories of ghosts and spirits, and that evil lurks in the depths of the forest.

There are more wooden houses and huts along the road. Soon we come to the outskirts of town. We wave to a UN Landcruiser as it passes and pause by a line of shop fronts. Some of the buildings are cement and brick, some are wood. Most of the owners live behind their shop front. There is an open-fronted chemist shop with a few boxes of pills in a wooden and glass display case, and several restaurants. They all have lockable doors or wooden or metal sliding shutters.

A red sign with white letters says 'Angkor Beer'. In spite of the poverty and lack of infrastructure the distribution of alcohol and cigarettes is a thriving business. Jim tells us there's a massive brewery near the seaport of Kompong Som and bottles of Scotch are on sale in most shops in the towns.

Part of the road-bridge has been demolished. Remnants of the buttresses and steel supports are still standing. It looks like it was built in the 1920s and blown up in the 1970s. It's been replaced with green Bailey bridge sections. The planks rattle as we drive over them. Children jump off the bridge into the yellow-brown water. We turn right along the sandy, coconut-lined riverbank, then left through grey wooden gates into the tree-shaded yard of a white-painted house. 'This is callsign 802, our location base,' Jim announces as we carry our kit into the large single-storey residence.

The huge veranda and floors are paved with red and yellow glazed tiles. In the 1920s it may have been the home of a French colonial administrator. Metal bars guard the unglazed windows and the French-style shutters are painted drab grey. Sparsely furnished with a few functional tables and a bamboo bookcase, it's just a temporary base for men and equipment for the duration of their task.

After sorting out our rooms and drinking some water we sit and wait on the airless veranda. Jim takes us to the map board and gives a general brief. 'Relationships with the local agencies are excellent. We're lucky because the senior UNMO here is a British colonel called Martin and all of the UN from the chief administrator to the soldier on the gate are helpful and friendly. He's asked us to clear a village called Chnang, which is here. The area is regularly patrolled and safe. He told us a few months ago that about forty kilometres north a commander called Mr Red shot several local people because he thought they were Vietnamese spies. Apparently they had a slightly different accent. Martin describes him as a *very bad man*. Draw your own conclusions. Fortunately, the local military say Mr Red doesn't have enough men to move out of his area.'

Jim then looks at his watch and says. 'Something's wrong. Mike and the team should have been here over an hour ago.' There's nothing we can do except wait. Eventually we hear the unmistakable approach of a Land Rover. Mike gets out, introduces himself and explains that he's been delayed helping a man injured by a mine.

THE NEXT DAY

It's eight o'clock in the morning. Nigel, Richard and I are sitting around the large wooden table with notebooks and pens at the ready. The operations officer stands by a shelf, upon which most of the mines, fuses and other types of ordnance found in Cambodia are displayed. Mike is tall and has the build of a natural athlete. He's been in Cambodia for nearly two years.

'Our objectives are to train demobilized Cambodian soldiers to clear mines, to identify and prioritize mined areas for clearance and supervise those operations,' he begins. 'We do all of this in co-operation with the other organizations working here, the biggest of which is the UN Mine Clearance and Training Unit (MTCU). Over the next few days we'll cover the technical aspects of mine clearance and demolition procedures and then I'll test you for real in those areas. After dry training we'll visit the field and take part in daily operations. This morning there will be a general introduction to mines followed by area familiarization.'

He turns to the shelves and says. 'These training aids are all free from explosive (FFE), which is why they're on display. In simple terms there are three sorts of mine: anti-vehicle, anti-groups of people and anti-personnel.'

Pointing at a light green mine the size of small circular tea tray and ten centimetres high, he says, 'This is a Soviet TM46 anti-tank mine. The casing is thin sheet steel and its total weight is 8.4 kilograms, 5.3 kilograms of which is TNT. When fitted with MV5 or MVM pressure fuses it has an operating force of 120 to 180 kilograms, so, theoretically, you could jump on it and it wouldn't go off, although I don't recommend it.'

We look at each other and Richard laughs.

Mike says, 'Don't laugh. People have done it.'

He moves forward and uses both hands to pick up an olive-green mine the size of a large baked-bean can with a three-pronged fuse screwed into the top. 'This is an OZM72, designed to kill or wound groups of people. About four kilograms of small steel shrapnel is blasted by about half a kilogram of explosive over a radius of approximately fifty metres. It's a bounding or jumping mine and it can be fitted with a variety of fuses. Over here you'll usually come up against trip wire initiation, which fires an igniter that sets off a low explosive charge in the base. This fires it out of its case into the air. There is a retaining wire linking the central detonator and the case. When it becomes taut the main charge explodes, sending steel fragments everywhere.'

He returns the heavy steel cylinder to its place on the shelf and holds up a brown bakelite mine. It's the size of a small, round tin of sweets and has a black rubber top. 'This is a Russian PMN anti-personnel mine. It contains 240 grams of cast TNT, which is a lot. Sometimes it kills the person who steps on it, or simply removes both their legs. Occasionally it may only result in the amputation of one leg. It's operated by 222 grams of pressure on the rubber cap. This simply forces the central cylinder down, which releases the striker into the detonator and then bang!' He puts it neatly in its place on the shelf before continuing.

'Anti-personnel mines like this have been laid in and around many villages in this area. Refugees can't go home because their villages and farmland have been mined. If they're lucky they may get taken to a hospital. Sometimes other people are blown up trying to rescue them. Medical resources are very limited and the local hospital is run by an aid agency, but it's better to see it than talk about it.'

As we emerge into the glaring sun I wonder if Mike's giving us an easy first day so we can acclimatize to the heat.

The market square is littered with rubbish and cow manure. Three light brown cows stand chewing the cud. Each has a rope through its nose, attached to a small boy. Concrete buildings with balconies and steel-shuttered shop fronts surround the square. About half of them have stacks of goods for sale, the rest look empty. The white paint has long since peeled and faded to grey.

We pass a magnificent yellow colonial house with grey-painted French shutters and a red tiled roof, surrounded by a wall and well-positioned palm trees. A second glance reveals peeling paint and rotting wood. 'That's the Governor's house.' Mike turns into the hospital entrance. 'He doesn't live there.'

The guard raises the metal barrier and waves. He wears a *kramar* wrapped round his waist and a battered blue peaked cap, like a parking attendant. Ours is the only vehicle in the compound. We park under the shade of the palm trees and he takes us to meet the Médecin Sans Frontières (MSF) doctor. She's here with her boyfriend who's a civil engineer. He's building the hospital. She explains that they are working alongside the Cambodian Health Ministry and the local medical staff intermittently get paid ten or fifteen dollars a month. They are short of blood. The local people won't give it because they believe it makes them weak and unwell. We all volunteer to give blood and then walk around the hospital.

Walking into the old building I'm immediately hit by the smell. It's a mixture of iodine, fish soup and bed-pans, with the unmistakable hint of rotting flesh. I turn into a dingy concrete room and wait for my eyes to acclimatize to the darkness. There are yellow and cream ceramic tiles on the floor.

A man my age is lying on a hard wooden bed. His face shows his pain, but he still tries to smile. His left leg is fine and so is his right, apart from the burns and the missing foot. The leg stops below the knee and is wrapped in a blood-stained bandage. I try not to stare, but I can't help it. I wonder how he will walk, grow rice and feed his children. Perhaps he'll end up begging like the other amputees I've seen.

I nod, smile and leave and walk guiltily down the corridor to meet a man in a heavy wooden wheelchair. One of his legs has been amputated well above the knee and the other just below. He probably stepped on a PMN. The stumps are wrapped in clean crêpe bandages. I think about amputation. One limb, bad. Two limbs, horrific beyond comprehension.

How would I cope? I can't imagine and I don't want to. I think I'd rather die.

I try not to stare. I smile and nod and say, 'Hello.' Without lifting his eyes, he grunts.

We spend the rest of the day meeting the key people in the agencies we'll be working with and learning more about the area.

The next morning at eight we sit eagerly around the table once more. We spend the day going through types of mine and how they function. Just before we finish Mike holds a green plastic mine the size of a tin of shoe polish in the palm of his hand. 'This is state of the art simplicity. The Chinese Type 72A. Only about 34 grams of TNT or TNT RDX mix. It's initiated by direct pressure to the rubber top. This forces a plastic diaphragm, with a metal striker in the centre, into the detonator. This in turn fires the booster charge underneath, which initiates the TNT moulded around the centre. It's a minimum metal content mine, which we are just able to detect.

Some of the soldiers around here call it the foot fucker. That's it for today. Tomorrow we go into the field.'

The journey takes an hour. They cleared the former military camp last year. The only sign of its previous use are the trench lines. The area around it is treeless and featureless.

The three of us watch from a safe distance as Mike prepares the first demolition. When a mine is found it's destroyed in situ by placing an explosive charge next to it. He stands up, looks all around, and shouts, 'Prong proyat moyna dee. Controlled explosion one minute.' He pulls the igniter on the safety fuse and walks back to the control point, maintaining his surveillance. As he reaches us he says, 'Lets see how good my timing is. I set that to three minutes. Remember this is 240 grams of TNT. Exactly the same amount as there is in a PMN.'

I watch the second hand on my watch. At exactly three minutes there is a thunderous boom and a small cloud of dust and debris. It is so loud. I feel it in my guts. Richard and I exchange glances.

After the demonstrations we visit the minefield to watch the teams working. It's a forty-minute drive through villages with small wooden and bamboo huts and through dense bush and bamboo. As we approach the Zil, a white-painted Russian lorry, a slim Cambodian with a wide grin directs us into a roped parking area. Mike introduces him as Mr Sok the truck driver, who speaks no English, but smiles a lot. He's got six kids and one more on the way. His wife cooks the food for the deminers.

A small Khmer man walks back down a red gravel road which we're told is coloured by locally quarried latterite. He introduces himself as Mr Houn, our interpreter. He's five feet five, slim and in his mid-thirties. He has a gentle, honest face, which seems somehow out of place here. He welcomes us and thanks us for coming to help the Cambodian people.

Jim briefs us on the site and we then go around with an individual guide. I'm paired with Mr Houn who shows me the control point, the administration area and the first-aid point and explains the function of each. We watch the deminers in their black uniforms working in their metre wide lanes marked with white tape. They feel carefully for trip wires, cut the vegetation, place it behind them, then sweep the ground with the locator. When the shrill electrical tone sounds they sweep again to identify the spot, prod carefully and dig to find the metal. 'We find many metal fragment for every mine,' Houn says.

'Don't they get hot wearing black?'

'No. Deminer prefer black. It more cool.' Mr Houn's dark brown eyes twinkle with humour.

At the end of the working day I travel back with him and Mr Sok in the Zil lorry. I enjoy talking to him and learn a lot about the villages and the history of this tortured land. 'Khmer Rouge make people dig big ditch.' He points to a dry, over-grown gully with such massive banks either side it's hard to believe they were dug by slave labour.

I ask him what it was like for him and his family in that time and wish I hadn't. He looks down and says quietly, 'My brother sick. He work slow. Khmer Rouge make him wait by side of track in bushes with two others. They come back with big stick to smash head and kill.'

When we get back to base Mike debriefs us on the day. 'Once we've finished training and testing you'll be partnered with another expat for several weeks and then, when you're happy and we're happy, you'll be on your own. General military skills, like first aid, communications and the ability to lead in a hazardous environment are vital. Character counts, because a lot of the time you'll be on your own and everything will be down to you. I'll just mention personal conduct;

because we work closely with other NGOs it's important that we behave reasonably, but I'm sure you don't need me to tell you this.

'The technical aspects of mine clearance are a prerequisite. It's a basic military skill, not a black art. The most widely used and effective method at present is manual. So far, for the conditions we're working in, machines aren't as efficient or cost effective.

'Manual demining is a combination of horticulture and archaeology. It's all about caution, professionalism and discipline. As you all know, it involves feeling for trip wires, cutting the vegetation, sweeping the ground with metal detectors and then prodding carefully and digging to find the metal. Battlefields and village sites are slow to clear because of metal contamination from mortars, shells and bullets.

'I can't teach courage, common sense, decency and enthusiasm. They're important and the boss thinks you've got them; which is why you're here.

'In the next few weeks look around you if you go into town in the evening. You'll see people who can't handle being in this kind of environment. Perhaps it's just this place, but it's like something gets a hold of them and they gradually give in to it.'

The next day Jim takes me, accompanied by Mr Houn and Mr Sok, to set up a new demining site in a remote forest village. The only access is an orange-ochre track through rice paddies dotted with tall trees behind the small logging town of Rhum. It turns from rutted clay to white sand as it leads ten kilometres into the vast forest, which stretches along the Thai-Cambodian border into Laos.

Chnang village is the last outpost before Khmer Rouge territory. Things are quieter now, but in the last few years there's been fierce fighting here. It's a sprawling settlement of wooden and bamboo huts under palm, mango and forest trees.

A river runs through the north of the village. In the wet season it's a torrent. In the dry season it's not much more than a large stream between deep stagnant pools.

As we emerge from the trees Jim points towards a clearing where rough wooden fence-posts surround an area of low scrub. 'That area's mined. It used to be a Vietnamese firebase. Nobody goes in there and it's one of the few fenced minefields in the Province. It's not a priority to clear, but the one in the village certainly is.' He laughs and points. Three water buffalo are wallowing in ponds. Their large horned heads and big hairy nostrils protrude from the water. A small boy sitting on the back of one of the submerged water buffalo waves as we pass.

On the southern side of the village the school has been rebuilt from local wood and clay tiles by a local NGO. It's big enough to take forty children from all the hamlets around, including those thought to be under the control of the Khmer Rouge. For the last few years there has been an uneasy peace. But the school can't open yet because the overgrown area adjacent to it is full of mines. There have been casualties.

Between the track and scrub of the minefield there is a strip of grass fifty metres wide where children graze water buffalo. The mined area used to be a military camp and a trench and raised bank mark its perimeter. Both Jim and Mike have been here before, done a full recce and got permission from all factions to clear the mines.

We establish the vehicle park, control point, first-aid point, administration and rest area near the school and then mark several metres outside the mined area where we know it's clear. There is one team of twenty deminers working in pairs so we measure and mark ten-metre wide lanes with a thirty-five-metre safety distance between each.

Once everything is clearly marked and everyone is fully briefed, the section commanders act as guides and take the deminers in small groups along the safe area to familiarize them with the layout. Next, the team leader supervises the section commanders as the deminers are deployed and work begins. We stop at two p.m. and return to base.

Later that evening Jim and I walk for five minutes to the market square. Only one or two houses have generators. A few motos ride past us cautiously trying to avoid the cyclists, all of whom have no lights. Across the river the palm trees are outlined against the breathtaking, star-laden sky.

The dancing restaurant plays deafening Cambodian and Thai'd music. A group of white cars and UN vehicles are guarded by a band of hopeful children. There is a race between amputees on crude metal crutches to be the first with the begging bowl. Jim tells me he tries to give something to the one who always arrives last; in this case a one-legged blind man led by a thin, ragged child.

We sit at a table outside a small open shop front near the dancing restaurant. The grey metal shutters are open, revealing a family home selling beer, Coke and whisky. In a small way they also trade gold and gems from the Khmer Rouge occupied area around Pailin.

The owner's wife is a thin woman with a gentle face, who wears a sarong and white blouse. She puts an oil lamp on the table and brings us two Cokes. We're too thirsty for beer. Jim points to a small group of stalls the other side of the square by the dancing restaurant. 'They sell food over there. The ice, crushed fruit and condensed milk is good, but don't try the eggs. They cook them just before they hatch so it's not so much boiled egg as Khmer fried chicken.'

I turn my chair slightly to look at the stars again. On the next table I notice a thin Khmer with a ragged moustache smiling and drinking a Fosters from the can. I catch sight of a pistol tucked discreetly in the waistband of his trousers. He nods eagerly and says, 'Hello.'

Jim has met him before. In hushed tones he tells me he's

the captain of the Special Police tasked directly by the Governor. They patrol the border areas and spy on the Khmer Rouge. Jim turns towards him and says, 'I haven't seen you for a while.'

'No. I capture by Khmer Rouge in forest. I lucky they no kill me. They not know who I am.' He grins and carries on.

'I tell them I love Khmer Rouge. They think I am poor man and no kill. Their leader very bad man. He kill everyone.'

His story is interrupted by the arrival of a large European, who greets Jim and sits at the next table.

The captain leaves silently.

'Hey! Whisky and beer.' The large European leans back in his chair and takes a long draw on a cigarette. As the woman scurries over and puts an oil lamp on the fragile folding table he emerges from the shadows. His head was shaved, but is now covered with grey-black stubble. He wears a fake designer T-shirt and baggy brown shorts.

I look at Jim and raise my eyebrows. He lights a cigarette and says quietly, 'Bulgarian, I think.'

The large man sinks most of the can of beer, looks into the shop and hisses, 'Got any nice stones?'

The shop owner looks nervously around him, disappears and then walks to the table. He looks about thirty. A clean white shirt hangs on his thin frame, and his black trousers look large and incongruous above his red flip-flop-clad feet He pulls a plastic bag from his pocket, puts a small cloth on the table and pours a selection of stones out. The Bulgarian rubs a fat finger over the stones and says, 'Okay, I see you tomorrow.'

Without looking up, the Cambodian says, 'Yes, sir,' folds the stones in the cloth, shoves them in his pocket and scurries back into the shop.

Swigging a second beer the Bulgarian turns and says, 'You guys British?'

'Yes.'

He slides his chair to our table and says, 'I've only got a few weeks left in this shit-hole. Then I go home.'

Pulling a photo from a thick wallet he points and says. 'My wife and kids.'

Without pausing for comment he stuffs it back, smirks and continues. 'I made sure I had a good time here. First few months I thought I'd save all my money. Then I get to thinking. I spend all my life looking after them; so it's time I enjoy myself. This fucking place gets to you. So I got my lazy gook interpreter to do some work and get me good girls. They do anything for dollars; these people are fucking dirty.'

He takes another swig and laughs. 'Have you heard the latest gossip about the UN soldiers guarding the base up north? When the Dutch took over they got pretty upset because the small kids kept coming up to the sentries and saying, "Okay mister. Blow job one dollar." Then there were the two interpreters from that base who got sent to the UN hospital with multiple anal lesions because the officers they were interpreting for told them it was part of their job to take it up the arse!' He swigs the rest of his beer, throws a few dollars on the table, grabs the whisky bottle and says. 'See you guys later.'

As I watch him disppear into the darkness, I remember Mike's words and wonder how long it took for him and those like him to become like this.

We decide not to go to the dancing restaurant tonight and walk home silently. I put out my clothes, ready for tomorrow, and climb under the mosquito net, think about the next day and drift towards sleep.

Sweat prickles on my forehead and back. It's unbelievably hot. I move my head to try to get some fresh air. I'm travelling through thick forest. In places the sun breaks through the canopy.

To my left there's a fallen tree with strangely contorted branches that has finally found peace among the leaf mould. Beyond it an enormous jungle tree towers above everything.

Out of the shade the sun is blinding and the heat overbearing. I feel slightly dizzy. I take a deep breath. The air is full of a beautiful sweet scent.

Directly ahead there's a grove of bamboo. I can still smell the scent.

Suddenly I'm falling and everything's gone black.

Now the heat's gone and it's cool, beautifully cool. I hear a splash and I feel the coolness of water. It's still dark, but I've stopped falling.

Now, I'm rising, floating upwards. Everything is happening in slow motion. I see vivid yellow and then bright, beautiful blue.

I wake with a start, like I've fallen off the edge of a cliff. I was dreaming, but it was so real. The heat, the smell, the motion and the coolness; I felt it all.

I've had this dream before. It was a few months ago, when I was trying to decide what to do. Afterwards I couldn't go back to sleep so I put the light on and read.

It must be the heat.

As I lie back a dog howls in the distance. Suddenly a burst of automatic fire blasts through the night. It's close; it must be from the bridge. The police and militia guard it during the hours of darkness. I can hear Khmer men shouting. There's another burst, then a long silence.

After five minutes a single pistol shot shatters, then becomes part of the night. I look at my watch. It's three in the morning.

5

TRIAL

I jerk the steering wheel to the right to take the Land Rover round the edge of the large tree root and straighten up almost immediately. I want to look after the shock absorbers. With metal detectors, first-aid kit, demolition equipment and six deminers it's a full load. Mr Houn the interpreter is sitting next to me in the passenger seat. The Zil, following behind, is being driven by Sok. There are about twenty women and children in the rear of the truck and about seventeen deminers.

The Land Rover rolls effortlessly across the sand. After the bumpy, potholed latterite roads it's unbelievably smooth. There's no room for lack of concentration though. I scan the sides of the track for more jutting roots. The trees vary in height from five to fifty feet; most are about fifteen metres. They all look the same, with large olive-green ribbed leaves the size and shape of a rugby ball. The locals use them for everything, from wrapping food to cigarette papers.

The loggers have taken the biggest trees. Occasional stumps stand like gravestones, but few towering trees still stand, their trunks hollow or disfigured, saved perhaps by their defects. Plants about a metre high line the side of the track. Some of them brighten my day. One has a plain white flower like a lily, another an elaborate purple trumpet, possibly an orchid.

A few bicycle tracks cross the wet sand and mud around

the deep puddles, signs of early-morning journeys by the village people taking rubber, wood, rice and anything else they can sell to the small gathering of wooden houses by the river. Last week I saw a small pig tied, legs upward, to a board on the back of a bike. I can still hear its squeals.

The track widens occasionally and winds to avoid the odd fallen tree. These points would make good passing places, but we've never seen another vehicle. It leads down to the wet clay quagmire of the flat paddy fields and on to the town of Rhum.

I hold my arm out of the window for the joy of the cool breeze. A small branch brushes my forearm. I glance at my watch. It's nearly 1.10 p.m. We should make it back slightly early, which will give us plenty of time to sort out the kit.

God, it's hot.

Trees and bushes either side of us limit visibility to a few metres. That and the remoteness of the place make me feel uneasy. This is definitely the boonies, the middle of nowhere. It must be the weather. The air is heavy with the threat of the monsoon. Charcoal-grey clouds darken the sky.

Through a gap in the trees I can see the angular, tree-covered mountains stretching into the distance – Khmer Rouge territory. I wonder what secrets lie there. The local people tell terrible stories.

I keep looking for tree roots at the side of the track, my gaze is drawn back to the gap in the trees. The clouds above the mountain are getting blacker. I never knew clouds could be so black. I narrow my eyes and glance towards the sun. They're edging closer and closer and now they obliterate it. The whole world seems dark.

The men laugh and chatter in the back of the Land Rover. One of them says my name. I turn to Houn, my interpreter, who says, with a mischievous smile, 'Deminer would like to do some more singing.'

I continue to watch for tree roots. The only thing that

comes to mind is the old school hymn. Not original, but at least I know most of the words. I sing the first line.

'Onlad Clistan solders marching as to war,' repeat my Cambodian colleagues, amid fits of laughter.

I am laughing because they sound like pratts and they're laughing because I sound like one. I look down the track and watch for anything unusual.

The stench of rotting flesh makes me catch my breath. I retch and try not to breathe in as I speak. 'Mr Houn, what's died here?'

'Maybe someone from village kill snake here, or forest cat die in bushes.'

'You mean they didn't eat it?'

He smiles indulgently. 'Cambodian people not eat all snakes.' I like Mr Houn. He is a quiet, good-natured and intelligent man. Like many, he had a tough time under Pol Pot, and many of his family were killed. Anyone connected to the previous regime, intellectuals, people speaking foreign languages and those too sick to work were eliminated or 'smashed' as Khmer Rouge records describe it.

We are approaching the large clearing at the edge of the jungle. I concentrate just in front of the Land Rover to avoid the bumps.

'Stop! Khmer Rouge!' shouts Mr Houn.

For a moment I wonder if he's joking, but I've never heard him raise his voice before. I find the sound of him shouting more shocking than the potential threat. I glance left into the bushes, because I expect them to be in cover. 'Where?'

'In front.' Mr Houn points.

Shit, he's not wrong. I feel sweat prickle on my face and the back of my hands tingle. There are at least twenty of them along the tree line at the edge of the clearing 250 metres away. My mind races and I can hear my heart beating faster.

'Stop!' he shouts.

What's the Zil truck doing? I check my mirror. He's still moving. Sok hasn't seen them yet. I wave and start to swing right. I might just be able to turn round and head back to the village. If Sok can get ahead of me we might just do it. Come on, look at me Sok! I must get his attention. My fingers flick to the horn.

The truck is slowing down. Shit, they've ambushed it. Three Khmer Rouge soldiers have just jumped out in front of them from the bushes.

As I look ahead again I can see AK 47s, AKMs and several RPGs. There is no way we can drive through. There are too many of them and they're too heavily armed.

Are there any other options? We can't go back either. There are six deminers and Mr Houn with me in this Land Rover and everyone in the Zil truck. If we try to reverse back and the Khmer Rouge start firing there will be a massacre.

I rub my hand across my forehead to stop the sweat running into my eyes. There are no other options. We have to stop.

My hand slips on the gear lever as I put it into neutral. I press my feet hard on the brake and clutch and turn off the ignition. The deminers have gone quiet.

We are sitting ducks. We have to get out. I turn to say so and all I can see is a scramble of black uniforms and arms and legs all trying to get through the back door at the same time. I smell a mixture of sweat, unwashed clothes and adrenalin. What's happening to the truck?

Everyone's jumping off. The men are helping the women and children from the village to get down. Looking around I get the feeling they think the best option is to put as much distance between them and the Khmer Rouge as possible. This certainly seems sensible; most have fought against them as soldiers.

I turn to the front. The Khmer Rouge are running towards us waving their weapons. This is a well-planned ambush. They

look like they know what they're doing. The men behind me
are slowly moving away. I hope to God nobody starts shooting.
Now I can see a few Khmer Rouge soldiers behind us too.
They must have been hiding in the bushes. We are surrounded.
What should I do?

There isn't much choice. I must try to communicate and
convince them we are friendly and neutral. The worst thing
would be to behave like a victim. I have to find the commander
and talk to him.

The Khmer Rouge soldiers are wearing Chinese olive-green
uniforms. They look a mean bunch. There is a soldier five
metres to my left who's running. He is holding an old but well
oiled AK 47. I'll try to talk to him. I walk towards him with
my hand outstretched to shake hands. I'll try and say hello in
Khmer and see what happens.

'*Soo-a s'day.*'

He glances at me, his face filled with hate, and carries on
running. Obviously not a good start. I suppose I'd better try
again. I wonder who's in charge?

Two soldiers jog past me towards the truck waving AK 47s.
They are shouting and gesticulating. I have no idea what they're
saying. They are hostile and aggressive, if not totally out of
control.

To my front a Khmer Rouge soldier about my age is moving
towards me. He is wearing the same Chinese olive-green
uniform as the others, but is carrying a Tokarev pistol. If I
remember rightly the weapon doesn't have a safety catch.

This must be the commander. I should try to introduce myself. I half raise my arms and start to walk towards him slowly.

As I get closer he looks perplexed. I smile, put my hands
together in a Khmer greeting, and bow. I hold out my right
hand.

I say hello in my politest Khmer. '*Soo-a s'day.*'

'*Soo-a s'day.*' He shakes hands and smiles the smile of a

man who has been waiting days to ambush somebody and has finally succeeded. His handshake is like holding a piece of dead wet fish. He heads straight to the Land Rover with two soldiers and begins to search it. There is nothing random about their actions. I think they're looking for weapons. Thank God we don't have any.

A soldier in a new olive-green uniform is running towards me. He's carrying an SKS with a rifle-propelled grenade. I think it's best not to move. He stops three feet in front of me and points the rocket at my chest. I can see his finger is on the trigger.

A trickle of sweat runs down my back. I breathe in. My chest and back ache.

He shouts. I don't understand what. He has wide, glazed eyes. As he shouts his nostrils flare like the snout of a pig. I look into his eyes and in an instant there is understanding. I don't like him and he doesn't like me. Still, this won't get me anywhere. I have to try to be sociable. I hold out my right hand and try again to introduce myself.

'*Soo-a s'day.*'

Pig Face responds by shouting some more and bringing the rocket very close to my face. I think he might try to shove it up my nose. I think I could be pushing my luck. Time to take a step back.

I bow humbly, but keep my eyes on him. He glances from me to the truck. He motions with his rifle in the direction of the deminers. I turn and start to walk. I can see Mr Houn by the Land Rover. His face is a mask.

As I get closer he speaks quietly. 'We must go over there or Khmer Rouge will kill us.' I feel like a defeated animal as we walk back towards the edge of the clearing. There are more Khmer Rouge behind us. The deminers and the village people are standing in a group. Soldiers with AK 47s cover them. We are made to stand in a semicircle. The soldiers motion with their weapons and start to shout. It reminds me of a scene from *The Killing Fields*.

'What are they saying Mr Houn?'

'We must walk backwards to bushes and stand still.'

Without looking behind we tiptoe backwards.

'*Chop! Chop!*' The soldiers shout at us to stop.

There are about twenty of them in front of us, weapons at the ready. Behind them in the middle of the clearing two soldiers are searching the empty Zil truck. Beyond them I can see the look-outs posted at the edge of the clearing.

There is more shouting. Mr Houn looks worried. 'They say we must take off clothes and put on ground.'

The deminers slowly take off their jackets. A few glance at me. The Khmer Rouge watch, fingers pressed on triggers. Pig Face walks purposefully towards me. I wonder if his grenade is fragmentation or blast?

Most of the blokes have taken their jackets off. Pig Face is getting excited again and shouting. Mr Houn looks worried. 'We must take clothes off and put on ground.'

Looks like I picked the wrong day to wear a boiler suit. Slowly I undo the leather belt around my waist and place it and the Leatherman pouch on the ground. I don't want them to think I have a pistol. The Leatherman multi-tool with built-in pliers is my most precious possession. I know they'll try to steal my watch, so I try to hide it. I put my hands behind my back, undo the strap and hold it in my fist.

I turn to Mr Houn; he looks worried. Not surprising considering that fifteen years ago members of his family were executed in front of him. I come from a different place. How can I understand what he's feeling?

He turns slightly, not taking his eyes off Pig Face. 'Khmer Rouge say you must take off clothes.'

I am not going to be a victim. I turn away from Pig Face and start to undress. I take off my watch and slip it inside my boiler suit and down my boxer shorts. As I take off the boiler suit I keep the watch pressed between my legs. I take a few steps backwards.

There is silence. One of the Khmer Rouge shouts and all of the soldiers advance slowly towards us. At the same time the men and villagers are walking backwards, their eyes fixed on the Khmer Rouge. They herd us back into a horseshoe of dense thorn bush. The only way to get through the thorns would be with a machete. There is no escape. There never has been.

They have a perfect crossfire and we are trapped. I look at Mr Houn. The unspoken thought passes between us. I look around at the sad, fearful faces and all I feel is the helpless, hopeless reality.

My throat is dry and my heart beats faster as I reconcile myself to my imminent death. I stand waiting for the bullets to rip into my flesh and mourn the innocent all around me. I look at Pig Face. His hate-filled face and burning dead eyes challenge anyone to move.

I try not to look into his eyes and confront him.

It might be possible they think I am a foreign military adviser. If this is their way of warning the UN and aid workers to go home, I'm in the wrong place at the wrong time. I keep my hands raised and try to smile. Mr Houn is standing transfixed on my right. He keeps his head down slightly as if trying not to get noticed. I glance to the left; one of the deminers is looking at me. I feel accused. I want to do something, but what? We can't run. We can't fight. People surround me, but I feel lonelier than I ever imagined it was possible to feel. I am responsible and powerless.

The young deminer looks at me again. This time I understand the questioning in his eyes. He's wondering whether or not to run. There's no doubt that a few, the fast ones, would make it. The women and children and the slow and unlucky ones wouldn't.

My brain flashes. I didn't know I could think this fast. It is amazing what adrenalin can do.

People running would give them an excuse to fire. The small thin soldier next to Pig Face looks like a boy, but looks can be deceptive and I guess he is at least twenty. The olive-green uniform hangs loosely on his scrawny body, sleeves and trouser-legs rolled up. His untidy hair and large yellow teeth make him look a demon runt. The AK 47 is ridiculously large in his small arms, but his thin childish finger strokes the trigger, more lovingly than nervously. I know I should pity him his disadvantaged upbringing and lack of education, but right now I'm low on sympathy.

Their faces remain impassive, but they are too poor to give anything away. All they've ever known is the jungle and fighting. The only thing they have to give is the very thing we want: life. They are aware of their power and not afraid to use it. For some of them it must be their greatest pleasure.

Only seconds have passed. It feels longer. I have to think. There must be a way, God help me, there must be something I can do.

The dark clouds are gathering. There is no sunlight and I know that it will rain soon. Perhaps the rain will wash the blood off our bodies. The monsoon rain usually starts in the afternoon. Maybe today it will be early. All we can do is watch with frightened eyes.

Pig Face shouts at me and waves his rifle, spitting venom. It hurts. This isn't fair. All I'm trying to do is make their villages safe. I can't give in to this bullying. Righteous indignation burns like a branding iron.

'Walk back here,' Mr Houn pleads.

For a second I am lost in my own feelings. The sight of Mr Houn close to tears brings me back. He thinks Pig Face is threatening to kill me if I don't retreat. He's been here before. I must do it.

Stumbling slowly backwards I see Pig Face has his eyes fixed on me. We are almost in the bushes and can go no further. Mr Houn is by my side. We stand surrounded; all eyes fixed on the soldiers.

I can hear my heart beating. Now they are sure they control us, they rush forward to our line of clothes and possessions. Pig Face squats opposite me, his SKS in one hand, the other rifling the pockets of my boiler suit. There's nothing I can do. The two young soldiers on either side with AKMs stay in position to keep us in order. They must be too far down the pecking order to share the spoils of war.

Pig Face takes my Leatherman, sunglasses, camera and money. I console myself with the thought that the camera was cheap, the amount of money small and the shades will be bad for his eyes because they're prescription-safety lenses. None the less I don't like being robbed. I wouldn't be disappointed if a bolt of lightning did its stuff.

The soldiers scuttle back to their previous positions. We wait.

The silence is shattered by orders shouted from a soldier, evidently in command, who sits in the Land Rover. Nobody moves. I look at Mr Houn. He's confused. The deminers look confused. 'Mr Houn, what was that?'

His look is somewhere between bemusement and terror. 'The commander say the driver of Zil, you and me must go to him. We should wait a while, maybe not move yet.'

I can understand his reluctance. Perhaps the Khmer Rouge will start by killing the intellectual, the foreigner and the technical man who drives the truck.

I'm an obvious target. I have nothing to lose, so I might as well see what happens.

I step forward slowly, trying to avoid looking into Pig Face's eyes and pick up my overalls. I struggle for dignity. I must look stupid, but it doesn't matter.

I walk through the soldiers towards the vehicle. Houn follows. The Khmer Rouge commander is smiling, holding his Tokarev.

I remember reading about the Stockholm syndrome. In the 1970s some bank robbers in Stockholm held a group of people hostage and the hostages formed close relationships with the captors. A good idea for me to do the same. I must make a positive effort to like the Khmer Rouge commander. He is standing in front of me, smiling. In Khmer society the smile can mean so many things. Lawrence's words come back to me. 'They can smile and kill you at the same time.'

I keep walking, smile fixed. Hands together I make the lowest bow possible while still keeping my eyes on him. It's not easy to look cool and dignified when you're only wearing boxer shorts and jungle boots, but I'm trying. There is a confused discussion between the Khmer Rouge behind me. Orders are being shouted.

I glance over my shoulder. They are still holding the deminers and village people in the same position. Houn walks round the Land Rover and gets in, resigned to his fate. The commander smiles and slowly waves his pistol back and forward from me to the driving seat. His message needs no interpretation.

As I approach the door I pause. I begin to unroll my overalls. Houn is now in the Land Rover, leaning forward, crouched and tense. 'They say you can put clothes on.'

As I start to do up the poppers I turn slightly, remove the watch from where it is wedged between my legs and slip it into my pocket. I do the rest up and slide into the driving seat. I hear the heavy splutter of the Zil engine to my rear. Sok is driving with a Khmer Rouge soldier next to him.

Six soldiers guard the deminers and village people. Another small group is heading south, which is odd because it's the direction of the town where any government troops (CAPF) will come from. One has a radio so perhaps they're going to observe to see if there is a reaction.

The commander is smiling like a double-glazing salesman who's just won the contract to refit the Pentagon. He's still holding the pistol, but this time it's not pointed directly at us. His finger rests on the trigger guard.

Behind me his soldiers climb into the Land Rover, they talk quietly and move things in the back of the vehicle. There is a shuffling sound, then I hear the back door slam. It's the moment in the film where the prisoner is thrown into a cell and the door is slammed and locked behind him.

The commander speaks. Houn translates. 'We have to go to meet his commander.'

I'm not surprised, but I don't feel like going. Can I argue? I smile until my cheeks ache and bow my head graciously. 'Houn, you know I can't understand everything they say. Please translate exactly and listen to everything. Explain to them that you are the translator and are not responsible for my words.'

Houn looks into my eyes and nods. We trust each other.

'Please say the rules of our organization. Say it is not possible to go. I will come back tomorrow and we can meet then.'

Mr Houn translates immediately without stopping to think. The commander laughs and plays with the pistol, stroking it like a favourite pet. Then he replies. Without shifting his glance from the windscreen Houn translates, 'We must go to meeting and then we go home this afternoon. It is only short distance. He promise.'

I know I shouldn't believe him, but I want to. Our position is not negotiable. My guts rattle. I know we're in the shit; the important thing is not to sink. Only when my last breath has gone can I give up. I have to keep as much control as possible.

I try to look confident and relaxed and nod my head earnestly as I speak. My guts feel like they've been hit with a barge pole. 'I agree to meet his commander and accept his promise we can return today, but I must make a radio call, it is the rule of my organization.' Houn translates like a machine.

The thin commander smiles and shakes his head looking slightly embarrassed, but his eyes remain snake like. 'Not possible, sorry. My commander will be very angry. It is against the rules of Khmer Rouge.' Houn translates with the look of a man about to be thrown into the lion's den.

The commander says, '*Yerng dtou.*'

I understand the simple command. 'We go.'

He waves his pistol and points to a track in the corner of the clearing. I turn the ignition key and the diesel engine rattles into life. Pushing the gear lever into first I gently release the clutch and slowly cross the bumpy clearing. I glance down at the Codan radio console. Good, it's still on. I have comms. In two and a half hours I'll be overdue so Jim will give me a call.

In the door mirror I see the Zil truck move off. The soldiers are starting to walk away into the west side of the clearing, while the deminers and village people stand like witnesses to the gunfight at the OK Corral. I am pleased they're safe. I feel a surge of relief. It fills a small corner of the emptiness I feel inside.

I look cautiously at my watch. It's 1.25 p.m. We were ambushed at 1.05 p.m. It's been the longest twenty minutes of my life.

I wonder what the future holds? I drive on slowly, trying to remember every tree and feature we pass. I want to know the way home.

There are fewer bushes now and the ground looks as if it was once cultivated, but is now used for grazing. There could have been a village here once. I can see a few sugar palm and mango trees.

The track is becoming overgrown. There are just two sandy wheel tracks. It's getting stuffy and all I can see through the windscreen are rain clouds. There's no sun to aid navigation, but I think we're heading due west. I haven't been in this area before. I'm surprised to see a few small fields with raised banks dug from the infertile sand; they grow rice here. It must be a poor crop because it's a lot drier here than on the paddy plains.

There is an uneasy silence in the vehicle. The soldiers look nervous. I can't imagine they have a conscience about kidnapping us; perhaps they're afraid of the CAPF.

My stomach tightens. I don't want to be caught in the middle of a firefight. I hope to God there's no immediate follow-up. I remember the wild, hard look in their eyes when we were ambushed; like wolves baying for blood. I expect that if their scouts see any troops they'll lie low and let them pass. Then they'll radio back to the commander and he'll just shoot us and disappear into the jungle. If that happened our only chance would be to run before they killed us; so I should be prepared to fight, but until then it would be suicidally stupid to consider that, or try to escape.

The smell of the soldiers' unwashed bodies fills my nostrils. They're lean and mean with a look that tells me the lights are on but nobody's home. Killing is an instinctive talent and I know these guys are good at it.

The commander grunts, making the kind of noise a farmer makes when driving ducks or chickens. He waves his pistol to the right, as if driving an animal with a stick. I push and pull the steering wheel and change down a gear to follow an ox cart track. We're heading east now, which is strange because their strongholds are north-west. Where are we going? Perhaps this is a deception. Mr Houn is lost in his memories.

The lane takes us through an area of scrub and low bushes. Steering with my right hand I place my left hand on my thigh and move my arm gently forward. It pushes my sleeve back enough to uncover my watch – 1.35 p.m., we left the clearing only ten minutes ago. It feels more like hours.

Behind me the soldiers are talking in low, excited tones. Suddenly the apparent winner of the argument shouts, '*Chop*'. It's a command that I understand. I brake and put the vehicle into neutral. I don't understand why we're stopping here. Perhaps they want to shoot us.

I eyeball the commander and smile, attempting to retain my dignity. I fight my desire to tell him he has no right to kidnap us and that he and his men are a bunch of ignorant gits.

For the last few minutes we've doubled back. We can't be too far from the clearing where we were ambushed. Why are we waiting? What's happened to the deminers and the villagers? The fear that the Khmer Rouge might shoot them gnaws at my soul. They wiped out hundreds of thousands when they were running the country.

A flash followed by a rumble of thunder electrifies the atmosphere. I try to smile reassuringly at Houn. I feel guilty about asking him to speak when he looks as if he'd rather be quiet.

'Please ask the commander, will there be a lot of rain?'

I understand the reply as he nods and smiles slightly. The commander looks amused, like a father of a young child who keeps asking stupid questions.

'I do not think it will be possible for our vehicles to continue if it rains. I will come back tomorrow to meet his boss.'

Houn translates cautiously. 'Not possible. We must meet today, then we go home. His commander travel long way and will be angry if we not see today.'

I catch his drift. In Cambodia it is not a good idea to make people angry just in case they kill you. There's a rattling sound behind me. One of the soldiers is trying to get out. The handle needs to be lifted all the way to the top to open the door. This is probably the first time he's been in a vehicle. I defy the urge to jump out and give a lesson in opening it. Houn gives some instructions. After more rattling and fumbling the door finally swings open.

The soldier darts towards the scrub. He wears tattered canvas chest webbing. I'm surprised to see he has four magazines; they're obviously not short of ammunition. He rests his hands on each end of the strap of his AK 47 and walks to the Zil truck, which has just stopped behind us. He looks up and says something to Pig Face, who stands on the roof of the truck cab and waves.

Within a few moments two soldiers emerge from the scrub. I am sure they were the ones guarding the men and villagers as we drove off. I feel a rush of relief. Three more Khmer Rouge come out of the scrub. Their field craft is quite good. Most of them have cammed up their webbing with branches and pulled their caps down.

The man in front walks to the truck and speaks to the soldier standing next to Pig Face. He talks into a hand-held radio, fiddling with the control buttons with strained concentration. Pig Face snorts and reaches forward to do the job himself. The radio operator turns away defensively and Pig Face wanders off to root around in the back of the truck.

The radio operator gives a shout. He seems to have got through. He approaches the Land Rover and makes a brief report to the commander, who nods and smiles as if he loves it when a plan comes together.

He gives instructions. Houn turns to me and says, 'We go slow. The soldiers will walk with us.' The commander grins his everlasting grin and motions us forward down the track with his pistol. I drive slowly. I wonder if there was ever a time when this track led to a happy, safe village where people smiled real smiles and didn't live in fear.

I let the engine tick over and keep to the speed of the soldiers walking. At the moment there's no chance of escape. Communication, negotiation and proving our neutrality is our best defence.

By now Jim will be wondering where we are. Usually we call base forty minutes before arriving. I was looking forward to seeing Lawrence and the boss. We had decided to make an effort for lunch. Jim had somehow magically procured HP Sauce to have with tinned ham, tomatoes and cucumber. This was no mean feat, as the local market doesn't stock such luxuries. It would probably have been easier for him to get a large sack of rocking-horse shit. I hope they don't scoff it all before I get back.

There is a flash and more thunder. Raindrops fall like giant tears as if the jungle is sobbing. I've never seen rain this heavy. Within seconds the soldiers are drenched. They have no thought of stopping. There's no shelter and I think they must still be afraid of a CAPF follow-up. Perhaps they're pleased the rain is so heavy, it might deter pursuers and cover our tracks.

Their companions sit silently behind me. They must be relieved they are not outside walking. The track is turning west again. We pass a few small fields of parched brown grass surrounded by built-up soil banks. They are filling with water and the promise of rejuvenation. Perhaps I was wrong about it being too dry to grow rice here.

We're moving slowly. The rattle of the rain on the roof stops conversation. The windscreen wipers can't cope. My nostrils fill with the smell of soil and fresh rain, which is better than the stink of my uninvited guests.

The thick clouds and heavy rain announce the arrival of night. The Khmer Rouge soldiers walk through the yellow-grey ethereal light like ghosts. Their black rubber Chinese sandals splash in the ever-deepening surface water. I'm surprised to see they're in loose arrowhead formation. Perhaps they're better trained than I thought.

The track is so infrequently used that it's flat. Deep ruts cause problems because vehicles bottom out; the front axle sticks fast in the centre of the track. If we go on to lower ground we'll almost certainly get bogged in. 'Please tell the commander I am worried we will get the vehicles stuck. I will come back tomorrow to meet with them.'

The commander coils his body back into the seat. He tilts back his thin neck and sticks his chin in the air like a cobra ready to strike. He reveals his venomous yellow teeth as he replies. 'Not possible. We meet his commander soon then we can go home.' Houn's face tells me I have pushed things far enough.

In the absence of an alternative I keep driving. So far my assessment of the situation is as follows: I'm a long way from home. I've missed lunch. I've just been kidnapped by a bunch of genocidal maniacs and it's seriously pissing down with rain. I'm having a bad day.

The rain starts to leak in around the door rubber and trickles down my arm soaking my overalls. Houn sits forward, his hands gripping the dashboard. The commander slithers away from the window to stop the water running down his arm. Houn jerks back to avoid contact. The commander leans back into his seat to make himself comfortable. He's enjoying the journey. He looks at the nearest soldier walking by the vehicle and laughs. He turns and speaks to the soldiers behind who share his joke.

They start to chatter and giggle. It reminds me of the scene from the *The Deer Hunter* when the VC play Russian roulette with the American POWs.

The windscreen glass is starting to steam up. The windows are closed and it's getting more difficult to breathe. I must keep trying. 'Please tell him my name is Chris Moon and I am British. What is his name?'

Silence.

Houn pauses, and narrows his eyes. Then he looks at me and says, 'Mr Red.'

So this is the legendary Mr Red.

Low scrub and trees have taken over the grazing land and there's no room in the dense jungle for the sugar palms and mangoes we saw earlier. I've seen heavy rain in Cambodia but nothing like this. Should I do every Englishman's duty and talk about the weather? I could tell Mr Red about snow, or the way the thorn trees sparkle in the chill of a clear, frosty morning on the chalk Downlands at home. Alternatively I could keep my mouth shut, which would probably increase our chances of survival and save Mr Houn a lot of stress.

Houn has a wife and two children. She runs a market stall, selling material and making clothes. His son and daughter are eight and six. They're always smart and clean and behave like angels. His family is a credit to him and they're very close. I hope they will see him again.

I must establish a relationship with Mr Red. I shouldn't be prejudiced. After all, why should I let ambush, abduction and death threats stop us from being friends?

'I have never seen rain this heavy.'

Houn's expression tells me conversation is a risk he'd prefer not to take. I can understand it, but we have to try. When Mr Red looks pushed I'll back off. The road ahead is straight and there are no trees I could hit. I'll set the wheel straight and watch him. It's a technique I learned on the farm to steer the tractor and watch the plough behind.

I watch Mr Red. He smiles again and this time looks at me before speaking. 'It rains more in the forest and it's cooler.' Houn looks surprised, as if the experience wasn't as bad as he'd anticipated.

We are starting to talk. Now we're on a roll, I'm going for it.

'There are many people who will worry about us. Can I tell them we are okay and going to meet the commander, and we will return tonight?'

After translation the response is courteous but uncompromising. 'Sorry, not possible. My boss will not allow.'

A tiny flicker of embarrassment replaces the smile. Perhaps he doesn't want to be responsible for our plight. Or maybe he just prefers to blame the feared commander who can't be challenged.

I sneak a look at my watch. We've been driving at snail's pace for two hours. Time has lost meaning; it's now just the movement of hands on a watch.

The track is narrowing, squeezed between trees and thick bushes. Soon we'll be in the jungle where the winding ribbon of sand is the only sign of human interference.

Mr Red rapidly waves his hand, which I take to mean, 'Please stop.'

He turns and passes the Tokarev to the soldier behind him and fumbles with the door catch before triumphantly wrestling it open. I examine the mirror. I can't see anything because the back window's steamed up.

I wind the window down. Water floods in. I quickly wind it up.

Mr Red is half out of the vehicle, watching the truck. He's trying not to get wet, which is impossible when it's raining so hard, but it's amusing seeing him try.

It's nearly three o'clock. By now Jim will know something is up.

Mr Red gets back in. He still can't quite work the door handle. He looks at me and laughs as he shakes some of the water from his soaked uniform. It's the Khmer way. I laugh back politely and start the Land Rover. I watch him out of the corner of my eye as we drive off. He hasn't asked for his pistol yet.

To stand any chance of keeping him to his promise of a return tonight we need to get a move on. These guys aren't going to let us go, so the only chance of release is to meet the commander.

Suddenly a staccato bleep signals an incoming radio call. Automatically I reach behind me to grab the mike. Someone has beaten me to it. The soldier brushes my hand away. I feel a rising urge to fight for the radio mike, but I know it's not sensible.

'It's no problem, just a radio call. They are wondering where we are. I'll tell them we will be back tonight.'

'*Dtay*.' The commander shakes his head. There is no need for interpretation, but Houn shakes his head too like a doctor looking at a mortally wounded casualty. 'They will not allow.'

Mr Red speaks to the soldier behind him who passes over the Tokarev. The message is simple. Keep driving.

Almost as rapidly as it started, the angry rain is easing off. I wind down the window. The damp, earthy smell of the jungle freshens the atmosphere. I rub the door mirror with my hand and in the smeared glass I see the Zil chugging along behind us. I can just make out Sok's face. Behind the wheel Sok is usually all smiles and flamboyant blasts of the air horn. When he drives through town, traffic parts and cyclists and pedestrians flee at the approach of this self-proclaimed King of the Road. I've been trying to get him to calm down for a while. I never thought of sitting in his cab with an AK 47 at his ribs.

On either side of the track impenetrable clumps of bamboo tower like castle walls. Droplets of water hang on the leaves and now glint like pearls in the sunshine that briefly lightens this wild place of darkness and uncertainty.

The wheel marks on the track are darker now showing soft black soil. If it gets any softer we might have problems. Ahead I see what looks like a log loading area, a clearing of crushed bushes and small trees.

Fifty metres beyond lies a stream. A flood of monsoon water has carved a sheer-sided crater across the track. The water is too deep and too fast to risk taking the Land Rover through. There's no room for manoeuvre and no margin for error.

I stop thirty metres from the stream to leave enough space to turn around. I switch off the ignition, take out the keys and put them in my pocket. I want to stay in control of the vehicle. I sneak a look at my watch. It's 15.45. We'll be pushing it to get back tonight, even if we leave now. I have to try again to persuade them to let us go.

Mr Red is giving orders and I can hear a soldier behind me grappling with the complex mystery of the rear Land Rover door handle. The handle is no match for Mr Red. He gets out and walks towards the stream.

I follow and stop a metre from the water. It's loud and looks deeper than I thought. The banks are nearly two metres high. A narrow ford has been dug. If we get the Land Rover stuck or washed downstream the chance of recovery will be virtually zero. Even with the raised air intake and sealed engine I'd be worried about getting water in the cylinders. With nearly a metre's ground clearance the Zil would make it, but I can't risk the Land Rover.

I look at the water. I know the Khmer Rouge haven't had a lot of experience of vehicles; I hope they believe me. If they force me to drive through this we'll be in trouble. It's my turn to shake my head and say, '*Dtay.*' Mr Red looks thoughtful and then speaks.

Houn translates. 'The water level will go down soon now it stop raining.'

I have to think about every gesture and expression to send the right messages. I feel like an antelope being watched by a lion. 'Do you think we should explain we are a neutral demining charity here to help the Cambodian people and ask him to release us?' I ask Houn.

Bravely Houn agrees to try and for several minutes we passionately explain our humanitarian mission and neutrality. As things are going well I think it would be a good time to pop the question again.

'We can't risk crossing the stream. The water is too high and my organization will be worried about us. Can we come back tomorrow to meet his commander?'

Houn's narrowed eyes and clenched fists tell me the negative answer before he begins to translate.

Mr Red scratches his head. As he lifts his arm I see he's wearing what I presume to be a fake gold watch. It has diamonds on the face instead of numbers. He's the only one I've seen wearing a watch. Discreetly I check mine. It shows about the same time.

Behind me six soldiers talk in low tones and point at the water.

I say, 'I'm worried we may not be able to cross back in the dark. Shouldn't we leave now and come back tomorrow?' Houn nods and deferentially translates my plea.

Mr Red's short answer makes Houn look as if he's been punched. He narrows his eyes, sighs, looks straight ahead and with an air of horrified resignation says. 'We are prisoners of war. We must do as told.'

Prisoners of war. I breathe in slowly. I wonder how much these guys know about the Geneva Convention?

6

WILDERNESS

I take a few steps towards the torrent of brown water. The sandy track merges into the rocks as it slopes down to the river. The banks are two metres of clay and rock. There are no large trees or stumps around that could be used as winch points. Judging by the steepness of the sides and the way the water is moving I guess it's about a metre deep in the middle. The depth isn't the only problem. It's the force of the torrent and the narrowness of the exit point the other side.

Mr Red shouts and points. One of the young soldiers walks obediently forward. Pig Face has joined us now. He and Mr Red are obviously good mates. The young soldier rolls up his trousers. He cautiously edges out into the surging water. It's only up to his knees but it's already hard for him to stand. Fighting to keep his balance, he struggles towards the middle. The water is nearly up to his waist.

I shake my head. He stumbles and throws his arms into the air. Pig Face and Mr Red snort with laughter as their human dipstick battles his way back to the bank. I wonder if they use the same technique to test if it's safe to walk through minefields.

Mr Red hisses at Houn who turns to me. 'We wait forty-five minutes. Then cross.'

There is no choice, but I'm going to try to keep as much control as I can. I glance behind. Sok is standing by the back of the Land Rover.

I nod at Mr Red, smile sweetly at Pig Face and walk

purposefully back to the Land Rover, making another set of footprints. I am going to conserve my strength and get my driving seat back before some baboon tries to pinch it, but more importantly I want to talk to Sok.

I catch Sok's eye and nod. He walks slowly towards me. His smile has gone, replaced by a worried frown. I can't imagine I look my normal happy self, even though I'm making a conscious effort not to stick out my bottom lip like a rolled-up sleeping bag.

Houn leans against the door, rubs the wet sand from his feet and bangs his blue flip-flops against the wing of the Land Rover. I glance around. The soldiers are either by the truck or talking by the river.

'Is Mr Sok okay?'

After a rapid, whispered exchange Houn says, 'He worried they will try to keep him prisoner to mend trucks. The soldier ask him if he know about vehicle. He say he just driver. He also afraid they find out he was in army then they kill.'

It's vital they don't find out that Sok was in the CAPF and Houn used to be an official in the provincial government. Sok might not be killed if they know he can mend trucks; but they might just keep him for an indefinite period as a slave.

'He's just a driver and you are interpreter for our charity. That is all we say. If the vehicles are stuck Mr Sok must pretend he is no good at getting them out and he's not a mechanic. Listen to everything they say and tell me what's going on.'

I can see a young soldier walking towards us. His AK 47 dangles from a frayed canvass sling; it's Chinese with a folding butt and bayonet and it looks well oiled and clean.

Sok smiles and nods deferentially as the soldier leans against the bull bar. It's strange in a society where age is revered to see a middle-aged man give so much respect to a youth, but he's the one with the gun. The soldier reminds me of one of the boys carrying out the executions in *The Killing Fields*. I'm beginning to wish I hadn't seen that film.

A few more soldiers join us. They view me with curious and suspicious glances. I feel like an animal in a cage. I won't be surprised if they start poking me with sticks.

Having done my best to establish cordial relations, I decide to chill out. I ease back in the seat and place my forearms on the steering wheel. It's good to have a break from driving. I'll delay as long as possible and say we can't cross the stream. Then I'll push for our release and arrange a meeting with Mr Red's commander. I need to get some sleep. No point in being stressed.

'Houn, why don't you sit down and relax. There's nothing we can do except wait.'

Houn nods and gets into the Land Rover. I've got him to sit down, but I don't have a hope of getting him to relax. He's the one with the memories.

Time ticks by, each second seeming longer because I count it.

Mr Red points at the river and says a few words, then walks back towards it. A glance at my watch shows that while I've been counting seconds half an hour has passed. I get out of the Land Rover and make more footprints in the sand. This time it is firmer. I'm surprised it's dried so quickly. The water level has gone down, but it still looks too deep and fast to risk crossing. The Land Rover won't make it. It's too risky. I'm not going for a long discussion here. I think I'll just repeatedly shake my head and say, 'No.' Here goes.

There is a strange reaction. Two soldiers by the stream are now having a heated discussion. The commander looks at the water and back at the vehicles, as if weighing up the odds. He starts talking to the soldier next to him who looks older than the others. They point at the stream and then back down the track. Mr Red looks at his watch and then discussions begin again.

I'm happy to leave them talking. Looking across to the other side of the river all I can see is trees, towering taller than any I have seen in Cambodia. This is the real forest. What a privilege to see it before it's all destroyed.

I turn my head in the direction of soft footsteps scuffing in the grass behind me. It's Sok. He moves towards Houn. He has empty eyes; there is something different about him. It's more than just the absence of his familiar smile. Something in his face has changed. He talks in rapid hushed tones. They look at me. Now I see something in Houn's face that mirrors Sok's expression. It fills me with sadness.

'Mr Sok say he hear the soldiers talking. If we cannot cross river they kill us and burn vehicles. They afraid government soldiers come.'

It's a simple soldiers' solution. Get rid of the problem and lie low. I wish there was one of them I could talk to who could see the bigger picture. We have to cross.

'Can we look at the river again?' I ask Houn. He nods.

Walking purposefully towards the crossing relieves the tension. It's good to do something practical. The Zil should be able to pull the Land Rover through. The ground the other side looks firm. As long as the tow is fast and I steer up stream it should work. I look at Sok and point straight through the stream and make it obvious I'm giving instructions. He plays his part well, looking confused and nodding a lot.

'We attach the winch cable from the Land Rover to the Zil putting it on free flow. When he gets to the other side I lock the winch and he tows us through. When we get to the middle he tows us fast.' I mime the actions.

Sok nods and goes to get the Zil, which he brings to a halt on the flat ground in front of the gap.

Pointing to the Land Rover I indicate that I'm going to bring it close to the rear of the truck. The soldiers watch and linger, occasionally pointing and nodding. I'm relieved they're not getting in the way. I turn on the engine and drive forward coming to a stop two metres behind the truck. Sok stands waiting by the towing hitch. He's in charge of his vehicle and I'm in charge of mine. We have an unspoken understanding. I unclip the winch hook from the bull bar and jiggle the winch lever on to free play. The greased cable runs smoothly. Sok lifts the jaws of the towing hitch. I pull the cable to make sure it's firmly held. Sok nods and walks to the front of the truck. The soldiers start to climb on the back. They don't want to get their feet wet. The engine roars as Sok guns the accelerator. Houn and I choke on the exhaust fumes. I pull up the slack in the cable to make sure it will run freely when the truck jerks forward.

The front of the truck plunges into the water. The stream must be deeper than I thought. Sok gives it more throttle. His timing is perfect. The back of the lorry drops into the water and it looks like it's floating. The wheels go underwater. The engine roars louder as he accelerates up the other side. The back wheels churn white water. The front rises; the engine screams. The back wheels are spinning. I take a deep breath. There's nothing I can do.

Sok keeps revving the engine. The four back wheels push the truck forward a fraction and then bite. It powers up the bank. As he eases off the throttle I check the cable. If he stops suddenly the cable may continue playing out and tangle. With a hiss of air brakes the Zil stops and I flick the lever across locking the winch.

The truck is at the top of the rise. Sok sticks his head out of the cab door and smiles, but it's short lived.

Four soldiers climb into the back of the Land Rover. One stands guard with AK 47 pointing to the rear. I'm pleased to see the change lever is on safety. Mr Red climbs into the front smiling and nodding.

Houn translates as he leans right to avoid touching Mr Red, reclining in the passenger seat. 'As soon as we meet his commander he will let us go.'

I stand alone, choosing the route. Dead straight through the stream and up the bank, then steer left to avoid a few small trees. I'll get right to the top of the bank and down the other side before I signal Sok to stop.

I take another look at the fast-flowing water and check my watch. It's 16.30. We've been here forty-five minutes. As long as we don't get forced downstream we should be all right.

I get into the driver's seat and switch on the engine. My passengers' faces are impassive. They have no idea.

The more weight I have in the vehicle the more traction I'll get and the less likely we are to be washed downstream. I'm glad the soldiers have got in. I grab the steering wheel in my right hand and stick my left out the window, thumb up. Sok is watching me in his door mirror; he lets the clutch in and takes up the slack on the cable. I do the same and aim for the gap the other side. We lurch forward.

I increase pressure on the accelerator. A bow wave surges round the bonnet. I can see water leaking in under the door. As we approach the middle of the torrent I check to see the wheels are in different tracks to the Zil. To get maximum grip I'll avoid the disturbed ground. My stomach hasn't felt like this since somebody took me stunt flying.

The bonnet starts to rise and I increase revs. The wheels churn and the dripping front of the Land Rover starts to grind upwards. This is the dangerous part. As the front starts to rise it pushes down the back end. I'm afraid the force of water will slew it round. We have to make it up the bank first time.

The wheels begin to slip. The truck tyres spin, throwing up grey mud. I keep my right arm locked on the steering wheel as we move forward a few inches. I hear the equipment falling to the back of the Land Rover. Smoke pours from the Zil exhaust and the engine screams. The front of the truck lurches over the crest pulling us up the hill. I hold my left hand out to signal a halt and drive on a few metres to take the tension off the cable.

I reel in the winch cable, without guiding it into the drum. It uses a lot of battery power, so it should never be used without the engine running. The Khmer Rouge cover the crossing. Mr Red nods and smiles.

Pig Face shouts. He has walked ahead a few hundred metres and is waving his arm and pointing. Houn tells me, 'They want you to drive through the forest where they point.'

I nod and get back into the Land Rover. The soldiers follow me and I swing around the Zil and head towards Pig Face.

The forest is eerily quiet. The ground is soft and wet. I frantically wave Sok past me. No point in us both getting stuck. If he keeps going with his higher ground clearance he'll get through; then he can tow us out.

We head off. The Zil speeds through the undergrowth. As he overtakes I feel the Land Rover start to sink into the mud, the wheels spin and we come to a halt. I put the gear lever in neutral and turn to Houn.

'Please ask the soldiers to get out and walk where the ground is soft. We need the vehicle to be as light as possible.' They obediently climb out.

I rev the engine and hold my breath. Magically I feel the vehicle move slowly forward. These Land Rovers are incredible. I try to keep the engine revs low to prevent the wheels spinning. Thank God I've got wide tyres.

The Land Rover inches its way forward. We're on solid ground. I stop beside the truck where Pig Face is pointing and shouting.

'We follow the trees. The commander will show us,' Houn says as the soldiers pile back into the vehicles.

Carefully I skirt the edge of the trees. The Zil follows and we drive through the forest as Mr Red directs. He turns frequently and speaks to the soldiers in the back. The trees, bushes and plants merge into one amorphous whole.

The crack of a gunshot echoes somewhere to my right. I glance at Houn, he grips the dashboard harder. Nobody says anything. I grip the steering wheel harder. If any of the Khmer Rouge had bumped into pursuers there would be a lot more shooting. It must be a signal.

Mr Red turns in his seat and talks to the soldiers again. Houn sits rigidly in between us trying not to touch him as we rock and roll over bumps. I catch his look and raise an eyebrow. I don't want to force him to speak unless he wants to.

'It's signal so commander knows which way to go,' Houn says.

The commander points right and nods. I steer in the direction I think the shot came from. We go down a slight hill, zig-zagging between the trees and come to a stop at the bottom.

Mr Red turns round and starts jabbering frantically to the soldiers in the back. They reply in the same tone. Houn sits impassively, 'We stop here and wait.'

I turn off the engine. The Zil hisses to a halt thirty metres behind. Time check. It's 18.15. It'll be dark by 19.00. I look out of the window. The forest floor is littered with dead, brown leaves. I wonder what will happen next.

The door handle rattles and Mr Red and his men pile out. Not wishing to be left behind I slip the keys in my pocket and join the Khmer Rouge as they mill about in front of the vehicle. Either because he doesn't want to be left, or because he feels he ought to, Houn joins me. Mr Red says something and walks away.

'He go to meet commander now,' Houn says.

A wave of excitement and dread make me respond immediately. 'Good. I look forward to meeting him.' I try not to look too desperate. 'We will accompany him.' I don't want to lose sight of the man in charge. He's responsible for us when we're with him. If we're alone with the soldiers they might get bored and use us for shooting or head-smashing practice.

I walk behind Mr Red, slowing my pace to stay behind him. When he starts to scramble down the bank I follow him and say, 'No problem. I am not tired. I look forward to the honour of meeting his commander.'

Houn follows and we leap over the shallow stream on to a small island covered with dead, leafless branches. The water flows slowly. This is not the same stream we crossed earlier, although it must flow into the Mekong near Rhum. This is a backwater compared to that.

Mr Red stands at the top of the bank and looks around intently. I find it hard to believe that this is the RV point. Most of the bends in the stream look the same to me. Even to somebody who knows the forest this must be almost impossible to find unless one group was approaching from the north side and the other the south. As long as they knew where they are relative to each other they'd turn right or left on hitting the stream and then simply follow it until they met. Yes then it would be possible

Mr Red shouts back to the soldiers by the vehicles. Nobody answers. There is a rattle of metal followed by a single rifle shot. The explosive crack fills the forest, amplifying the silence that follows its last resonating echo. It must be a signal. Perhaps to let them know which way to turn when they reach the stream.

We stand waiting in our own private silences. Anxiously, Mr Red scans the undergrowth for his commander. Houn

stands with arms crossed, looking at the ground. I watch and
wait, enjoying the last, optimistic rays of evening sunshine.

I am preparing my speech. Once I've met the commander
and explained, we can go home. I tell myself it's a misunder-
standing that can be sorted out very quickly.

The sun sets behind the trees, momentarily leaving a blood-
orange glow. It's 18.40, just dark enough for the fluorescent
hands on my watch to start to look bright. Dusk will soon be
replaced by darkness. The insects are emerging from their
daytime slumber. Strange how you can always hear them, but
seldom ever see them.

I sense some movement in the bushes about fifty metres to
my right. I turn and strain my eyes and ears. Twigs snap and
more branches rustle. It's getting closer. Mr Red makes a noise
like a bird. A similar sound, a cross between a pigeon cooing
and a peacock screeching, comes in reply. These guys do great
animal impressions.

Mr Red looks relieved as a short figure emerges from the
undergrowth. He's wearing the same olive-green combats and
black rubber sandals, but is distinguished by a stained, brown
wide-brimmed trilby hat. He's thin and looks old. With a faded
red check *kramar* draped around his neck and his sleeves rolled
up he looks more like a farmer than a soldier. He walks quickly
down the bank, jumping deftly over a large pool. With my
speech prepared I walk confidently towards him. I beckon
Houn to follow.

He nods a greeting to Mr Red and says two or three sentences
without stopping. He's obviously in a hurry to get things sorted
out. I stop and hold out my right hand expectantly. He pauses,
shakes my hand rapidly, turns to Houn and repeats the gesture.
He looks at me, delivers two short sentences and scrambles in
the direction of the vehicles. Before I have a chance to speak,
Houn captures my attention. He looks pained.

'The new commander say not worry, he no have authority to kill us yet. He take us to the Khmer Rouge headquarters.'

So we're not going home.

Of course I don't believe them. They lie all the time. I know that. I step over the stream and climb the bank. I use both hands to pull myself up, then I turn and offer my hand to Houn. He accepts and I feel a little better. We have to be positive.

'I'm sure he's being kind to us. He doesn't want us to worry.'

'Yes, I think he try to reassure us. So we not so afraid.' Houn avoids my gaze as he speaks.

'Yes, it's good of him.' I carry on walking towards the Land Rover.

The man in the trilby talks to the soldiers. I get back into the Land Rover to await his directions. Mr Red is relegated to the back. I drive into the dusk with no path to follow. I try to avoid using the lights. I want to keep my night vision, and I think they don't want us to draw attention to ourselves. I have no idea which direction we're heading. For all I know we could be going in circles.

Eventually the commander signals for me to stop. The soldiers get out and stand around the vehicles involved in what sounds like a Chinese parliament. I can see their silhouetted gesticulations. Each one has a view on the direction of our travel. I'm not getting involved or we'll be here all night.

Mr Red and another soldier are trying to operate a small, hand-held radio. It's a commercial machine, the same type the CAPF use. I've seen them for sale in the local market. They're cheap but I don't know what the range is.

Houn interrupts my thoughts. 'They are sending soldiers to check which way we go. We can use vehicle lights and go slowly.'

I drive forward slowly. On my right the Zil struggles. We

creep forward, start, stop, stuck. It's a nightmare. The darkness of the forest is beginning to smother me.

A Khmer Rouge soldier walks to my left with his AK 47 at the ready. I don't know what for. He occasionally points and waves directions to the commander. His outline almost merges with the shadowy trees.

Somewhere behind me a single shot breaks the silence. I check the door mirror, stomach churning. The Zil chugs slowly behind. I decide the shot sounded close, but not that close. There is a murmur among the Khmer Rouge soldiers.

Houn turns and says, 'We stop and wait here.'

I switch off the engine.

7

NIGHT

Houn speaks in a soft monotone. 'We stop here for tonight. They say we lost.'

I pull over to the right-hand side of the track. The Zil passes and stops fifty metres in front. The Khmer Rouge climb over the sides dragging out an unruly assortment of webbing and pouches. I grope behind the seat trying to find my rucksack. I want my *kramar* to beat off the bugs.

The mosquitoes from the forest carry malaria. I have applied the repellent religiously every evening, and now when I need it most I don't have any. Being kidnapped wasn't on my list of things to do today, so I left it by my bed.

I put the clean red and white check cloth around my neck. It smells of the powder that Madame Bong uses to handwash our clothes in the big aluminium bowl on the veranda. I do up my collar and tuck in the cloth at the back of my neck. That's where they bite the most. Intermittently, I flick the loose end of the cloth in front of my face to keep them away.

Equipment rattles and bangs as the Khmer Rouge climb out of the back. The commander walks over to Pig Face and they talk. Two of the soldiers have torches. They use them for a few seconds, then turn them off to save the batteries. I enjoy looking at my watch without fear of theft. The luminous hands say 20.30. I'm surprised it's so early. It feels like we've been driving for ever. I wonder what the night will bring?

Pig Face points at the back of the truck and shouts to somebody there. A soldier passes him a small package, which he unwinds and shakes out. He ties both ends to the back of the Zil and climbs into a hammock leaving one leg dangling lazily outside. The commander looks in our direction and says something to Pig Face. He lifts his head, nods and gets out of his hammock. They walk slowly towards the front of the truck. I haven't seen Sok get out yet. His Khmer Rouge escort climbs awkwardly down and speaks to the commander. It looks like they're telling Sok to stay in the cab.

Unless they throw us out, Houn and I will sleep in the Land Rover. I want to keep control of the vehicle and at the moment it's more comfortable than anywhere else. If we keep the doors shut it should keep the mosquitoes out too. More of JJ's words come to mind: 'Any fool can be uncomfortable in the field.'

'I think we should sleep in the Land Rover. It will be quite comfortable on the foam cushions from the side seats in the back,' I suggest to Houn.

'I will try to speak with the soldiers,' he replies softly.

My legs feel cramped. I need to stretch them. I open the door and stand up. Looking behind I see a group of five soldiers by the small stream. The faint smell of wood smoke mingles with the earthy jungle air. I hear the crackle, hiss and spit of a starting fire and watch as the orange light shows the green of the soldiers' uniforms and the colour of their skin.

The flames flicker and jump. I'm impressed. We've only been here a few minutes and they've already made a fire from wood and leaves soaked in the monsoon four hours previously. They must feel safe and confident the CAPF aren't looking for us. The scouts they left behind this afternoon would have seen any follow-up troops. I don't know where we are or where we've been. All I know is that we're in their territory and they feel at home.

I lean against the side of the Land Rover. It's comforting to touch something familiar. In the distance a soldier moves slowly down the track towards us. He carries a long SKS rifle in one hand and a dead bird swings limply from the other. The hunter pauses as he crosses the stream and puts the bird and the rifle on the bank. He bends over, rapidly scrubbing and splashing his hands. Then he joins his companions, squats by the fire and deftly plucks the feathers. It's about the same size as a pigeon. He beckons the smallest soldier and points to the stream. The boy picks up a small axe and walks away from the dancing light of the fire into the shadows of the night. Minutes later, he returns clutching a handful of sticks.

They split and flatten the carcass on to the sticks and start to roast it. A soldier takes a small bucket with a wire handle to the stream, fills it with water and returns. They suspend the rice pot over the fire.

Low, conspiratorial voices drift from the direction of the truck. I turn to see the commander and Pig Face walking towards me. I don't want to draw attention to myself. I open the door and slip back into the driving seat, gently pulling it closed. They pass without looking and join the group around the fire.

'How are you feeling Mr Houn?'

'Fine thank you.' He replies in a monotone, hunched forward, looking directly ahead.

A Cambodian friend told me that during the Pol Pot period prisons were often ordinary houses. There was no barbed wire and at night the guards slept. In Khmer Rouge territory there was no point in running because there was nowhere to run to. He told me how they spoke kindly to some victims, telling them they were being released, then shot them in the back as they walked away. At least they didn't have to go on experiencing the agony of uncertainty. Waiting and thinking, 'May be any minute now.' But I'm not ready to think about dying yet. I have too much to do.

'I'm sure we'll get out of here once we talk to the senior commander's commander. Don't worry.' I try desperately to reassure Houn. I get the feeling I'm not doing a terribly good job.

'Yes, I hope so,' Houn replies mechanically.

A soldier walks up to my door. I open it and smile. He waves his hand behind him, says a few words and walks off in the direction of the barbecue.

Houn turns to me, 'The soldier say there are mines all around here.'

Maybe there are. On the other hand the commander said earlier they didn't know where we are. 'What do you think?'

'I not sure.'

I think through our options again. I have to communicate with someone at a senior level. If I can explain that we're neutral, that we're clearing mines to allow Cambodian farmers to work their land and to prevent poor people being hurt surely they'll release us. On the other hand they've already given their permission for us to work in the village. Mike visited them months ago and cleared it with everyone. They've executed a well-planned operation. Why do they want us?

My thoughts are interrupted by a tapping noise. The boy soldier is knocking politely on the passenger window. Houn opens the door. After a brief exchange he says, 'The soldiers say we sleep in Land Rover. You go in back. I stay here.'

I nod agreement. 'I'll need to move things around.' I walk to the back and move the stretcher, first-aid box and demining equipment to one side. I try and make a flat space big enough to stretch out on. I remember JJ's words again. I need a good night's sleep. I have to be at my best for the meeting with senior Khmer Rouge. I've managed to find one of the cushioned seats. I look around for the other. I crawl out backwards.

I get out cautiously and stand up. One of the watching soldiers reaches in past me. He puts the other seat cushion down, says a few words and then walks away.

'If you stay there you will be okay. They will bring us some food.' I am surprised the soldier helped me. What did he mean when he said we'll be all right if we stay here? Does that mean we'll be killed if we try to leave?

I nod politely to the soldiers and say, 'Or-gon.' They smile and turn back to the barbecue. I close the door to keep the mosquitoes out and lie back on the makeshift bed. It's good to relax. I'm tired. It's been a strange day. I still have no idea of what's going on and why. At least now I have a chance to talk it through with Houn.

We go through everything several times and are none the wiser. I'm surprised to discover they think I am a Russian military advisor. The Soviet Bloc advisors left five years ago.

There is another knock on the passenger window. I sit up. I can't afford to miss anything. The soldier hands a heaped plate of rice to Houn and disappears. A battered spoon lies each side and the charred bird carcass sits on top. The plate is chipped white enamel with a blue rim, like the one I fed my cat from when I was little. 'It's kind of them to give us the bird,' I say.

'Yes maybe some of soldier pity us. Sometimes they treat well before they . . .' Houn stops and holds out the plate of rice. I put it on the seat between us.

'We should eat as much as we can,' I say with no trace of hunger. I eat a few spoonfuls avoiding letting my teeth make contact as I chew. The rice will be rough milled. It probably contains stone fragments.

Houn sits, motionless. 'Please eat,' I implore.

'Yes I am.' He spoons a few grains of rice into his mouth. I pull a piece of meat from the bird and start to chew. It's rubbery. The taste reminds me of the smell of manure.

We try and force down rice. Houn manages two mouthfuls.

After a long silence, I realize it's useless. 'Please thank the soldiers for the food. I can't eat it because I'm feeling slightly unwell. They have been walking and must be hungry. They can eat it.' I decide not to tell them it tastes like shit.

The soldier returns and takes the plate. 'He thank us and say no problem.' We are confined to the Land Rover and Sok to the truck. I tell Houn not to worry for the hundredth time and lie back on the seat cushion. I've slept in the front of a Land Rover before. He should be comfortable. He's short enough to stretch out.

There's no point in thinking of escape yet. I have to try to negotiate our way out with the equipment. I need to be sharp tomorrow. God help us. I'm tired. I'm overcome by a sense of sadness. All I can do is hope and pray.

The plastic seat cover is soaked in sweat. When I wake I know exactly where I am. I force myself back to sleep. I must rest.

*

I awake, instantly alert, to the first light of dawn. There's no point in dreaming of being somewhere else. I have to face it. The sun will be up in forty minutes. Houn sits hunched forward in the same position he was in last night. One look tells me he hasn't slept. 'Did you get some rest?'

'Yes, I sleep for a while, thank you.'

I won't embarrass him any more. I wish I could do more to help him.

'I must go to the toilet. I'm going to go out the back.'

'Yes, no problem,' he replies. I creep out the door and walk back towards the stream. I can see a soldier wrapped in a green nylon hammock. Nobody's looking. I tiptoe past him and relieve myself by a tree.

I'm thirsty. This stream is the only water. The Khmer Rouge drink it and they're still alive. I find the best place to drink. The water is running over gravel and through sand into the round clear pool. I should drink boiled or sterilized water, but I have no choice. I scoop my hands and try some. It's nectar. I drink.

Two soldiers talk quietly by the truck. They're at least 300 metres away. The others are still in their hammocks. No one's watching me. The tentacles of temptation are reaching out. The stream-bed is rocky. There's no way it can be mined. I could just run down it. I'd have a minute or so, maybe five, before they realized I've gone. I'm sure I can out-run them. I've better boots, I train most days and I've got a lot of stamina. They can't cut me off. The odds are in my favour. The question is where do I go from here?

I hear JJ's voice. 'If you're lost without a map, go downhill until you find a gully, follow it to a stream and that'll take you to a river.' I'd have water and fourteen hours of daylight. The river goes through Rhum.

What about the equipment and Houn and Sok? I look behind me. The Khmer Rouge aren't watching me, but I can't do it. If I get it wrong they'll have a good reason to start shooting. All things considered, our best chance is still negotiation. At least I can console myself with the knowledge that I'm a volunteer prisoner.

I walk slowly back. Houn hasn't moved. I slam the door, loudly. I'm keen to get going. I want to meet the commander, talk and then get the hell out of here.

'Do you think they know where we are?'

'I don't know,' Houn replies as Pig Face kicks people out of their hammocks. Two soldiers walk off in different directions, ahead of the Zil.

The commander speaks. 'We drive through the jungle to find the road, then we go to the headquarters.' He waves and nods, which I take to mean go. I drive slowly past Sok; I wave and try to look cheerful. He nods.

*

I'm not sure if it's dried overnight, but the ground is firmer. We're out of the lowlands. Daylight is easier and faster.

Finally we reach the yellow brick road. It doesn't look well used, but the sandy track is even. I'll be able to do at least thirty kilometres an hour on the straight. In the distance there's a figure in the centre of the track. As we get nearer I see a Cambodian wearing green combat trousers and a bright orange Bermuda shirt. He looks a fat and friendly figure, but rumour has it so does Pol Pot.

'We stop here. They get some fuel,' Houn says as the commander greets the man in the psychedelic shirt.

After the noise of night insects and engines the forest is remarkably silent. I can see a junction through the low trees and clumps of grass. Sok appears, accompanied by two soldiers. 'They say Mr Sok will drive the Land Rover to get the fuel. We stay here and have breakfast.'

My heart sinks. I don't want to give up control of the vehicle. How do I know they'll bring it back and Sok will be safe? 'No problem. I will get the fuel. You can come and they can have breakfast.' Houn's face falls. He doesn't like the idea of disagreeing with the Khmer Rouge.

A tense discussion follows. Sok has explained the lorry takes petrol (*saeng*) and the Land Rover diesel (*masoot*). They don't have petrol. The commander eventually nods and points at the Land Rover, which I take to be agreement. The fat man in the Bermuda shirt climbs into the back. He has a round cheerful face, but for all I know he could be their torture expert.

It's 07.15. The sun is shining. There's a more relaxed atmosphere. Mr Fixit is in the back with his friendly fat face and two soldiers with AK 47s. Mr Red has been trusted to ensure we return and sits next to Houn.

Suddenly Mr Fixit shouts '*Chop!*' and jumps out the back door. He doesn't wait for the vehicle to stop and falls over as his feet hit the ground. He laughs loudly, revealing his deep embarrassment, brushes off his bright shirt, quickly gets up and begins exploring the undergrowth. He walks off the track and back again several times. Houn turns and looks as if he's trying not to laugh.

'He says it around here somewhere. It is hidden.'

That's great. Mr Fixit's hidden the fuel in a secret place in the jungle, but it's so secret he can't find it again. Looks like we're going to be here a while. I drive on, pausing every few minutes for Mr Fixit to leap out the back door and run into the jungle. After ten minutes of stop start, he returns waving excitedly. We follow.

About fifty metres from the track two fifty-gallon drums are covered with branches behind a bush. I'm surprised he found it. There are no obvious reference points and it can't be seen from the track. When we take the branches off I can smell diesel. I reverse back as close as I can.

A bucket and improvised funnel sit between the drums. Mr Fixit and the other soldier can pour the diesel. I don't mind it on my hands, but if it's all over my clothes I'll stink.

The Land Rover doesn't need the fuel. It has extended tanks and will go another 400 kilometres, but it would be stupid not to take the opportunity. I don't know where or how far we're going. I'm worried about the Zil. It might run out of fuel some time tonight. There's not a lot I can do.

They fill the tank until it overflows over their arms and legs. They jump back, clicking their tongues and laughing self-consciously. It looks like the fuel has been hidden recently. I wonder if the Khmer Rouge have other vehicles nearby? Maybe the loggers brought it in. Perhaps Mr Fixit is a logger. He looks too fat to live in the forest. They've gone to a lot of trouble to get the fuel here. The kidnap has been well planned.

The sun is bright, but the coolness of dawn still lingers in the shade of the trees. The return is faster than the drive out. For the first time I know where we're going. Early morning sunshine makes the world a better place. We're still alive. I check the time, it's nearly 07.50. Normally we'd have done over an hour's demining by now.

The soldiers are sitting around the junction in small groups. From a distance this could be mistaken for a Scout camp. As we arrive the commander tells us we're going to his divisional headquarters. Within minutes the fire is smothered in sand and the soldiers are on the vehicles. The track is flat; there are no tree roots. We're averaging twenty-five kilometres an hour.

The commander and Mr Red talk in conspiratorial tones. I slow down as we approach a blind corner. There are thick bushes either side of the track. Abruptly the commander raises his hand and shouts '*Chop!*' I stop. In the door mirror I see the Zil do the same.

Houn jumps out and stands in front of the Land Rover. It's the first time I've seen him move so fast. He beckons me quickly with his hand. What has he heard that he hasn't been able to tell me?

I walk over to him and turn to see two soldiers climb into the back and start going through the kit. They pass back a few items. Mr Red gives instructions. Now they're going through our rucksacks. There's not much worth stealing now. Pig Face has taken the best of my kit. The humiliation smarts. They start to take the TNT from the explosives box. That's the last straw. 'What the hell are they doing?'

'They are robbing us.'

'I'm not putting up with this.' I look at two of the young soldiers and try to catch their eyes. One stares vacantly back and the other looks at the ground. I turn to Houn to give instructions. There are tears welling in his eyes. I'm not being fair. I should do it myself. I'll take the kit back from them. I begin to walk past him. As I do he touches my arm and says, 'Do not go near them. They will kill us.'

Maybe that's what he heard. Was it worth the effort of

taking us any further or will they just kill us here? They could say we tried escaping. No one would ever know. They can do it and I can't stop them.

Mr Red takes four blocks of TNT and puts them in a green canvas backpack. It looks uncomfortable. They talk for a while and point towards the Zil. The commander gives instructions. Mr Red and five soldiers amble off. Pig Face waves and makes a joke from the back of the truck as they walk past.

We get back in the Land Rover. There are four soldiers with us, including the commander. There's an awkward silence. We try to pretend nothing really happened. After an uneasy moment the commander speaks. Houn nods and says, 'We go to headquarter to meet senior Khmer Rouge commanders.'

'I am keen to meet the commanders.' God I'm keen. I need to talk to someone who can understand me. Why we are here and what we are doing is so simple. It's hard to imagine a task that should be more acceptable to any rational human being.

Houn told me they asked him if I was Russian. If they think I am they'll kill us all. I hope I get the chance to prove that I'm British. If I'd lived in the jungle for fifteen years with my information on the outside world coming from Khmer Rouge radio I wouldn't be able to tell a Russian from a Brit. I've heard stories they still believe the Vietnamese occupy Cambodia.

I listen to my own breathing. I've never felt this lonely. The injustice, frustration and uncertainty are overwhelming. Finally I admit this could be it; the end of the road. God help us. If it's possible for a soul to cry out, then it must sound like this. I need to meet a Khmer Rouge commander who can see beyond the end of his nose.

'Please explain I am from Britain. I work for a charity that has come here to help the Cambodian people by clearing mines. We're neutral.'

'Khmer Rouge senior commanders. They will decide.'

'What is this commander's name?' I ask.

'Mr Keun.' I get the impression the conversation is over and he's done enough talking. It's coming up to nine o'clock. There's no point in being bitter. It won't help our case and it gives you bad karma. The track's good. We're moving fast, at least twenty kilometres since the junction. I try to make conversation, but I'm left feeling even more empty and isolated. They can't understand charity. They hear the words, but their hearts can't grasp the concept.

The trees are taller now and the soil less sandy. I can see where the folk tales of beasts and evil spirits come from. Sok told me when he was fighting in the forest years ago he saw a snake that had swallowed a deer.

'The headquarter here.'

Ahead there is a tree at least a hundred feet tall. Nothing grows under its thick leaf canopy. It's magnificent. To the left there is a small field hacked from the jungle. Tree roots and weeds stick out from a thin crop of cassava. At the end of the field there's a small thatched hut.

The commander takes off his trilby and wipes his forehead with the back of his hand. 'We park Zil and Land Rover under the big tree. We only stay here a short while then we go to the big headquarters to meet the senior divisional commanders.'

It's cool under the shade of the enormous tree. I hadn't realized the sun was so high in the sky and the heat of the day had arrived. It's 10.30. The lorry pulls up alongside. Mr Keun and a few of the soldiers walk over to the hut to greet a soldier sitting behind a large old-fashioned field radio set. I expect once they've reported in we'll move on. I should meet the soldier and learn what I can. I can't afford to miss anything.

On the far side of the hut there's blue plastic sheet covering what looks like a heavy machine-gun mounted on an air defence tripod. I can't imagine they've been under air attack since the Vietnamese pulled out six years ago. The government have got a few jets and helicopters, but most of them aren't airworthy. The weapon covers any possible advance from the direction of CAPF territory.

I can see the ring sight. It looks like a Russian 12.7mm DhSK heavy machine-gun. It must have been captured or perhaps they bought it. They've tied plastic around it to keep out the dust and rain. It's the same blue sheeting the UN gave to refugees when they were repatriated from the camps on the Thai border. I can't see a lot of ammunition, but that doesn't mean they haven't got it. Perhaps the machine-gun is a show of strength for our benefit.

Mr Keun nods and says something to the radio operator. Houn and I bow, smile and introduce ourselves. 'This is area political officer. He operate radio as well.'

They invite us to sit down with him in the hut in the shade. Mr Keun shouts into the bushes. A footpath leads downhill at the back of the hut. The bank is steep and I presume it leads to a river. They would have to settle near a water supply. A woman aged about forty in a faded sarong walks slowly up the path. She looks genuinely pleased to see Mr Keun. She glances in our direction, then averts her eyes. Directly behind her there are two young children. She squats at the side of the hut, grabs a few pieces of charcoal from a pile underneath the raised wooden floor and makes a fire. She starts to boil a battered, blackened kettle. I'm unsure how to greet the woman or if I should. I bow, place my hands together and make a polite Khmer greeting. She ignores me, her gaze glued to the ground. The children cling to her sarong and hide behind her legs.

The hut is constructed around four wooden corner posts. Irregular boards are nailed to cross-beams making a floor a metre off the ground. Short grass thatch attached to poles the length of the roof is overlayed like tiles. There are three nylon hammocks hung between the posts. One black and two green.

'The commander say you can sit in hammock and rest.'

It would be rude not to. I climb on to the floor and flop into it. I swing gently like an idiot, watching the soldiers chatting around the Land Rover. I'm a victim of my own politeness. On the other hand, it would be foolish to upset them. Our position is not very negotiable.

The radio operator nods. He's very tall for a Khmer, nearly six feet. His pock-marked face is covered in spots. He's too old to be an adolescent and they don't usually get spots here, so he must have a skin infection. Poor bloke.

He's wearing green combats and blue flip-flops. His gangly, awkward frame perches on a fold-up seat joined to the radio. A green panel with white control dials and black buttons houses what looks like a Morse key. There doesn't appear to be a speaker or headset. I can't see if it's dynamo or battery operated, or a connection to an antenna. I've never seen anything like it.

There's nothing I can do except sit and wait. Mr Keun speaks to the woman who I assume to be his wife. She pours thick condensed milk from a can into a mug and adds boiling water from the kettle. I'm surprised to see the milk. It must be a long walk to the nearest market; perhaps they trade with the woodcutters. Mr Keun passes the cup to Houn. The spoon is sticking out the top. He hands it to me and says, 'You should drink this.'

I stir in the viscous yellow blob at the bottom of the mug. The water goes creamy. I sip the scalding hot fluid and savour the sweet, safe, boiled water. I'm thirsty. I don't know when we will eat and drink again. I take another slurp and pass it to Houn. We soon finish the mug. A soldier reaches over and slides it across the floor to Mrs Keun. She refills it and slides it back.

I don't want to look greedy or make them think I'm too

expensive to keep. This is the last one I'll have. We thank them politely and pass the mug back. Mr Keun now takes economical sips. I glance at my watch. It's nearly eleven.

Suddenly the Land Rover engine shatters the calm. I start to leap out of the hammock, but stop myself. I sit up, roll out of the hammock and sit on the edge of the hut floor with my legs over the side.

Pig Face is sitting in the front of the Land Rover revving the engine. I was told we'd only be here for a few minutes, so I left the keys in the ignition. How could I have been so stupid? I know I can't trust anybody.

There's a loud grinding of gears. Eventually he finds reverse and takes the vehicle back slowly. He turns awkwardly then drives down the track. He almost stops then lurches forward as he changes gear. Perhaps one of the loggers, in fear of his life, gave him a few driving lessons. But it doesn't look like he's had many. The soldiers watch him and laugh. He does a clumsy five-point turn at the far end of the cassava field and returns.

I watch, humiliated. There's nothing I can do. Can I risk saying something to Mr Keun? I try not to look angry, but to convey polite anguish instead. The gears grate and the Land Rover jumps as Pig Face lets in the clutch. His driving's not improving and he's getting more brutal. I try and catch Mr Keun's eye. I shake my head and look worried, as if to say the vehicle will be irreparably damaged. He looks at me, then shouts across to the spectators by the tree. A young soldier runs after the vehicle shouting, then ambles back to the shade. Pig Face drives slowly back and switches off the engine.

'What did he say?' I ask Houn.

'He tell them not to drive vehicle because it waste fuel.'

I get back in the hammock. At least they've stopped. I'll never leave the keys in the ignition again.

It's a pleasant sensation gently rocking, but after twenty

minutes I've had enough. I get out and sit with my feet dangling over the side of the stilted floor. Mr Keun is asleep in the other hammock. Perhaps kidnapping people is as tiring as being kidnapped.

8

BUTTERFLIES

The political officer isn't talkative. We sit there in silence. Wherever you are, whatever you are doing, waiting is always the worst bit. What are we waiting for?

'I look forward to meeting the senior Khmer Rouge as soon as possible,' I say hopefully.

Houn quietly replies, 'Yes I tell them, but commander is very tired and he want to rest. Maybe we go soon.'

They always say soon. They promised us we could go home yesterday. They promised we could go once we'd met Mr Keun.

Mrs Keun works by the charcoal fire. I'm surprised she can get two pans cooking over the same small fire. She chops what looks like the leg of a deer into small pieces on a section of tree stump. She fries it in a pan and adds black pepper-corns. It looks better than last night's bird. Mr Keun carries on sleeping.

I look at my watch. It's nearly 11.50. Two young soldiers help Mrs Keun by the fire. She spoons rice into faded plastic bowls and adds spoonfuls of deer meat. They pass them round. Houn and I get one each with a spoon. The soft lean meat has been cooked to perfection. This is some of the best food I've had in Cambodia.

I try not to eat more than any one else. I could easily manage another bowl or two, but I don't want to draw attention to myself. If it comes to the crunch it just might tip the scales if we need a lot more food than they do. Behind the hut there is an ancient moped. It's in bits. The wheels and engine are missing. It looks beyond repair.

A young soldier wearing red plastic sandals and green combats is sitting next to Houn. He talks enthusiastically, but looks shy and too young to be a soldier. He should still be in school. His young face is disconcerting because it has the eyes of an old man.

The fields around the hut are planted with cassava or sweet potato. The red stalks and oval-shaped green leaves are just visible. In a few months the crop should be two metres high, if the thin, dry soil can support it. Farming is a safe subject. 'Do they do much farming here?' I ask.

We talk with the boy and learn they have a few cows and near the river they have some rice fields. The river is very close. It's just behind us.

Suddenly I sit back and listen. I can hear a faint buzzing. A familiar droning in the distance. No, I'm imagining it. It must be an insect. I strain my ears and scan the horizon. I'm sure I can hear it. I'm certain. In the far distance I can see a faint black dot, like a fly in the sky. It's getting closer. I'm sure it's a helicopter.

I keep my head down. There's no point in drawing their attention to it. I look at the heavy machine-gun under the plastic sheeting and wonder how much ammo they have and if it works? There's only one reason a helicopter is flying in this area. It has to be looking for us. No one else has noticed it yet. I hold my breath. Please God, let it come closer.

The fields must be visible from the air and they should see the vehicles parked under the tree. The noise gets louder and closer. Pig Face and the soldiers by the Land Rover stop and look up. They put their hands to their eyes to shield them from the sun. Mr Keun wakes, walks to the edge of the hut and peers up. I walk forward so I can get a good view if the helicopter circles. Everyone is silent.

It changes course, as if approaching the clearing to check it out. Perhaps they can see the vehicles! The helicopter circles. It's flying high and wide, sensibly keeping its distance. The soldiers are mesmerized. So far no one has gone near the gun. It remains heavily wrapped in the plastic sheet. Let's hope it stays that way.

The helicopter is white. I can't make out any markings and it's not close enough to see the outline of the pilot. I think an American contract company flies it for the UN. I'm sure they've seen us. I take a few steps forward and glance anxiously at the machine-gun. I hope they don't think about having a go.

It circles again, wider this time and maintaining height. It comes in range. All eyes remain fixed on the helicopter as it completes a third circuit and heads off in the direction it came from.

They wanted to let us know we were being watched. It was too high for them to see us, even with binoculars. The UN has strict flying restrictions – aircraft has to stay out of small arms range. All that will have been reported so far is the vehicle sighting. No one will know if we're dead or alive.

It's nearly 12.10. The helicopter will have seen us just after 12.05. Even if they think we're still alive what can they do? No military can enter the forest without the Khmer Rouge knowing. If any force comes near they'll shoot us and run.

Mr Keun and the soldiers are still peering into the sky. 'Please tell the commander they saw us. That's why they circled three times. They are very worried about us. He must take us to his senior commander now.' I feel suddenly cheerful.

After a pause Mr Keun shouts instructions. The three soldiers nearest to him walk off and pick up their AK 47s and tatty webbing. The others remain squatting on their haunches in the shade of the tree. Mr Keun and the political officer exchange a few sharp words. I'm surprised he hasn't reported

My parents on their wedding day. ▶

▲ A summer holiday on the Isle of Wight, aged four – the year England won the World Cup.

Me as a snotty-nosed schoolboy. ▶

MY FATHER IN HIS PRODUCTIVE GARDEN WITH A PRIZE PLUM TREE.

IN MY PARENTS' GARDEN WHEN I WAS A 'PEASANT' – AS DEMONSTRATED BY MY BLUE 'BENNY' HAT.

▲ 4 PLATOON rugby team.

OFFICER CADET IN
CEREMONIAL DRESS FOR
FIRST PARADE AT Sandhurst
(WHERE I NEVER EXHIBITED
A NATURAL TALENT FOR
MARCHING IN EXCEPTIONALLY
SHINY BOOTS). ▶

PHNOM PENH BY THE SIDE OF THE RIVER MEKONG.

THE SECURITY REGULATIONS AT THE FORMER KHMER ROUGE
INTERROGATION CENTRE (TUOL SLENG), PHNOM PENH, CAMBODIA.

THE SECURITY REGULATIONS

1. YOU MUST ANSWER ACCORDINGLY TO MY QUESTIONS...DON'T TURN THEM AWAY

2. DON'T TRY TO HIDE THE FACTS BY MAKING PRETEXTS THIS AND THAT. YOU ARE STRICTLY PROHIBITED TO CONTEST ME.

3. DON'T BE A FOOL FOR YOU ARE A CHAP WHO DARE TO THWART THE REVOLUTION.

4. YOU MUST IMMEDIATELY ANSWER MY QUESTIONS WITHOUT WASTING TIME TO REFLECT.

5. DON'T TELL ME EITHER ABOUT YOUR IMMORALITIES OR THE ESSENCE OF THE REVOLUTION.

6. WHILE GETTING LASHES OR ELECTRIFICATION YOU MUST NOT CRY AT ALL.

7. DO NOTHING, SIT STILL AND WAIT FOR MY ORDERS. IF THERE IS NO ORDER, KEEP QUIET. WHEN I ASK YOU TO DO SOMETHING, YOU MUST DO IT RIGHT AWAY WITHOUT PROTESTING.

8. DON'T MAKE PRETEXTS ABOUT KAMPUCHEA KROM IN ORDER TO HIDE YOUR JAW OF TRAITOR.

9. IF YOU DON'T FOLLOW ALL THE ABOVE RULES, YOU SHALL GET MANY MANY LASHES OF ELECTRIC WIRE.

10. IF YOU DISOBEY ANY POINT OF MY REGULATIONS YOU SHALL GET EITHER TEN LASHES OR FIVE SHOCKS OF ELECTRIC DISCHARGE.

TWO CHILDREN WHO ARE
VERY LUCKY TO BE ALIVE, HAVING
JUST WALKED THROUGH A MINED
AREA. WE SAW THEM WHILE
CARRYING OUT SURVEY WORK;
THEIR FAMILIES WERE RECENTLY
RETURNED REFUGEES WHO HAD
NO IDEA THE AREA SURROUNDING
THEIR HUT WAS MINED. ▶

▼ DUSK IN CAMBODIA.

PLANNING AND
MAPPING WITH
CAMBODIAN
COLLEAGUES.

DEBRIEF WITH UN OFFICER
IMMEDIATELY AFTER OUR ESCAPE
FROM THE KHMER ROUGE. ►

▼ INSPECTING THE DEMINER'S
TOOL KIT IN CAMBODIA.

SOM ON, WHO SURVIVED
AGAINST THE ODDS, NOW
TEACHES WOOD CARVING AT
THE JRS CENTRE NEAR PHNOM
PENH, HAVING REGAINED
SOME INDEPENDENCE BECAUSE
OF A HAND-POWERED
WHEELCHAIR PROVIDED
BY MOTIVATION.

THE TOP OF AN OZM72 MINE MARKED FOR DESTRUCTION. (*John Rodstead*)

the sighting of the helicopter. Maybe the station he communicates with is only manned at certain times or perhaps the radio is a deception. There's lot of that here.

Mr Keun gives the word and we're off in the Land Rover again. The helicopter must have worried him. I follow the track downhill into the shade of bamboo and bushes, the sort that grow near water. The Zil follows.

'There is a river ahead. They make a Khmer Rouge bridge with logs under the water.'

I don't think they do it to avoid detection from the air, it's just the easiest way to make a bridge. They take large tree trunks, cut one surface flat and wide enough for tyres and submerge them to make an underwater tramway. The ends are buried in the riverbank. As long as the tyres stay on the logs it's fine. 'I'll need to walk across before we drive it,' I say.

As the water surges into my boots it feels more like a hot bath. Sunlight dances across the sand and dark green bushes and reeds, accompanied by the rippling of the water. Under any other circumstances it would be a joy to be here. I step forward cautiously, I expect it's slippery. A soldier overtakes me on the other log tramway. The tree trunks are enormous.

The crossing is about twenty metres wide. There must be two logs joined in the middle. The water is clear and I can see the riverbed. It looks like soft sand. There's a small gap where two logs join. I rock both sides with my feet. There's no movement.

The other bank is flat dry sand. As I check to see where each end of the trunk is firmly buried in the ground I can feel them watching me. I step on to the other tree trunk and walk back.

I hope we'll be coming back this way later today.

I slip suddenly as my foot jams in a gap. If the lorry takes this too fast the impact could force the logs apart.

The Zil rattles slowly towards the river and gently bumps on to the logs. Two soldiers walk two metres in front to guide the wheels. I hope they don't slip. A body would be crushed like a matchstick. Sok stops in the middle and very gently takes the gap.

Once over the other side he stops the truck at the top of the bank. The soldiers walk back across the logs to guide us in the Land Rover. When we get to the middle I stop, then inch forward. I feel a bump.

Sok stands on the bank and watches. In his black trousers and shirt he looks more like one of the Khmer Rouge than they do.

The right side of the vehicle rises. I hold my breath. In a smooth movement we roll magically forward. There's another slight bump as the back wheels cross the gap. Sok is standing with the two soldiers. His eyes are fixed on the ground and they are full of sadness.

Houn says ominously, 'We must leave truck here. There is not enough fuel to take it to the area headquarters. His man will look after it for us. You pick it up tomorrow.'

We always start with full tanks first thing in the morning. Driving solidly for about sixteen hours and going through boggy ground uses a lot of fuel. There's probably just enough to get to the edge of the forest if we take the track rather than the scenic jungle route. It makes sense to leave it here, but it's ours and I don't want to lose it. 'How far is it to the next headquarters?'

'Long way. They say we drive all afternoon. Commanders there will decide what to do with us.' Houn looks down as he finishes speaking and folds his arms.

There's no guarantee we'll be returning, but at least we're allowed to take Sok with us.

Mr Keun waves his hand and the soldiers get back in the Land Rover. Our conversation is over. Houn sits hunched in his usual position. Mr Keun climbs in and says something to the soldier behind him who fiddles in his rucksack. I drive on. There's only one track to follow. Out of the corner of my eye, I see the soldier passing a package to Mr Keun, something wrapped in a plastic bag. He takes off two elastic bands and pulls out a large grey pistol.

I try not to stare. Why does he need it? Does he think we'll try to escape? Is he taking us to a place where he can hide our bodies? The worst feeling is helplessness.

The track is now only occasionally shaded by large trees. It seems hotter and more humid here. In the gaps between the trees a variety of lush green plants soak up the sunlight. I've often wondered what it is like in the forest. There's more space between the trees than I'd expected, but the undergrowth is impenetrable. The clumps of bamboo are as thick as fortress walls. I persist in trying to establish a relationship. 'The forest is beautiful. You live in such a beautiful place.'

Mr Keun smiles and looks out of the window. He cradles the pistol in his lap.

Houn smiles nervously. 'He say when there is peace in Cambodia you come back. He will take you in forest so you can take photograph.'

Does that mean he doesn't intend to execute us this afternoon. Or is he just being polite?

Ahead there's a hole in the right-hand side of the track. I swerve round it. It's about forty centimetres deep and wide. What's it for? After twenty minutes we come to another one in the same position. A large log has been placed in it. It's in line with our wheels and it's about the same size as an anti-tank mine. 'What are these holes for?'

'The soldiers say they dig for anti-tank mines. If government soldiers come they can bury mines quickly,' Houn replies.

I nod my head. Very clever. 'Are there any anti-tank mines buried on this track?'

Houn speaks slowly to the soldiers in the back. They talk for a disconcertingly long time. 'They don't think so.'

I fight my desire to stop and shout, 'You don't fucking think so! Do you know what'll happen if we drive on one?' After a pause I stop and say, 'Please make sure there's no chance this track is mined.'

Houn leans forward and turns around to face the soldiers. After a brief exchange he says, 'They haven't put any here recently and a few logging lorries have driven this way before. They say you drive.'

At the top of a sandy bank the trees become thicker and there's a heap of rusty metal and several twisted chassis. The soldiers speak to Houn and point. He says, 'Many year ago Vietnamese soldier come to fight. So they blow up with anti-tank mine, shoot soldiers from trees and run into forest. They kill everyone who come here.'

Mr Keun's Tokarev looks the same as Mr Red's. Perhaps they've only got one and have to share.

Sweat tickles my forehead and back. It's unbelievably hot. I put my head close to the window to get some fresh air. For some reason the forest looks familiar. In places the sun breaks through the vegetation. To my left there's a fallen tree with strangely contorted branches that has finally found peace among the leaf mould. Beyond it an enormous tree towers above everything. The available sunlight beside the giant is taken by a small clump of bushes. Adjacent to these a rotting tree trunk lies among dead brown leaves.

Out of the shade the sun is blinding and the heat overbearing. The combination of the motion of the vehicle and watching the familiar landscape makes me feel like I'm floating. I feel dizzy. I take a deep breath.

I inhale a powerful scent of perfume.

'What's that smell?'

Houn speaks briefly to the soldiers. 'Sandalwood.'

I'm mesmerized by the view of the forest on my left. I've been here before. I glance ahead and line up the steering wheel to keep a straight course for the grove of bamboo ahead. I lock my arm on the steering wheel and look out of the window. I remember it all. The overpowering scent of the sandalwood and the extreme heat.

Suddenly I'm falling.

It's dark. The heat's gone and it's cool, beautifully cool. I hear a splash and I can feel the cool closeness of water.

I've stopped falling.

It's still dark.

Now I'm rising, floating upwards. Everything is happening in slow motion. It's like falling through a window in time.

All I can see is vivid yellow. Now everything is bright, beautiful blue. I wonder if I've been shot? How stupid of them to shoot me while I'm driving.

I squint and peer into the strange mixture of yellow and blue merging before my eyes. I blink. It's outside the vehicle. The colours are fluttering in front of my eyes. Now I can make out the shapes. Thousands and thousands of butterflies fill my vision. For a few seconds they dance in front of us, then flutter away as we emerge into the sunshine.

The butterflies are more beautiful than anything I can imagine. Even in the blackest darkness there might be a faint light. Perhaps we're not as helpless or hopeless as we think.

I'm shaken. I remember where I've seen this place – it was in my dream. I'm sceptical when I hear tales of the extraordinary and powerful feelings of an external force. If somebody told me about this experience I'd find it hard to believe, but I know where I am and what I've seen. I wonder what the others think?

'The butterflies were beautiful. Does Mr Keun often see things like this?'

'Sometimes they see tigers.'

My heart leaps. To be somewhere where these magnificent creatures still live wild is a privilege.

'Are there many tigers in this area?'

'Yes. Sometimes Mr Keun goes into the forest to shoot tigers with AK 47. They sell to traders.'

'How close does he get before he shoots?'

'It takes long time. They have to get close, at least seventy-five metres. They have to go into forest for two, three days.'

Tiger hunting is a subject Mr Keun is comfortable talking about. I'm sure we've been told a lot of lies, but I don't think this is one.

'Are there many in this part of the forest?'

'Not so many now.'

That's hardly surprising, but now doesn't seem a good time to argue the case for the World Wildlife Fund. Mr Keun holds the pistol loosely in his right hand. He avoids my glance and looks out of the window. They never look us in the eye. He makes a half-smile and speaks but keeps his gaze fixed on some distant tree. Perhaps he's worried I'll start talking to him again, about how beautiful the forest and butterflies are. How can they be unmoved by such beauty?

Houn tightens his grip on the dashboard and says, 'Stop here. He go to speak with commander at headquarter.'

A track merges from the right. It's the first junction we've come to since we crossed the river over two hours ago. I've no idea where we are.

Mr Keun puts on his hat and strides away purposefully. A soldier follows a few paces behind. We sit and wait in the heat and silence.

Houn moves over, relieved to have more space. The back door opens and the soldiers get out, AK 47s at the ready. One walks to the back of the vehicle and stands on the track. The other walks to the front. It's 14.30. I get out hoping it will be cooler. In a few moments the Land Rover will be like an oven.

Houn joins me. We lean on the bonnet. It's a great comfort to be together and able to talk.

'What do you think?' I am eager for any scrap of knowledge.

Houn keeps his eyes fixed on the ground. 'Senior Khmer Rouge have meeting to decide what to do. They will not allow us to see headquarter. They think we are enemy. They will interrogate us.'

I feel slightly sick. 'Do they really think I'm Russian?'

'Yes. Mr Sok tell me soldiers ask him.'

'What did he say?'

Houn's eyes haven't moved. 'He say no.'

I take a deep breath. I'm relieved.

'But he not think they believe him.'

We are like drowning men, desperate for something to cling to. I wonder what the Khmer Rouge headquarters is like and what weapons they have. The soldiers are taking guarding us seriously. The youngest leans on the other side of the Land Rover, watching us curiously. The other is at the back covering us with an AK.

I need to go. No point in being embarrassed. Dignity is not skin deep. 'Please ask the soldier if I can go over there to the toilet.'

'Yes, they allow.'

I disappear behind a clump of bushes, savouring the privacy. First I have to check the colour of my urine. I haven't had a lot to drink today, but it's not too dark. Good, I'm not dehydrated. I drank stream water this morning, then I had the milk at the hut. If the water was going to give me trouble it would have affected me by now. Ominously it feels as if the world's about to fall out of my bottom. I attempt a controlled explosion. The result is firmer than anticipated. The large soft leaves of a nearby tree are always useful. You have to use the right ones or you get a rash.

As I bury it I wonder if that's the last crap I'll have. I wash my hands in leaves and sand and retie my laces. Now I'm as ready for anything as I can be.

All too soon I have to return to the Land Rover. It's only a few metres, but I try and make it last as long as possible. I lean on the wing and look around. Sok is lost in thought. Perhaps he's remembering his children. Houn and the older soldier are talking.

The only links these Khmer Rouge have with the outside world are their occasional journeys to their relatives in border villages, people entering their territory and Khmer Rouge radio, which isn't known for its impartial reporting. There are frequent broadcasts alleging the CPP (Cambodian People's Party) are Vietnamese puppets. The Khmer Rouge was ousted by Vietnamese invasion in 1979. They fled to the forest keeping control of the country's two main sources of wealth: timber and the sapphire fields around Pailin.

The Vietnamese were Russian backed, hence the CPP's weaponry is Russian. There are rumours of foreign military advisers. If they think I'm Russian, I'm the enemy. I'll try telling them again. 'Please tell them, I'm British. I work for a charity. We help the Cambodian people by clearing mines.'

After a discussion Houn says, 'The soldier say he went to see his family and the village had well dug by foreign organization.'

I say, 'We are like that, except we clear mines. How often does he go to see his family?'

The older soldier and Houn speak. 'Maybe once a year. Now the Khmer Rouge are calling many soldiers back from rest of Cambodia to fight.'

We talk. The older soldier wants to be wealthy so when the fighting stops he can return to Cambodia a rich man. He tells us of gold buried in a Wat in the jungle. Nobody can get it because the area is so heavily mined. I'm not offering my services to clear a safe route, but I'll keep it in mind as a last resort. If the soldiers take us into the forest to kill us I'll try bargaining.

He says people near the edge of the forest bury their gold at night underneath their houses. It's the only place they think is safe. They're afraid of each other and trust nobody. When the Khmer Rouge go to the villages they never find gold. That's why he thinks they bury it, because that's where he would hide it if he had some. He wants to know if our metal detectors can find gold. I lie. I explain they can only find iron and steel.

We wait.

Sok looks out of sorry, empty eyes. Tears don't look far away. He wants to know who'll feed his six children if he never goes home. Usually, he's a bit of a talkative wheeler-dealer, but he's gone quiet now. Sok told me he had a lot of children to make up for all the Khmers who died in Pol Pot's time. He repeatedly tells the soldiers he's just a simple man who drives the truck. I keep telling them too.

I wonder what they're saying about us in the Khmer Rouge headquarters? If they torture us I wonder how they'll start? We'll probably be tied up first.

I don't think they'll hold us for long. We'll either be out of here or killed very soon.

I strain my ears. I can hear a vehicle. It's not a lorry, probably a four-wheel drive. A white pick-up speeds to the track junction and skids to a halt. Mr Keun emerges from the pick-up with dust flapping his hat. He says a few words and everyone gets back into the Land Rover.

It's a fairly new Toyota pick-up. Probably one of the many donated by the UN at gunpoint. The doors have been res-prayed where the black UN markings used to be. Six soldiers are squashed in the back amid a mass of AK 47s and RPGs. The soldiers laugh and point at us. We're the new boys in their playground. The RPGs are all loaded. They clutch them in one hand and hang on to the side of the vehicle with the other.

The driver leans across, nods and waves his arm for us to follow. He has short-cropped hair, looks athletic and is probably in his late thirties. He smiles a full toothed beamer and waves his arm frantically again.

'Commander say follow that car.'

If I wasn't so preoccupied with our impending execution I'd think that was funny.

The driver looks like the man in charge. He has an air of confidence that marks him out. He speeds away, creating another dust cloud. I don't want to be left behind. I glance at the speedometer. We are doing nearly fifty kilometres an hour. We bump along the jungle track in a constant cloud of dust. Every now and again there's a jolt and we're thrown about as we wallop over large tree roots. I've never gone this fast in these conditions. He's a good driver.

This must be killing the shock absorbers. What the hell? I could be dead in ten minutes. Why am I worrying? I might as well enjoy the drive. I'll leave enough distance between us just in case he stuffs up and rolls it. If there's an accident we're on our own. Houn wedges himself firmly between the dash and the seat. As we come to a straight I put my seat belt on. Mr Keun has shut his eyes.

I'm not sure what I'd expected. Perhaps, an old Khmer Rouge commander dressed in black surrounded by thin henchmen with frowns and hard eyes. We would speak in broken French. I would explain we were here to help the Cambodian people by clearing mines and that we're neutral and apolitical. He would ask questions. There would be understanding and he'd allow us to go back to work because what we were doing was good.

In a worse case they might believe I'm a foreign military adviser. When he didn't get the answers he wanted he'd get angry. The worst might happen. We'd be interrogated separately. We might go before a Khmer Rouge court in a bamboo hut where frightened people would watch, relieved it was us and not them. They would clap and shout the right things at the right time. The chairman would have a microphone and we would have no defence. He would be there to pass sentence and we would be there to die.

Then again they might give the order without us knowing. We would be taken to a field or a place on the edge of the track. The soldiers might be kind. They'd feed us and lie, saying we were going home. We'd be shot in the back or the head. It would be quick. Houn thinks it'll happen that way.

Worst of all we'd be given to someone like Pig Face. We would be tied up. They would get scorpions, rope, fire and bamboo splinters. There would be pointless, stupid questions. They would laugh and we would scream.

Whatever I was expecting, it wasn't this surreal jungle race.

I brake as I see the rear of the pick-up bounce over a large root. Everyone is thrown into the air in a jumble of arms, legs and weapons. Two of them are still holding RPGs on their shoulders. They're pointed straight at us. They all laugh and rub their bruises.

As the back wheels jolt over the root I hear a thud as a head behind me hits the roof. Unlucky. It's followed by a bang as the equipment thrown into the air returns to the floor. The pick-up speeds ahead. I can't keep up. I'm not going any faster. It's not safe.

Ahead I see a soldier perched on the tailboard catapulted into the air as the wheels bounce over rocks. I brake. He throws his arms forward as he falls. The soldiers grab them. He lands on his stomach on the tailboard. His legs flail as he's pulled in. They laugh while he rubs his stomach.

I change up and down and steer round rocks and ruts, trying to keep up. The pick-up pauses at the top of a wooded hill then disappears. It's the first time he's slowed down for anything. At the top I stop.

Thick bamboo covers the side of the hill. The track has been washed away and there's a steep drop into a rock-strewn gully. The gradient falls to the right as well as down. The pick-up tilts precariously and the soldiers lean left to stop the vehicle rolling. With wide grins and waves they dare us to follow.

Usually I'd dig into the side of the hill for the left wheels and pull the earth down to level up for the right wheels. I'd also move any large rocks likely to damage the axle and sump. This time I'm just going to go for it. If he got down there then so can we. I can't let them beat me. 'Houn, tell everyone in the back to lean left.'

Shouts and the sound of rattling equipment fill my ears. I grip the steering wheel to stop myself slipping into Houn. He wedges himself, gripping the dash and the seat back. Mr Keun falls against the door and pulls his hat over his eyes again. I hope I haven't misjudged our centre of gravity. I shout, 'Keep leaning left.'

Miraculously we reach the bottom to find the pick-up has disappeared. There are now deep ruts in the dry grey soil, most likely made by logging trucks last wet season. Soon we climb out of the lower ground, back to sand and trees. The forest flies past as we race along the track once more.

Up ahead there's a clearing. Apart from the gully it's the only memorable feature. The rest of the jungle is a blur. It's nearly two or three hectares covered in long grass. Beyond it the track bends sharply right. It's nearly 16.30. We've been driving an hour and a half and there have been no junctions or turnings. I tell myself to remember the gully and clearing.

The pick-up slows as it approaches another gap in the trees. The ground is cultivated and thin crops are just visible in the dry soil. Ramshackle huts with sides and roofs of brown thatch are dotted among small fields. There's a pagoda in the centre. It's a central meeting place, not a religious building. They use the same word. It's new with a tin roof and straight wooden beams. A house made from the same materials stands next to it.

'Stop and wait,' Houn says.

A group of soldiers guard the edge of the clearing. There are two large tree trunks and a heap of rough timber. The pick-up stops long enough for the driver to say a few words then speeds off towards the centre of the village.

A soldier talks to Mr Keun through the open window. Houn clenches his fists, looks down and says quietly, 'You must go with soldiers. We wait here.'

I park by the small pile of timber and quickly stuff the keys in my pocket. On my right three soldiers are squatting under the shade of a tree. They get up, wave me forward and start walking. I march a pace behind the one in front. Two of them follow me. I look over my shoulder. Houn stares through the windscreen. Sok has stuck his head out of the side of the Land Rover to watch me disappear.

Around the edge of the clearing there are small fields of maize and cassava. The crops look thin. Life for the people here must be hard. Each of the huts has a vegetable patch. Rows of spindly yellow tomato plants and melon and cucumbers sprawl over sticks leaning against the side of the houses. As we approach the first one, a dog rushes to the corner and barks. It senses strangers. It yelps as a soldier scores a direct hit with a stone. They laugh like it's the funniest thing they've seen in ages.

In front of us a woman in a sarong that's been washed so many times it's faded grey walks towards us carrying a battered tin can of water. I put my hands together to bow and greet her. She looks terrified. She turns around and walks rapidly in the other direction. The Khmer Rouge ignore her.

There are about twenty huts. Most are bamboo and reed thatch, but a few have hardwood planks on the floor and sides.

Near the pagoda there's a long house. It looks like soldiers' accommodation. Three lie in hammocks near the door. As I get closer they raise their heads. There are no smiles.

The track leads to the other side of the clearing. We turn towards the pagoda. The first building looks like a general's house – two storeys and a five-metre radio antenna. The other building is a tin roof on a wooden frame. Instead of walls there's a low wooden fence a metre high to keep the dust and dogs out. There are two entrance gaps. To the left of the pagoda, there is a large clump of trees. Among them is a concrete building next to a well. It looks like a washroom.

Three sides of the ground level of the house are boarded. The other side is left open. There's a concrete floor and a wooden wall down the centre makes it into two rooms. We stop at the first. There's a table and two chairs. The soldier motions me to the chair nearest the wall.

I sit down. He stands behind me and the others walk away.

A soldier peeps around a mango tree opposite, scrutinizes me and disappears. I strain my ears. What are they doing to Houn and Sok?

Wood smoke drifts through the trees. Maybe they use that area for cooking. I wonder why they split us up? Do they really think I'm a Russian military adviser? I don't want to be killed for being something I'm not.

Someone shouts and the soldier leaves.

The folding metal chairs are like the ones sold in the markets. The boards on the wall are evenly spaced. The house looks well built. Tyre tracks stop opposite the house. Perhaps the pick-up is parked here and reversed down the short track. The ground outside is littered with cans and plastic food wrappings.

Between the house and the trees there are six spindly rose bushes. They have beautiful small flowers, red, yellow and white. I'm surprised to see them in this place.

I've heard stories.

They hung people by their hands and beat them with rods, rope or bamboo. Sometimes they'd tie them in the hot sun and leave them to get thirsty. In the wet season there was water torture, repeated drowning and the beatings. Scorpions and venomous centipedes held with pliers and played slowly over the body made the victim beg to be smashed in the head with a hoe, or shot.

9

A CLEVER MAN

The time is 16.40.

I play with my watch. It's comforting to touch something familiar. Time is relative and more precious than I'd realized.

I wonder what happens when you die? Faith is being sure of what you hope for and certain of what you cannot see.

I hope Houn and Sok are okay. I strain my ears. At least there's no screaming.

I can hear a large water-container being filled by buckets somewhere near the trees.

In the distance, angular, tree-covered mountains stretch into infinity. It's a fairytale landscape. I wonder if Thailand lies beyond the mountains.

The table wobbles when I rest my hands on it. It's the sort the local carpenters make. I feel the surface. The local wood is always hard and heavy.

Out of the corner of my eye I see movement through the gaps between the boards. It's slow and quiet, somebody taking a step then pausing. I watch the corner. The shape moves faster. The driver bursts round the corner.

He smiles, showing his teeth. He looks me in the eyes and shakes hands firmly. His hair is short and layered back. He looks clean. He walks to the other side of the table. Before sitting down he says awkwardly, 'I would like to help you.'

He speaks slowly, struggling to pronounce each word. He holds a plastic-covered book, a notepad and a red pen in his left hand. His forefinger is stuck in the page as a bookmark. He regards me intently. 'You speak Thai?'

I shake my head. 'No.'

He frowns. 'I speak Thai.'

He opens the book, presses it down with his fist to keep it open at the right page and takes the lid off his pen. He consults what I think is a Thai/English phrase book and scribbles notes in his exercise book. 'What country are you from?'

'I am British.' I keep it simple. This could be the most important question I'm asked.

He consults the book and makes a few notes. 'Nationality?'

'British, United Kingdom.' I speak slowly.

He reads then laughs, as if witnessing something ridiculous. 'Where is your organization from?'

'United Kingdom.'

He studies and makes more notes. 'Why you come Cambodia?'

'To help the Cambodian people by clearing mines.' His interrogation technique is excellent. He wants the truth and he's getting it.

He's wearing a copied American combat jacket. They're made in Thailand. Some are ferried over the border to the local markets on motorcycle trailers.

'Name?'

'Chris.'

He makes and consults notes. 'What you do in Cambodia?'

I stress our neutral status. Occasionally he pushes the dictionary across. I look up the word and point to the meaning in Thai. Communication is slow but effective. I have no margin for error.

'When you come Cambodia?'

'Six weeks ago.' He had time to speak to Houn; perhaps he's looking for verification. Beyond our courtesy is a search for the truth and a battle of wills.

He says, 'Why you have Zil truck?' I think he knows it's a Russian lorry.

'Low price.'

'Who you work for?'

'A charity clearing mines. We give equipment and teach people the work.' It would be wrong to assume he understood me. I write every word and show him in the dictionary. There's something different about his eyes; there is a hint of understanding.

'You pay Khmer people?'

'Yes. Truck driver and interpreter here. Good Khmer men. They are my family. They like Khmer Rouge.' I write slowly and clearly.

'Why you come my area?'

I try not to sound angry. 'Soldiers attack and make us come.'

He laughs. He knows we were kidnapped. 'Who you work for?'

He doesn't wait for an answer. He puts the lid on his pen, gathers his books and beckons me with his hand as he heads for the pagoda. Inside there are two long wooden tables and a variety of chairs, some folding metal, some wood. At the far end there's a white plastic board with red and green pens hung on the beam. I'm surprised to see it, but it wouldn't be too difficult for him to send somebody shopping to the local market or Thailand.

'Where you from?' he asks.

I write, 'United Kingdom, UK.' He checks again and laughs.

A soldier emerges from the bushes 200 metres behind the pagoda. He's carrying something wrapped in a huge leaf. He folds it back to reveal ten silver fish slightly smaller than his hand. It must be a good catch. They look pleased, but not as excited as I am.

I rub the board clean and write in large red letters, 'Where you catch fish?'

The commander points to the rear of the pagoda. The ground drops downhill. It's covered in bushes and creepers. Everything beyond a few metres is a mystery, but at least I know the direction to the river.

The commander asks again, 'Why you come Cambodia?'

I show him the words in the dictionary. 'To help Cambodian people by clearing mines.'

He stares at me, then shouts an order. A soldier runs out from the trees and disappears down the track. He walks to the table, gestures to a chair opposite him and says, 'You have a good heart.'

I sit down and sneak a look at my watch. It's 17.05. We've been talking for nearly half an hour. Two soldiers bring in Houn. He places his hands together and makes a low bow. The commander asks a series of questions then gestures to the chair next to me.

Houn stretches and leans back. 'Before they not trust me. Now he say they will use me as interpreter.'

The commander closes his book and speaks.

Houn stares incredulously, then narrows his eyes. He looks utterly perplexed and says. 'We are the reason he is here. Sometimes he hear a voice inside his head. This morning he was going to a distant village to solve a problem, but the voice tell him, Stay here. This afternoon there will be something important to do.'

How could he know? What did he hear? Was it just a coincidence?

I can't explain because I don't understand, but I'm grateful. This morning I'd done everything I could and gone beyond desperation.

I remember the flash of yellow and blue and the beauty of the butterflies.

Houn continues. 'The people call him Mr Clever, because he went to primary school. They ask him to solve problems.

He told the Khmer Rouge commanders he would deal with us.'

Soldiers are hanging around the edge of the pagoda. They keep staring at me.

'The commander of another division capture us. Mr Clever not invite us here, but he will try to help us,' Houn says.

The command structure is confusing. Even though they kidnapped us nobody is responsible for us. From what I've been told and seen the regional commanders have a lot of autonomy. Communication is difficult. Rumour has it Pol Pot sends written instructions to the regions via trusted messengers. They have problems getting through to the headquarters by radio. Each divisional commander is the local warlord. They can do what they want as long as they don't make Pol Pot angry.

We have escaped execution this afternoon, but for how long?

Houn sits forward and clenches his fists before he speaks. 'This evening he invite us to eat with him. First you park Land Rover by his house then we can use his bathroom to wash.'

I park the Land Rover, then from nowhere I'm passed a pink plastic bottle of shampoo. A soldier shows me to the bathroom. It's built from hollow Cambodian bricks rendered in cement. Like the pagoda and house it's recently constructed. The wooden door jams on the wet cement floor. There's a squat toilet and a corner water tank built of brick and cement. They must fill it with buckets from the well.

There are no windows, just narrow gaps at the top to let the light in. I take off my boots to avoid making mud marks and stand on the wall of the water tank. I peep through the gaps. Two soldiers are asleep in green nylon hammocks. Nobody is watching.

I force myself to use the toilet and take off my overalls. The wet floor is delightfully cool. I'd forgotten the heat. I scrub my boxer shorts and socks. They'll dry as I wear them. The smell of the shampoo is luxury beyond belief. It makes me realize how bad I smell. I fill the small plastic bowl and lift it above my head. Slowly I pour the water. Its coolness makes me catch my breath.

I wash, using the water and shampoo sparingly. I must be a low-maintenance guest. I put my clothes and boots back on. Now I feel more like a civilized human being and less like a caged animal.

I return to the pagoda and pass the shampoo to Houn. 'You'll enjoy that.'

'Yes I think so.' For a second he grins. He keeps his head down, but his eyes register everything around him as he scuttles to the washroom.

Mr Clever and the others have gone. I walk around the pagoda. Sitting in the corner nearest the general's house is a large wooden bed with a pink mosquito net. There's no mattress.

A hundred metres away there's a small hut, where a woman sits in the doorway cradling a silent baby. I look around. This place is visible to the whole clearing.

Houn returns. We sit at the table. It's great to have the chance to talk freely. 'Where is Sok? Is he all right?'

'Yes, no problem. He stay with soldiers. They know he just driver.'

Sok is good at looking after himself. As long as they don't find out he was in the army he'll be fine. 'I like Mr Clever,' I say.

'Yes, but we cannot trust Khmer Rouge. Maybe soldiers want to kill us.'

Beyond the clearing there is no sign of the presence of man; just sky, trees and mountains stretching for eternity.

'What have the soldiers been saying?'

'They ask many question and I hear talk about attack military base. I not know where.'

Just before seven o'clock, two women start to put food and cracked china bowls on the table. They bring small tin oil lamps, which light the pagoda in a gentle orange glow. As they put the food down they avoid looking at us and try to stay in the shadows.

Mr Clever introduces us to four other commanders. We don't get told ranks or names. Anonymous hands emerge from the darkness delivering rice and plates. Mr Keun sits on my right. He looks sheepish. Houn is on my left and Mr Clever sits opposite.

A soldier dumps a dirty cardboard box on the end of the table. He tears it open and pulls out shiny blue cans of Tiger beer. If I ever get out of here alive and tell people, they'll never believe me.

We all have a beer and I wish them good health.

It would be wrong to assume none of them speak English. It's possible Mr Clever understands more than he lets on. He's certainly quick. At every opportunity I try to establish a good rapport.

The food is excellent; fried fish, some deer meat with chopped pepper, bony chicken and rice. I don't know when we'll eat again. I scoff as much as I can without drawing attention or looking greedy. Even Houn has found his appetite.

What about Sok? 'Is Mr Sok all right?' I ask.

'No problem. Commander say he eat with the soldiers. He get on very well with them.'

Mr Clever says he wants to help us, but there are no plans or guarantees. What's behind the polite smiles? I want his personal assurance we won't be harmed.

A British officer serving with the UN told me the Khmer Rouge invited a group of UN officers to eat with them. It became a well-known event. At the end of the evening all eight were shot dead. There were rumours the soldiers were drunk and rude and misbehaved. The official version reported unprovoked executions. Either way it's a good reason to be careful.

Houn stops eating and translates, 'Each Khmer Rouge commander responsible for own territory. He can only guarantee our security in own area. Maybe we have to leave through his territory.'

As long as he's not lying and nothing changes it means we're safe with Mr Clever. Now I have to convince them we have to keep our equipment. I explain the importance of our work. Mr Clever is interested in mine clearance. He wants a demonstration tomorrow. He says we should wear a special uniform so they can recognize us as deminers. They will leave us alone. I draw the minefield warning sign. We tell them the deminers will wear it on a badge. We also agree our vehicle wings should be painted red for recognition. Mike, our training and operations officer, suggested it some time ago.

They're being polite, but I don't know what lies behind the nods and smiles.

He says they have difficulty contacting the Khmer Rouge hierarchy. Often they have to make their own decisions. It has not been possible to tell the headquarters we are with him.

Mr Clever is our patron and protector. He wants to know if I've had malaria. I haven't. I'm worried; perhaps it means they plan to keep us for a while.

I leave food in the bowls just in case the cooks haven't eaten. I thank them for the excellent food.

Houn nods and listens to Mr Clever, who says, 'Goodnight,' and leaves.

Houn turns to me. 'You sleep in pagoda on bed with mosquito net. I sleep with Mr Sok and soldiers in long house.' They get up and go.

There's nothing I can do. I put my hand on Houn's shoulder and say, 'Get some rest. I'll see you in the morning.'

'Yes, I hope so.' He follows the soldiers into the darkness.

I feel my way round the bed, making sure the mosquito net is outside. I climb under. It's hard, but I'm very lucky to have the net. I take off my boots and massage my feet. I'll keep my socks on. It's good to be alone and not having to worry about every word and movement.

We might be killed tomorrow.

Do they have sentries? I've seen soldiers each end of the clearing.

I need to stay healthy. Malaria is a problem here. I must think about the food that I eat, everything I drink and every aspect of hygiene. Discipline is everything.

I peer through the darkness. By the corner of the hut there's an orange glow. Somebody is smoking. I strain my eyes. Can I smell smoke? The light darts off. It's a firefly.

The night is a dangerous time. It was when the Khmer Rouge did their killing. People were taken from the huts where they slept to be shot or smashed in the killing area. If that moment comes I'll fight, but I have to keep the element of surprise. I hope Houn and Sok will be okay. I'll wake up if there's shooting.

Women and children live in the huts. Their husbands and fathers are Khmer Rouge soldiers fighting a long way from here. They don't often come home. The village people walk with their eyes down. Nobody laughs. There is no joy here. It is a place of sadness.

I'm sorry for my family. At least I know what's going on. They won't know if I'm dead or alive. As I start to drift off to sleep I remember the butterflies.

Sleep comes in short bursts. The distant barking of a dog and sometimes just the night insects wake me. I am instantly alert. I can hear breaking sticks and footsteps in the dark. I hold my breath and listen. Are they coming for me?

I can hear breathing. I grab my boots, slip them on silently and do up the laces. Behind me a shape merges into the shadows and disappears behind the hut. A sentry?

At first it was good to relax. Now I want to do something to get out of here. I listen. A dog barks on the other side of the clearing. I should try to sleep again. This wooden bed is hard. Cambodia is tough on your back. I force myself to sleep.

I wake up. The inescapable fact that I have lost my liberty sinks in. I am a prisoner. I wonder if today will be my last?

A soldier with an empty, hollow face appears from behind the nearest hut. I am sure they're watching me. I should have spotted them last night. Good job I didn't stray from the pagoda.

I sit up on the hard bed and feel the coolness of the early morning. It is the first time I've felt cool since I've been in Cambodia. I look beyond the clearing to the jungle horizon. A woman walks round the far end of the pagoda to the bamboo hut, carrying a battered bucket of water. I saw her yesterday. She's very thin and, in spite of her youth, has the face of an old woman.

I stand up to say hello. I'm sure she won't run away today. But in the instant she looks at me her face is full of terror. As she looks at the ground her expression changes to pity.

It reminds me of the child's face in the village where they slaughtered the pig.

I look around me. This place is full of shadows and desperation. It's the first place I've been where the children don't play.

I stand up. The sun is rising over the mountains. The wooded pinnacles stretch across infinity in a landscape older than time.

A dawn haze caresses the tree-covered mountains. The light of the sun glistens like diamonds on damp, distant leaves. It reminds me of the butterflies.

I feel the warmth of hope and I realize it doesn't matter what they do to me. They've stolen everything. I've been humiliated. I thought I was about to be killed.

What's important is that whatever they do to me I can still feel hope. I can still see beauty.

Two soldiers are sitting under the mango tree near the fire. I point to the toilet. They nod agreement. Afterwards I return to the pagoda and sit down. I know Houn will be over as soon as he can. He emerges from the long house and speaks to the soldiers. They give him permission.

After greetings I get to the point. I don't know how much time we have. 'What do you think of our situation and Mr Clever?'

Houn speaks with the expression of a man walking on thin ice. 'I think he good man. He will not kill us but others may. I thought last night meal would be our last.'

Our lives are in the balance. I keep trying to increase our options and create opportunities, but I have to be realistic, I don't call any of the shots.

I decide there's a psychological advantage in occupying the pagoda. I have to try to make it our territory. A split second of deference or hesitation may come in useful.

Mr Clever emerges from his house. He speaks to a group of soldiers then waves us over and gets straight to business. He wants a demining demonstration.

I remove a detector from its bag, instal a battery and switch it on. I mark out a lane and explain where the imaginary minefield is. 'If there are areas around here where mines are injuring people we want to help. These detectors only work with special rechargeable batteries. You can't buy them anywhere in Cambodia or Thailand.'

As he translates Houn shoots me a look that makes it quite clear if we ever get out of here he won't be volunteering to come back with me.

I pick up the shears and cut four or five weeds so I can pass the detector carefully over the ground. The machine bleeps in two areas. I place the detector behind me, pick up the prodder and carefully dig towards the first. I uncover a beer can ringpull. I then repeat the process and find a second. I tell them again. 'It uses batteries from Germany.'

When I get to the end, Mr Clever explains he uses a tractor with the tyres removed and chains wrapped around the wheels. He then makes somebody drive it through the minefield.

I decide not to tell him he'd be lucky if they detonated 50 per cent of the mines and that I don't believe him; although it could be the reason the tractor is in pieces at the end of the clearing. He thinks his technique would be faster. I don't argue. I want to keep the equipment.

Houn says, 'Soldier want to know if it find gold.'

I imagine a terrified family with a small necklace or pair of earrings hidden under their house. 'No. It only finds the metal in mines.' I look at the ground as the sweat runs down the back of my neck and hope nobody has any gold to hand to prove me wrong.

The commanders nod and discuss. I think so far I've done all right. It's not a lot of use to them. I carefully repack my gear.

Now they turn their attention to the vehicle. I know what's coming next. 'They want to drive.' I get in. One of the commanders joins me and Houn gets in the middle. Quickly I push the small gear lever forward into low ratio. I think of as many things as possible that are wrong with the vehicle. 'It is very difficult to start.'

I flick the ignition key on and off quickly. 'It's not good at starting.' I hope Mr Keun doesn't remember it started first time yesterday.

Houn says, 'They wish to drive Land Rover.'

The commander reverses it back and drives slowly towards the long house.

I hold my breath slightly as he changes gear again. He's only gone a short distance but to get some speed he's changed up three times. I think he's in fifth now and still struggling to do twenty-five kilometres an hour.

I try not to laugh. What will they do if they find out I'm taking the piss? I look at Mr Clever, shake my head and say, 'The vehicle is very weak and slow.'

The driver returns, shakes his head and gets out. I think he left the keys in the ignition.

'This vehicle not powerful. Commander's vehicle better. Now they know why we not keep up yesterday.'

I agree and point out a few more faults. There's a dent on the front wing, caused by a tree stump when we were driving through the jungle. I tell them it will have to be welded or the vehicle won't work for long. I'm pleased Houn puts all his effort into interpreting. It's difficult for him. After my last statement he gives me a sideways glance. I may have pushed my luck a bit too far.

Mr Clever walks over and cups a small red rose in his hand. Houn says, 'He bought roses in Thailand and planted them for world peace. He hope one day Cambodia will have peace.'

A confused medley of emotions rips through me. I remember the roses. I examine Mr Clever's face. I can only find what I think is sincerity. We talk. His family had flowers in their garden when he was small. His mother and father live in Phnom Penh now. They're in their seventies. His father used to be a Khmer Rouge colonel, but he's been retired for years. He says he can't visit them or leave Khmer Rouge territory, there are too many people who will kill him. His eyes tell me he's not lying.

The flowers are beautiful but look as if they need watering. I would love to pick up the rubbish, to dig a hole and bury it and then find stones and make a border for the rosebed. I agonize for several moments wondering what he'd think. He just sees the flower and not the area around it. I always want to see the bigger picture.

'There is something he want to show us,' says Houn looking even more confused than me.

We follow him to the house and into the next room. We haven't been in here. Close to a television there's a twelve-volt battery. Crocodile clips connect black and red leads. I try to keep thinking televisions and videos and not electric shocks.

He puts a video into a VCR player, fiddles with the battery terminals and then presses the television on button. Suddenly Thai pop music blares out and a beautiful girl sings and dances. There are two volume settings, off and very loud. As if from nowhere the soldiers appear. They're mesmerized.

I make it clear that I'm enjoying the treat. He shows us the video case and says, 'My favourite singer.'

This is becoming increasingly surreal.

Just after six o'clock we're invited to breakfast. Mr Keun sits next to me. He keeps his trilby on as he spreads several spoons of sugar over his chilli and noodles. He sips Tiger beer slowly from a cracked china cup. I down as much boiled water as I can.

We discuss our release. I apply as much pressure as I dare and tell them how worried people will be about us. I suggest there will be big problems if anything happens to us. I push things as far as I can and take a step back.

Mr Clever furrows his brow and sits forward lost in thought. After a few minutes he smiles and starts talking excitedly as if he's found the solution to an insoluble problem. 'He will come with us to make sure we have security in his area and show us the way, but we cannot go out the same way we came in. That's another commander's area. We have no security there.'

No security. I think I get the message.

Mr Clever and the commanders talk and look at their watches. I pull my sleeves down. Houn sucks his lips then says, 'They let us go at two o'clock after lunch. The commander must make it safe for us.'

We're being released with the vehicles. Elation rushes through me. But we're not there yet. When we're back in safe territory I can relax.

Something catches my attention. I'm astonished to see a figure in a vivid saffron robe walking slowly down the track. I didn't think they allowed Buddhist monks to practise. In the Khmer Rouge years all of them (an estimated 63,000) were put to death.

The wizened old monk potters to the house, places his hands together and continually bows. A soldier speaks with him then gets Mr Clever. They talk. He takes the old man to a chair near the video.

Everyone is occupied. I speak with Houn. 'I'm surprised to see a monk.'

'Yes, some Khmer Rouge now allow people follow old ways.'

The monk frequently places both hands together and bows very low. It's strange. He has no begging bowl.

It's seven o'clock. We're left alone. I must learn everything Houn knows. We compare notes. We think Mr Clever is a decent man. Without his patronage we're dead.

The loud pop music blares again. Mr Clever walks to the front of his house waving his arms in all directions, beckoning everybody to watch his video.

I bow and greet the monk, a meagre crop of white stubble bristles on the side of his otherwise bald brown head. He bows and reveals a toothless grin. His eyes are like dark pools; perhaps they hide secrets. He won't look at me or Houn. He stares self-consciously at the ground and only occasionally glances at the video. He's out of place and uncomfortable. Is it the technology or is it the young girl dancing? I watch him. Then I realize: it looks like fear.

Sometimes his eyes dance nervously towards Houn and I. He is a tired, frail old man exhausted by the burden of reality.

The pop music screams at full volume. The girl dances and gyrates. The soldiers love it. I try my best not to look a party pooper.

After the second showing of the video, Mr Clever disconnects the crocodile clips and the soldiers disappear to the long house. He points to the Land Rover. 'We can drive him to his village. He is old and weak. He walk a long way.'

We help the old monk into the back. It's probably the first time he's been in a vehicle. As usual Houn is in the middle, trying to avoid any physical contact with Mr Clever.

I drive off and rapidly achieve twenty kilometres an hour. I've been directed to the west side of the clearing. We came in on the eastern side. I want to know what lies beyond my immediate horizon. On the left side of the track a thin crop of maize struggles for survival.

As we start to rise uphill the soil changes to sand. I shift into top gear and rev the engine high, to try and give us what feels like a reasonable speed. The engine noise is loud. Mr Clever turns to Houn and says a few words, pointing at the gear stick. I start to break out in a cold sweat.

'The commander he say you change small gear stick into high and then we go faster.'

I thank Mr Clever profusely for his helpful suggestion as I change into high ratio. I scan his face, trying to decide if he knows I wanted to put them off the vehicle, or if he thinks I just don't know. I can't decide so I change the subject. 'It is nice to meet the monk. It is kind of the commander to let us take him home.'

Mr Clever nods and speaks to the old man. Houn looks surprised. He turns and says, 'The commander allow people in his area to live as monk. It is old Cambodian way. But life hard here for people.'

He must struggle to fill his begging bowl. It's not surprising he's so thin.

I'm surprised Mr Clever hasn't told me to stop, but with two saffron robes the size of bed sheets hung on the bushes it's a fair bet a monk lives here. As we slow the old man speaks. He glances briefly at us, places his hands together and bows several times to Mr Clever and gets out. I help him.

A timid, hairless head peeps through the gap of the doorway of the spartan bamboo hut and disappears. Mr Clever speaks and waves to the old man. As I watch him disappear I realize how sorry I am to see him go. Houn looks at me with wide eyes and says, 'Commander allow you to thank old man. Monk walk a long way to beg him not to kill us.'

The monk is living proof the commander is not an extremist focused entirely on black pyjamas and genocide. He's allowed the monks freedom to live as they wish. The old man showed amazing courage asking for our lives to be spared. I turn off the engine and follow him. He turns round; I place my hands together, bow and say, '*or-gon*' – thank you – several times. He puts his hands together and bows. For a brief second we share understanding of the need to try and do what's right. I hold out my right hand. He grasps it with both his. Then he walks away as if I no longer exist. The present becomes the past.

I'm glad we're going back to the clearing. I don't want Sok to think we're leaving him behind. He's standing outside the long house looking down the track. The soldiers are still sitting under the tree looking bored. Mr Clever speaks again.

'This afternoon at two o'clock we leave to return to our work.'

I try to control the flood of relief. I have to remain reasonable. I mustn't get emotional. This is the second time he's told us. I scan his eyes for traces of deception. I think he means it. Houn looks at me uncertainly and says, 'He want us to have special lunch so we can part as friends. They cook now.'

10

HOPELESS

Under the mango trees three men, one who looks fat for a Cambodian, are busy chopping pork and plucking chickens. I look at my watch. I'm not going to be robbed next to Mr Clever. It's just gone ten o'clock. We sit on a wooden bench, facing the house and talk. He thinks one day after a last great battle, there will be peace in Cambodia. In this guerrilla war, the prospect of one last great battle seems unlikely.

Suddenly I strain my ears and hold my breath. I scan the horizon. Far in the distance I can hear a helicopter. The noise gets slightly louder. The others can hear it now. The soldiers run around like headless chickens pointing all over the sky. Mr Clever, Mr Keun and the other commanders have a frantic discussion and rush off. Mr Clever moves under his house and stays there.

I see it. It's very high, like a black dot on the right-hand side of the clearing. It's set on a course straight for us. No! It's turning away.

They haven't seen us.

The helicopter changes course again and circles. Maybe it's checking out a clearing. Now it resumes its original course.

It's getting closer. He's doing an area search. He must have seen the clearing

I walk to the corner of the pagoda to get a clear view and shield my eyes against the sun. The helicopter starts to circle. Mr Clever looks scared. So would I if I were him. 'Tell him it's a UN helicopter. It is unarmed.'

Mr Clever points at the sky and back at the village, his wide staring eyes follow the helicopter. Houn speaks quickly, 'The Vietnamese drop bombs on a village he was in. Many people die.' Terror can only be truly understood by those who have experienced it.

The helicopter must have seen the Land Rover. It's high, but I can see it's white. I hope it doesn't try to land. That would be suicidal. It comes closer and turns to bank around the clearing.

Soldiers are running everywhere, grabbing weapons and ammunition, some taking cover and some standing in the open. I know it's not Vietnamese, but I can't see the UN markings yet. We're not going to be bombed, but if I were Mr Clever I might think differently. I have to reassure him. I say. '*Dtay panyaha*, no problem. UNTAC helicopter. UNTAC.'

Mr Clever says a few terse tense words to Houn. 'Commander not see UNTAC markings.'

They might try to shoot it down. I have to convince him not to give the order to fire. I point at the helicopter. As it turns the markings are clearly visible. 'Look UN, UNTAC, UNTAC.' I try to keep my voice calm and confident. I point and smile, giving a thumbs up. I try again. 'UNTAC, UNTAC.' The markings are clear. He must be able to see them now.

Houn clenches his fists as he speaks. 'Commander cannot see the markings.'

But they're obvious! I point again. 'UNTAC, UNTAC.' I nod my head and try to look reassuring.

I'm scared. There are good people in that helicopter. They're trying to help us; they don't know what it's like down here.

Without warning, the deafening sound of automatic weapons erupts around the clearing. I've never heard so much shooting at the same time. It's fucking loud.

The shooting shatters my hopes. It was going so well. The

commander had offered us security and we were going to be released.

I know the helicopter's out of small arms range. I can't hear a heavy machine-gun and I haven't seen any SAMs, so they should be safe.

Mr Clever and I exchange glances. He looks away at the ground. The commander didn't give the order to fire. All my fears are justified. The lowest common denominator rules supreme in this place of darkness.

The helicopter heads away from the clearing. I'm surprised he changed course. I'm sure he was out of range, perhaps it's fitted with kit that picked up the incoming fire, or maybe a fluke shot went through the airframe. He definitely knows he's under fire, he's dispersing chaff. Thousands of pieces of foil designed to confuse surface-to-air missiles flutter out of the back.

As it moves further away the soldiers gradually stop firing. Occasional bursts are followed by shouts. They're saving their ammunition. Eventually the shooting stops completely.

Who gave these people guns?

Mr Clever looks at me through narrow eyes.

Houn speaks with the resignation of a condemned man. 'Commander not invite us here. Now helicopter come he cannot guarantee our security.'

If this was a film there would be dramatic music, but this is reality and all I can hear is my heart pounding. We exchange stares.

The helicopter changes course again. It's going to circle the clearing. I want the commander to see I'm not afraid of it to prove it's not going to attack. I walk to the Land Rover and wave both arms.

Houn interrupts my impersonation of a windmill by hissing and gesturing frantically. 'Come here, come here. You make commander angry.' Houn looks like he wishes he were some-where else.

'Sorry.' I scuttle back and say, 'No problem, no problem.'

Mr Clever looks unconvinced and gives instructions to Houn. 'He say we drive to clearing. If UN helicopter it will follow . He has big machine-guns near here. Maybe he get.'

'No! No! It will not attack. They must not shoot.'

He speaks to Mr Keun and the soldier with the flat face. They shoulder weapons and walk towards us.

It makes sense to drive the Land Rover away. I'm sure the heli will follow us. I nod agreement. The same soldiers who brought us are clambering into the Land Rover. Mr Keun gives directions. 'We drive to big clearing.'

I know where it is but I'm not going straight there. I will not leave Sok. I take a detour to the long house.

The commander starts waving his hand and speaking to Houn. He shouts, 'You go wrong way.'

It's not far now. I can bluff on the amount of time it will take to translate. 'I am getting Sok. We must take him. I can't leave him. Keep them talking.'

After an exchange Houn shouts, 'They say go to clearing.'

As we reach the long house my heart drops. I can't see him. Mr Keun jabbers away to Houn. I drive to the other end. Sok is with the soldiers, absorbed by the helicopter.

They're all shouting at us.

I shout, 'Sok,' and point my thumb to the back of the Land Rover. He moves faster than a cat squirted with a hosepipe and clambers in.

I speed away and then I remember. I've just been telling them the Land Rover isn't fast. I hope they're all concentrating on the helicopter.

Soon we reach the clearing. Mr Keun gives instructions. 'You drive to middle of clearing. We wait here.' As I stop everybody piles out.

I'm driving through long grass. There could be tree stumps. I slow down and scan the vegetation. It's bumpy. I guess I'm in the middle now. I turn in a wide sweep and put on all the lights and the hazard warning. I grab the keys and rush round to the other side and open the door. That should attract their attention.

I wave and start to do star jumps. That should tell them I'm alive. I can't imagine there are many Khmers in blue boiler suits that do star jumps. The noise of the rotors gets louder. Perhaps they think I'm giving them a signal to land.

Shit.

The Khmer Rouge will try to shoot it down.

Things aren't going as well as I hoped.

I sprint across the clearing. The soldiers and Houn are under the trees. There are only three soldiers. Their expressions combine terror and confusion. Their AK 47s are at the ready. The only thing between them and the helicopter is me.

If I stand with my back to the helicopter it'll prove I know it won't attack us. 'Please tell them the helicopter has no gun.'

I wonder if this will precipitate our death: we'll be in trees by side of the track where our bodies will never be found. Houn will look at me and say, 'We must wait here.' They would be a few paces away. Just too far for me to get to them and fight. There would be a burst of automatic fire and that would be it. I wouldn't have time to thank Houn for his friendship or tell him that I still believe in the end right wins through, even though we might have to die trying to prove it.

The sound of the rotors changes as it banks. The Khmer Rouge grip their AK 47s and look up with faces full of suspicion.

It's 10.17.

The helicopter circles three times then flies off in the direction it came from.

I watch it disappear.

It's mid-morning. They must have been flying a while. I

wonder if it's short of fuel? I follow the direction. It's the bottom right of the clearing. I think that's south-east. If we can escape that's the direction to head. It would be at least six days' walking, maybe more.

Mr Clever walks towards us and says, 'You must speak to helicopter on radio.'

I'm elated, but I can't speak to the helicopter. Our radios aren't compatible and I've no idea what their frequency is, but I don't need to tell them that. Somebody should be monitoring our radio net.

I switch off the engine and reach behind for the radio mike. It's not there. A young soldier in red sandals reaches in his little rucksack and passes me the mike. I plug it in and press the pre-set call button. I think the tone registers an acceptance. I bite my lip and wait.

Nothing.

Mr Clever talks and points at the radio.

If the call was accepted their volume automatically comes on. It's worth trying. 'Hello 803, this is 1247, radio check.'

Nothing. I try again. I mustn't get emotional.

I cell call the other locations. I can't get through. We're out of range.

I try retuning the antenna. It's not working.

If anyone is monitoring this frequency they should hear me. 'Hello all stations, all stations, SOS message. SOS message.'

I have to give them time to respond.

It could be I'm so far out of range I can't get through, but I'm sure the first cell call registered.

Mr Clever wanders off to sit in the sun and kick his front tyre. The soldiers talk among themselves.

I struggle to control my desperation and quell my desire to scream into the mike.

I keep trying. 'Any station, SOS message. SOS message.'

I test all channels. Nothing. The loneliness returns.

Mr Clever shouts a few words to Houn. Houn says, 'Stop now. We go to commander's house.'

Mr Clever sits in his house looking worried. I get the impression we're not welcome. He really thought he was going to be bombed and now he doesn't know what to do.

Things have changed. We're not going home at two o'clock. Maybe we never were.

The Khmer Rouge command group are in deep discussion. We wait outside. They occasionally look at us and point to different places around the clearing. Mr Keun walks away and spends a long time trying to use his hand-held radio.

'Can you hear what they're saying?' I ask.

'No.'

'Don't worry we'll be fine.' I say it again, perhaps as much for my benefit as theirs.

I have to convince Mr Clever he's not going to be bombed. He might think the helicopter will report our position, then attack aircraft will be sent. Perhaps that happened to him before.

I must assure him we're grateful for his good treatment. If he hadn't intervened yesterday afternoon, we would have been executed. He's a friend now.

The soldiers leave Mr Clever in the house. Now's my chance. I walk forward. 'Please tell the commander we're very grateful for his help. He's a good man and I want to speak with him.'

He gives a short answer. Houn's face falls. He stares at the ground, stunned.

I ask, 'What did he say?'

Houn replies without lifting his eyes. 'He find us tiresome.'

I try to speak, but my throat is too dry. I struggle for composure. 'I understand he's busy. I do not wish to trouble him. We will wait in the pagoda.'

At least we have some space. I try not to look shaken. 'Don't worry, we'll speak to him later. Tell Sok it's okay.'

Houn runs his hands through his hair and says, 'Yes. I know.'

We sit at the table.

At least someone knows where we are. But what good is that? I've got to get out of here or take the consequences. My biggest concerns are Houn and Sok. They're my duty.

Mr Clever strides purposefully towards us. He rubs his hands and talks for a while. Houn says, 'Now it change. He can't help us. We are responsibility of commander who bring us here. We must go back that way. After lunch we leave.'

He didn't mention our security. I keep believing we're going to be released. Then I'm crushingly disappointed. I know I shouldn't trust them. I have to accept uncertainty, in spite of my natural desire to hope.

Behind Mr Clever I see a little man running frantically across the clearing. He dashes between the huts and through the cassava fields. He's about fifty, very thin and wearing a *kramar*. His feet are bare and he's clutching a piece of white paper. As he reaches us he bows slightly and pants. He points to the other side of the clearing, then the sky. He keeps glancing at me and looking away. He speaks to Mr Clever and points into the air again.

Mr Clever takes the paper. I crane my neck. It's in Khmer. He reads the letter twice, smiles and dismisses the messenger. The old man jogs away, occasionally looking back over his shoulder.

Mr Clever waves the paper at us and speaks in short bursts, giving Houn time to explain. 'This letter not polite, but he understand it. It tell him we are neutral, what you tell him already.'

The helicopter was dropping leaflets. They probably didn't know they were under fire. Still they were well out of range.

I say, 'The helicopter only dropped letters. There are many people worried about our safety. They want us to return to our work.'

It's 10.45. He's told us after lunch we can go. I want to skip lunch, but I don't think it would be polite to tell him. He's probably saved us from execution again and insulting him would be stupid.

I watch the minutes tick by.

Through the strained silence I can hear a distant buzzing. It's the helicopter. I wonder if they've refuelled?

Everyone leaves the pagoda to search the sky. The soldiers run around shouting. Most of them are heading towards the long house. A woman in a nearby hut picks up her baby and runs across the clearing towards the trees. Another woman follows her, dragging two screaming children.

Mr Clever and the soldiers point at the heli and have a heated discussion. We watch. 'Houn, What's happening?'

'They discuss what to do. Mr Clever not help us. He not invite us here. We go back to other area immediately.'

I glance at Sok and nod my head towards the Land Rover.

Mr Keun walks towards the Land Rover and shouts to his soldiers, the same soldiers who brought us here. I say thank you and goodbye to Mr Clever. No hard feelings, I like him.

It's just gone 11.55. As we drive away I see Mr Clever peering into the sky with his hand shading his eyes.

I don't know if the helicopter is following us. They should be able to see the track through the trees. I drive as fast as I can without risking damage or loss of control. Mr Keun is holding a hand-held radio.

Suddenly he raises his hand and shouts, '*Chop.*'

Shit. What now?

I stop.

Mr Keun gets out and stands in the shade of a tree and speaks on the radio. I switch off the engine, hoping Houn will be able to hear. I glance at him, raise my eyebrows and nod in the direction of Mr Keun.

The soldiers get out. Sok moves to the front and leans on the bonnet. It's too hot in the Land Rover. Houn and I join him.

'He has radio message. We must wait here.'

The sand on the track is dry and dusty. The only sound is the insects.

We wait.

In the distance I can hear a vehicle.

Mr Clever's pick-up swerves past us and skids to a halt. He picks a large leaf from a nearby tree, walks to the centre of the track, puts it down and sits on it. It's a cool move. I'm fascinated. What next?

He crosses his legs like Buddha. I get out and sit before him like an eager student.

He tells us it's a shame we can't stay for lunch and he's sorry our departure was so rushed.

I have to agree. It was going to be grilled pork and ginger. It looked good. He says he enjoyed meeting me and wishes me good luck in my work. He hopes I'll tell people the Khmer Rouge are not all totally genocidal. He wishes us well on our journey, gets up, bows and shakes hands.

We get back into the Land Rover. Just as I'm about to drive off he runs up, pokes his head through the window, waves and says, 'God Bless.'

I drive on, elated and confused.

It's 12.20. It'll take us about two hours to get to Mr Keun's village. From there we might make it to Rhum before nightfall.

We could stop in the town by the small military camp and drive back in the morning. It's too dangerous to move on the roads at night.

We're heading in the right direction. Or are we?

I wonder if my family knows where I am?

I expect the lads have put bets on when we get shot.

I keep my eyes on the track. The Land Rover is our lifeline. If we break down or get stuck we're stuffed. I must look out for the mine holes.

The track ahead disappears into a tunnel of trees. This must be the gully of the butterflies. I hold my breath and hope to see their magic again.

We drop into the shade and splash through the stream. I can feel the coolness, but they've gone.

We've been driving for nearly an hour. We pass a rock outcrop.

A soldier with a flat face speaks to Houn, who immediately says, 'Stop. He sick.'

I don't want to. I'm in a hurry. But the last thing I want is a Land Rover full of vomit.

The soldier gets out and walks around moaning. He rubs his head and holds his stomach. I look at my watch, then try to see into the forest.

The soldiers mutter, shake their heads and make clicking noises with their tongues. After a few minutes Mr Keun says something. The soldier gets back in.

'Is he going to vomit?' I ask.

'No, he sick.'

I try to summon some sympathy. 'What is the problem?'

'It is first time he go in Land Rover.'

I put my foot down and, out of the corner of my eye I see flat face craning his neck like a dog to get some fresh air from my slightly open window.

I try not to laugh.

It's payback time.

Then I relent. I wind down a window then stop. I turn around and push back the sliding window in the back. He didn't know it was there. I get them to open the one the other side. As we drive on I can feel the breeze. It's better for all of us now.

It's nearly five past two.

I wonder why we never see any wild animals? I know they're out there, I've seen piles of dung.

We drive round a bend.

There are tyre marks and ruts on the right. It's familiar. The river confronts us. I brake rapidly.

Something's missing.

Where's the bloody truck gone?

I don't throw my teddy bear out of the cot very often, but I can feel a sense of humour failure coming on.

11

MULTIPLE CROSSINGS

I give Mr Keun a look that says, 'Give me back my lorry you bastard.'

He looks away, disinterested.

I take a deep breath. 'Where is the Zil?'

'One of his men move, to protect it. He will get soon.'

There are tyre tracks in the sand on the far bank. I hope it hasn't shifted the logs.

I go to check. The hot water fills my boots.

I can only hear the sound of the river. The baking sun glints on its surface.

In the middle I stop. I've been careful not to stir up the mud, but I can't see anything, the water's too murky.

The log has moved a few inches up and forward. I can just put my foot across the gap. It will be like driving up a small step.

There probably won't be enough fuel to take the Zil all the way back through the forest. If we can find it we'll drive as far as we can and return with a military escort to recover it.

'Commander say we must eat lunch with him. Please drive over now,' Houn shouts from the riverbank.

How nice.

'Please ask two soldiers to walk on the logs, like before.'

As we approach the middle I increase the revs. The vehicle suddenly lurches to the left and the front drops down. Water starts coming in under the door. Houn rolls into me then pulls himself upright. Equipment crashes down behind me. I increase the revs slightly. Nothing happens.

I try reversing. Nothing. We're stuck fast. I push the gear lever into neutral. 'The tyre has stuck between the logs. We'll have to try and winch out.'

He looks at me with sorrow in his eyes.

On the other side of the bank there are no winch points.

I step off the log. To my horror I sink into the muddy sand. The water is nearly up to my waist.

Behind me the soldiers are talking and pointing. Mr Keun gets out and walks carefully along the log, then stands watching from the bank.

The soldiers avoid the deep water. They point at the winch and start jabbering. How can they be so stupid? Even they should have seen it has to be attached to something.

I shake my head dramatically. 'The only way we can get out is by using the Zil to tow us.'

Mr Keun sends two soldiers.

Eventually they return. They say they can't find the man or the truck. He's gone to another village.

The others keep pointing at the winch and jabbering at Houn. They're in front, behind him and to his side, giving instructions. He turns to me. 'They say we should use winch.'

I know that. The question is how?

I climb back into the Land Rover, rev the engine and hold my breath.

We're not moving; then there's a slight shift. Slowly, inch by inch we move forward.

Suddenly there's a thud.

The rear of the vehicle skews left.

I look underneath. The front tyre's wedged between the two logs. The rear left wheel can't touch the bottom because the rear axle is resting on the log.

I don't want to think about what'll happen to us if we can't get the vehicle out.

The soldiers start pointing and jabbering again.

If we can get the front wheel unwedged I can try winching. It won't damage the back axle if it slides along the wet log. I start to show them.

They argue among themselves.

The next thing to try is to dig out the log. We should be able to get it from the other end. I make a digging gesture at the end of the log. Two soldiers shake their heads and talk about something else. Sok gets a digging hoe out of the back of the Land Rover and starts work. After a long explanation three soldiers help to manhandle the log.

I drive forward a metre and try to get on to the log again. It's too high. The front axle sticks on it and the wheel churns like a paddle steamer.

It's nearly half past two. We've been here twenty minutes. The Khmer Rouge have another Chinese parliament as they watch Sok and me work. They start giving Houn directions. I'm glad I can't understand them.

Houn politely explains each of their orders and I politely explain why each of them won't work.

Sok and I dig the log out from under the axle. Three of the soldiers have a discussion then grab the log. They push and pull in different directions and ignore our instructions. One of them points at Sok then shouts at Houn.

'What's he saying?' I ask.

Houn bites his lip and clenches his fists before speaking. 'He think Mr Sok is mechanic because he know how to help you get vehicle out.'

'Tell him he isn't. We do this many times. That's how he knows. When we finish here they'll know as much as Sok.' I look at the soldier and shake my head, then I wipe the stinging sweat away from my eyes and carry on digging.

I watch the soldier nod as Houn explains. Now I make a show of giving Sok instructions every time we do anything.

We pull a log from under the back axle and winch forward another metre before it sticks in the mud.

I start to dig it out.

Everything goes quiet.

Someone has switched the engine off.

Shit. The winch drains the battery. I always leave the engine running. It's probably too flat to start again.

I splash my way to the driving seat.

Houn just stares and says, 'Sorry, the soldier switch off. I try to tell him, but . . .'

I put my hand on his shoulder, 'No problem. I understand.'

I get in. God help us. If this doesn't start, we've had it.

I twist the key. The engine coughs then slowly fades into the whirring noise of the starter motor.

I try again.

The engine turns, slows and clicks.

I switch off and wait. I wipe my muddy hands on my trouser legs.

I give the key another go and press the accelerator. It coughs then miraculously starts. 'Please tell them we must leave the engine running, or there will be a big problem.'

The soldiers jabber as I dig. The two in front want to pull the log one way, the two behind, the other. At this rate we'll never get out of here.

More sweat stings my eyes. Finally I jump on to the log and scream, '*Chop.*'

The Khmer Rouge look at me. There is a stunned silence.

I grab the soldiers on the far bank. I point and mime digging gestures by the log. Next I grab the moron pulling the wood the wrong way and make him push. I climb back on the log, point at the other soldier and make him pull.

Houn and Sok look at me, wide-eyed.

What have I done?

Nobody shouts at the Khmer Rouge.

I think I've gone too far. I've made them lose face.

They'll probably lose it and beat me. That's why Houn and Sok are looking at me that way. They've seen it before.

The silence continues. The soldiers stare.

The one with the flat face is the first to move. He nods at me then grunts at his mate and starts digging. Gradually the others start work.

Houn starts breathing again. If we have guardian angels, mine must be doing a lot of overtime.

Soon the logs are dug out. A combination of winching, pushing, digging and sweating gets the Land Rover across. Houn and I laugh and cheer as we drive triumphantly up the bank. Then we remember where we are.

I leave Sok revving the engine as I wash off the sand and mud in the river. We reel in the cable and drive the short distance to Mr Keun's headquarters.

'Commander invites us to eat lunch.'

I bow and place my hands together to greet his wife. She doesn't respond; her eyes are fixed firmly on her feet.

The wooden floor is a metre off the ground and makes a good seat. I stay near the edge because I'm soaking and I don't want to get their mat wet. Underneath the hut two or three thin chickens scratch and cluck as Mrs Keun busies herself over the rice pot.

We go through the whole negotiation process again. I think about every move I make, every nuance in my expression. Mr Keun stops often to ask questions. I can understand why they find it hard to believe what I say. They probably think everybody lies as much as they do.

With a combination of pleading and pressure I argue our case. They agree our work is a good thing and understand why

I need the Land Rover. I ask him for a guarantee of our security to transit his area.

There is a long silence.

After a few moments Houn almost smiles. 'We can leave in our vehicle after lunch. He guarantee our security. Some soldier will escort us.'

The soldiers will want to eat and I can't offend him by saying I want to go now. So I attempt to make polite conversation.

We talk about tiger hunting. Mr Keun sees tigers as something of a nuisance. They've eaten his cattle. He must know what he's doing to clean kill one with an AK 47. He says he shoots it in the head or in the heart; then he tells me about the forest and how they sometimes go off for two weeks, living off the land. We talk about tigers and butterflies. We're getting on really well.

The young soldier in red plastic sandals walks past, carrying an enormous heap of fresh steaming tripe. It looks like they've just killed the cow to feed us. That's a real honour. It's a delicacy here. I nod and smile at Houn.

Mrs Keun chops it up and throws it in a dented aluminium pan. She boils rice. Soon the feast is prepared. We all have a plate and a spoon. None of them match, but it doesn't matter.

I don't want to offend them. I try a spoonful. It tastes exactly how I imagined lightly cooked cow intestines would. I keep chewing.

On the other side of the hut the two young soldiers are having an intense discussion. I'm curious. 'Houn what are they talking about?'

He looks at his food, frowns and quietly says, 'One asks, "How is the sick cow?" The other says "Very horrible, it just die. We are eating it."'

I wonder how many other things I've misunderstood.

We ask about the forest and get as much information as possible about the route back. The sandy track is good for a few hours, then it diverges into different paths. Most of them lead out of the forest; some are dead ends. In places it's boggy, but the logging trucks usually get through. I try again to get the Zil back. They say they don't know where it is. I arrange to pick it up at a later date.

Mr Keun grabs a green canvas rucksack, one of the few possessions in his house. He undoes the cord and rummages inside. He walks over and gives me what looks like a tiger tooth. It still has a few bits of flesh on the base.

Houn says, 'Commander give you this.'

'Thank you.' I hold the tooth tightly. The shiny end is smaller than the root. I wonder if the animal was young? The tip is purple.

I like Mr Keun. I want to understand more about his life and how he ended up here. I look around the hut. The most modern thing here is the heavy machine-gun wrapped in the blue plastic sheet. They're struggling to survive; so are the tigers and so are we.

Nothing ventured nothing gained. I say, 'Please thank the commander and his family for lunch and their hospitality. We must leave now.' The man with a flat face walks over, picks up his AK 47 and starts walking towards the vehicle.

Houn says, 'We go now. The soldier will guide us through forest. He go to village to see relative.'

Sok beams for the first time in days.

I thank everyone for their hospitality; we shake hands.

Elation rushes through me. We're going home. But we're not safe yet.

It's good to be back in my Land Rover. Houn has the front seat all to himself. Sok and the soldier are in the back. He's only carrying his AK and webbing. I have to cover the ground as fast as possible. I can't risk damaging the vehicle, but I have to drive as fast as I can.

'Please tell the soldier I will take him where he wants to go. When we get out of the forest I will guarantee his security. I will make sure he is well looked after.'

After a brief exchange Houn says, 'No problem, from edge of forest soldier can walk to his village.'

We can identify him as Khmer Rouge. Once he's out of his territory that means he could be killed. I want him to see the benefit of us getting out of the forest quickly.

I pull back my sleeve and look at my watch. It's 15.20. Twenty past three; that's a time I will never forget. The time I regained my freedom and left with my colleagues and equipment. We take a lot of things for granted.

Getting out of the labyrinth is going to be an adventure. I'll follow the most used track. I'm confident I can get us through quickly and be in Rhum before night. We have to be out before then. The darkness is dangerous.

'Please ask him how long he thinks it will take us to get to Rhum.'

'Maybe nine or ten o'clock tonight.'

I change into fourth and press the accelerator. We surge ahead. I can fit new shock absorbers next week. It's great to drive where you want to without somebody pointing a gun at you.

We are going home, with our equipment, to carry on our work. It's good to be alive. Freedom is like air. You don't miss it until you don't have it. I take a deep breath. It's good to be free.

There is a faint roar in the distance. It sounds like a Zil. The engine noise is very distinctive. It must be ours. 'We'll stop the Zil and tell the driver we have permission to take it back. He can walk back to the village.'

Houn smiles and nods.

Things are really getting better. I knew we'd get out. There's always hope.

The familiar roar of the engine approaches. The vegetation either side of the track is like a wall. I slow down as we approach a corner, then pull over to the left and stop.

Suddenly a battered blue Zil careers around the corner. It's the wrong colour. It should be white. About twenty heavily armed soldiers are clinging to it; some perched on the roof and some on the bonnet.

Everything is happening in slow motion. Pig Face is sitting on the front wing clutching his SKS with an RPG on the end. I feel like I'm falling into a black hole. The horror has returned.

He turns, shouting and waving at the driver to stop.

They look as surprised to see us, as we are to see them. The lorry halts. It's blocking the track. There's no way round it.

Pig Face leaps off and runs to the window. His face is full of anger and his eyes full of hate.

He ignores us and speaks to the soldier in the back. A few of the others also get off the truck. We're completely surrounded.

Pig Face stares at us, rubbing his eyes with one hand and clutching his rifle with the other.

'What's he saying?' I whisper to Houn.

He glances sideways. 'He wants to know where we go. Maybe he surprised they not kill us.'

I recognize some of the soldiers. It's the same bunch who ambushed us two days ago. There are about six whom I haven't seen.

The driver is a thin weasel of a man with a bum-fluff moustache. He wears no shirt. The inside of his windscreen is crawling with flies.

In the passenger seat there's a man aged about fifty or older. He wears tattered green combats and a floppy green jungle hat.

Instead of eyes he has narrow slits which reveal nothing except the absence of a soul. A black, straggly goatee beard perches at the bottom of his wide, bony face. I presume he wears the hat to hide his horns.

All my instincts shout danger.

Pig Face goes to the lorry and he speaks to the man in the front seat who nods and points at two soldiers.

Houn turns. 'We must stay here,' he says very quietly. 'He say switch off engine.'

Pig Face returns and shouts at Houn. Two soldiers follow him. He climbs back on the truck and the rag-tag demons drive off.

Houn says, 'We cannot leave. He tell the soldier to keep us here.'

I'm tempted to drive off, but we have a soldier in the back with an AK 47, and two outside. I wonder if there are any more ahead?

I think I could deal with the soldier in the back, but the boys at the front and rear of the Land Rover look ready to shoot. The most sensible thing would be to go back and speak to Mr Keun.

I get out. Behind I can hear the soldier doing the same. I have to speak with him. We're safe with him. 'We must go and speak with Mr Keun.' I realize I am pleading.

I start to walk back up the track. The soldier gets out of the Land Rover and says something to Houn. The boy at the back moves out of the shade and walks towards me, pointing his AK 47 at my chest.

'Stop. They not allow,' Houn shouts.

I walk back and lean against the driver's door. The old soldier stands behind me. Sok and Houn come over. We want to be together. He stands with his hands by his side, clenches his fists and says, 'We have to wait here or they get angry.'

Neither of us want to use the word kill.

It's 15.25. I enjoyed our few minutes of freedom but now that's just a memory. The boy soldiers squat on the other side of the track in the shade. They're twenty metres each end of the vehicle. It would take a few seconds to run to them. I've no chance. Occasionally they speak to each other, the rest of the time they balance on their haunches, watching us like buzzards.

Perhaps our release was just a charade. On the other hand they looked as astonished to see us as we were to see them. Pig Face either wants to execute us or he isn't happy about us keeping the Land Rover, or both. By now the Chinese parliament will be in full swing. I want to be part of that process. It will be easier for them to kill us in the jungle than waste time taking us out.

I have to speak with Mr Keun. 'I must speak to the commander. Please tell the soldiers they can come with us.'

Without lifting his eyes Houn says, 'Not possible. They not allow. The soldier are ordered to stay and not let us move.'

At the edge of the track there is a tangle of creepers and bushes. It's too thick to run through, but you could walk a little way in. If they shot us here, they could roll our bodies into the undergrowth where they'd never be seen.

What can I do? I can't give up. I always thought I'd have the chance to fight, but there are three of them and they'd shoot me before I could get to them. Houn and Sok wouldn't want to join in and might get killed in the process. There's a saying: there are no atheists on the battlefield. Now I can understand why. God help us.

Sok looks at me with empty eyes and Houn just stares at the ground. I try desperately to be reassuring. 'Don't worry. When I speak to Mr Keun everything will be all right.'

'Yes I know.' Houn does not sound reassured.

To be killed for what I am is bad. But to be killed for

something I am not is a total bummer. Please God, help them to understand we're just trying to do something basic and right. Help us get out of here alive.

It's a beautiful sunny day. It's hot. The sky is butterfly-blue. As I look up I feel I could reach out and touch it.

I grip the tiger tooth.

If they're going to do it, I wonder how? The soldier behind us looks kind. He'd probably say, 'You are free to go,' and as we would walk away there would be, shots, point blank and we'd fall into the jungle. Tigers would devour our bodies.

This is no good. I'm starting to think like a victim. But it's strange. I'm not afraid, just nervous and sad. Sad for Houn and Sok and our families. I can't give up without a fight. Failure is not an option. 'Please tell the soldiers I must speak with Mr Keun.'

Houn asks reluctantly. 'They told we must not move.'

The roar of the Zil signals their return. The boy soldiers stand up. I don't know why I call them boys; they can pull a trigger as well as any man. Perhaps better. This time there are only about ten soldiers on the truck. Pig Face jumps off the front bumper and stares at us triumphantly. He bares his teeth in a big smile.

The man with the goatee beard clambers awkwardly down; it's a long way for his short legs. A small battered black bag hangs on a strap around his neck. It could be a map case or a document folder. He tips back his hat to reveal long matted hair. He's the only one not carrying an AK 47 or rocket launcher, and is not much bigger than a dwarf, but he's as broad as he is tall and looks fiercely strong. Some of the soldiers look afraid of him.

We don't want to be boxed in by the bushes so I walk towards the soldiers. Houn and Sok follow. We form a line across the track. Behind us the boy soldiers keep their positions.

Without taking his eyes off them Houn says, 'They want talk to us, we sit here.'

Pig Face speaks to Houn, who swallows and says, 'We leave Mr Keun's territory. Khmer Rouge official headquarter never know we here. Now UN not know where we are.'

Pig Face continues, dead pan as if pronouncing sentence. As he finishes he nods to the man with the beard. He says, 'We enter another Khmer Rouge area. This is commander.'

The devil with the beard smiles to reveal black teeth and an enormous pink tongue. I place my hands together and bow. He nods slightly and smiles again. His tongue is too fat for his mouth. He would have been in his prime during Pol Pot's reign. He's how I imagine the Khmer Rouge recce troops would look; the ones who took people from their huts at night, those who ran the killing fields.

Houn nods.

The only thing that moves in the commander's face as he speaks is the position of his mouth. He says a few words and then pauses gesturing with his hand to Houn. 'We in area of new Khmer Rouge commander. We have no security.'

I go through the whole process of who we are and what we're doing. I don't need to explain how we got here because Pig Face is standing behind him, but when I make the point we didn't come here of our own free will he laughs. I tell him that if anything happens to us there will be serious repercussions. He pauses and plays with his wispy beard, then says the forest is a big place and he moves around a lot. I keep things polite and deferential; making him angry is not what I want. My heartbeat quickens and the sick feeling in my stomach increases.

'He say we have no security. We must arrange with him,' Houn says.

We're back to square one. Maybe they've always planned to kill us. The back of my head itches. I scratch it and think the piece of shit opposite me is about as low as human beings can get.

The devil pops out his pink tongue and points several times at Houn while he delivers his lecture. When he finishes he smiles at me and licks his yellow and black teeth.

Houn stares silently at the ground. He looks like he's been smacked with a shovel. I glance at the commander again. I give Houn a few seconds before I ask, 'What did he say?'

Houn looks up slowly and clears his throat. 'He recognize my voice. He hear it on government soldier radio.'

The back of my hands and neck prickle. There's a strange sensation moving from the pit of my stomach to my throat. They're telling him they mean to kill him. I fight to stay calm.

I put my hand on Houn's shoulder and say. 'All I want is to get out of here with Houn and Sok. They are my family.' I nod at them as I say their names. 'What does the commander need to guarantee our security?'

There is a pause and some discussion.

Houn says, 'Commander worry we not get through jungle because our Land Rover will get stuck.'

I reach in my pocket and take out the keys. I hold them on the open palm of my hand and say, 'Can he guarantee our security?'

He takes the keys, says a few words and grins triumphantly.

Houn lifts his head. 'Yes, now he know he can guarantee our security.'

I struggle to maintain some dignity. 'May we take our personal belongings from the vehicle? Which way do we go?'

There is a big discussion among the soldiers. The commander nods and Houn says, 'Yes, they allow.'

I pass Houn his small rucksack. It feels slightly heavier than usual. Sok never brings a bag to work, but he follows us over. I grab my daypack and the two empty water bottles from behind the seat. The first-aid box is close enough for me to shove in some field dressings and the drips before they notice. I put my *kramar* on top and zip up the bag. There are several large straw sun hats Jim bought for the blokes. I grab one. If we're walking it'll be useful. I try and persuade Houn and Sok to take one, but they shake their heads and say the sun won't bother them. It's true, but their hollow stares tell me they don't think we're going anywhere.

I touch the steering wheel one last time and walk away. I can't think of any other four-wheel drive that could have made the torrent, the mud and the river. If we hadn't got through them we'd certainly be dead. I learnt to drive on one of these. I remember my first driving adventure when I hit the church wall and then a decade later driving the old Land Rover round the field under Dad's instruction. It's like losing a friend.

The flash of memory fades as Pig Face shouts instructions to a soldier in red plastic sandals and one of the other boys. They nod, put on their frayed webbing, grab their AKs and jump on the back of the truck.

A soldier runs down the track, clutching a faded Chinese rucksack. He gives it to Pig Face, who unties the top, takes out a small wooden box and puts it carefully in his pocket.

The devil explains that the soldiers have to return to the forest. They will escort us some of the way. We can ride on the truck.

It's just gone five past four. Our negotiations lasted four and a half minutes. We're not dead and they haven't started beating us yet, so I guess they can be classed as successful.

Sok puts his hands together and bows several times to the commander, then jumps on to the back of the truck. Just as I start to follow him, the commander shouts.

Houn translates. 'They say you go in front.'

Good. I gesture Houn in first. He'll be safer there. I bow, thank the commander in Khmer and wish him farewell. He's amused at my attempt, or is that smile his only facial expression?

As I climb in I say to Houn, 'Please say loudly so they can all hear, I thank the commander for his guarantee of security.'

The engine roars. There's no silencer. Like most things on the lorry, it's fallen off.

I hope this will be a long journey, not a short one to a hole or fire.

Pig Face climbs on the front and sits on the bumper. I would never allow one of my blokes to do that. If the truck goes over a rut he could fall under the wheels. It couldn't happen to a nicer guy.

The cab smells of perished seats, petrol and sweat. It's hot. The flies buzz incessantly across the windscreen. The driver is a thin young man with unkempt hair. He wears a *kramar* around his waist and no shoes. He doesn't smile.

Pig Face peers over the top of the bonnet, lifts back his head and snorts. I wonder whether we've jumped out of the frying pan into the fire.

It's unbearably hot. Sweat sticks my back to the cracked plastic seat cover. There's a can of oil and a dirty cloth at my feet. I clutch my daypack. More and more flies invade the cab. The window is only half down. I try the handle. It's broken. I force it down as I wind. Gradually it opens. Occasionally the driver flaps a cloth at the windscreen to clear the flies so he can see where he's going.

The truck lurches over the occasional tree root, but Pig Face remains frustratingly steady.

'Do you think they're taking us back to Rhum?' I ask.

'We cannot trust the soldier,' Houn says, then pauses. 'Maybe they want to kill us in the forest.'

On that basis, as long as we're moving we're safe.

'Please ask the driver where he's from and how to get to Chnang.'

Houn says the driver works here all the time. In seventy kilometres the track disappears into the forest. It's easy to get lost, but he knows the way. Families of Khmer Rouge soldiers live in small groups on the edge of the forest growing rice. Nobody ever goes there without Khmer Rouge permission. There are two places belonging to the dead. We will pass through one. Ten years ago the Vietnamese and government soldiers attacked. The villages were burnt and most people killed. Their ghosts joined the demons in the forest. Now the village belongs to them and we must be careful not to make them angry.

A thirty-kilometre ox cart track leads from the last Khmer Rouge village to Chnang. There's another safe village called Sai. Both are on the southern edge of the forest. He thinks we might get to Rhum some time late tonight. It's further than I thought. I look at the rev counter and speedometer. Neither work. He probably doesn't know what a kilometre is.

Houn interrupts my thoughts. 'He say he not like Khmer Rouge. This morning soldier on front of truck tell him to drive twenty soldier to base of Mr Keun. He hate Khmer Rouge. He want to know if we do.'

'Tell him we really like the Khmer Rouge. They are my friends,' I reply.

Houn gives me a sideways glance then carries on talking. Thank God I can trust him to translate exactly what I say.

We learn more. He thinks the Khmer Rouge soldiers live in small huts in the jungle. They appear from nowhere to take cigarettes and money and make him drive them round, especially when they have something to carry. There are no mines on the tracks. Anyone they think is Vietnamese or a government spy is killed. It's about a nine-hour journey from here to Rhum. I look at his wrist. He doesn't have a watch.

The forest has changed. The thick tangle of bushes and

creepers has been replaced by magnificent trees. We are crossing a range of hills that look like mountains, but once under the canopy prove to be more modest.

As we move into a valley I can see a clearing below us. Nothing is growing there; that's odd, because there's plenty of sunlight. I stick my head out the window. It's still hot, but cooler than the stinking cab. As we get closer I can see an enormous tree stump, hacked to the ground by myriad chain-saw cuts. There are piles of sawdust, and the stump is the size of a bomb crater. I wonder how many generations it takes for a tree that size to grow?

As we drop into a hollow I glance through the cracked back window. Sok is the only one who looks comfortable. The rest are struggling to hold on to the cab or each other. The ground must be boggy. There are no mudguards. Wet lumps of liquid grey clay are catapulted off the wheel. Only Sok, who's sitting between the back wheels, avoids them.

Up ahead there's a fork. Both tracks look equally over-grown. With an impressive display of agility, Pig Face puts his arm in the centre of the bonnet, stands on the front bumper and turns around. Holding his SKS in his left hand he waves the driver to the right. Without acknowledgement he obeys and we trundle downhill, flanked by bamboo.

The driver revs the engine like fury. We start to climb the other side of a gully and the vehicle starts skidding. Lumps of mud thud on to the cab roof. The truck slides and spins to the top of the hill.

We only just make it. It wasn't steep. Why was it so difficult?

There is a drop into another gully. The track has disap-peared. We squeeze through gaps in the trees and bushes. The driver flicks the flies off the windscreen again. He bites his bottom lip and tries to change down a gear. There is a noise

like a badly-oiled chainsaw. He tries again and this time gets it
into gear. Just before we reach the bottom, he revs the engine
to gain momentum to take us up the other side.

We almost reach the top. The vehicle spins and slips. Mud's
thrown everywhere. Pig Face jumps off and runs up the rise.
As the truck halts the driver leaps down, walks a few paces and
relieves himself. This is a chance to demonstrate a degree of
independence. Pig Face has gone and the passengers will be
recovering from their mud bath. I spring out of the cab, nod
at the soldiers, walk to the front of the truck and go through
the motions.

It's a struggle, I think I'm getting dehydrated.

I join the others. Houn is getting some fresh air. One look
at the wheels tells me why the lorry is struggling. The tyres are
as bald as a Buddhist monk's head after a pagoda shaving
party.

Pig Face shouts. We climb on. The driver reverses back,
aims at an area covered in grass and charges up the hill again.
This time we make it.

Occasionally Pig Face turns to wave instructions to the
driver. We're following gaps between the trees, guided by
particular landmarks: a bank, a gully, an exceptionally large
tree. It's probably a Khmer Rouge footpath. We move through
thin scrub and join a sandy track.

The driver mutters to Houn. 'He say soldier live near here
and not want to carry his bag.'

'Are there more Khmer Rouge between here and the edge
of the forest?' I ask.

After a discussion Houn replies. 'He think so. Khmer Rouge
always know when people come into the forest. They have
many spy and can hear tractor and lorry.'

Pig Face halts the truck, takes his SKS and rucksack and
walks down the track. He goes about a hundred metres then
turns off to the right.

The passengers scrape the mud off their bodies. Sok stays where he is, possibly because he's found the best seat and doesn't want to lose it.

It's six o'clock; it'll be dark in under an hour. I don't like it here. Neither does Houn.

There's the crack of a rifle shot. Everyone takes cover.

As the echo of the shot fades, I strain my ears. There is nothing.

The soldiers talk quietly and finger their AKs nervously. The driver and two dirty passengers hide in the bushes.

Suddenly there's an explosion. The thunderous boom echoes around us. It must have been half a kilogram of TNT at least, and it was close. Maybe a mortar or an RPG?

The eldest soldier waves the other two to the shelter of the track. He presses the safety catch down and takes up a fire position by the cab. Sok leaps off and joins us. We squat by the side of the track.

My guts feel like I'm on a roller-coaster.

I hate waiting.

Maybe we should try to escape? I glance across the track. The boy soldiers are facing us with their guns ready. No chance.

'Houn, please ask the soldiers if they know what is happening.'

After a rapid exchange they say they've no idea. They don't think the CAPF could get this far without them knowing.

The old soldier at the front speaks to one of the boys, who climbs quickly on to the cab. He shields his eyes from the evening sun and looks around. He shakes his head and climbs down.

If we could get close enough I might be able to hit one and take his gun. They're on the other side of the truck. There are three of them. Get real! I haven't got a hope. They're too far apart. We'll have to wait. If I start fighting and fail, we'll certainly be shot. There's another slight drawback; they've got guns and I haven't.

Eventually Pig Face ambles back. He says a few words to the soldiers, then squeals. The two frightened Khmers emerge cautiously from the bushes. The driver gets in the cab.

Houn's expression doesn't change as he says. 'He fire the rocket at us for a joke.'

I look around. Nobody's laughing. Well done Pig Face. That was a real thigh slapper.

The two boy soldiers are left to guard us and the others disappear to look for the track. It's nearly six thirty and the light's fading. The night insects start to chatter and the mosquitoes bite. I pull out my *kramar* and put it round my neck.

It's hot. My throat's dry and there's no water.

I must take the opportunity to butter up our guards. I like the one with the red plastic sandals. He's bright and keen to talk. The truck has to go to Rhum to get petrol. He says they've been allowed to visit their families. They live in a village with seven huts, twenty kilometres from Chnang. Everyone there is very poor.

The Khmer Rouge can't go in there now because it's too dangerous. People are angry about what happened to us. The local military sent soldiers there to protect the people from more Khmer Rouge attacks. The Khmer Rouge think they'll be killed if they enter the village.

He says some of the Khmer Rouge still want to kill us, but he doesn't. He thinks what we're doing is good. Some of his relatives have been killed by mines. He says we have done well to survive and congratulates us. I tell him I can guarantee his security around Chnang.

The others return, shouting they've found the track. We retrace our route, drop into a shallow gully and emerge through a gap in the bushes on to the yellow brick road.

Pig Face stops the truck, shouts through the window to the

driver then disappears into the darkness. I'm not sorry to see him go.

'What did he say?' I ask Houn.

'He tell the driver to get us out of here tonight.'

Eventually we slither to the top of a slight incline. I say, 'What is the road like to Rhum? Are there any wet areas?'

'The driver say good and dry. No problem.'

'How much fuel does he have?'

'Just enough to go to Rhum.'

12

DARKNESS

The lights don't work, but even if they did none of us would want them on. I can't see anything except the track and it's going to be a long night. I shove my daypack against the side of the cab and try to sleep.

It's a vain attempt. We jolt and roll all over the place. I don't feel like sleeping, but I force myself to go through the motions.

A sharp jabbing pain in my right elbow and head instantly wakes me. The lorry lurches. Houn falls over my legs. We've gone over a massive bump. I hear screams from behind. All I can see through the back window is a huddle of dark shapes. The driver grips the steering wheel and carries on regardless.

I can feel a trickle of blood in my hair just above my ear. I touch the side of the cab at the same level. There's a bolt sticking out.

Houn pulls himself back on to the seat.

There's a loud banging on the roof and shouting. The angry Khmer screams are clearly audible above the roar of the engine. The driver ignores them.

Following the line of the track through the trees ahead I can see the stars. Across the track I can see a raised ridge. I yell, 'Be careful' in Khmer. The driver slows slightly and we bounce over the mound. I brace myself against the door and try to get a closer look at it as we pass. After five metres it disappears into the bushes.

I peer through a gap in the undergrowth on the right where

I see another grassy bump. It's in a straight line, perpendicular to the track. After about thirty metres it turns a right angle before disappearing into a bush. It must be the edge of an old paddy field.

I turn to Houn. 'Please ask where we are.'

'He say close to the village of ghosts.'

We drive on through the shadows, then magically we emerge into a vast clearing. The glittering sky consumes me. I lean out of the window and stare upwards.

The clearing is flat and surrounded by the black edge of the forest. On the right a group of palm trees are silhouetted against the dark blue sky and shining stars. It's like a Christmas card.

The lorry slows. The engine roars. We stop moving.

The driver grinds it into reverse and the engine roars again. Slowly we move back a few inches and stop. He grates back into first gear and tries again. The wheels spin helplessly. He repeats the futile exercise several times before the silence takes over.

I stick my hand out of the window, open the door and jump down to escape the heat. My throat burns. I'm dehydrated. I sink to my ankles in mud. The axles are bogged in too.

I wipe the sweat from my eyes and pull my feet out of the shit. A veneer of lovely grass covers the stinking morass. That's Cambodia.

It's seven thirty. This is the end of the road.

Twenty metres in front of us, two palm tree stumps stand like broken tombstones. One is just a few metres tall, the other four or five metres. Their tops are jagged and their outline is burnt black. I walk forward.

Suddenly I stumble into a muddy hole. I run forwards, trying to keep my balance, then fall. I scramble up quickly. My head's spinning. I've twisted my knee.

I reach the palm tree stump. There's a round hole through the edge, probably made by a rocket which took off the top of the tree. I can see a small star twinkling through the hole. Around me the ground is dotted with shallow craters; some contain water, some are overgrown with grass.

I touch the charred trunk and for an instant I can see how it was.

A village, huts and palm trees in bright sunshine. Suddenly, the boom of explosions, screaming chaos. An incoming rocket. A mortar. The Khmer Rouge soldiers in thin black cotton run for their weapons and take fire positions. A boy soldier with a wide face and flaring nostrils like a pig shoots two men in the back as they run away. Women drag their children towards the forest. Screams. The deafening rattle of machine-gun fire. I hear the crackle of fire and feel the fierce heat as bamboo and thatch are consumed by orange inferno.

Slowly I take my hand off the charred stump and walk back painfully towards the lorry through this place of ghosts.

I look up at the sky, mesmerized. A shooting star leaves a glittering trail before it disappears beyond the blackness of the treeline. What beauty. What beauty.

Houn is walking towards me. I point with my right hand. 'Look! Look!' Too late, it's gone. 'It was a shooting star.'

He stares at me blankly so I say, 'A small star, flying in the sky, with a bright burning tail. Have you seen one?'

He nods. 'Oh, yes. I see before.'

We walk a few paces away from the lorry.

'What will happen if we stay here?' I ask.

'If more Khmer Rouge come, they kill us. They only give us permission to pass today.'

I nod my head and think. There's only one option. 'Can you and Sok walk all night?' I ask.

He looks confused. 'I think so.'

'I'm sure you can. We should be able to do six kilometres an hour, with breaks. No problem.'

If we can't it doesn't matter because I can carry him, thanks to the army. The PTIs who took us for exercise sessions after long marches, when every muscle ached, have given me the strength and confidence. I know I can do it. If you've trained beyond normal limits it's easier to deliver the goods when it counts.

'We have to get the two young soldiers to walk to their village. We go with them; then follow the track to Chnang. Can you ask them to come here?'

I move further from the lorry. I don't want the others to hear us. They're all busy at the back, trying to dig it out.

As the two young ones approach I say, 'This is a bad place. There are many ghosts.'

Houn hunches his shoulders and stands rigid. They discuss things for a while. The boys nod.

Houn says, 'Many people die here.'

'I know. They will be angry if we stay.'

I pause to let the message sink in. 'Have they walked to their village from here before?'

'Yes. It take nearly one day.'

I speak slowly, allowing Houn to translate each sentence. It gives me time to think.

'They know I have got many vehicles out of the mud, but this one is impossible. We could wait days and days before somebody comes to pull it out. There's nowhere to sleep here. We should walk. We will get there before midnight.'

The two soldiers have a brief discussion.

Houn raises his eyebrows. 'They say yes.'

It was easier than I thought. I'm not prepared. We need to get our daypacks and Sok. 'If they wait here, we get our bags. We will tell the others.' I walk away as I speak, so they can't object.

I reach into the cab, grab my pack and feel inside to check nobody's taken the first-aid kit. I shove my *kramar* on top, zip it up and throw it on. I grab the straw hat and press it on my head. It might make me look stupid, but I'll be glad of it when the sun comes up. I snatch Houn's bag and put it round my neck. 'I will carry this.' He's just behind me and tries to take it. I pull it sharply back. There is a ripping sound. I feel a flood of remorse. It's not heavy so I should let him. I must respect his dignity. I check the straps. It's all right.

'I'll get Sok. You explain to the driver.' I move to the back of the lorry where Sok is squatting. The hole he's digging around the wheel is filling up with water. I grab his collar and indicate the boy soldiers. I put my finger to my lips.

As I approach Houn I can hear shouting from the back of the lorry. He says, 'Driver angry. We should give money.'

'He knows I have no money. It's been stolen and it was the Khmer Rouge who made him drive through the forest, not me. I prefer walking.' As I finish speaking I take a few steps backwards and beckon Houn.

He says, 'He know Khmer Rouge soldier come tomorrow. What he do?'

'Tell him to do what he usually does. He comes here all the time.' I take another few steps back as I talk.

Houn has another discussion. 'He say many ghost here. We must stay or they angry with him.'

I put my hand on Houn's shoulder.

I take him round the front of the cab where they can't see us. 'One soldier in front. Then Sok. Then you. Then soldier and me last. We go fast now. Tell the soldiers I have seen the ghosts and they say we must leave.'

I carry on walking. Houn explains as I push him and Sok gently forward.

The soldiers set off at a good pace. I pause and watch the

driver. It doesn't matter what he thinks or does now. We've got more AK 47s than him.

I stay slightly ahead of the soldier in the red plastic sandals as we start across the clearing. It's 19.45. We have nine hours before daybreak. The ground is grassy and uneven. I place my feet cautiously and keep glancing upwards, hoping to see another shooting star. They say there is a track on the far side of the clearing. It goes through the forest to their village.

Out here we can still see clearly. Near the tree line it gets darker. I wonder how much darker it will get? I drop back.

The ground is dryer now and we're following sandy tyre tracks through the grass. Both boys are wearing their chest webbing with four magazines. That's a lot of rounds. They hold their weapons at the ready. When we left both had them on safety.

Now I can see the track through the forest. It's hard and dry. It should be good walking. The trees cast dark shadows and the white sand glows a strange grey in the blue light.

I guess we're doing six kilometres an hour.

In the distance the track disappears into a tunnel of darkness. It's probably bamboo. I raise my voice. 'We should hold the person in front. Then we will stay together. We must go very slow.' I put my hand on the shoulder of the boy in front. He laughs. We edge slowly into the darkness.

I step forward carefully, moving my hand on to the boy's neck. It's thin, fragile like a pigeon's. He's very light. I'm probably twice as strong and four stone heavier.

I could slip my right arm round his throat, grip my left forearm with my right hand and twist his head back. I'd snap it first time. Crunch. Then I'd rush the front soldier in the darkness. Neither of them would know anything about it. I'd keep the weapons, but carry the bodies into the forest and hide them.

I want vengeance. They deserve to be killed, because of what they have done to us.

Then I realize that the spirit of evil does not just lurk in the shadows of the forest. It waits, ready to strike, inside all of us. If I let it consume me now, I am lost.

I relax my grip and move my right hand back to his shoulder. I put my left out to feel for the trees.

13

GHOSTS

I can see a faint blue glow. I strain my eyes. Now there's a tiny white spark, followed by several more. I can make out the dark outline of tree branches. We emerge into the blue-grey starlight, out of the shadows, and lengthen our stride.

After an hour and a half the first soldier stops by a fallen tree and sits down. His mate joins him. 'We rest here,' Houn says.

They all look tired. Our speed's good and I'm not sweating too much, but I've got a headache and my throat's parched. 'You and Sok okay?'

'Yes, no problem.'

I swallow, to try and relieve my dry throat. 'Are there are any more soldiers around here or in the village? Also, do we go through any mine fields.'

Houn turns to talk to them.

Occasionally he explains their answers. We follow the track to their village, then keep going to Chnang. It's the only track. The boys say there are two mined areas between here and their village. Neither of them know who laid them. They've always been there, but they're sure the track is safe. There are no Khmer Rouge patrols out tonight. No soldiers guard their village and there are no mines around it, so we can walk straight in.

I want to keep moving. We have to get out before daybreak. I pace up and down, hoping they'll take the hint. They rise wearily and continue. The boy soldiers keep stomping along like beasts of burden, with their AKs and chest webbing. I'm impressed. They're doing better than I thought.

The track is rutted and uneven, but it's still dry. The imprints of water buffalo and ox hooves in the baked clay make it feel like we're walking on cobblestones.

We march on silently. There's no need to talk and no one's got the energy. We're all thirsty, but there's no water. We must get to the village.

The soldier in front slows, looks around him and sits down by the side of the track.

It's about ten o'clock.

I squat opposite them so we can talk. 'How is everyone?'

After a pause Houn replies, 'Everyone tired. Not usually walk this fast.'

'Yes, but we are doing well. Does anybody feel sick?'

There's another discussion before Houn answers. 'Everyone thirsty and tired. Nobody sick.'

Good, the pace is right. 'How much further?' I say.

'They think we halfway.'

We enjoy our rest.

The boy soldier without the red plastic sandals speaks to Houn.

'He say you shouldn't sit there.'

I'm curious. 'Please ask him why.'

'Because there are mines.'

I look around me. I'm sitting on the edge of a deep rut made by an ox cart. Behind me there is an area of short grass about two metres wide, then the vines and bushes takes over. The ground is well trodden and baked hard. There's no sign of recent disturbance. I check for trip wires. The others are mute with exhaustion. I carefully retrace my steps and stand in front of them. 'Where are the mines?'

They chat for a while before Houn replies, 'Someone told him in jungle, over there.'

'Are there any mines on or near the track, anywhere where we are going?'

'They say no problem, track fine.'

'Excellent. We go.' I start walking. They overtake and fall into place.

We march on and on. It's like a dream.

When we get to Rhum I'll believe we're free. Until then we're not safe.

The soldier in front stops. He speaks to his companion, then disappears into the bushes. 'They not sure which way. Night time everything different.'

He returns. We continue. Without warning he leaves the track, gingerly steps round a thorn bush and tiptoes sideways between the trees. He rapidly reappears and beckons us to follow.

It's a narrow path through the bushes. It must be a short cut. Or is it a trap?

These boys would do exactly what they were told. If their commander said they had to take us to a certain place and kill us they'd do it. 'Where are we going?'

'They say this path go to village,' Houn says.

We emerge into a small open area of rice paddies. The fields are under water and in places I can see the reflection of our shapes against the star-speckled sky.

For a while we head towards the tree line, then turn left. There is a pause as we negotiate a wide ditch. It gives me the chance to look around. So far I've just been concentrating on keeping my feet from slipping. The bank in front of us is fenced on one side with bamboo sticks and beyond it a group of palm trees surround a hut built on stilts.

To our left another hut stands, isolated, on the edge of the paddy.

Nobody makes a sound. People here have every reason to be afraid of the dark.

The soldier in front whispers to Houn who turns and whispers to me. 'We wait here. He borrow torch from his friend.'

He creeps to the hut on the edge of the paddy, leans against the step and speaks quietly. Somebody inside replies then I hear things being moved. A light shines inside the hut then vanishes. The soldier creeps back.

'Can we get some water to drink?' I ask.

'Yes, they thirsty. They will show us. I very thirsty.'

The promise of water gives our tired bodies new energy.

Trees either side of the track lock branches and everything is black. The dim torchlight guides our footsteps. We group together to make best use of it. We're walking over rough dried mud. The soldier with the torch moves to the left and starts walking along a buried log. To his right there's a pool of stinking mud.

I jump clear of the puddle at the end and follow them through the trees. We stop underneath a hut. He climbs up the ladder and lifts back the sack nailed over the doorway. After a murmured exchange he steps back down and runs under the hut. He stops by an enormous clay pot and shines the torch above his head. He grabs a battered aluminium bowl hung on a nail. My friend in the red sandals removes the flat wooden lid from the pot. The other soldier scoops the water, lifts the bowl to his lips, throws his head back, and drinks noisily.

He repeats the process several times before passing the bowl to his mate.

We all drink in turn. In spite of Houn's protestations I wait until last. He has three bowls. Perhaps that's how he manages to go all day without drinking; he's like a camel, drinking at night and storing it up.

It's passed to me. I roll the soft sweet water around my

tongue. I drink again and again until my stomach's full. I've lost count of the number of bowls.

I persuade Houn and Sok to have more. We could be walking all night and I don't know when we'll get the chance to drink again.

'Where is the track to Chnang?'

'They will show us. It may be twenty kilometre.'

We hang the bowl back up, put the lid on the pot and disappear into the darkness. As I step on the log I hear the water slosh in my stomach.

Once back in the starlight the torch is switched off. Batteries are expensive and it's a long walk to the market. The grey path leads through the shadow of the trees, past a fence of bamboo branches, then curves right to a group of sugar palms. A small hut sits in the middle. The soldiers stand under the hut and quietly call the occupants. They take off their webbing and sandals, unsling their AKs and climb the ladder.

The glow of an oil lamp lights the hut and Houn says, 'They invite us to rest.'

Deciding it would be rude not to I take off my boots and climb the ladder. Two children are asleep in the far corner. A thin old woman with a face like soft leather crawls across the floor and puts the oil lamp near the doorway. She wears a sarong and a stained and faded pink blouse. The floor of the hut is made from split bamboo and the sides look like woven palm leaves. The thatch roof is so low everyone has to stoop or squat.

The woman speaks to the boys and ignores us. 'What did she say?' I ask.

'She tell them not leave their guns and ammunition around the house, it very untidy.' Houn crosses his legs and sits down.

The woman withdraws to the side of the hut as they hang

up their webbing and put their guns neatly in the corner. Then
they sit, heads down. They're home, so they can give in to the
tiredness. All I want to do is get to Chnang.

We talk. The boys will spend the next few days helping to
plough the fields and plant rice. I look around. The only
possessions in the hut are a small pile of clothes, a big rice pot,
an old knife and a few spoons. It's immaculately clean. The
woman says nothing. She just kneels and looks at the floor. I
try to learn where there might be Khmer Rouge or CAPF
soldiers. At this time of night anybody with a gun or grenade
is dangerous. They think there are soldiers at Chnang to
protect the village from a Khmer Rouge attack. Before when
the government soldiers came, they stole everything including
the rice and burnt the houses. There might be more mines laid
there now.

It's not easy to tell the difference between the boy soldiers
now because they've taken their sandals off. One of them is
falling asleep. 'Can we go now?' I ask.

'Yes I think so. They wish us good journey,' Houn says.

As I put on my boots I glance back at the boys. They sit
silently, lost in tiredness. Their legs are crossed and their heads
hang low. They don't lift their eyes or say goodbye. I wish I
could give them something, like a radio, a pocket-knife or an
education.

I climb back up the ladder and hold out my hand. 'Or-gon.'
The first boy reaches out and shakes it weakly. The second is
as cautious. Neither lift their eyes.

I step down. We join the track and turn right. It's about
eleven thirty.

I must have absorbed the water; I've got a new lease of life
and feel like running. I try not to race off. I keep looking over
my shoulder and listening. Apart from the sounds of the night,
there's nothing.

I keep my eyes on the hut. The light's out and there's no

movement. The boys are probably asleep already. Now it's just the three of us. I stop and whisper, 'We should be silent all the way. Will there be any soldiers at the village?'

'Yes, maybe at edge. Nobody move at night except Khmer Rouge, so they will shoot us,' Houn replies.

We are demining the south side of the village. I haven't spent much time on the north. Our approach will be through unfamiliar ground. 'Will they have laid more fragmentation mines this side of the village?'

'Yes, maybe.'

There are a few huts near the river. Several years ago the Khmer Rouge crept in and laid Chinese-type 72 A anti-personnel mines around the ford where most people cross. The result was devastating. In the dark we should get a local to show us the safe route. 'When we get to the village we stop at the first house and ask where the soldiers are. Then get them to show us the safe route through the river. Okay?'

'Yes. No problem.' Houn and Sok nod.

I shake our rucksacks to make sure nothing rattles and we start walking. This time I'm in front.

I keep glancing behind and ahead.

The incessant chattering of night insects, the dark shadows of the trees on the grey track and the blue tinted starlight always look the same. Sometimes I glance up, hoping to see another shooting star.

Suddenly my heart stops. I can see the silhouettes of two men with guns. My pulse pounds in my ears and I hold my breath. They haven't seen us yet. I raise my hands. Houn and Sok stop. I turn, put my finger to my lips and look at each of them. Silently I step over to Houn, put my hand on his shoulder and point. He freezes.

As I point I feel a breeze. The silhouettes move strangely and I rub my eyes. It's the shadow of two bushes, not two soldiers.

We power on through the night. We're moving faster than before. There isn't time to stop and rest. I keep looking and listening. When we get near the river I'll find a stick that I can use as a trip-wire detector. They might put POMZ 2s or MON 100s on the track at night.

Sometimes we stop again to peer at shadows or to listen to the noises of the night. I pull down my sleeve to cover the luminous dial of my watch. It's nearly one in the morning. Four hours until daylight.

Behind us there is a small hut hidden from the track by trees. I whisper to Houn. 'We must be near the river. Ask the people who live there if there are any soldiers or mines near here, and get them to show us the safe way to cross.'

'I try, but they will be afraid. If they have gun maybe they shoot.'

'No problem, we can hide in the trees. They won't know where we are.'

We walk back down the track like schoolboys about to ring on someone's doorbell and run away.

Houn calls gently to the occupants. A frightened voice asks who he is and what he wants. He replies he's a woodcutter who's been lost in the forest. He must get to the village and he needs to know the way through the river.

A face emerges from the black space of the doorway. A thin man climbs down. He adjusts the *kramar* around his waist. He's unarmed so Houn approaches. They talk for a while before he turns and says, 'Okay.'

We move forward. As the man sees me he jumps and starts jabbering.

'He think we are ghost,' Houn says.

I bow and smile, then start down the track. He follows cautiously. At the river he points. Houn says, 'That side best. He say no soldiers and no mines around Chnang.'

'You believe him?'

'Yes. He simple man. He believe we are ghost of people the Khmer Rouge took into forest and killed.'

I walk into the stream. My feet sink into the sand and hot water floods into my boots. I turn to thank the man, but he's already running back to his hut. I whisper, 'I think we should stop until daylight in Chnang. There are soldiers and fragmentation devices near Rhum and there could still be Khmer Rouge between here and there.'

'Yes. I think so,' Houn replies. 'I have friend there.'

We pause by the palm trees. This must be the centre of the village. It looks completely different in the dark. We tiptoe around until Houn is sure it's the right hut. I fan my face with the straw hat while Houn quietly wakes up his wife's distant cousin's friend. An old man and an old woman appear and stare at us in silence.

We speak quietly. They touch us slowly then shake hands. They laugh. We're not ghosts. We're alive! They shout to the next hut. People come to look. They congratulate us for escaping with our lives and tell us the Khmer Rouge told people around here we would be killed.

The flicker of an oil light fills the front of the hut. Rough wooden planks a few metres wide are covered by the thatch roof making a small front balcony. I drop my hat and rucksack under the boards.

The hut is walled with woven palm leaves. The floor is about a metre off the dirt. I lean against it and keep my feet on the ground. I don't want to take my boots off. I can't relax. We're not back in Rhum yet. The border villages are still full of darkness, distrust and fear.

Two small children sleep inside the hut. The old woman fusses over them, speaking gently and stroking their heads. She tucks the pink mosquito net around them, lifts up the small tin oil lamp and shields the wick with her hand as she returns to the open front of the hut.

The little boy and girl have always lived with their grand-parents. Their father was killed in the fighting. It no longer matters for which side. Their mother died soon after, from cholera. The grandparents are worried they might die before the children are old enough to look after themselves.

We talk about security. I want to know if the road between here and Rhum is safe. People appear from the darkness, stare at us and walk away. A muscular man with a big grin shakes Houn's and Sok's hands and smiles a lot. Houn introduces him as the new military commander who was sent here with reinforcements following our kidnapping.

He tells us they were all very surprised when it happened. The senior military commanders didn't think the Khmer Rouge had the strength to mount such an operation in this area. He says some of them may have been special forces sent by Pol Pot. He congratulates us on surviving and assures us the road is now safe. They've put more soldiers on the road to Rhum and the edge of the town is better protected.

I ask how many more soldiers and he says maybe five, but he's not sure. The road is fifteen kilometres long.

They pass us bowls of rice and fresh chicken soup with lemon grass. They give me the honour of having first go at the chicken's feet. I get Houn to explain it would be against my custom because I'd be unhappy if we didn't share equally. I manage to get away with it.

Sok relates our experiences, miming the actions. Houn helps out, supplying details. He does an impersonation of me trying to shake hands with the Khmer Rouge when they ambushed us. They laugh and point. He does a good one of Pig Face holding the RPG and shouting. His helicopter sounds are excellent, much better than his AK 47 noises.

They deserve to laugh and be happy. I sit on the sideline, isolated by my feelings of sadness. It's very early on Sunday morning. In thirty hours I want to start demining. But we can't do it without the kit.

We finish the rice and chicken soup. The old woman washes the bowls in a dented bucket. The old man tries to haul me into the hut to sleep under the net. Perhaps rudely, I refuse. I want to sleep on the balcony because I'm hot and I want to be the first to know if anyone comes near. By way of compromise I accept the small pillow he proffers. I look around. We are safe here. The only danger now is the road between here and Rhum. I can take my boots off. I feel my socks. They're almost dry.

I cover my face with my *kramar*, put my hands in my pockets and lie back on the pillow. The irritating high-pitched whine of a mosquito fills my right ear. I feel a tickle as it lands so I smack the side of my head. I rewrap my face and try to sleep. The boards are hard. I want to leave at first light.

On Monday I'll try to get the kit back. I'm not sure how. I'll talk it through with Lawrence. I doze and watch the darkness disappear.

It's nearly five. 'Is it safe to leave yet?' I whisper.

'I think so,' Houn replies.

We wake up Sok and thank our hosts profusely. A few people are stirring in their huts as we leave, but the village is still in the ghostly grey light.

It's good to walk now before it gets too hot. I push the sun hat back and look ahead. The track is clear but as we turn every corner I wonder what lurks in the bushes.

After twenty minutes it is daylight and I recognize the fallen tree and broken remnants of a fence marking the second minefield outside the village. We soon reach the muddy water-hole where the boys bring the water buffalo to sit.

The sunlight turns the dewy-coated leaves to gold. In the

heat of the night it's hard to believe dawn could ever be cool enough for dew, but it is. I stroke some of the larger leaves as I pass. The water drips off my fingers.

We've been walking for over an hour and keep to the side of the track so we can run and hide if there are soldiers. Hopefully we'll see them first.

Soon we'll reach the clearing. There's no cover and we have to cross it. If they want to monitor movements to and from the village this is the place.

As we approach, I move into the trees. I signal to the others to wait in the bushes and creep forward. I drop to my hands and knees and crawl. I stop behind a large bush with thick waxy leaves and listen. I can hear the sound of insects and the rasp of my own breathing. On the far side a bird squawks. I scan the trees.

I crawl back into the bushes, keeping a look-out for snakes, then make my way back to Houn and Sok. 'I think it's safe. Are you happy?'

They both nod and we creep out into the clearing.

There are no signs of the ambush three days ago. All that remains are our memories. But something's not right.

I'm being watched. From behind I hear a snort. I turn round. The sun is behind us; it's hard to see.

Four hundred metres away there is an ox cart being driven by a little man in a battered brown trilby. A large figure sits behind him. They're gaining on us.

Sok looks at me with wide staring eyes. Houn cups his hands around his forehead and squints into the sun. After a while he says, 'No problem. People from village go to market.'

We walk on.

The toothless old driver grunts, tips back his dirty battered hat and waves his stick as he passes us. The felt is misshapen and there's a dark ring above the rim where ribbon once prevented the felt from fading.

The oxen snort and one licks its wet nose with a huge, pink, sand-papery tongue.

Before we get the chance to greet them, the large lady in the back speaks.

'They want to be sure we are not ghosts,' Houn says.

I thank them and offer greetings.

'She congratulate us for surviving. Always everyone die. She happy we alive. But she pity us.'

Compassion: I had begun to doubt it could exist here. I walk to the cart, take off the straw hat and give it her.

She smiles and the little man laughs as she puts it on. As the cart disappears she waves. Houn says, 'They go ahead, tell people in Rhum good news. We alive.'

I watch them disappear. The straw hat with the pink rim looks a lot better on her than it did on me.

14

LIGHT

13 JUNE 1993

Tall coconut palms surround a large wooden house. The roof is ridged with large clay tiles. Square timbers buried in the ground support the heavy-boarded walls and floor. The wood is bleached grey by the rain and sun. Underneath the house at ground level there are several large sacks of rice and a moped. It looks in working order. The children run to the gate and cheer and wave.

As we circumnavigate a large lagoon containing a mixture of green slime and buffalo shit I can see the line of houses. Some have grey sheet-metal roofs and some have terracotta tiles.

We stop and look. No one needs to say anything. We know we've done it.

Houn turns to me, eyes burning. 'I want you tell UN and everyone what Khmer Rouge did.'

I nod. 'I'll try.' Life's not always fair, but we should still try and make it that way.

Short of going back in with the local military I know there's nothing that can be done, but I don't have the heart to tell him.

On the outskirts of Rhum there are spacious wooden houses on large plots of land. Most of the people are farmers or traders or both. As we approach town people run over to us, waving and saying hello. Men come up and shake our hands.

Children start to follow us and women hold up their little ones to see us and wave. More people are running out of their houses. Just for an instant we're all happy. I can feel the goodwill. The sun's shining and the bright blue sky is cloudless.

Everyone's smiling and no one's afraid. Houn says, 'They think Khmer Rouge kill us. They happy we alive and thank us for clear the mines.'

Just for a moment we are a community. I nod my head and turn away. I don't want him to see that I am crying.

I wave and say, '*Or-gon.*'

A well-built man aged about sixty is riding a bicycle towards us. His grey hair is cropped short. He wears old brown trousers and a patterned shirt of orange and yellow, like the ones sold on the market. A dollar to the locals, seven dollars to the UN. He stops in front of me and shakes hands. His smile reveals two missing front teeth.

'This commune chief. People tell him we alive. He very happy and come welcome us,' Houn says.

I am pleased there are no other foreigners here. They would not understand.

His appearance and method of transport mean he's probably an honest commune chief. Kindly he offers me a lift on the carrying rack of his bicycle. They don't think a *joo-un bor-ra-dtayh* should walk. I can't accept. Why shouldn't I walk like everyone else?

In the distance a man aged about fifty is bumping down the rutted clay road on a battered moto. As he reaches us he does a U-turn and stops. He's dressed like the commune chief except in blue. He secures his cigarette in the corner of his mouth then shakes hands. He turns to me and pats the rear seat of the moped.

I keep on walking.

'This district chief. He try to send message to Khmer Rouge. But he hear we dead. He very pleased we alive. Where you go?'

'To the UN post.'

'He want to take you there.'

I don't want to offend him, so I reluctantly sit on the back. Just as I try to get my legs either side on the footrests he drives off. I stumble and end up sitting side saddle. Frantically I grip the seat with both hands. Every time we go over a bump my legs fly in the air. I start to laugh. The others have no trouble keeping up with the moto. Even though we're travelling at walking pace, staying balanced is a lot harder than it looks. I try to grip the seat.

We bump up the baked clay track on to the latterite highway through the centre of Rhum. The police post is only a few hundred metres away. Outside it I've seen a massive white satellite dish. This is definitely the right place to send a radio message.

We stop in the small car park. There are no vehicles and the brick and cement building looks empty. The others wait shyly as I walk to the doorway. I knock. 'Good morning.'

It's eight o'clock. I thought the UN started work then, perhaps it's later on Sunday. A nervous-looking Khmer man rushes down the corridor putting on his clothes. He doesn't speak English, but his French is reasonable. I learn that CIVPOL are pulling out and that there's only one man here at the moment. He'll be out soon too.

I join Houn and Sok on the Vietnamese concrete seat. We thank the district chief for his kindness. He smiles and rides away.

Several minutes later a short North African policeman strides down the corridor doing up his zip. We converse in a mixture of French and English. I ask if I can use his radio to get someone from my base to come and pick us up. He says the satellite link doesn't work and he's just guarding the equipment. He doesn't have a radio and is supported by the military base down the road. The Norwegian CIVPOL will arrive at eight thirty, so if we'd like to wait he can arrange a lift.

He tells me he's heard about a very serious incident: three people taken by the Khmer Rouge. Everyone says nobody can do anything. I tell them they don't need to because we're out.

He stares in disbelief, then throws his arms in the air, laughs and says he is pleased to see us. He asks if we want some tea and understands when I say we should walk to the camp as soon as possible. I must let base know and get Houn and Sok back to their families.

The UN are sharing the CAPF camp. Blue and white painted oil drums and coiled barbed wire mark the entrance. The UN troops are starting to pack up to leave. In the centre I find a soldier and ask if we can use their radio to speak to the UN provincial headquarters. He summons the lieutenant.

The short, portly Tunisian officer arrives breathless and beret-less, clutching a clipboard. He laughs a lot and says he's pleased we're alive. I am touched by his sincerity. He introduces two colonels from the CAPF, both wearing civvies. They give us a warm welcome. We all keep shaking hands. I've met one of the CAPF officers before. He says he didn't think he'd see us again and laughs. They couldn't do a follow-up operation because they were told the Khmer Rouge would shoot us and destroy the vehicles if they went anywhere near Chnang. The militia was strengthened in the village, but that's all they could do. They were all surprised the Khmer Rouge had the strength to mount the operation. He didn't think they had that many men.

He doesn't ask awkward questions that might compromise our neutrality and suggests I visit his friend at the next division down the road if I'm serious about getting the kit back. He thinks it's possible.

The TUNBAT officer is switched on. He's already made the radio call to HQ and says my base will be notified. I know my

Australian mates in the Communication Centre will inform everyone. He thinks there will be plenty of people to offer us a lift home and invites us to have some tea.

The platoon dining room is in the centre of the camp. It has a tin roof and open sides. It's surrounded by a low wooden wall to keep the dogs out. Four tables are covered with a thick blue and white plastic tablecloth.

It's a relief to be in the shade. A teapot and several glasses are brought. The TUNBAT officer keeps pouring tea and smiling. I'm grateful; the walking has given me a raging thirst.

Two UN Landcruisers arrive and halt in a cloud of dust. One is marked CIVPOL. Two enormous Norwegian policeman climb out, head and shoulders taller than the people around them and dressed in blue shorts and immaculate light blue shirts. They're an impressive sight. I recognize the sound of a Land Rover engine. It's Lawrence and Colin. I walk straight over. I know they'll have done everything possible. I never doubted that.

I shake hands with the boss. He says, 'Yesterday, I said to Lawrence we had to face the fact we might never see you all again. Out here it's over, one way or the other, very quickly. You've done well. It reminds me of the time when a friend of mine waited for me to emerge from a forest in Korea. They'd all given up on us. My whole company was posted dead. I was pleased when we did a tactical withdrawal at night through the Chinese lines not to lose a man. The adjutant was happy to see me, but the CO never spoke to me again, because he had to explain to the brigadier why we weren't dead!'

I introduce them to Houn and Sok and the TUNBAT officer.

I knew Lawrence would be straight down to collect us. Amid the hustle we have a brief chat and I'm relieved to have the chance to get their views. I have every confidence in both of them and I've done everything I can, but I'm not sure where to go from here. I'm exhausted and confused. There are so many things I want to understand.

Lawrence introduces me to a French UNMO called Geoff Petit and a UN human rights official. Geoff, an athletic-looking military man, is clutching a map case. He says, 'Good to see you. Come on, I'll show you where you've been.'

I'm relieved to see Lawrence is looking after Houn and Sok.

The blue plastic tablecloth feels sticky. I take my hand off it. The boss sits on my left and studies the map. He's every inch the immaculate retired British officer in jungle boots, neatly-pressed lightweight trousers and khaki shirt. I realize how unshaven and dirty I am in comparison.

Geoff is on my right. He folds the map to show Chnang. 'This is an American map from the 1970s; not all of the villages shown exist now.' He points with his pen. 'You were taken here. The helicopter flew over all villages in the area looking for the vehicles, but found nothing. We were low on fuel and checking the last village when we saw two vehicles under a tree. I told the pilot to circle.'

He looks up and frowns, as if troubled. 'We didn't know if the people on the ground were still alive, but we thought if they were at least it would reassure them to see the helicopter.'

He grips the black roller-ball pen tightly and half smiles. His expression tells me how difficult it is for those trying to compel circumstances over which they have no control.

I say, 'I'm grateful. After that it was possible to make the commander take us to his superiors.'

I tell them what happened. The TUNBAT officer scribbles as I speak.

The French officer rearranges the map and points with his pen to a tiny village in the middle of the forest. 'This is where we sighted you the next morning. By then we'd searched the whole area and were low on fuel. We were on the point of giving up when we saw two white vehicles. One looked like a stolen UN pick-up. I think it was taken from another area. We were astonished you were taken so far into their territory so quickly.'

They look aghast when I tell them about the shooting. They had no idea. They were still well out of range. The minimum height restriction is there for a good reason.

'We followed a white vehicle to a clearing where we saw somebody put the lights on, open the doors and run into the trees.'

The Norwegian policemen quietly make notes in their pocket books as I give the rest of the details. When I finish the boss gets up. 'Right, well thanks to everyone, let's go. We've still got a lot of mines to clear.'

I shake hands with them. 'Thanks for the tea.'

The nearest Nordic giant says, 'We would appreciate your help with two current murder investigations.' Like most Norwegians out here his English is perfect.

'Of course.'

'There have been reports two local men were murdered in March about thirty kilometres north of Chnang. A brutal Khmer Rouge soldier who terrifies the locals abducted them and a commander called Mr Red shot them in the back. We think it could have been the same people who took you.'

I nod. 'Yes, I think it was. You should get your interpreter to speak to Houn and Sok. They may have heard things.'

The other policeman beckons his interpreter and sends him over.

We're going back to base. Somewhere I can sleep, eat and wash. I remember imagining Sok walking to the gate and waving to me like he always did and then Houn politely bowing and hurrying home to his family. It was my dream. Now it's going to come true. Lawrence takes a few photos of us and drives us back.

I thank everyone again and climb into the Land Rover. The

three of us sit in the back, grinning. We don't need to say anything. Lawrence and Colin are in the front. Lawrence is an excellent driver, but it feels strange to be a passenger. I want my Land Rover back. We discuss our plans for kit recovery.

Colin says, 'After you've had two months' leave you can worry about that.'

I swallow hard. I'd rather have my head boiled than have two months' leave. That would be giving up. I tell him I don't want it and explain that I'm keen to carry on with our work. I also make the point that I don't keep things bottled up and if something bothers me I tell people. Once I've had a good night's sleep I'll be fine. The boss agrees, but says I should take it easy for a few days. Lawrence thinks it would be a good idea to have a change of scenery. I'll arrange a two-day trip to Phnom Penh. It suits me fine. I can have a computer lesson from Lawrence and go out for fish and chips with Duncan.

When we get back to base Jim has organized a reception committee. I'm really pleased to see him. We shake hands on the basis that hugs are too girly. I pause and look around. I know what's special about these people and why I can feel goodness around me. All of them can see beyond their own noses.

I want to understand what happened. I still feel confused. The days drift by and I fight to sort myself out. I understand that even though I lost my liberty for just a few days I must regain my sense of control. Every time I want to go to the toilet I look for somebody to ask permission, and I tell myself, 'get a grip.'

It is not until I go running that I feel properly free.

As I run out of the gate I turn right and take the usual route to the rice fields. Within minutes I'm soaked in sweat. I pass through two small villages where I wave to the children. They laugh and shout, 'hello, bye bye', and try to run with me for a little way. As I leave them behind I look at the skyline.

The setting sun is the colour of a ripe tomato. A line of distant palm trees is silhouetted in front of it. It reminds me of the day I arrived and went running with Lawrence. As I run back along the river I realize that if you allow yourself, you can be a prisoner for ever.

At every opportunity I go back to Chnang to try to negotiate with the Khmer Rouge and start work again. But now there are rumours the Khmer Rouge soldiers have put a price on my head. They're trying to lure me into the border areas so they can kill me.

No one was more surprised to hear the reason for this than me. Recently Mr Red and Pig Face were shot dead when they visited a border village. Life's not always fair, but we should still try and make it that way.

15

WORKING IN CAMBODIA

JUNE 1993 TO DECEMBER 1994

I'm immersed in our work. Days merge into months and time is only measured in small achievements such as clearing a village site, taking a few refugees home or teaching one of my Cambodian colleagues to do something they didn't think they could do.

Sometimes it feels like I've always been here. Home is a distant memory detached from this reality.

After six months, I moved to Banteay Meanchey on the Thai border.

As the loaded pick-up truck speeds past me the fine orange dust cloud from the latterite road fills the Land Rover. I catch sight of a dozen Cambodians in the back with *kramars* wrapped around their heads. They try to stick their heads high to escape from the dust, but it's a useless gesture.

Not even a giraffe has a neck long enough to avoid the fine red dust from this latterite road. The faster vehicles travel the more dust they make. I can feel it getting up my nose and I sneeze twice. Now I start to cough. This foggy dust is dreadful.

I'm going to have to go for a long run tonight to get all of this stuff out of my system. If work commitments allow I run for forty minutes or an hour before our daily admin radio call at six thirty.

When I moved up here I found a running partner. Martin

is a British doctor working in the government hospital on a
VSO project. He's a general practitioner with five years' experience in Britain. In the rural areas of Cambodia, where 80 per
cent of the population live, the infant mortality rate is one of
the highest in the world. His commitment, professionalism
and energy have saved countless lives, but he often says it's a
drop in the ocean.

I glance at my bare forearms which are now coloured red-
brown. I can even taste the dust.

For a while the thick cloud obscures the dazzling sun and
brilliant blue sky. Being enveloped in the dark dust is like a
temporary trailer for hell.

The wooden houses with grass thatched roofs are all covered
in a layer of dust and I still can't believe that people actually
live so close to the road. It fills the air. It's easy to forget how
poor and miserable many of the people's lives are here.

I brake quickly and change down a gear. There's a small
shelter by the side of the road and I can see two children
waiting to sell cigarettes and sweets to passers-by. These are
usually farmers riding bicycles to the fields. Sometimes they
are leading their water buffalo or an ox cart. They buy the
cheap high-tar cigarettes.

Most of the older men have revolting hacking coughs. Out
here, where TB is a problem, nobody has heard of lung cancer
and the large tobacco companies have an emerging and
increasing market. Several of the major brands employ school-
girls wearing their T-shirts and baseball caps to promote their
cigarettes. There are no health warnings.

Thinking of some of the victims around here: the homeless,
the disabled and the dispossessed leaves me with a hollow gap
filled with melancholy. No time for potentially depressing
thoughts though. It doesn't help anybody and I have too much
to do. I have to get to the minefield. They need some kit

dropped off and I've got a meeting with the commune chief to discuss settling hopeless refugees on some land we cleared.

Now I'm leaving the village I speed up and call in my position on the radio. Once I've had my meeting and checked the site I've got some survey work to do in the hospital. Being able to use the United Nations Development Programme net is a great help to the aid agencies in the area. With hand-held radios we can speak to anyone within a forty-kilometre radius of the town.

The radio net is much more important now because since the UN troops have withdrawn the level of robbery and security problems have rocketed. In places there is sporadic fighting and things change rapidly, so the radio is a lifeline.

As the Land Rover approaches a bridge I change down and look over the side of the wooden abutment into the muddy water below. In the wet season this is a deep raging torrent. Now in the dry season you'd get a small canoe stuck in the trickle of water. No chance of surfing or sailing around here; especially at this time of year, which was why we had some T-shirts printed with 'Banteay Meanchey Surf and Beach Club' written on them.

After my meeting I drive back to the hospital. We do a weekly survey to see where the mine casualties are coming from.

The International Committee of the Red Cross provide medicines and medical professionals to train local staff. By mandate they only deal with war wounded and an American Quaker organization supply a small team to work in general medicine. Martin, my running partner, is one of them provided after a government request to VSO.

As I drive through the gate and park under the palm trees I pass a woman in a well-washed sarong clutching a small, wizened baby. With wide brown eyes she shows me her limp dysentery-dehydrated child and softly asks for help. If they get a drip in straight away the child might have a chance.

The only thing I can do is take them to Martin. I beckon her to follow me.

We walk past the old part of the hospital. The TB ward is a magnificent traditional Khmer wooden building with a clay tile roof. Long and dark, it stands on huge wooden stilts. The floorboards are nearly two inches thick. It was built by the Khmer Rouge as a traditional Khmer medical centre. They had a herbal pill made to their own district formula, which cured everything; or not. I've been told they also used to give intro-venous infusions of coconut milk to the people they wanted to live.

I wonder how many people died cutting the wood by hand and bringing it out of the forest and how many more died in the hospital from disease and lack of proper treatment?

I look around. If the patients were crammed in, several hundred could get into the building at a time. Over several years that's a lot of people. I look around at the flat fields. It must have been somewhere nearby, or maybe they took the bodies on ox carts and dumped them at the regional killing field.

I see Martin the VSO doctor doing the rounds with his Cambodian counterpart. He looks up and smiles as he takes the pulse of a thin smiling man. When he's finished he says, 'Hello. As you can see, we've had to start putting them outside. I hope the new ward's finished by the time the wet season comes.'

I reply. 'It's a sign of your success. People aren't afraid of the hospital now you and the Red Cross are here. I'm afraid I've brought you one more.'

He walks over, reassures the woman, looks at the baby and says. 'We need to get a drip in straight away. Thanks. I'll see you later.'

He shouldn't thank me. All I've done is present him with a problem that means he won't have time to stop for lunch.

Walking back I pass an emaciated man lying on a reed mat on the metal-framed bed. His breathing comes in irregular snorts. He's in a mumbling coma, his jaundiced yellow skin and the sweet sickly smell of malaria tell me what he's dying from.

I check the time. I have an indestructible Swiss diving watch, a recent birthday gift from Kate and Ian, my sister and her husband. It's my prize possession. As we walk into the surgery unit run by the Red Cross I look through my notebook. I'm always surprised to find how many of those injured by mines knew they were in a mined area, but decided they would starve if they didn't take the risk to get firewood or grow a crop. I go into the intensive care ward and am shocked to see a man with no legs.

What is left of his thin body is covered in sweat. His wife is sitting on the side of the bed trying to cool him with a bamboo fan. The little that he has below his waist is covered with a *kramar*. He looks as near death as any man I've seen.

As I approach he opens his eyes and tries to speak. I move closer and like a drowning man he suddenly grabs my hand. His grip is tight, alarmingly tight. I can feel him clinging to life. If only I could give him strength. Tears of desperation run down his face as he repeats one question like a mantra: 'How will I feed my wife and children?'

His daughter sits silently on the end of the bed. Her Daddy doesn't take up much space now. The little girl is about four years old. She rocks and cradles her two-year-old sister, who has a runny nose and a hungry look.

He keeps holding my hand. I feel awkward and tell him he must live for his family. I know some people who will help him to learn a new skill and he'll be able to work to support them. He tells me his name is Som On. He was a major and joined the government army to fight the Khmer Rouge because they had killed his parents. He was blown up while they were attacking a remote Khmer Rouge base. It took days to get him to hospital. He doesn't remember it. His wife watches and fans him with a look of resignation and despair.

He won't loosen his grip. After half an hour I have to go. I prise my hand away.

Fernanda the Spanish head nurse for the International Committee of the Red Cross sees me leaving. Outside, she gently shakes her head and smiles. That's what she did last week, when I brought in a man from a remote village who'd been bitten by a viper. He had a leg the size of a tree trunk, but we still had to help him. For three days he mumbled and salivated into oblivion.

She quietly says. 'He has a bad infection. It's amazing he's hung on for so long.'

I say. 'He'll make it.'

'Maybe. Miracles happen. We always do everything we can,' she says.

I reply, 'I know. You always do.'

I leave feeling inadequate and sad. There isn't much I can do for him. He's just another sad story in the on-going tragedy of Cambodia.

I can't help him, but I know a man who can. I'll write to Kike. He's a gentleman in the true sense of the word. He's a Spanish monk working with the Jesuit Refugee Service. With a pleasant manner, keen brain, several degrees and the sort of clean-cut good looks women love he could have been president of a large corporation or a professional sportsman. Instead, he chose to work for JRS. Everybody says they do excellent work helping the disabled. Some of the people who work for JRS speak four or five languages, have several degrees and run projects which give the possibility of hope and a future to people who have neither. In a way they could be described as

God's special forces. They don't preach or procrastinate. They just cut the crap and get on with it.

I write Kike a note and get back to work.

On rare occasions I travel to Phnom Penh. This time I'm picking up some new metal detectors. Ebinger, a German company, has made them to HALO specification. They've been independently tested and I'm keen to get them into the field. I'm also getting Khmer translations of our SOPs and a Land Rover maintenance manual that Lawrence has sweated buckets to produce. There are no garages here, our vehicles will only be maintained if we do everything.

Sometimes I still need to check the map when I'm travelling around Phnom Penh, but I know where most places are. It's rumoured the street numbers were assigned in accordance with the number of paces from the central post office. I haven't had time to check it yet.

As I drive through the thronging mass of Phnom Penh motos I glance sideways for the painted sign of a photocopier and park in front of the shop. The pavement is deserted, but the road still streams with cyclos, motos, a few cars and four-wheel drives. The generals usually drive Landcruisers with blacked-out windows.

As I walk into the shop a voice behinds me shouts. 'All right Harv? What are you doing down here?'

It's Neil. We were in the same platoon at Sandhurst and by a quirk of fate we've both ended up clearing mines in Cambodia. He's a few pounds heavier than the last time I saw him; but then again probably I am too. He's working for the Cambodian Mine Action Centre.

I reply, 'Admin run and yourself?' as I search for some shade.

Neil wipes the sweat from his forehead and says, 'It's a bit warmer than Thetford.'

After remembering old times we get engrossed in the future

of funding for demining in Cambodia. Suddenly I feel a soft
nudge, then a push on my right upper arm and hear a soft
whine. A man is standing so close to me; strangely and
invasively close. Simultaneously the smell of a very unwashed
body fills my nostrils. It's so bad it makes me wretch.

I turn to look at the beggar. He's standing in line with the
sun so I'm temporarily blinded by the light. Then he puts his
face in front of mine and nods at the Land Rover. His hair is
long and matted and his face is pock-marked. His eyes sing
desperation. He quietly repeats two Khmer words. He says
'mine and please' again and again.

I take a step backwards and am shocked to see he has no
arms, just six-inch bony stumps.

Neil says, 'He's reading the Khmer mine-clearance words
on the Land Rover. That must have been how he lost his arms.'

I search my pockets for money. I don't think I have any.
Neil beats me too it and pushes a few dollars into the man's
top pocket. His shirt is nylon and is creamy yellow in a few
places, but most of it is the filthy colour of the street.

He smiles, bows his head and moves a small bony stump
near his shoulder.

As we watch him shuffle away Neil says, 'I don't think I'd
want to survive something like that. I've started looking for
flying jobs.'

Later that afternoon the very efficient Suthy, who took over
Duncan's job when he left, gets the detectors cleared through
Customs. The next morning I leave just after first light to make
the ten- or eleven-hour drive up country. Outside of the major
cities it's not safe to travel after dark. If I doubt we'll arrive
well before last light we'll stop in Battambang, and complete
the journey the next day.

The deminers are accommodated five kilometres the other
side of the small town of Sisaphon. In the surrounding village
sites, many now overgrown with scrub, there are countless

minefields that with the current level of resources will take between five and ten years to clear.

By the time we finish work on Saturday afternoon we're exhausted. It's seven in the evening. I walk the short distance down the road to Martin's house. The ambient light from the stars creates a land of shadows and secrets. The last eighteen months have taught me this is what this place is.

I take off my shoes and walk up the steep wooden steps to the veranda where the rattle of the small diesel generator is masked by the sound of night insects. Martin has two guests, Huw and Heather, a husband and wife team who work a hundred kilometres down the potholed and dusty Route Five in Battambang. It's the main road connecting the two major cities with Thailand. In places it's like a rutted farm track.

Heather is an ophthalmic optician. Huw is a lawyer working on the establishment of the judicial system and human rights issues. I've met them before. Huw is a former Hong Kong Police officer who grew up in Africa. He's also a natural athlete, excelling in all sports including martial arts. He's a black belt and is the sort of person everybody wanted to be friends with at school. I've decided to call him 'school bully'.

We sit on the veranda hoping for a cool breeze and discuss the plight of an estimated 40,000 refugees around Sisaphon. They've fled from the fighting in front-line areas. The government troops have pushed back the Khmer Rouge advance and it's hoped that they'll be able to return soon to what's left of their homes. Many of them are displaced, landless and hopeless. They haven't planted crops and they survive on rice handouts from the World Food Programme and UNHCR.

Huw talks of human rights abuses, injustice and corruption, which make the air heavy and all of us silent.

His contract will be up in a few months. I ask, 'Will you stay?'

'We have to go back because Heather's only got a one year leave of absence from the eye hospital. What about you?'

'They've asked me to move to Mozambique. I should get there just in time for Christmas.'

16

AFRICA

Through the burning and stinging I fight to focus my mind. I'm going to be lucky to get out of this alive. I think I'm going to die. All that's left is what I believe is right. I will fight the pain and try not to moan. I will try not to lose control.

I feel totally alone.

I know the SOP is to remove the casualty from immediate danger and no one should be injured doing this. My first priority should be to make sure nobody else gets hurt. The next step is first aid and evacuation of the casualty. I must send a casualty report (CASREP) to the back-up team on the road. It feels like ten minutes has passed since the blast, but I know it is hardly a second.

I shout in a controlled voice. 'Frank, I'm a casualty. I have been blown up walking down the safety lane. Lower right leg is blown off. Right hand is badly damaged. Get on the radio and see if the US AID helicopter is able to do a CASEVAC. Only the two medics should come into the lane with the stretcher. Do you understand?'

Frank shouts urgently, 'Yes, Sir.'

I am confident he has and that he'll follow the SOPs. He's a good man.

I sit forward and raise my right leg to keep the mangled

stump off the ground. It feels surprisingly light, but then again it would because the heaviest bit is missing off the end. The stump is bleeding a little and a clear fluid is running out the end of it. I can see the drips making the soil darker as they land. My hand is starting to bleed.

I try not to move my right hand because I don't want to damage it any more. I lean back on my elbows and then by pulling with my left leg I am able to crawl and shuffle back to the seat of the explosion. It's only a metre or so. I have to know what kind of mine caused my injuries.

My mind races. I'll be lucky to get out of here alive. One of the blokes must have missed a mine. This is the first time in the eighteen months they have been working they have ever missed a mine. I start to laugh. The irony is too much.

I have always tried to lead by example and I've always said that if one of my blokes missed a mine I wanted to be the first to know and I am, so I can't complain!

I wonder what happened? Perhaps someone came in last night and deliberately laid it to catch somebody today.

If it was a PMN, which has a large amount of metal, then the deminer should definitely have found it, so that will be an error of drill. The PMN usually leaves fragments in the ground which allow it to be identified. These are a rubber sealing ring the size of a washer, some metal fragments and occasionally particles of the Bakelite housing. The Portuguese 969 leaves virtually nothing behind and so far we have only found these two mines in this area so it's likely that it's one of them.

As I reach the hole I sense a burning in my left ankle. I look down and see that my sock has melted to the flesh and is soaked in a mixture of blood and plasma. I wonder what other injuries I haven't registered yet. It's a race against time. I must check the hole before the pain overtakes me and while I can still speak.

I reach forward with my left hand and feel the soft soil. The hole is deep. A mine found with a locator and destroyed in situ using explosives leaves a much shallower crater than a mine detonated underground when somebody steps on it.

Even taking this into consideration the crater looks very deep so it may have been below detector range.

I sift through the powdery soil in the crater. The soil does not feel as hot as I thought it would, which again points to the fact that it may have been a very deep and powerful explosion.

I sift the soil with my fingers and find no PMN fragments. I feel a surge of relief. At least it wasn't a PMN. There is such a lot of metal in a PMN that if one was missed it would mean the deminer made a mistake. It is likely the missed mine was a 969, which might well have been out of detector range.

My mind is racing. Everything is happening in slow motion. My left sock has melted to my ankle and is smarting like hell. I laugh. The least serious injury hurts the most. Now I feel a scalding soreness all over my legs and right arm. What's left of my right hand is a raw ache. I must not give into the pain.

The medics will be here soon so I must get myself into the safest position for them to pick me up. I shuffle back on my elbows pushing with my left foot. I only need to go a metre.

I lie back on the shortly clipped bush grass of the safety lane and I feel as if I'm burning. The right sleeve and leg of my thick cotton boiler suit are shredded to rags, but it seems to have done its job of keeping flash burns to a minimum.

I look at my forearm and I can see the veins, which normally stick out strong and greeny blue, have almost disappeared. I know I'm going into shock. My throat is consumed with a burning thirst. It is on fire. It is getting worse. Sleep beckons. I know I could just drift away and die.

I hear a shocked moan behind me. The medic looks at me with wide staring eyes. He puts the trauma pack down and stares briefly in horror at the stump of my leg. I wonder what other injuries I have? I have been wearing body armour and eye protection. At least I can see and I know I have no stomach injuries.

I wonder if I've had my balls blown off.

The thought is terrifying and I fight off a rising surge of panic. As I face the prospect I tell myself it doesn't matter because I'll still be the same person inside. That's the truth. I thrust my hand between the popper buttons of my fly and pull up my boxer short elastic. I peer down and see blood around my groin.

I gently put my hand down.

I breathe deeply. I check the bits. They're bleeding slightly, but everything is still intact. Thank you God! Having completed the internal boxer shorts inspection I really must give thanks to the Almighty. Things could be worse.

I sit up and look at what's left of my right leg. The limp pink flesh clings to the stick of jagged, blasted bone and it's losing fluid fast. So is my mangled right hand and my left ankle. I feel like I'm on fire.

Even if they pump saline into me I'll probably die of shock before I get to hospital.

I lie back and look up at the butterfly-blue sky.

They say when you're dying your life flashes before you. It's not quite like that, but I'm acutely aware of my surroundings, of the people I've known, my friends and family, the places I've been to and the things I've done. They all seem to merge into one.

When I went for my initial interview in London, Guy showed me photographs of a faded wooden schoolhouse and a sandy playground. Nobody knew the play area had been mined until three children lost both legs. I recall hollow-eyed amputees begging and bereft of dignity. I remember the smell and the emptiness in their eyes.

I frequently visited the clean Red Cross hospital in Cambodia where Martin worked. Long lines of beds containing frightened amputees stretched endlessly like graves in a First World War cemetery. I remember the kindness and decency of those who treated them.

Everything seems to make complete sense, and yet I didn't think my life would end like this. I'm so tired. All I want to do is sleep. I know that if I do there will be no pain. I'm not ready to die, but the silent siren beckons. It's the easy option. No pain, no disability, no credit card bills.

I'm dying. In this moment I have to pray. I manage to whisper, 'God help me.'

I lie back and wait but I'm not sure what for. A vision of the future perhaps. A sign that all will be well?

There's nothing. Nothing at all.

I'm looking into the abyss.

Suddenly I'm swept over the edge by a rush of pain. My lower right leg feels as though it's being cut off with a blowtorch. I grit my teeth and take slow, deep breaths. I will not cry out. I'm not the first or the best, but I remember Captain Wiltshire's memorial on the church wall.

Yesterday the whole team was running up and down here. Being blown up in a cleared lane is unbelievable. They've never missed a mine. It's like being struck by lightning. It was either below detector range, deliberately laid last night to get someone today, or one of the blokes didn't do what he was told. I'm always so careful. How could it happen? Why me?

But that's a real loser's attitude. Life's not fair. I chose to be here and I'm still the man in charge. The buck stops with me.

I take another look at the stump. I've got to get used to it. It's not going to grow back. I've also ruined my best pair of shoes.

I sit up. The two medics have laid out the orange stretcher next to me. The good thing about these plastic fold-up stretchers is that it's easy to wash the blood and crap off. They reach over. I think this is going to hurt. They lift me up gently and put me on the stretcher. I'm surprised they take so much care. I can't feel anything except the burning in my throat. It's like someone's poured petrol down my gullet and set fire to it.

Sam comes running down the lane. He stops by my side and looks at me, wide-eyed. His mouth is half-open, as if he's trying to speak, but can't find the words. After a second he manages, 'Don't worry, Sir. We'll get you out of here.'

I keep asking him not to call me 'Sir'.

'I got through to the US AID helicopter on the radio. It's lucky he's close. He said we should take you to the other side of the airfield and wait.'

They carry me slowly back down the lane. Ahead I can see a few deminers running down to help. Their expressions show shock and confusion. Some of them start to moan. Apart from that everything is silent. This is now a high risk area. If there was one mine here there could be more. Our SOPs state it should only be the medics and the commanders involved in a CASEVAC. The others should not be here. I'm losing it; I should have said something as soon as I saw the first man. I'm still the programme manager. Sometimes there are accidents during evacuation because people panic. I lift up my head and shout, 'Stop.'

Everyone freezes. I turn to Sam. 'Get everyone out of here and close this site. Nobody goes down this lane unless you dig the whole bloody thing up. Switch to digging. Get them out of here now.'

Sam's a good man. I like him a lot. He shouts a few instructions, everyone does what he says; the medics pick up the stretcher and carry on.

If it wasn't for the pain, the fire in my throat and the fact that I think I'm dying the stretcher would be quite comfortable. I lie back and look at the sky again. I know I must get to hospital. Once I get there I'll be fine. All I have to do is get back to base. They'll warn the hospital. Do they know? I lean up and speak to Sam. 'You did send the CASREP didn't you?'

'Yes, Sir. Rupert will be waiting at the hospital. Just relax.'

I lean back. I'm burning hot and getting hotter. I'm dying of thirst. I lift my body armour up slightly to try to get some air. I'm dying of thirst. I must have some fluid. It's like I'm breathing in flames. I must have some fluid. I lift my body armour up and feel my guts. There's no blood and they feel okay. The kevlar's done its job. I have no peritoneal injuries. I can drink. I'm so hot. I have to stop sweating. I should take it off. 'Sam, can you take my armour off? I'm so hot.'

They stop and gently put me down. I sit up and reach to my lower back to undo the Velcro strap. They help me. The medic's good. They're kind. I feel slightly cooler, as if I've moved from a gas grill on 'high nine' to one that's on 'high seven'. But my throat's getting worse. I turn my head to look for Sam. He's by my side. I look at him and say, 'Please give me some water. My throat's on fire.'

He shakes his head. 'I'm sorry, I can't. You're not supposed to let the casualty drink.'

'But I have no stomach injuries, so you can. I must get some fluid in. It's okay. Please, I'm dying.'

Sam stares at me and shakes his head. He looks close to tears. 'I'm sorry, Sir, I can't.'

I'm not being fair to him. By conventional thinking he's doing the right thing. But I know I have no stomach injuries so I know I can drink. I'll have to get them to put the drip lines into me before my veins go down. I look at my arm. Shit I can't see my veins. 'Get me to the helicopter.'

They pick me up and run. They've lifted me on to their shoulders. I'm really high up. I hope I don't fall off. I can't remember if I wrote in the SOP that stretchers should not be carried at the high port. If I didn't perhaps I should. It's a long way down. I look up at the glorious blue sky. It's getting closer.

My right hand is seriously injured. I cradle it carefully in my left and look at it. It hasn't started to gush, but I know it's bleeding a lot. More importantly it's drenched in plasma. I can feel it trickling down my wrist. I think I've stopped sweating, which means the signal my throat is sending is correct. I'm dying of thirst. I don't want to look at my hand. I know it's shredded. I shouldn't move it. I was carrying a prodder and it got blasted through the palm. I wiggle my fingers gently. They move slightly. Great! I move them again. They still work. That's good news. It'll be repairable.

I want to know where we're going. I lift my head and look ahead. There are trees and the grass is long. We're nearly there. I lie back and look at the sky again. The blue is getting more and more beautiful.

My watch was on my right wrist, but now it's gone. I've lost my watch. It was supposed to be a high-quality Swiss indestructible. Probably not quite as indestructible as it needed to be.

I measure time in breaths. I am lucky still to be breathing.

I've lost count of the number of breaths. I am being lowered. I try and raise my head. I see the outline of a shiny yellow, black and white helicopter, incongruous among the African trees and long grass. It is silent, ready and waiting. How strange, it's as if they've been expecting me.

The chopper door is open and the front left seat has been taken out. The stretcher bearers' pace slows and they lower their load. I prop myself up on my left elbow and look ahead. The pilot is standing directly in front. He's a good bloke and I like him a lot, although we've only briefly met. It's lucky he's here.

'Don't worry we'll have you out of here in no time.' He looks at my injuries and I think he goes slightly pale. I can't imagine I look good.

He says, 'Right, lie Chris on the left side. I've already taken the seat out. The medic gets in on the right behind me.' He glances back at me, narrows his eyes slightly and bites his lip. 'Don't worry, we'll get you there soon.'

I think he's trying not to let me know I look like shit. It's kind of him, but I know the score.

The burning intensifies. The fire in my throat is spreading through my chest. I'm getting weaker and all I want to do is sleep. I think dying must feel like this. I sit up and look at Sam. 'Tell the medic to get two lines into my arms and run in the Ringer's solution as fast as he can. I don't want to die from lack of fluid.'

I watch as Frank explains. The medic, nods. He knows the drills. The reason we didn't stabilize in the lane was because I told them not to. I decided it was a high-risk area and ordered everybody out. I was worried it would be hard to control the blokes. They'd all come to see what was happening.

I can hear the pilot behind me. 'That's it. Lie the seat cushions in the front.'

The medic puts on clean surgical gloves and rips open the sterile dressing package. He places a field dressing gently on my hand, wraps the ends around my wrist and ties them together. The dressing starts to show a red stain.

The pilot walks round, checks the helicopter and tells everyone where he wants them for take off. He says, 'I'm ready as soon as the medic is done.'

I look down. I struggle for composure and fight the pain. The stump of my leg is losing a lot of fluid, but it's not bleeding, it's been cauterized by the blast. There's no need to dress it. When a mine goes off the explosion drives soil, bits of bone and shoe into what's left of the limb. Strictly speaking I should get it dressed, but I know they'll have to cut it off a long way above the bit that's missing. What I really need is a hospital and antibiotics to control the spread of infection.

It's my leg and I'm still in charge. We won't bother to wait for the medic to dress it. I shout, 'Don't worry about the leg dressing, it's not bleeding. Let's go. He can put the drip lines into me in the helicopter. He must do that.'

I watch the medic as Sam explains. He nods. He knows what he's doing. He was a FRELIMO medic. I think the East Germans trained them. On handover David told me that last year they had two doctors out here doing six months' medical training and supervision each and they also had several nurses providing first aid and refresher training. I'm in good hands.

They lift the stretcher and take me to the side of the helicopter. The faded blue of the deminers' uniforms is all around me, like a curtain. I'm going down. They're so careful it doesn't even bump.

They lift me clear and start to feed what's left of my legs through the door. I try to help but strong arms pull me back. The medic smiles. I'm helpless. They alter the angle slightly. I get ready to try to raise my right leg. I don't want to bang the stump.

The pilot shouts, 'Pull him back, bend his legs back at the knees and then sit him in.' He used to be in the Army Air Corps. I'm lucky he is around.

I try to help but they've already started to move me out and bend my legs. The best thing I can do is relax. I'm lifted sideways. I feel my backside on the floor of the helicopter. As the arms release me I put my left hand on the floor and push forwards so I can lie down. The limbs sting and smart and the blasted bones ache deeper than I could have imagined pain could be felt and all the time it seems to be getting worse.

I lie back. My head isn't quite on the cushion. Kind hands gently lift my head and move the padding so my neck is no longer tilted back.

'Right, everyone back over there,' the pilot says. 'Saul, you make sure they're all out of the way. I'm taking off.'

When everyone is clear of the rotors he checks the controls and flicks a series of switches. I look at the medic and nod encouragingly. The helicopter belongs to USAID and it's only been in this area a few days. I don't think it's flown before.

The pain is getting worse. I want to scream and I'm afraid I might. I clench my teeth and take deep breaths. The rotors start to turn and the engine noise gets louder. The pilot looks at me. I can't quite see his face, but I think he's doing a visual to ensure the casualty is calm and not going to interfere with take-off. I lie still.

The tail lifts off first, then we're airborne. The grass shimmers in the downdraft and we start to rise above the trees.

The noise is deafening.

The burning in my throat is getting worse. I would not have believed it possible. The medic is by my side and starts to open his orange bag. David did a good job finding those and buying them from South Africa.

He gets out two drip lines and two clear plastic bags of Ringer's solution. He unzips an inner pocket, removes a shiny metal hook and carefully loops it through the radio headset hook on the roof.

He puts on another pair of clean surgical gloves and picks up the drip line and needle. I clench my teeth again and breathe faster and faster. My throat burns more fiercely with each breath. I move my head from side to side and try not to cry out.

I look out of the window and watch the trees fly past beneath us. We're flying over the bush. We still have a long way to go. I force myself to lie still. I'm getting weaker and weaker. All I want to do is go to sleep and escape from this.

I turn my head back to the medic. He's put the needles in my elbow joints and I didn't even feel them. All I want to do is cry, 'Water. Water. Please give me water,' but I can't speak.

My throat is too dry and my voice doesn't work. I'm worried. In books and films people cry for water just before they die from traumatic injury.

I see the trees rush past the side window, then I look up at the sky. I turn back as the medic turns the drip on. Wait, I don't think he's run them through. If he hasn't, the air from the lines will probably kill me. I can't afford to take the chance. I sit up and try to explain, but when I speak nothing happens. My voice still isn't working. I point. He looks at me sympathetically and pats my shoulder. He thinks I'm delirious, shocked out of my wits. He tries to lie me back down. I try to resist, then realize how weak I am.

I have no choice. I lie back. He reaches again for the switch. There's only one thing I can do. I'm fighting for life. I sit up and lash out with my left hand. Then I pull the line from the inside of my right elbow with my left hand. My right hand doesn't work so I bite the hard plastic end of the needle and pull my arm away. It comes out, so I let go with my teeth and watch it drop on to my dirty blood-stained overalls.

I have to put out the fire in my throat. Ringer's solution is isotonic; the same concentration as blood. It's absorbed almost immediately through the gut wall. I have no stomach injuries, so I can drink. It's not standard medical procedure, but I feel like I'm dying from lack of fluid. I've never been closer to the edge of panic.

I hold my right arm awkwardly to the side and reach up with my left. The bag is soft and warm. I push it up and off the loop. Out of the corner of my eye I see the pilot turn his head. He's wondering what's going on. I'm sorry I can't explain.

My mind races. I didn't know I could think this fast. The inferno in my throat is consuming me. I think my head is about to explode.

I am moving my left hand towards my mouth. I watch the

liquid in the clear plastic get closer. It's the elixir of life. I bite through the plastic and the warm liquid floods into my mouth. I tip my head back and gulp greedily. Relief floods through me. It's better than diving into a cool, blue pool on a scorching day.

In a moment, though, I realize that it has not subdued the burning in my gullet, just stopped it getting worse. I must have more.

I sit up and grab the other bag. I bite more carefully this time. My neck and shoulders are wet. I know I should be taking smaller mouthfuls, but I can't help gulping it. I need it so much. Soon it's all gone. I feel a little better, but I'm still thirsty. The poor medic. I turn to him, rub my stomach with my left hand and give him a thumbs up. He understands now. He's using the medical scissors to make a hole in a haemocoel bottle. He passes it across. I hold it to my mouth and drink.

I've had nearly three litres. Now I know I'll get to the hospital alive. I see the bush whizzing past. The nose of the helicopter is pointed down and we're flying several hundred feet clear of the trees. He's going like fury. My leg and hand smart like they've been placed in boiling oil. I don't know how much more of this I can take without passing out. I mustn't go to sleep. I want to cry out and scream. I must fight it. I'm afraid I might let myself down.

I take deep breaths and keep watching the bush zoom underneath. The noise of the helicopter is thunderous and relentless. The landscape and the blue sky float past. I hope we get there soon. I'm not sure how long I can hang on.

My right hand has swollen up. The bandage around the wrist is cutting in. It's throbbing and aching with strangulation. I lift it up to try to undo the bandage ends. I can't do it with one hand. The medic takes it carefully and unties the knot. He slackens it off and re-does it. It feels slightly better.

I hold out my left hand to shake hands. If I'm going to die

I want to bid him farewell; after all he's one of my team and we're on the same continent. I hold his hand and collapse back. The surgical gloved hand has a grip stronger than mine. At least I'm not crying like a baby; even if I'm as helpless as one. Now I truly understand the importance of faith, hope and charity.

I look to the ground again. There are fields and several small houses. We must be getting near to the town. Gradually there are more houses. And a tarmac road. The buildings are white. We circle around for a while and then start to descend. I sit up.

Below there is a blue flat-bed van. Rupert and Marjolaine are standing close by. She's the Action Aid doctor, and like their programme director here, is good news. I sit up straight and give Rupert a thumbs up. I wouldn't want him to think I'm wibbling.

We touch down. Rupert watches and waits. I think the pilot has given him a thumbs up because he's given a thumbs up to the pilot. The engine gets quiet and the rotors stop. He bends down, leans forward and runs under the rotors to the door. He opens it and says, 'Don't worry mate, we'll soon be sitting down having a beer and a chat somewhere cool.' I'm lucky he's switched on. I'm doubly fortunate because he's our best medic.

They start to lift me out carefully. In army first-aid training they always tell you to 'reassure the casualty'. Now I can really understand why. I need desperately for someone to tell me I'm not going to die and that everything will be all right.

Marjolaine looks slightly shocked. I was due to meet her and some other aid workers to talk about medical care in remote rural areas one night this week. This wasn't the plan.

As they lift me out I feel weak and tired, but I have to know. 'Do you think I'm going to die?'

'No,' Marjolaine replies. 'You just won't be quite as pretty as you used to be.'

I've never been called pretty before and it's not high on my list of priorities, so that's all right.

Once we get clear of the helicopter Rupert looks around then gives a thumbs up. The engine whines and the rotors whirl. The chopper rises, turns and then heads back the way it came.

I'm lying on a board in the back of the truck. I'm disorientated. The hospital is the enormous single-storey concrete building nearby. I'm not sure if we're at the front, the back or the side. I lie back and look at the sky.

They put me on a battered trolley and wheel me in. I feel elated. I got here. I knew that if I could make it out of the minefield I'd live. They take me into a white-painted, concrete-walled building. It reminds me of a slaughter house I visited with the Young Farmers' Club many years ago. I think they're speaking to me, but I can't make out what's going on. I know I shouldn't hang around here. I must get on the next flight out to South Africa. That's the drill once the casualty is stabilized.

The trolley is black foamy plastic; the sort that can be sterilized. It's probably quite uncomfortable, but my nervous system is a bit preoccupied right now.

They cut off my clothes. I hear the scissors. They examine the wounds and search for other injuries that are not immediately apparent. Very carefully Marjolaine looks at my hand. They keep talking but I can't hear what people are saying. All these things seem to be happening around me. Rupert goes to check aircraft availability. Marjolaine says, 'We will stabilize you and fly you out as soon as we can. Is there anything you want?'

'I drank two litres of Ringer's solution and a bottle of haemoceol on the helicopter,' I say, 'And I wouldn't let them give me morphine.'

She stares at me with disbelief.

'I was wearing body armour, so I knew I had no peritoneal injuries, and I thought I was dying from lack of fluid.'

'Were you sick?'

'No. It tasted good, and I felt a lot better after I'd drunk it. Would it be possible to have something for the pain?'

'I'm sorry, I can't give you anything. You're going into theatre very soon. It won't be long now.'

She hurries away and I lie back. I'm trying not to think about the pain. On my right there is an African lady with her leg in traction. It looks like a traffic accident. I catch her eye. Here I am, naked and blasted. I must look like something from another planet. There's a cheap cotton curtain pulled around the lower end of the trolley. I have more privacy than I thought.

I hear movement on my right. I turn my head to see a Mozambican dressed in white cotton trousers, smock and apron. The apron and smock sleeves are covered in blood. On top of his head sits a white cotton cap.

He walks to the base of the trolley and produces a pair of scissors from his pocket. He glances at my face, then down at the stump. With his other hand he pulls something near the stump. I didn't think I could possibly feel any more pain, but I was wrong.

I turn my head to look at the woman. She stares back, oblivious. I can feel the scissors cutting through my flesh. The orderly must be tidying up the stump for surgery. I wonder if he knows that I can feel every cut. I wonder if he cares. I lie motionless. I will not cry.

The woman's large brown eyes stare at me vacantly. I turn my head slowly from side to side. As I face her again I wonder if she lay here and watched Orlando die?

Pain stabs into the blasted bone. I take deep, rasping breaths. I keep thinking that the pain can't get worse, but constantly I'm proved wrong. How much longer can this go on?

I'm lucky Marjolaine and Rupert are here. But I don't know this guy and I don't trust him. I'm naked and helpless. What's he doing to me?

I feel the loose pieces of flesh being pulled again. He's cutting off the ragged flaps around the stump. I raise my head slightly. He looks at me ominously for a moment, then gets back to work. He locates a strand of muscle. Beads of sweat prickle on my face. I will not cry out. Each snip of the scissors is like the thrust of a red-hot poker.

Why is he doing this?

He's tidying me up, but he doesn't look like a doctor. Another wave of pain builds and roars. I want to scream, God help me.

They're going to give me a general anaesthetic soon, aren't they? I am suddenly terrified. If they are doing this to me now, what will happen when I'm unconscious?

He stops cutting with the scissors, and starts hacking. I feel the metal tearing at my flesh.

He must have found a big piece of muscle, or a tendon. 'Agh—' I stop myself before I scream. I've had enough. He shouldn't be doing this.

I sit up. If he does it again I'm going to shout for help or punch him.

He turns immediately and walks out, taking the pieces of dirty, severed flesh in a small white enamel kidney-shaped bowl that has a chipped blue rim. Maybe he's taking them for his lunch.

I don't want to be left alone here. When they give me the general anaesthetic I'll be unconscious. If Marjolaine and Rupert aren't around I might die.

I lie back. The woman's expressionless eyes are still locked on to me. I try to smile.

A door rattles somewhere to my right then Rupert appears, dressed in a green theatre gown.

'Rupert,' I blurt out. 'Please don't leave me alone. The hospital porter's just been cutting bits off my stump with scissors. You won't leave me will you?'

'No mate, don't worry. I'll be here all the time.' As always when the shit hits the fan, Rupert's as cool as a cucumber. He's not the sort of bloke to jack his mates. I'll be fine with him and Marjolaine.

I catch a glimpse of her fair hair over Rupert's shoulder.

They wheel me into the operating theatre. Several people in green gowns are talking and getting things ready. I don't understand what's going on, who's doing what. I can't see beyond the pain. I try to be as co-operative as I can.

I feel a rumbling in my guts and then a series of jabbing cramps. I urgently need to have a dump. I turn and look for Marjolaine. She's on my left, speaking to the surgeon. When I look at the medical equipment, they put a sterile cloth over the tools. They don't need to. I've seen the stainless-steel amputation kits before. There's the huge hacksaw, and the coiled wire saw with two metal loop handles. There's also the sharp chisel scoop, the scalpels and the large, coarse-cut files for honing down the bone. I know what's coming.

My stomach cramps. 'I'm sorry to trouble you,' I say weakly, 'but I need to go to the toilet.'

All medical activity stops. There is a stunned silence. She says, 'What, you mean now?'

'Sorry, I urgently need to do a big job.' An ominous gurgling in my guts makes me hold my breath.

She translates into Portuguese. Then there's a frantic flurry of activity. The green clad figures instantly take a few steps backwards. A man on my right, the anaesthetist I think, shouts urgent instructions to someone in the corner.

The orderly in the abattoir uniform ambles towards me,

carrying an enormous stainless-steel bowl. Now he's wearing a surgical mask. He stops and holds out the bowl. What am I supposed to do now?

I'm desperate; I can't hang on any longer. 'Is it all right if I go here?'

'Yes,' she says. 'Can you manage?'

I shift sideways, turn to my right and aim. I'm weak and racked by the burning agony of shattered bone. I avoid going too close to the edge. I'm not going to risk falling over. I feel the side of the bowl cold against my backside.

I relax slightly and prepare for the first controlled explosion. The result is standard. I relax further for the second. Another normal result. I totally relax for the third. Suddenly there is the most enormous detonation, followed by a volcanic gush. It smells revolting. Thank goodness they're all wearing surgical masks.

My guts ache. When it finally stops I reach for several handfuls of the green paper towel that is so useful on these occasions.

Where did it go? Did I miss? No, the floor's clean. I think the overflow has gone down the orderly's white Wellington boots. Oh dear. Life's not always fair. Thank you God.

Somebody helps me wash, then normal medical activity is resumed.

Marjolaine says, 'Because you drank all that fluid I'm going to tube your stomach. It would be dangerous if you vomited under the general. This is a plastic tube with a lump one end. It's sometimes hard to get the tube down. It would help if you can relax and try to swallow once the bulb on the end of the tube reaches the back of your throat.'

Emptying my stomach is easier than trying to rehydrate a corpse. I knew they'd have to do this. I've tube fed a lot of sick calves, so I know how difficult it can be. I lie back as she feeds the clear plastic tube into my mouth. When the large bulbous end touches the back of my throat it makes me gag. I force myself to swallow.

The tube is taken behind my head and I hear the flow of water into a bowl.

A few seconds later someone says, 'Don't worry, you'll be fine. Now we're giving you a general anaesthetic. You won't feel any more pain. You will be okay, don't worry.'

That's what I used to say to sick animals as I stroked them while the vet was putting them down.

I see a small hypodermic, held in an anonymous surgical glove, approaching my forearm. I don't feel the injection. There's a murmur, then Marjolaine says, 'Please count to ten.'

That won't be a problem. They'll probably have to give me two doses. 'One.'

'Two.'

I think there are four people around me in green gowns.

'Three.'

There's Rupert and Marjolaine. The other two must be the surgeon and the anaesthetist.

'Four.'

The smell of disinfectant fills my nostrils. I wonder how many people they've chopped here.

'Five.'

I'm tired.

'Six.'

Yes, more tired than I thought.

'Seven . . .'

17

FLYING

For the first time I feel cool, away from the torturous heat. It is as if the demon tasked with my torment has switched off the blowtorch he has been playing up and down my body and gone for a tea break.

I lie still, drinking the coolness.

Breathing seems hard work, and as I try to blink I realize my eyes don't feel like opening. I try to work out where I am.

I can't smell anything at all.

I am trying to move my head. I can feel something coarse under my chin. What the hell is it? I try to move my left hand. I know there's something wrong with my right hand and I can't use it. I must save my strength. I will not give up. I will fight.

I think it is more sensible to keep still.

'Stay cool,' I say to myself. 'Stay calm.'

I need to work out where I am. I flex the fingers of my left hand; the coarse sensation on my skin is fabric. I struggle to remember. I start to drift and I see and smell the texture of something similar that I have touched before.

I return, momentarily, to a place I used to go in my childhood. I am confused. Then things become clearer and I recognize what I am feeling. It is a blanket.

This is a really good sign. Someone has been kind enough

to put a blanket on me. I am being looked after. I feel a surge of relief, but where am I?

Why is there no heat and pain?

I must work out what to do next. I know I'm on a journey. The important thing is to keep moving in the right direction. I must take stock of where I am.

Today I was blown up, walking in a safety lane.

My lower right leg was blown off. I must get used to not having one.

My hand is bad, too. Really bad.

I'm still surprised that I was blown up in a cleared area. At least I know it wasn't a PMN, because I didn't find the fragments. Oh well, as Forrest Gump says: 'Shit happens.'

I can hear a noise. A deep, vibrating noise.

I still don't feel able to move. I don't know why. It is not sensible to move when you are badly injured. I must stay still and conserve my strength.

I open my eyes and try to focus. I blink. It's dark. There's a green light in front of me. More of a glow than a light. I can also see a small red one.

I can feel the vibration of the noise through the floor that I'm lying on. Why is it dark? It must be night. I turn my head slightly. I can see the dark outline of a seat and a man silhouetted against the green light. I must be in an aircraft. The noise I can hear is the engine. The soft green light is coming from the instrument panel.

Good to know that the engine sounds so powerful. I think it must be a twin-prop. The plane must be going to South Africa. I move my head slightly; someone is next to me. It's the outline of a slim, fit-looking woman.

'Do you have any chest pain?' she asks gently.

I recognize the voice, the Belgian accent. It's Marjolaine, the Action Aid doctor. She's a good egg. I am really lucky. A doctor is looking after me. I try to speak, but my voice doesn't work. I try harder and this time I manage something between a croak and a grunt. 'No.'

Interesting question. I can't understand why she's worried about my chest. Perhaps it's because we are at high altitude. No I'm okay. I'm going to make it. Nothing wrong with my chest. What about her chest? She leans forward slightly and I decide now is probably not a good time to start thinking about that.

'Try to keep your right arm still.'

I nod slightly and grunt. My right arm is motionless and I don't feel able to move it.

'You must tell me if you have any chest pain. Tell me at once.' Strange that she seems so agitated. I feel fine. I can't think what's bothering her. It feels so good not to have the pain. I must have been given morphine. Good stuff this. First time I've ever had it. Seems to work all right. Makes me feel sleepy though . . .

I am conscious again, but somehow things feel different. I know I'm in the aircraft. I remember Marjolaine was speaking before I blacked out. I'm confused. Things feel slightly odd. I look down and I can see her sitting next to me. She looks worried. I can see the pilot flying the plane. And outside, the vastness of the night.

There is a blanket wrapped carefully around me and the clear plastic oxygen mask is held over my face by a thin, white elastic strap. My eyes are closed and I am sleeping. I look calm now. The breathing sounds strange, but it is still happening, so that's good.

I feel as if I have been here before. I think that I am on the way to somewhere familiar, but I am not sure. I drift around for a while and remember going to a place like this when I was a child, a friendly place I sometimes glimpsed when I was saying my prayers before going to sleep. An enormous place with many rooms.

Long distances are short and colours and patterns start to merge.

I turn around and look back.

I drift back into myself and sleep.

I have no idea what time it is, or how long I have been sleeping. The aircraft is dark, except for the green glow. I expect they are giving me oxygen because of the altitude. I know that there is something wrong, in addition to the leg and arm injuries, but I'm not sure what.

The highest vibration of engine and propeller drones on, then seems to fade. The crew seem agitated. We are being swallowed by the African night. Is the night my enemy or my friend? Somehow I am indifferent. It feels as if the darkness is offering me an invitation to join it. I do not wish to go. Oblivion is tempting, but I know I have to stay with the light. Where there is light there is hope.

The plane will get to its destination. I have to believe that I will get to mine. I'm fine now. I'm going to make it.

No, wait. I feel like I am drowning. I am sinking and fighting for breath. God! Don't let me sink. Help me breathe.

Miraculously, it feels as if there is a hand under my chin, just holding my head above the water. I *will* make it. I have done the hardest part. I got out of the minefield. But now I'm tired, so tired . . .

I can hear a man's voice, South African accent. The voice of competence and authority. He sounds like a man who knows what he's doing. 'No, you listen. Clear it now or he's dead. If we don't get clearance now I'll punch any immigration official who gets in my way.'

Now his voice is close, almost conversational. He must be talking with people in the plane. I attempt to open my eyes. I catch sight of an orange boiler suit. Now my eyes are too heavy to stay open. I try to keep listening.

'I think we'll get clearance soon. As soon as we do we'll go and we'll need to be fast. This is life or death, man. I hope we're not too late already.'

This doesn't sound encouraging, but I'm not giving up now. I'm fine. I've got out of the minefield; I'll be all right now. I'll make it.

'We have to get him to the hospital,' Marjolaine says.

'I know. How is he?'

'Still breathing.'

'Good.'

There is shouting in the distance. The South African in the orange overalls says, 'Good,' again and I feel myself being moved. I think they are paramedics.

I feel like I'm being carried. The people moving me are strong and confident. I feel reassured.

I can hear a helicopter. I think I am outside it.

I am fading again, fading fast.

The darkness beckons. I only realize when I start to emerge from it. I have no idea how long I've been unconscious. Time has lost its meaning.

I can hear the helicopter. It's loud. I try to open my eyes. Not as easy as I thought. I try harder. I can see lights. I feel a slight bump. I think the helicopter has landed. Now I am being lifted. I must be on a stretcher on the outside of the helicopter for them to get at me so quickly.

I can see bright lights around me, or are they above? My ears are filled with noise. I can feel the heat of the engine and the draught from the rotors on my face. I smell aviation fuel.

Capable hands lift me on to a trolley and almost instantly we are moving. I can see the back of a man and a woman on each side of the trolley in front of me. They are leaning low and running as we go beneath the rotors.

There are bright lights ahead and a large building. The ground must be smooth for them to be able to run with the trolley. These nurses must be running really fast.

I hear a thud. Then there is a slight scraping noise. It must be the trolley going through the plastic swing doors. There is a clean, antiseptic smell.

All I can see are the lights above me. They are going by very fast. This is confusing. The lights are above me. I must be looking at the corridor ceiling. It is clean and white and new.

If only breathing weren't so hard. I feel as if I am sinking. I try to move. It is hard . . . too hard.

I have no idea how long I have been unconscious. The last thing I remember was arriving at the hospital. Now all I know is the brightness of the light.

I turn my head slightly to avoid the glare. As I turn it further I see two beautiful blonde women, dressed entirely in white.

I blink.

They are dressed entirely in white and they are smiling. They must be angels. I have died and gone to Heaven.

I look at them again and smile. Thank goodness I went to church. Heaven is just as I hoped it would be. They're blonde and beautiful. Thank God!

My rejoicing is interrupted by a professional, male voice.

This isn't how I imagined God would sound.

'Hello, my name is Dr Ken Boffard. You are in Milpark Hospital, Johannesburg. You have been injured and we're going to take care of you. We're starting off by putting some blood into you, because you seem to have lost rather a lot.'

I feel someone putting a needle into my forearm, but it doesn't hurt.

'I hear that you used to be in the British army. I did some medical training with them.'

I'm feeling sleepy. I can't keep my eyes open any longer.

I almost touch a beautiful blue sleep, but it flits away, out of my grasp, like a butterfly.

Pain sears my right leg. It's agony beyond imagination. My

right hand feels like it's being held against an angle grinder. The burning is a memory now. This new, raw pain is worse.

There is darkness all around me.

I am floating, lost in silent space.

Suddenly I'm zooming downwards, down, down, down.

The airfield and the ghostly skeletons of the military buildings rush towards me. The small town and road disappear. They are real and important, but not relevant to the destination of this demon-driven journey.

I can see the family's bleached, broken bones. We're not sure, but we think the remains are of two adults, a child and a baby. It was probably an olive-green OZM72. One of them initiated it, either by snagging a trip wire and pulling out the retaining pin, or by stepping on the prongs and exerting more than three kilograms of direct pressure. The base charge fired it a metre into the air and then it exploded, showering lethal metal fragments across a thirty-metre radius. One adult skull is more or less intact. They say someone took the other.

The trees and bushes around the airfield fill my vision. The short clipped grass is a dry green-brown. The ground is uneven and there are occasional hollows and holes. This used to be a rubbish tip, not that any of the poor souls who once scratched a living here could afford to throw anything away.

I look around me. There is evil here, hiding in the shadows. It lurks, always watching and waiting for a hapless victim to cross its path. I keep looking, but I can't see it.

I force myself to wake from the nightmare. I know I must be dreaming, but I can't escape. I'm held in this nightmare and I must try to escape. I force my eyes open. Bathed in green light, one of the angels sits by my side.

I relax and slumber grabs me again. I avoid the shadows now, and stick to the light. I turn around and suddenly I'm out of the wood and walking into a large building. There's a party. The sound of raucous laughter. The air is heavy and hot.

I walk past the bar. There's a waiter carrying drinks. I bump into him and say sorry. He offers me the tray. I take a cool glass of water with three small ice cubes floating in it. It's so good because my throat is dry. I put the empty glass back on the tray and walk on.

I'm in a hurry. I must find them. There are people I know. I have to find them and speak to them. I need to ask them to do something urgently. People could be blown up. They could be maimed and killed. I have to stop it. I must warn them. They can't hear me. I shout louder and louder, but they're deaf. I keep trying but I can't make myself heard. I try to show them, but they won't look. I keep shouting.

I can't work fast enough. The phone keeps ringing. I rush off to answer it and return each time to a bigger stack of paper. I pick it up now, and move to a bigger room.

People keep interrupting, which is a shame, because I've got so much to do. Not to worry, I'm getting through the work faster now. I reach forward and rearrange the papers and stack the boxes. I'm sorting things out.

There is so much to do. I should stay and watch the blokes, but there's no time. I have to leave; there is a job that must be done up north.

Suddenly the guard runs in, shouting and screaming. He says there's a traffic warden coming. All hell breaks loose. People run around screaming and trying to hide. Eventually I calm them down and find out that they've parked all our Land Rovers outside on the street. There are no parking restrictions in the town, but the provincial government employed him because they thought they ought to.

In Africa, corruption is occasionally a problem. I assume the warden took the job for the bribes. Then I think again. Maybe he started as a man of principle, but gradually let the tentacles of temptation take hold.

I run out the door to move the vehicles, but I emerge at the airfield. I'm confused. What's going on? I walk along the path and suddenly, whoosh, I'm lifted up so that I can see all around me. The panorama of trees, buildings and bushes stretches ahead. I look down. All I can see is the sandy dusty soil between the clumps of grass.

Suddenly there is the blast of an explosion. All I can feel is the force, the thunderous boom. Then everything is quiet. But it is the uneasy silence that follows devastation, a brief calm between storms.

Another explosion follows. It's so loud it hurts my ears.

There's a tense pause, then another monstrous blast.

I'm blown up again and again, caught in a time warp.

I'm dreaming. I must be dreaming, but I don't know how to wake up.

'Mr Moon,' a voice is calling.

I want to answer, but I can't wake up and I can't speak.

I'm being flayed alive. I never thought anything could be this bad. My fingers feel like they're being shredded on an acid-covered cheese grater. The palm of my hand is being worked on with a red-hot chisel. I try to move it and there's an explosion of pain. I move it more slowly. The pain eases a fraction.

'Mr Moon.' A man's voice.

'Mr Moon, can you hear me?'

It must be the doctor. I try to speak, but only manage to groan. My eyes are too heavy to open.

'Can you hear me?' he says again.

I force a shaky reply, 'Yes.'

'You're in hospital in South Africa. You were injured in an explosion. Do you remember?'

'Yes. I had my lower right leg blown off.'

'That's right. I'm the surgeon looking after you and I have to tell you that I have just amputated your right hand four inches below the wrist. There was a remote chance we could have saved it, but it would probably never have functioned. Reconstruction surgery would have taken over two years and it was likely that it would then have had to be amputated anyway.'

I'm curiously relieved. He's told the truth straight away, and I still have a life. I want to get out of here as soon as I can and get back to work. I don't want to spend the next two years in limbo. It's far better to get rid of it now than mess around. I've heard people get phantom pain after an amputation. That's why my hand hurts. I say, 'Thank you. I want to get back to work as soon as I can.'

I'm tired and fogged by sleep.

'Are you in pain?' he asks.

I say, 'Yes, it's quite sore.'

'We'll give you another morphine injection.' He turns to give instructions to someone behind him. I think it's a nurse.

I try to open my eyes, but I'm too tired. I can't feel the syringe. The doctor speaks again. 'You'll probably have strange dreams because you have a very low haemoglobin count. We're trying to get it back up as fast as we can. Don't worry, it's quite normal. If you need any help at all just call for the nurses. They'll be close by.' His competent voice fades into the shadows, or is it me who's leaving?

The night is full of confusion, pain and strange dreams. I fly back to the minefield and see the crater and hear the deafening explosion again and again.

The pain in my leg consumes me. I think I must have moaned. The nurse speaks through the darkness. 'Are you in pain?'

I try to speak. I say a few words and now I'm full of shame. I think I may have let myself down. Did I swear when I described how my leg felt? As I try to remember, sharp teeth gnaw at my right hand. I fade back to sleep.

I open my eyes to a grey-green light. It must be daytime. I

don't know how long I've slept. It could be morning or afternoon. I'm in hospital. This is intensive care, so they must keep the curtains closed to see the heart monitors. I move my left arm. Soft, warm tubes brush against it. A blood bag hangs on a stainless-steel hook above me. I watch the bright blood drip into the reservoir.

I put my hand to my face. I feel something plastic. It must be an oxygen mask. I don't know why they're giving it to me. A new nurse and somebody else approach my bedside. The nurse says, 'Hello. How are you? Do you feel that you want to pee, but can't?'

How could she know that? I need to and I can feel the pressure building up, but I can't go. I sit up slightly and nod.

'That's the effect of the morphine. We'll need to put a catheter in.'

Now I understand. I should have remembered. As I lie back the sensation of a large tube being inserted into a tract designed for one-way traffic of an easy flowing fluid is unmistakable. The discomfort then gives way to relief as I feel my bladder emptying. Then the stumps tingle and writhe. It must be the nerves. It wasn't as bad as I thought, but then again, nothing ever is. These people know what they're doing. I'm so lucky to be in a good hospital.

I must rest and get better. The back of the bed is raised, so I'm almost sitting up on the pillows. It makes it easier to breathe. I can't understand why I'm still so short of breath. I can feel a thick plastic sheet between me and the mattress. It's warm. I'm covered by a sheet and a grey woollen blanket with small airtex holes.

I wonder what time it is?

Where did my watch go?

I think I was wearing it on my right wrist. The nurse is sitting at a desk. Monitors, consoles, charts and patients records surround her. Every bed in intensive care is clearly visible from her control point. The other medical staff walk between the beds, tending the silent patients. Am I the only one who's conscious? She glances up at me several times then asks, 'Are you waking up?'

I reply uncertainly.

'Relax and take it easy. Can you remember what's happened to you and why you're here?'

'Yes.' I glance at the white bandage around the stump of my forearm. It's strange to think that until yesterday my strong right hand was there and now it's gone for ever. But I'm still alive and I have to concentrate on getting fit. I have to get on with it and I can only do it alone.

'Your boss is on the phone asking how you are. The cable is just long enough to reach you. Would you like to talk to him?'

I sit up further and nod. Right now there's no one else I'd rather talk to. I know he won't get emotional and he's one of the few people who will understand my way of dealing with all this. I'm not sure what to do about the oxygen mask so I pull down the elastic slightly to speak. 'Hello, I'm fine thanks. Still alive and I've got an arm and leg the other side so I don't really see what all the fuss is about.' I hope I don't sound too brittle.

'We've heard that you're coping amazingly well. Sue is in constant touch with your family. They've taken it very well and are fine. Is there anything you want?'

I'm quick to respond. 'I don't want to cause any trouble and I don't want anybody to come out here. I just want to get fit quietly. I knew that if I got out of the minefield alive I'd be fine. Thanks to you and everyone for getting me to such a good hospital.'

Before going I'm made to promise that if I want anything I'll let him know. He tells me that Guy the HALO field director's sister, Caroline, will pop in to check everything is all right because she lives nearby.

The nurse in charge comes over. Her badge tells me her name is Mandy. She asks if I have any clothes, which makes me realize that I'm naked. Not that it matters, I'm covered by the bedclothes. I look at my chest. Several sensors are stuck on with medical tape. The electrical leads disappear into a machine on my left. She glances at the monitor and says everything looks good. I turn my head and can just see a series of fluctuating lines. I can't begin to work out what they all are.

From the bottom of the bed she lifts up my small green daypack. 'The hospital administrator has put your passport in the safe. This was sent with you.'

She unzips the bag and passes me a pair of glasses. 'Now you're waking up you might want these.'

Well done Rupert. Thanks for packing me some kit. I reach out for them and then realize I'm trying to use my right hand. Mandy pretends not to notice. Examination of the lenses reveals pit marks and a thick dusty film with occasional lumpy white specks.

She pulls out several T-shirts and a pair of shorts. 'I'm going home now. I'll take these and wash them and I'll get my husband to come and have a chat. He's a medic in the Defence Force so you'll have a lot in common.'

I thank her. She tells me not to mention it, puts the bag within reach of my left hand and disappears. When I get fit again I'll try and do something for people who aren't as lucky as I am.

The material on the lenses fascinates me. I pick off several white particles. They feel hard as I roll them between my fingers. I think they must be bits of bone. Unfortunately they're not big enough to keep as a souvenir. I touch the small holes in the lenses. The toughened plastic did a great job. Attempts to clean them on the sheet prove unsuccessful so I put them back in the bag and use my spare pair.

Periodically the nurses check my monitor, then fill out

charts and tick boxes in the folder at the base of the bed. The surgeon returns. I wonder when he gets time to sleep?

He wants to know if I'm in pain. It's not so bad now, it just feels like someone's peeling my toes and holding an electric sander on my hand. I tell him it's a bit sore and he prescribes a self-administering intravenous hand pump. It's designed so patients can't overdose themselves, and self-administration is thought to be more efficient.

I enjoy the luxury of time to think. I realize that for the last few years I've always been so busy. I remember a passage from one of my favourite books, *To Kill A Mocking Bird* by Harper Lee. It's the story of a lawyer's struggle for justice amid the prejudice and violence of Deep South USA in the 1930s. He sends his fourteen-year-old son to read to an ancient, cantankerous morphine addict with a terminal illness who wants to break the habit. After she dies he explains why he sent him, saying, 'I wanted you to see what real courage is, instead of getting the idea that courage is a man with a gun in his hand. It's when you know you're licked before you begin but you begin anyway and you see it through no matter what. You rarely win, but sometimes you do. Mrs Dubose won, all ninety-eight pounds of her. According to her views, she died beholden to nothing and nobody.'

I don't want to be dependent. Once they take the pump out I won't take any painkillers. I'm just going to have to get my brain around phantom pain. For all I know I could have it for the rest of my life.

I'm surprised, but very grateful the doctor can spare a few minutes to talk to me. I want to understand what's happened. I explain to him that the most terrifying thing about being blown up was the burning in my throat and the weakness I felt when I thought I was dying from lack of fluid. I tell him how I was certain I had no peritoneal injuries because I wore body armour, which was why I decided to drink the drips. He says it's unconventional, but right on the basis that I'm still alive. He checks my ears for blast damage and says it should repair. He also tells me I have some blast damage to the lungs, which will heal, and that I was very fortunate to survive such a massive loss of blood.

'A healthy man has a haemoglobin count of sixteen. If it drops rapidly to below four, as a result of traumatic injury, it's usually fatal. Yours was two when you arrived. It's miraculous that you survived.' He says with a smile.

He says he was sorry he didn't get the chance to meet Marjolaine and the pilot.

I float through the day, unaware of time, but grateful to escape the discomfort in brief periods of sleep. As I wake up and emerge from my dreams I fight the temptation to deny that anything's happened. All I really want to do is go back to sleep and pretend I'm somewhere else and that I still have all my limbs. I know it's not healthy though, so each time I force myself awake and feel the thick bandaged stump of my right arm before trying to sleep again.

Somebody offers me some water. I don't want it, but I think it would be a good idea. Under supervision I force myself to take a few sips.

They bring me the phone again and ask if I want to speak to Helen from Cambodia. She's an old friend doing a socio-economic study on the effects of antipersonnel mines. She sounds astonished to hear me. 'Are you all right? What happened?'

'I'm still alive and I'm not sure. I was walking down the cleared lane and put my foot on something that went bang.'

'That's what the lads in Battambang guessed had happened.' The phone line from Cambodia crackles. 'They send you all the best.'

We chat for a while. It's great to hear from her. Although I've just said something, I can't remember what it was. It must be the drugs. Plus I'm quite tired.

After a brief sleep I phone home to reassure everyone I'm fine. I explain to my parents that I don't want any fuss and I want a bit of peace and quiet to recover. My mother sounds a bit excited, but I suppose that's natural. The next thing I need is some South African currency. I phone my sister, who is an accountant, and ask her to transfer some cash through to the hospital. Last year I gave her power of attorney for my bank account, which was definitely a good idea.

Day merges into night and I snatch brief periods of sleep. The hospital routine starts early in the morning and a nurse whom I haven't met before tells me she'll be looking after me today. I keep thinking I understand everything that's going on and that I remember what happened yesterday, but I don't think I do, because for the first time I notice a plastic clip with a black plastic lead attached to my finger. I follow the cable to the monitor and play with the clip. It falls off and a nurse rushes in, asks me if I'm still alive and puts it back on again.

I can't eat yet, but I'm allowed orange juice. It's cool, fresh and invigorating and throughout the day the nurse makes trips to the kitchen to keep me well supplied.

Caroline, who is Guy's sister, pops in and says hello and checks to see that there's nothing I need. I'm quite drowsy and probably not very good conversation, but it's great to speak to somebody with a similar perspective on life. The nurse told me earlier that I'd feel confused for a while. I think someone else has visited who gives me a carved wooden owl. It's beautiful.

When I wake several hours later the nurse asks if I want to watch television. I hadn't noticed the set in the corner of the room. I watch an educational programme on small builders constructing houses in the South African townships and then one on how to set a table and eat with a knife, fork and spoon.

I go back to sleep and emerge into day three in intensive care. The nurses are washing me with large soapy flannels, which they rinse and then rub the soap off. Soft towels skilfully dab and dry. I feel much fresher. Somehow they change the sheets without moving me out of the bed. I'm not sure how they do it; it's like a well-rehearsed party trick.

I try to avoid giving myself a pump of morphine and search for sleep.

There is a stabbing, nerve-shredding pain in my right hand, except that it's not there. I try to think. Nerves from the hand have been severed and are sending confused messages to the brain. It's therefore logical to assume that real stimulation of the nerves in the stump should counteract the phantom pain. Carefully I lift my left hand, making sure the plastic thing on my finger stays in place, and then whack the stump of the arm against it.

Shit, I've done it too hard. I hold my breath and wait for the pain to subside. I gently massage the stump. The phantom pain subsides and I relax.

A woman approaches, carrying several sheets of paper. She introduces herself as the hospital administrator. She hands over some faxes and lends me a few books to read. People are so kind. The faxes are from friends. Most of them are humorous, particularly the ones from the military.

I get a call from Ken. He's an Australian who ran the vehicle fleet for the UN in Northern Mozambique. He only left a few weeks ago and now he's in South Africa with a large engineering company. In spite of working long hours and his plan to travel the rest of Africa as soon as possible, he says he's coming in to see me.

The day moves in and out of focus. The television news is disturbing. There were shootouts in the townships. The pictures show a bloodstained road and the devastated aftermath of hand grenades and AK 47s. People are screaming and wailing for the dead. The newsreader says, 'The taxi was crammed with people when a car drew alongside. Passengers in the car then raked the taxi with automatic fire and threw several grenades before speeding away. This is the latest outrage in the taxi wars.'

The nurse fills out the mysterious health charts at the foot of the bed and takes my temperature.

'That's terrible. It's all linked to gangs and crime. This place is becoming more and more violent.' With my teeth clamped to the thermometer I ask her to tell me more. I'm shocked to learn that some nurses in hospitals near the townships are so fed up with seeing the results of violent crime that they're leaving nursing. As she checks the thermometer and finishes the charts she says, 'The police are really good though. They get officers there right away when patients attack medical staff.'

Ken arrives and we amuse ourselves thinking up exchanges relating to my change in physique. My favourite is, 'Pull yourself together man. Didn't you see the sign that said don't feed the crocodiles?' He's cheerful and down to earth. He asks the nurse when I'm allowed to have a beer. The answer is some time next week, which will be when he returns from his work in Tanzania. Before leaving he gives me his contact numbers and insists that if I need anything I should call.

I doze and watch television.

A smiling, white-bearded face appears. 'Hello, I'm the hospital counsellor. In cases of traumatic amputation it's hospital policy for me to talk to all patients.'

My initial reaction is to tell him I'm fine, that I don't and won't have any problems coping and I don't want to waste his time when there are others who probably need his help. I pause, and on reflection decide this would be a defensive reaction, indicating poor judgement, emotional instability and a certain lack of intelligence.

I explain that I still don't really understand how I was

A PARTIALLY UNCOVERED PMN2 MINE. (*John Rodstead*)

PMN mine. (*John Rodstead*)

A PMN MINE, PARTIALLY UNCOVERED. (*John Rodstead*)

A Chinese Type 72A mine. (*John Rodstead*)

DEMINER CLEARING AROUND A CHAPEL IN MOZAMBIQUE.

MOZAMBIQUAN FAMILY AT THE GRAVE OF THEIR ELDEST CHILD,
WHO WAS KILLED BY A MINE THE DAY AFTER THEY RETURNED TO THEIR
VILLAGE FROM A REFUGEE CAMP IN MALAWI.

▲ Deminers working in Northern Mozambique.

◄ Demolition training in Northern Mozambique. (The author considers this his most photogenic angle!)

Explosion caught on camera in a remote area of Northern Mozambique.

Day 4, Milpark Hospital, Johannesburg – when I realized my dreams of entering the world arse-kicking contest might now be unobtainable.

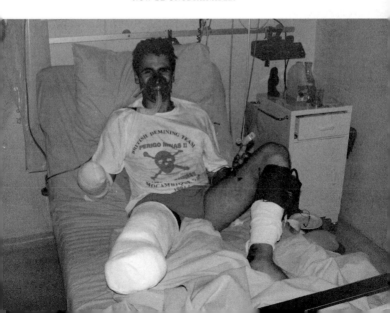

PREPARING
TO RUN THE
LONDON
MARATHON,
APRIL 1996.

HAVING COMPLETED
THE LONDON MARATHON
WITH BOB COPSEY.

blown up, that I'm quite happy to talk about it and the reason I don't want my nearest and dearest rushing to see me is because I need peace and quiet to recover, and I don't like fuss. I realize that all this has come out in a bit of a rush.

As he sits down I see he's wearing a skullcap. He must be Jewish. I make a mental note not to make any jokes about how close I came to circumcision. He says, 'Do you always think about things so much?'

'Yes, but at the moment because I'm drugged and slightly under the weather, it takes me longer to crank up the brain, so it's more noticeable.' I ask him about himself. He's an interesting man and the first psychiatrist I've met. I'm relieved to find he has a sense of humour and we seem to have a similar outlook on life. He's surprised I'm more concerned about how the mine was missed than I am about my injuries. It's easy to explain. I was there because I've had the privilege of doing something I passionately believe is right. Most mine victims don't have the luxury of choice.

Our conversation is similar to the one I had with Ken, except that we're spending more time discussing the meaning of life and the rational arguments for the existence of God. He understands why I'm concerned that it may be harder for my friends and family to deal with my injuries than it will be for me. I enjoy talking to him. He's a bright man with a great sense of fun. He appreciates people are different and is sympathetic to my view that attitude is everything and that each of us can cope with this kind of difficulty and do more than we think.

After resting and trying not to acknowledge the pain for several hours I get another visitor.

Mike says, 'This is no excuse for not meeting in Maputo for that beer.'

It's the first time we've met since working together in Cambodia. He's just arrived in Mozambique to run the UN accelerated demining programme. It's his first weekend off and he's hired a vehicle and driven eight hours to call in and see me. I'm grateful he's arrived early enough to go to the airport to pick up my girlfriend who has ignored my repeated pleas not to visit. She works in Cambodia, for an aid agency. I know she'll be upset, it's only natural, but I'm not in a position to look after her and I need time to recover. When I take the oxygen mask off to speak to Mike I'm surprised how short of breath I still am.

We talk through the sequence of events. We both agree it was lucky I was walking fast, have a big stride and was wearing a groin protector. If my legs had been closer together I would have lost part of my left leg as well, a large flash burn on my left shin and ankle prove that. The thick cotton overalls I was wearing undoubtedly prevented more serious burns.

It was unlucky that I was carrying a metal prodder. The force of the explosion ripped it through my hand and it shredded the palm bones irreparably. Mike tells me he knows of a deminer who was blown up in a lane while carrying a metal detector. It was blown out of his hand with such force it flayed all the flesh from the bones of his arm.

I have enormous respect for Mike's opinion. The opportunity to talk through with him what could possibly have happened is the best therapy possible.

We discuss how an explosive device could be located in the cleared area. If it wasn't deliberately laid by someone after the area had been cleared then it must have been missed for one or a combination of the following reasons: a) it was buried below metal detector range; b) the detector was faulty; or c) the man in the lane and those supervising him had a procedural problem.

In any post-incident analysis it's easy to be wise. Hindsight is a wonderful thing.

I say, 'When mine clearance programmes have been running for over a year it can be a dangerous period. It's when the local staff take over field supervision from expatriates and sometimes their perception of risk may be different. Perhaps we reduced our expat numbers too quickly?'

'Maybe,' Mike replies. 'But you know sometimes, in spite of everyone's best efforts, accidents happen despite everyone's best efforts.'

'I still can't understand how the mine was missed. And why did nobody step on it the day before, when they were in the lane treating Orlando?'

'I'm afraid that's probably a question you'll ask yourself for the rest of your life,' Mike says. 'On a different note you'd better be fit by September so you can come to the US because I'm getting married then.'

I grin. 'I'll be there.'

Mike checks his watch and heads for the airport. I drift back to sleep and try to ignore the rising tide of discomfort in what's left of my right leg.

When my girlfriend visits she's upset and doesn't think any of my being blown up jokes are funny. I'm not a believer in going around with a bottom lip like a prize marrow when life deals a bad hand. My view that we have totally different attitudes to life is confirmed and in spite of doing my best to console her I seem to make things worse.

She does some shopping for me and I reflect quietly on the best course of action. We're all ultimately responsible for ourselves and I have to deal with this in my own way. When she gets back I try to explain. I need all my energy to recover alone and don't really have enough to try and make sense of this for her.

She stands and looks at me then says, 'I'll see you tomorrow.'

I haven't got the strength to carry on explaining. I must rest. I have a temperature and an infection so they need to operate again.

18

SALAMI TIME

The trolley rolls smoothly over the gleaming floor tiles. I raise my head to watch the people we pass. Some of them smile, some look embarrassed. After being bed bound, going down the corridor is a real adventure. It's become a regular trip. I've done it quite a few times now.

I wonder what the open stump of my leg looks like?

I won't allow myself to be nervous. If I allow myself to think negatively I know I'll be afraid.

The porter turns a corner skilfully and pushes the trolley through the large double doors. I think this is the fifth time we've done this.

The operating theatre is cavernous and empty except for the lights and medical equipment. The air is heavy with disinfectant. There are no windows and the electric lights are always bright. They're all waiting and kitted up for surgery. They don't put their masks on until they've had a chat. I think it's a smart move. It makes the whole thing much more personal.

I've been in hospital about ten days. I hope this will be the last amputation and that they've reached the last of the dirt that was blasted up into the leg because there's not much left below the knee now. I stick my head up and say, 'Hello, I've only come back because I want to hear another of Wayne's jokes.'

The anaesthetist responds with a story about two cows. One says to the other, 'Moo, moo. This BSE is worrying. I've heard they've got it all over France and Germany, but they call it JCB there because the farmer just digs a hole, buries the cow and doesn't tell anyone.'

The other cow replies, 'It doesn't bother me, because I'm a duck.'

It's time to get down to business so I ask for the usual short back and sides and then go to great lengths to position myself exactly where they want me on the slab. As they prepare the injection I thank God I'm lucky enough to get such brilliant treatment.

'Right, that's it. I'm just going to give you an injection and then ask you to count to ten.' Wayne's voice is as relaxed as always.

I feel a slight tingle in my arm. I look at him and he nods to let me know I should start counting. 'One, two, three, four.' I think to myself that I don't feel at all sleepy. There's nothing difficult about having an operation. All you have to do is lie there and try to count to ten. I'm tired. What comes after five?

Wayne tells me another joke, but when I wake up I can't remember the punch line so I keep racking my brains. Whatever was chopped off in the operation is momentarily less important.

The plastic mattress cover makes a noise like a child unwrapping a present as I wriggle to try and get comfortable. I wonder how long I've been asleep? My leg feels sore so I give myself a pump of painkiller and lie back. I think this is the fifth time they've had to salami slice the infected bits off the stump. I look up to the drip stand. There is a milky white bag of antibiotic. I hope it works. I want to keep my knee.

Christ. Is it still there?

I pull back the sheet and slide my hand along my right thigh. I feel the bulge of a kneecap under the thick bandage, then lie back against the pillows, relieved. I won't feel any lower because it's tender.

I wake up as the nurse checks my pulse. They've run out of places to insert the drip needle, so they've had to use a vein in the back of my left hand. I've had to suspend my attempts to teach myself to write.

My head is thumping. Maybe I'm dehydrated. I force myself to drink a glass of water.

The phone rings and it's my old friends John the fisherman and his wife Clare. I'm lucky to have access to a phone. It's great to speak to them. I'm tired and confused. I can talk and make sense, but then I forget what we've just said. The doctor tells me it's caused by all the general anaesthetics and it'll wear off.

Several of my friends from the Irish aid agency Concern have travelled vast distances to visit. Friends of my parents who belong to Rotary contacted the International co-ordinator and several charming people have come in to say hello. One of them said I should consider myself 70 per cent South African by blood, given how little I had when I arrived.

One couple told me their son was injured several years ago in Angola while serving in the military. He was in bad shape when he returned because his mates sent him back with a gin and tonic drip.

The faint sound of squeaking wheels signifies the arrival of the dressing trolley. The nurse parks it by the bed and prepares things. As always we have a laugh and a chat.

Gently and skilfully, the bandage on my forearm is removed. The hand was amputated four inches below the wrist. There's a large T-shaped scar nearly the length of my forearm. It branches out at the end of the stump. Blue cross-stitches are clearly visible in parts of the thick, dark crusty scab.

The flash burns where the blast went up inside my sleeve are well scabbed over. The burns are superficial and I pulled off a large scab the last time they dressed it. Underneath it the hairs and skin had grown back.

The nurse applies liquid iodine dressing, a fresh bandage and then fills out the paperwork and pushes the trolley off in the direction of her next appointment. As she leaves, Jack from USAID arrives. He's in Johannesburg for meetings and has made time to visit. It was his helicopter that took me to the first hospital. The last time he came I wrote a note to the pilot thanking him for the flight and apologizing for being a restless patient. My writing looked like a six-year-old's. Jack is good company. A friend of Ken's arrives to check on me while he's away.

When they have time they take me out in the wheelchair and push me around the outside of the hospital so I can feel the sunshine and breathe fresh air. The hospital is a modern building. The front is like a well built marble-clad office block; the rest of it is more functional. It inspires confidence. Around the back the older brick built buildings house the nurses' accommodation, administration and laboratory buildings. The hospital is on three floors and exudes excellence. Inside the hospital is like any other. It smells of disinfectant.

A small pole and hook on the side of the chair holds the drips. When I shave in the morning I see that my face is thin and gaunt. My clothes hang off me and I know I'm weak. When I was trying to get into the wheelchair a slim nurse went to help me and I said, 'Careful you might hurt your back.' She picked me up effortlessly and carried me like a child, cradled in her arms.

I know I don't look healthy. One of my young visitors had to rush off and throw up the other day. They all wanted to know what happened when I was blown up. If people ask me I don't mind telling them. I suppose it's only natural that they're curious. Strangely enough I hadn't started telling them the really gory bits when he puked.

The hospital's sliding electric doors whirr and clunk open. Like one of Pavlov's dogs the sound signals a nice experience and I start to imagine the feel of the sun on my face and the wind in my hair.

I manage to avoid salivating on the kind nurse. She's a pretty blonde from the old country. Her family are farmers. She says people are old-fashioned where she comes from. She's still training, but next year when she's finished maybe she'll return.

The sun warms my face and a cool breeze chills my arms. She says. 'Isn't that a lovely warm breeze?'

I don't want to say I find it cool, so I say, 'Yes it's great to be outside.'

I can hear a car. I scour the car park. I need to know here it is. I can't move out of its way. It might hit me. It gets closer. I can see it now.

The car passes and I peer up to see the driver's face. It's low down here.

The nurse pushes me across the car park and round the corner of the hospital.

When I'm alone again I try to sleep. I can't sleep for more than a few hours at a time. It's hard to find a comfortable position, because whenever the stumps touch the bed or any pressure is applied to them I wake up. I don't want to take sleeping pills although I know all I have to do is ask for them. I remember Mrs Dubose, all ninety-eight pounds of her.

I wake early in the morning, and lie happily looking around me. I am so lucky to be alive. I watch the news and the OJ Simpson trial. I lie back and before I know it several hours have passed. Time flows like sticky porridge. Everything I do takes so long. I watch my small travel alarm clock to see the minutes tick past. Today I must remember the time. There's a film I want to watch this evening. It's been advertised for the last few days. I try to sleep in the morning and afternoon so I'll be able to stay awake.

It's *A Few Good Men*. When it's over, I look at the little

black clock with the green second hand racing around. It took me all day to prepare to watch a film. At least I can remember everything that happened and I understood it, so things are improving. I think about the film and remember some words someone said to me years ago. I can't remember who or where it was. *All it needs for evil to triumph is for good people to do nothing.*

I doze in fits and starts and suddenly the droning of a helicopter wakes me and I'm back in Mozambique, lying on the floor, looking at the medic and the pilot. It's all so real. I can see the trees rushing by underneath. Above me the clear blue sky is perfect. I struggle for breath. The heat is unbearable. I fight to control the burning in my throat and the inferno searing my right arm and leg. All I want to do is give in and go to a place where there's peace and no pain. But I can't give up. I lie on the floor of the helicopter and the vibration makes my spine tingle.

The engine and whirring of rotors gets closer and louder. I try to move, but I'm paralysed. I know that if I can lift my head or tense my muscles I'll wake up. I keep trying, but I can't escape the horror.

The noise starts to fade. Suddenly I move and I'm free. I'm awake. The helicopter was bringing a casualty. It's one in the morning. I know the emergency team will be running the stretcher from the heli-pad into the hospital and down the corridor to the treatment room. I remember watching the clean white ceiling and the lights glide above me. I hope the patient makes it.

Movement in the corridor near my door makes me open my eyes. The silhouette of an angel shines in the doorway. 'Are you all right?' a gentle voice enquires.

'Fine thanks. I hope whoever arrived in the helicopter will be.'

'Me too. Does the pain stop you sleeping?'

'No. I'm just drifting off again; the helicopter woke me.'

As I drift back to sleep I try to discipline my brain. It's natural my subconscious has some sorting out to do, but I can control the way I go to sleep and I can wake up when I want to. All I have to do is wake up, tell myself my dreams aren't real, think about something pleasant and go back to sleep. It's simple. I just have to get my brain around it.

In the dark of the night when I wake with pain and uncertainty I remember Som On and the others. Most of them have to beg and live in constant degradation. I promise myself I'll try to do something for them and the others with no voice.

With the arrival of morning I wash and shave, careful not to dislodge the drip needle. It takes nearly half an hour. I smile at the two nursing assistants who help cheerfully with water and towels. It's a dignified occasion because they provide me with a soapy flannel and turn their backs as I give my private parts a thorough wash. We always chat about their children, who are close to leaving school, and their concerns about crime and violence and what they'll do with their lives. I have the usual breakfast cereal and sleep. I need to be awake this afternoon because I have an important visitor.

Alistair, who advises the British government and audits their programmes, has been sent to investigate the accident. It's his second visit.

The day flies by. I emerge from sleep to see him walking in with my large rucksack and document bag. I don't know why I'm surprised, he's an old soldier, it's the sort of thing he'd do. He drops the rucksack and smiles. He doesn't give any indication that I look like shit, but I know I do. Whatever I look like, I feel worse, but I'm not going to tell anyone. I have a headache, I'm confused and the stumps hurt like hell.

His task isn't easy. Due to logistical constraints he's only had a short time on the ground to investigate the site. He thinks he may have found evidence of a booby trap. He believes there may have been a device buried deep, designed to get people clearing the mines. If it was, it certainly worked.

We discuss the possibility that there was a trip wire, and immediately discount it because so many people had travelled up and down the lane, the vegetation cut and the ground cleared.

We discuss booby traps again, then Alistair goes back to the airport. He has to fly back to London, write his report and then head to Asia to do another job. I forget to remind him to make sure he collects Air Miles.

The view out of my window is of a brick wall. I've decided it's a very nice red-brick wall. We've become familiar because we've spent so much time looking at each other. If you look from the other end of the room you can see a garden with small trees. When I'm sure nobody is about I push the drip stand to the end of the bed and stand up on my left leg. So far I haven't been caught. I don't move away from the bed, so if I get shaky I can sit down. Standing even for a brief period makes me dizzy and exhausted.

I spend the rest of the day eating fruit, which the nutritionist advised me to eat. The doctor walks in and says, 'That's good, keep it up. Have you been yet?'

'No, not yet,' I reply.

'How long has it been now?'

'Ten days.'

'Keep trying, and keep eating lots of fruit. I think the natural methods are the best. If something doesn't happen in the next few days we may have to give it a push. I mean that metaphorically speaking, of course.'

The arrival of the next morning heralds a new determination. I've been looking at the stainless-steel bed-pan for days and I'm resolute that today it will see active service. After breakfast I place the bed-pan in front of me and stare at it, but nothing stirs. I try for several hours and then I feel a slight movement. After endless pushing and straining I realize how dreadful childbirth must be.

After more agony I start to get a result, a loud metallic clank as it hits the pan and a feeling of intense relief. Good job it was stainless steel.

Later on I suddenly feel I may need to go again. I pull the emergency cord to summon a second bed-pan. I was right. I am embarrassed to find I've filled up the container and it's so heavy I can't lift it. I cover the pan with the paper lid and press the button for assistance. A nurse kindly and discreetly gets rid of it. She doesn't comment on the chokingly bad smell that fills the room.

Some time later the doctor pops his head round the door and gives me a thumbs up. 'Well done. We think it's an all time hospital record.'

I lie back and do the exercises to rebuild my leg muscles. It's also a great way of avoiding bed sores.

Carl the physio has told me what to do. My goal is to be able to do five times as many reps as he's suggested within five days. I never thought lifting your own limbs could be such hard work, especially since they don't weigh much now.

'How are you doing? I finished work early and I've come to pick the wife up, so I thought I'd see how you were getting on.' It's the medic from the Defence Force. He tells me about the violence in the townships. As a front-line medic he's treated some appalling injuries. The most horrific of these are what they call necklace injuries. A tyre is placed around the neck of the victim, the rim filled with petrol and then ignited. In most cases the casualty dies a slow, agonizing death. If they live, they're permanently disfigured. This barbarity is beyond comprehension.

He tells me nearly all the victims he saw died. Some of them had inhaled the burning petrol. I remember when I thought that death was the easy option.

After he's gone I wonder how long it will be before I can walk again. Some people think I might be able to run again, though some say I won't. I say I will. Yes I will.

The doctor and consultant examine the stump and knee. The consultant says, 'Good news. The infection is under control and we think it's now safe to close the wound. I've also spoken to physio and they're getting you some crutches. The right one will be an elbow crutch with a Velcro strap, but within the next week or so you should be up and about.'

Every day I try to get a little stronger and do something I didn't do the day before. I'm still only sleeping a few hours at night. The rest of the time I feel as if I'm in limbo. I am aware of my surroundings and have no problem having a conversation, but I find reading difficult, and anything that requires me to concentrate.

Some people from the Embassy have brought me a copy of *The Economist* and a magazine on African wildlife. Sometimes it takes me hours to read a single article.

They've removed the intravenous morphine applicator now. If I'm in pain I must let them know and they'll give me tablets. Every morning at eight o'clock the nurses change shifts. 'Are you in pain?' the nurse in charge asks. 'If you are we can give you something for it.'

I always smile, think of Mrs Dubose and say, 'No, I'm fine thanks.' For all I know I could have phantom pain for the rest of my life. I'm just going to have to get used to it.

I've been in hospital for ten days now.

The physiotherapist arrives with an enormous package wrapped in brown paper. It feels like Christmas. Out come the crutches. As promised, one has a normal plastic handle and the other a padded armrest with a Velcro strap.

She sets them to the correct height and I watch like an excited child. Carefully I put the stump of my arm on the rest, place the sleeve over it and press home the Velcro. The thick bandage around my arm offers some protection. With her steadying my shoulders I start to move cautiously around the room. We emerge into the corridor. I don't have any shoes. There is still a thick bandage around the flash burn on my ankle, so I probably wouldn't get one on anyway. 'Take small steps,' she says. 'You can't risk falling over yet.'

She's talking sense, so I curb my enthusiasm and try for total control. It's hard work. We've only been a short distance and I'm panting more than a very fat person who's just climbed the stairs up the Empire State Building. She says, 'You're short of breath because your haemoglobin count is still low. Take it easy. We'll go back now.'

When I sit down on the bed I realize I'm drenched in sweat. I'm forced to admit it was harder than I thought it would be.

The physio sensibly takes the crutches away and hides them until I've had a few more supervized sessions. Gradually we go further and further down the corridor and eventually I reach the hospital entrance and thank the administrator for the loan of the books. On the way back I feel dizzy and short of breath. I can't get enough air, my head starts to spin and I begin to wobble. The corridor floor and ceiling are trying to change places. I have to say something. 'I'm feeling faint.'

I stop and struggle to stay upright. The physio says something to a nurse and they get me a chair. I sit down ponderously. I feel several pairs of hands supporting me.

'Breathe slowly and deeply.'

I keep trying. I look at the floor and fight for breath then it suddenly gets closer and ... I know I fainted, but as I come round I've no idea how long I've been out. The hands are still supporting me and they say, 'Take it easy, just sit there and get your breath.'

I do just that, then I ask, because I have to know, 'How long was I out?'

'Only a few seconds,' she says.

I breathe deeply and normally then blurt out, 'How embarrassing. I've never fainted in my life. It's the sort of thing girls do in films. I've got my breath back now. I think I'll be fine.' The nurses help me up and point me in the right direction. It's no big deal for them, all in a day's work.

I have to sort this out. I now know how I felt before I fainted. Next time I'll stop and rest at the first onset, so I'll be able to move around alone. After some discussion, the nurses and physio agree. After a few hours' rest I go a short way down the corridor on my own. The next day I go to the main entrance and sit in one of the comfortable chairs.

On the way back I meet a man in a wheelchair with a high double-leg amputation. He's about fifty and has short-cropped silver hair. He's wearing shorts and a brown and white check shirt. He's the first amputee I've met since I became one. As I pass him I smile and nod. He says, 'Hello, you're doing well on those crutches. What happened?'

I explain. He says that after five years you get used to it and it doesn't bother you as much. 'What happened to you?' I ask.

'Oh I've been like this for over fifteen years. It doesn't bother me so much now; I've had plenty of time to get used to it. Where are you from?'

'England.'

'I went there a few years ago. I was in the bowling championships.' He sits back in his chair and swings his arm. 'I'm just in to have some treatment. I hope. I don't want any more taken off my bowling hand.'

He smiles. I try not to look embarrassed as I think, you poor bastard, all this for twenty fags a day.

On the return trip I rest in the waiting area. The seats are soft and the sofa provides a comfortable place to rest one's stump. There are potted plants and it doesn't smell like a hospital. People speak or smile as they pass and offer generous words of encouragement. I'm moved by their kindness. This is a good place to think. I have to accept that I've lost two very useful bits of my body but I must focus on what I have, rather than what I don't.

As a child, when things weren't going well I used to thank God for the fact that I had two arms and two legs. Now I'm even more grateful for the fact that at least I've got one of each.

I arrive back in my room as the phone rings. I get there just in time. A voice says, 'Hello, it's Mum. Your father and I are really worried about you, and I mean really worried. The rehabilitation expert, the psychiatrist, rang me and said that it was amazing how you'd coped with the amputations. He said you had no stress problems, you were rational and reasonable and that you were as sane as he was.' She pauses. 'That's why I'm calling. If you're as sane as a psychiatrist then we're really worried. They're all barking mad you know. You'd better go and drink beer with your army friends and start behaving normally again.'

I get the update on friends, family and the garden.

I remember the garden. Beyond the patio doors there's a large paved area which leads to the oval pond. We dug it just after Dad retired. It took three days of hard graft with pick, shovel and crow bar. I loved it.

Their red-brick house was built on the site of a farmyard. The ground was full of rubble. To make a garden we dug and levered out bricks, flints and limestone staddle stones. We used the best of the stones to make a rock garden around the pond. The rest was used as hard core for the paths and greenhouse foundations. The pool was stocked with delicate pink and yellow lilies and coy carp.

We spent a further three weeks digging out the rubble, raking up the stones and concreting a path around the perimeter. I did most of the donkey work and Dad did the fancy bits.

We reseeded and rolled the lawn and I dug and mulched the vegetable garden and flowerbeds with barrow loads of horse manure from the nearby stables. We usually worked silently. When I was younger we used to talk a lot, particularly when he was teaching me how to shovel efficiently or hold the hammer correctly. Now we're both perfectionists. He never had to say when he needed more cement, or the wheel barrow emptying, I could see. When we stopped for a tea break we'd have a chat and a laugh. I'll never forget the smile on his face as he laid the last brick in the path and it fitted perfectly.

Now yellow and blue iris and a host of rockery and herbaceous plants surround the pond with colour throughout the year. A strip of perfectly groomed lawn separates the water garden from the path and greenhouse, where Dad nurtures freesias and gloxinias. In spring the heavenly scent of freesias fills the house and in summer the gloxinia blooms are like huge trumpets.

The lawn swerves down to a wooden summer house, amid shrubs and flowering cherry trees. The vegetable garden fills the bottom right-hand corner and along the side nearest the grass a line of apple and pear cordons blossom pink and white in the spring and abound with fruit in the autumn.

In the centre of the lawn stands the circular rose bed.

I'd planned to grow roses one day and sit outside in the summer evenings after I'd mown the lawn. I'd look at the flowers and smell the fresh mown grass. I'm reassured to know that some things haven't changed.

19

NO BOTTOM LIPS

'Is there anything you need?' the boss asks. The phone line is eerily clear. It sounds like he's speaking to me from next door, not two continents away.

'Yes please, some footwear. Something like a plimsoll or boating shoe that doesn't slip. Just one, a left one will be fine.'

After our conversation I put the receiver down and struggle to untangle the cable with my left hand. It's a constant battle. I have to keep the small, Formica-topped table tidy. Mounted on a grey painted tubular frame with casters, it slides under the bed and provides a firm surface. It's the centre of my world. I eat my meals from it and use it to store magazines, books, the phone, Get Well Soon cards and several hundred weight of fruit.

I get back to my routine: occasional expeditions down the corridor on my crutches, isometric bed exercises, wound dressing and treatment, attempts to read and long periods of sitting in a stupor. I sit or lie in bed thinking, then look at the clock and see that hours have passed. Sometimes I pick up the clock, shake it and listen to it ticking to make sure it's not broken. My loss of ability to estimate the passing of time means, at least, that I don't realize how long I've been feeling really crappy.

It's been an unusually hot day. My back is running with sweat and is stuck to the sheet, even though the window is open.

When visitors ask, 'How are you?' there doesn't seem to be

any point in saying, 'Not bad thanks, I'm glad to be alive; but my arm and leg hurt a bit.' It's not fair on them. What can they say? 'Funny that, it's probably because they've been chopped off.'

The next day Richard, who is going to take over my job in Mozambique while I'm a sickie, walks into my room and presents me with a Harrods bag with the boss's compliments. I pull out a pair of boating shoes, a book and some chocolates. He also gives me a bundle of letters and cards from friends in Cambodia.

The shoes have arrived astonishingly quickly. I check my clock and try to work out the time scale. Allowing for flight times and travelling from London to the airport, the boss must have gone shopping as soon as he put the phone down.

I offer Richard a chocolate. As I examine the shoes, he says, 'Apparently, they don't sell them singly.'

The last time we met was five months ago in Cambodia. He was taking over the location I was running and I was moving to Mozambique. 'This is becoming a bit of a habit,' I say. I run through the work in Mozambique. 'There's a black book in the office where I noted every job I had to do, ranging from presenting the accounts through to getting the radio antennae fixed. These are prioritized on a scale of one to five and completed jobs were ticked in the box. The only major change is that when the UN left, the rents dropped. We could get more space for the same money, so we moved to a bigger building.'

I go through what I can remember about the sequence of events in the minefield and mention Alistair's comments about the possibility of a booby trap. Richard's already been briefed in London.

There's one area where more training might be needed. It's only a minor point, but I might as well mention it. 'The medic was fine, but it's worth checking when they put in a drip that they run the lines through. You can get them to practise sticking needles in you. It doesn't really hurt.'

Richard laughs. Later he gives me the news from Cambodia. They've completed the three village sites that we started, and the large mined area we cleared is now a new village for the homeless. Three thousand people who were previously destitute, dispossessed and desperate to escape the fighting now have the chance of a future.

I know Richard will do a good job in Mozambique. As he leaves to get his flight I remember the day we flew to Cambodia with Jim and Nigel. I'll never forget the heat when we got off the plane in Phnom Penh, and the strange dream I had about the jungle when I was trying to catch up on my sleep. Was it a warning, or just a coincidence?

I reach over and pick up the pile of cards and faxes. One of my old friends from the army has sent me a little book entitled, *He won't get far on one leg*. I replied by asking for an entry form for an arse-kicking contest.

I recognize the writing on one piece of paper. It's from Houn. He's sending best wishes from the blokes. It reminds me of when I was fit and strong and we walked to our freedom.

I decide it's time to get some more practice on my crutches. I put on my new shoe. I spend ten minutes doing up the laces with one hand. Fortunately they're long laces, which makes it easier. I walk slowly up the corridor to the entrance hall and back again, pausing to rest at the usual places.

I feel much safer with a shoe on. In a quiet stretch of the corridor I gradually accelerate, then try for maximum speed. I'm surprised how fast I can go. I struggle for breath, but power ahead. My eyes start to fill with sweat. Suddenly my left foot slips and I lurch forward. Quickly I stick the crutches out to steady myself and recover my balance. My heart thumps like a base drum and I try to stand still as I recover my breath. I don't want to think about what it would feel like to land on the stumps.

I take a few more paces before I feel faint. It's time to rest on one of the window seats. As I look back down to the entrance hall, I promise myself I'll leave here under my own steam. I think I'm getting stronger. I've done thirty metres more than I managed yesterday. I head back to my room and crash on the bed. My head is thumping and I'm panting like a dog who's spent an hour chasing a rabbit. Now I've set my first goal I'm terrified I won't be able to achieve it.

The inescapable reality is that I felt less tired after running ten miles before I was injured than I do now, and all I've done is the length of the corridor. I'm frustrated and angry, but what can I do?

I just have to accept reality. I will fight to overcome disability and face the fact that sometimes I'll lose. The only thing to do is relish what I can do and be thankful for the present. The way to deal with the tiredness is to enjoy the chance to rest. I'm knackered. I close my eyes, massage the stumps and lie back and think of England. In a week or so I'll be fit enough to travel.

I wake up late in the afternoon. It's almost the time for changing the dressings. My arm is starting to heal and the doctor thinks they'll be able to take out the stitches. The nurse cuts them with a curved scalpel and pulls them out with tweezers. The blue thread pricks as it's tugged through the scab. I clench my teeth and watch with fascination. A few threads stick and some of them are so well buried they need to be dug out. At the end of the stump the T-shaped scar merges with the scab. The nurse's nimble fingers remove the last stitches from the long scar on my forearm, then she dresses it again and leaves.

I watch the news. The Queen is visiting South Africa. With

President Mandela she receives a tumultuous welcome. I follow the royal visit with fascination; it's much less depressing than the OJ Simpson trial.

After following the day's events it's time for handwriting practice. I turn to pull the table closer, but can't reach it. I realize I've tried to grab it with my right hand. I can still feel it. The tendons that operated it are still in my wrist and although it hurts when I move them it's like I can still feel my fingers.

To control the phantom pain they have given me a Tens machine, a small electrical pulse generator that's battery operated. The theory is that the electrical impulses give real stimulation to the nerves and override the confused messages from the severed nerves in the amputated limb. It's not easy to attach and arrange the wires with one hand, so I haven't used it that much.

Instead I continue to massage and gently tap the stump and find it helps more than the machine, or maybe it's just easier. I still can't sleep for more than a few hours at a time. I keep waking up when I move and can't find a comfortable position to lie in.

The doctor visits and we discuss rehabilitation and false limbs. There are so many things I don't understand. It's reassuring to know there are false legs held on by Velcro straps which are quick to take on and off. Throughout all the treatment I've received the medical staff always explained exactly what was happening. I've never been left wondering what was going on or what might happen. There's a saying 'knowledge dispels fear'.

I sit back, doze for a while and then as my strength returns turn on the television. I'm glad I've got the remote control. There's a repeat of an education programme about eating with a knife and fork and basic building techniques for township houses. It's followed by a documentary about bears in North

America. The angel walks in smiles and says, 'You have a visitor.'

Neil visits me. Another quirk of fate has placed us in Africa at the same time. I heard he'd finally got a flying job, so he'd be able to get enough hours to give him the experience he needed. Unfortunately there were maintenance problems and he ended up without a plane. When he heard I'd taken a few weeks off to go to hospital and he was in Johannesburg he tracked me down.

'What will you do next?' I ask.

'I'm going back to England to look for other opportunities in aviation. I'm taking your experience as an omen!'

I remember the company defensive position exercise at Thetford when the British winter turned arctic. We struggled to survive a week in temperatures lower than minus ten. At the time it was the toughest thing we'd done. I say, 'Do you remember that exercise in Thetford in the snow?'

'Yes. Eddie threw his teddy bear out the cot. Surprising there weren't more low flying teddies, when you think about it. It was colder than a penguin's bum.'

I smile. 'There's no point in wibbling. It doesn't achieve anything.'

I catch up on what the aid and development agencies are doing and his work in Jo'burg, until he suddenly looks at his watch. 'I've got to go to this work meeting. I'll be in again soon. Let me know when you want to go to the airport. I've got a hire car. I can give you a lift. I've told everyone you'll be sorted out in less than six months.'

Several hours later the doctor appears clutching a folder with my medical records. Steel-rimmed spectacles give Doctor Boffard a reassuringly academic air and he's got just enough grey hair to show he's nothing to prove. He's an expert in trauma injuries and is the consultant looking after me. I am fascinated to learn what happened and the treatment I've received. He always explains everything. The consultants and surgeons work long hours. He frequently appears in the evening and early in the morning to check how I'm doing.

I'd trust him with my life. In fact I probably owe it to him. He was the surgeon who treated me when I first arrived.

He smiles. 'When you first arrived I thought it would be at least six weeks before you would be well enough to fly. It's now been just over three and you're fit enough to leave hospital. You've made an amazing recovery, both physically and mentally. There are no infection problems and the wounds are closed and healing well and you obviously have no trouble getting around. The next stage is for you to get false limbs fitted and to learn to use them. Roehampton Hospital in London is the most convenient place for you to go. It's also an excellent rehabilitation centre. I've spoken to your boss and he's arranged everything. The travel insurance company say someone should accompany you on the flight. Whoever it is should be strong enough to pick you up just in case you fall over.'

I phone the HALO office and speak to the boss. He understands why I want to make my own travel arrangements – I want to control as much of my life as I can. I don't make a good invalid. I telephone the insurance company.

I have to see this as the first problem-solving exercise since the accident. My aim is to get safely to Roehampton, causing the minimum amount of disruption to everyone concerned. The insurance man tells me that every day he arranges travel all around the world, but rarely gets to visit any of the destinations. We check through flight times and dates.

I switch on the television and watch the rugby. He phones me back to let me know which flights are available. Travelling back sounds more complicated than I anticipated; the flight is not direct. Suddenly the All Blacks get a try and he asks me the score. In the ensuing conversation I learn he's six foot five and eighteen stone and his name is Steve. I ask if he would like a rapid return trip to London. He checks then accepts, which leaves me time to watch the rugby.

I'm transfixed as I watch the power of the pack. Now the ball's out and one of the All Blacks on the outside wing is making a run for a try. He holds his head high, clutches the ball to his chest with his right arm and steams down the field. They can't catch him and now the full back is on him, but as he throws himself in for the tackle the forward swerves sideways and palms him off perfectly. Now he cuts into the middle of the pitch and the crowd goes wild as he scores without opposition. I sit back and relax. I'm breathless.

Their speed and strength is awesome. For a moment it felt like I was running with him.

At eight thirty I clean my teeth and collect my washing and shaving kit. I wear shorts and a T-shirt. I can't get long trousers on over the bandage around the stump.

I use the crutches to position myself in front of the toilet, then I put them in the corner and carefully sit down. As always there's a nervous reaction in the stumps, it's like an electric shock. I grip my soap bag in my teeth, slowly return to the bed and start to pack up the table. I put my cards and books in the daypack, one item at a time. Things don't fit in and the bag keeps moving as I try to push them in. I have to take it all out and do it again several times.

I pack everything except my clock and the book I'm reading.

I find it hard to read. Concentrating is difficult, but this autobiography of a First World War pilot is fascinating. The boss sent it to me and it's become a treasured possession. The author joined the Royal Flying Corps at eighteen when war was declared, and his friends were killed, one by one.

A friend of mine who was clearing up after the Gulf War told me about an American EOD team that had a run of bad luck; in a series of unconnected incidents the section were killed until there was just one left. He committed suicide. Perhaps it's harder for the ones who are left behind.

As I finish packing I glance at the clock. It's ten thirty. In the past, I would have taken ten minutes to do all that. At least I can feel pleased I've been able to do it myself. I'm going to have to plan much more in advance. I'm excited about going to the airport and flying back home. I have to look upon it as a new challenge. I almost wish I were travelling alone, just to prove I can do it.

I get my crutches. When I get to the corridor leading to intensive care, I glance at the white ceiling. I stand there awkwardly, like a little boy confronted with a room full of strangers. A nurse opens the door, sees me and says, 'Oh, hello.'

I don't really know what to say. She beckons me inside. I move to lean against the door to prop it open. Inside there are seven people propped up in their beds. Their grey, ghostly faces are partly hidden by oxygen masks. The heart monitors paint the room faintly with intermittent colour. I know where they are, and where they might go. The air is heavy with it; death is somewhere close.

The nurses must be busy. I'm embarrassed. I was in here three weeks ago. They've had a lot of patients since then, I'm just one of many. I mumble like a child told to thank his host. 'I'm leaving today, I wanted to say thank you . . .'

I turn and swing back towards reception suddenly relieved to be alone. In the entrance hall I sit and think. I've always been independent; I've never had to ask anybody to do anything for me. That's all changed now.

I walk to the administration office to collect my passport. Then I go through the glass doors and stand outside. It's a grey day. A fine drizzle makes the neatly-laid orange road bricks glisten. I watch cars hiss down the road, leaving a trail of spray.

Now it's time to see how far I can go without stopping. I almost make it back and pause just past the place where I fainted to avoid repeating my mistake. With the rhythmic tap of my crutches, I swing back to my bed. I'm exhausted.

The nurse comes in with the trolley and gives me a small plastic bag. The vivid red and yellow capsules look quite beautiful. I don't intend to take them, but it's a long flight and I don't know how I'll feel. Steve said it would be sensible to have them because once in the air there's only aspirin and paracetamol. In a way it's going to be worse for him than it will be for me.

Ken, has just got back from Tanzania. He and Neil are coming to the airport to see me off. The moment has arrived. I say, 'I don't need a wheelchair, thanks. I promised myself I'd leave hospital under my own steam.'

They understand. I say my goodbyes and thank everyone. I make good progress down the corridor. We all walk together. It's possible to go surprisingly fast on crutches, even when you're weak. The drizzle has turned into a torrential downpour. It's the first time I've been on a really wet surface and I'm afraid I might fall. I get into the car and we head for the airport.

Even with the windscreen wipers on full it's hard to see where we're going, but I enjoy the journey. It's a treat to be out. When we get to the airport they get my crutches from the boot and we head to the restaurant. The three of us sit at a table and have a chat and a beer while Steve takes my passport and baggage and checks us in.

It's good to be sitting here chatting away like everyone else. Except that now I'm not like everyone else. I have only one beer. I don't have as much blood as I used to. It's late on Saturday afternoon and the airport is full of people. To go to departures we have to go to the top floor. It's sensible for me to use a wheelchair now.

When it's time to board we all cram into the lift. Ken and Neil steer me towards the departure area. The place is packed with travellers, some ambling, some frantic. A group of people stand near the chromium railings, waving to their departing loved ones. I'm steered skilfully around them.

A portly Indian gentleman waddles through the terminal towards me. I'm transfixed. He's not looking where he's going. He pauses occasionally to look at the departure screen. He is short, balding and middle-aged. His black silk shirt is unbuttoned, revealing a fair amount of chest and two gold medallions. His belly hangs over the top of his belt. His black trousers are too short, revealing white socks and crocodile-skin shoes. Sweat streams down his face and the hair he's combed to hide his baldness has slipped forward on to his glasses. In his right hand he carries a huge black suitcase. He lurches towards us, bashing into passers-by.

I stare in horror as he looks over his shoulder and steams directly towards me. The suitcase is on a collision course with my stumps and the crowd is so thick there's nowhere we can move to. There's nothing I can do to protect myself. I shout, 'Excuse me!'

He doesn't hear. I shout again but he just keeps on going. I push my left hand forward to protect the stumps and brace myself to take the pain. The image of a ripe peach being smashed with a mallet fills my mind and terror grips my guts.

Suddenly the wheelchair stops and Ken leaps in front of me. With his left hand he deflects the suitcase, with his right he pushes him away. He glances at me and laughs, then his expression changes. Our eyes met for an instant and I know that he saw my fear.

Ken walks in front of me from now on. As they shepherd me through the throng I try to hide the fact that I'm hyperventilating and sweating like a pervert in PVC at the world spanking championships.

I think back to a time a few months ago. It was Christmas Day. Ken and I were the only aid workers left in town. We were sitting in a café eating some samosas (because they didn't serve turkey), when four young men walked over to our table shouting. Two of them looked very drunk. One of them deliberately charged into me.

As he hit me I tensed my stomach muscles and exhaled, at the same time I jerked my elbow out to protect my face. I didn't feel it, although he may have done. Instantly I got up and jumped away saying, 'By the wall.' Ken was already there. If four of them were going to have a go we were both confident of defending ourselves, but wanted them to come from one direction.

We made conciliatory gestures and said, 'Nao problem. Nao problem.'

They watched us. Two faces showed hesitation and uncertainty and two showed drunken rage and stupidity. I always try to avoid trouble. If they try it I can defend myself, but it's not what I'm here for so I shout, 'Policia! Policia!'

A few people at the bar shout at them and as a policeman in a grey uniform starts walking over from the road they run away.

We laughed and sat down and turned our chairs slightly so we could see who approached us. I was strong then and I wasn't afraid. Now I'm weak and disabled. I can't even make a plane journey on my own or carry a cup of tea in the café. But I'll fight and one day I'll be strong again.

I say goodbye to my mates and we head towards the plane. I try to think of something appropriate to say as I leave, but I can't, so I just say exactly what I'm thinking. 'I know it's going to be tough, but you can be sure I won't be hopping around with a bottom lip like a prize marrow. Thanks for coming to see me off.' As we go towards the gate a member of the airline staff takes over pushing the chair and Steve protects me from passing passengers.

We are flying via Zurich. They put me on the plane first. At the aircraft door I get out of the wheelchair and go slowly down the aisle. Using crutches in small spaces is easier than I thought. As we get to our seats in the front of the economy section Steve gets several layers of sheepskin out and puts it on my seat. Initially I thank him and accept it because I think it would be rude not to. A few hours into the flight I realize that because I'm a lot thinner and I've still got a few flash burns, sitting is uncomfortable. Without the sheepskin padding I would be in agony.

We're on the left-hand side of the aircraft and Steve is in the aisle seat, which means I'm protected from the hand baggage as passengers bump along to their seats. At the moment I'm a good person to sit next to on a plane because there's not much of me to get in the way.

People stare in shock at my bandaged stumps, look at me, look away and often look right back again. I'd probably do the same. I draw comfort from the fact that if somebody over-does the staring I can tell my six foot five companion to ask them not to.

I try to read, fight to find a comfortable position and snatch some sleep. When we land at Zurich I wait until everyone gets off. Then I leave the aircraft and swing up the ramp to the gate. There is a golf buggy waiting. I share it with a woman in her twenties. She's on crutches; her ankle is in a cast. Steve goes to check our transfer details. As I sit next to her I say, 'Oh dear, that looks a bit uncomfortable. Was it a skiing accident?'

She nods, 'I had some bad luck and took a tumble.'

'I had some too. I was working out in Africa for a charity. I was in a remote area of Northern Mozambique when a lion tried to eat me. Fortunately it only got to the hors d'oeuvres.'

When Steve returns there's an awkward silence.

I try to sleep on the plane, but the stumps are too uncomfortable. London is wrapped in a grey drizzle. It's strange to be pushed through Heathrow airport in a wheelchair. 'Excuse me, madam. Mind your bag please, sir.' The airport authority man pushing is an expert.

Steve pushes our luggage trolley on my right side and we hop into a taxi. We emerge into a cold, late March morning, shrouded in low cloud. It's always good to be home. The journey seems like a moment of freedom.

Roehampton Hospital has been a rehabilitation centre for the wounded since the First World War. I know roughly where it is and I vaguely remember seeing it in *Reach for the Sky*, the film about Sir Douglas Bader the heroic, legless RAF Pilot.

20

WHAT FUTURE?

28 MARCH 1995

The hospital is a vast and sprawling web of temporary constructions linked by cavernous, well-decorated corridors, and it has the unmistakable aura of war. I can feel it. The long passageways and low buildings are a memorial to a time of greater sacrifice than we can claim.

Reception directs me to Accident and Emergency where a charming nurse has found me a chair and gone to check my details. I balance my daypack on my lap and hold it still with my stump. I unzip it and try to pull out my book, but it's packed in too tightly. I give it a tug and the bag falls to the floor. I try to bend down and pick it up. I haven't done anything like this yet and my balance has gone. I lurch to the right. Shit! I think I'm going to fall off the chair and land on my stumps. I grab the seat with my left hand and just save myself. I sit back upright and pull the bag closer with my foot. Cautiously, I pick it up and try again.

I wrestle for a few minutes and eventually persuade the book out of the bag. I put it down and start to read. After a few minutes my left arm aches. I never realized that holding a book with one hand was so difficult. I put the bag on my lap and rest my aching hand on it.

I'm in the midst of an astonishing dogfight. Suddenly the bag slips off again. I'm just about to say 'bugger' when I see a little girl two seats away looking at me, so I try to change it to 'bother'. Her mother gives me a disapproving look. Perhaps I've been in the bush too long.

Right, that's enough of sitting still. I'm going to have a look around the waiting area. I try to put the book back in. After several minutes I finally succeed. My stumps are uncomfortable. I rub them and reach for my crutches. I feel tired but restless. I realize I'm used to lying down most of the day.

· I get on my crutches and move around the waiting area. Several pensioners and two young men sit with faces as grey as the drizzle outside. A few seats away a woman waits with one child who looks about six and another of four. I smile at the children, then decide to move on. I have to face the fact that I probably look like an extra from a horror film. I don't want to frighten them. As I return to my seat a man about my age passes me with a well-bandaged hand. There's a small blob of red that has leaked through the dressing. It reminds me of the Red Cross flag. It must be a really nasty cut. Ouch! Poor bloke.

It's early on Sunday morning. Most of the patients look like DIY injuries or sick children. The nurse told me the Saturday night drink- and drug-horrors have all been dealt with.

I return to my seat, start juggling with my bag again and then give up as the nurse returns. She says I need to go to the other end of the hospital. The ward is expecting me. I get my crutches, but she smiles sweetly and suggests a wheelchair. I know it makes sense.

The cheerful green doors and huge heating pipes compliment the calming light green of the walls. The warren is well sign-posted at every junction. It needs to be; I wouldn't be surprised to encounter a group of ramblers with their maps out

A large black and white photograph demands attention. First World War officers and gentlemen in top hats stand in front of a stately home playing croquet; they are being watched by a formidable group of ladies wearing long dresses and a bearded, bemedalled gentleman in uniform who looks like the King. I catch sight of a caption that says something about helping the war wounded.

The wheelchair slows slightly. We're going up. The hospital is on a hill, so the buildings are at different levels off the motorway corridors. There are now windows to my right and double doors that are open. I peer out. I can see the stately home in the photo. It hasn't changed.

The bricks look almost bruised and bloody, but the four-storey building stands strong and defiant, in sharp contrast with the line of temporary drab huts stretching away to its right. I wish I could paint.

The prefabricated ward buildings have faded, creosote-painted pine walls and large, white, wooden-framed windows. They are like a line of beach huts. In one of the windows I see an old man sitting in a red dressing-gown, staring into space. He turns his head slowly and for an instant we exchange glances. His grey face, slow movements and piercing stare tell me his life is draining away from him.

I would like to stop, but I can't because somebody else is controlling the wheelchair and she's got more important things to do and other patients to deal with. The nurse delivers me to the Limb Surgery Unit before disappearing back to Accident and Emergency to remove saucepans from children's heads, stitch their cuts, care for elderly people who've fallen, and be threatened, abused and attacked by drugged and violent people.

The pink folder containing my medical records from South Africa is handed to the staff nurse. I am taken to my room and asked to get into bed to wait for the doctor to examine me. They have to put me in isolation. The infection they particularly worry about is MRSA, which is resistant to all known antibiotics. I've heard about it. It stops wounds healing and is untreatable. I hope I haven't got that, it sounds a real bummer. There's a toilet across the corridor, just for me.

Through the wheelchair-wide swing door, most of the outside wall is taken up by a metal-framed window. Against the right-hand wall there is a small television on a wooden table, and near the corner a chunky white ceramic sink with a mirror above. There's a built-in cupboard opposite. The tubular-steel bed juts out into the room. It looks like there is just enough space to get round it to the sink and cupboard in a wheelchair.

Behind the bedstead there is an oxygen line, electrical points, call button and wall light. I put my daypack on the small bedside table. They leave my crutches in the corner of the room. The staff nurse helps me settle in. She tells me to try to stay off the crutches and only use the wheelchair. 'We want the swelling in what's left of your leg to go down as quickly as possible so we can fit a prosthesis.'

As she disappears I try to think about the future, and not the short-term loss of mobility.

She returns with a wheelchair and fits a short padded leg rest to the right side. I stare at it, wondering how to avoid pushing myself round forever in bloody circles.

After accepting a cup of coffee, I wash and shave. This is the first time I've been in hospital in the UK. Until just over three weeks ago I'd never been in hospital. I don't know much about rehabilitation, but I'm going to do my best to learn.

A tall man in a dark suit comes into the room and introduces himself. It's not until we've shaken hands that I realize he automatically held out his left hand. He's clearly had a lot of experience of dealing with traumatic injuries. 'The surgeon will check that your wounds have healed and that false limbs can be fitted. They have saved as much of your limbs as they possibly can, but occasionally more surgery is required so that a prosthesis can fit properly. The time it takes to learn to walk on one will vary, depending on the height of the amputation and so on. A ballpark figure would be two months.' He pauses. 'I'm afraid you have to remember that a false limb will never be as good as the one you've lost.'

I hope I don't need any more surgery. I thought that was finished. I want to get back to work as soon as I can.

We talk for a while about what I did before the accident and he's particularly interested in what I want to do next. The charity has asked me if I'd like to deal with admin and logistics in London. They made it quite clear when I was in South Africa that I have a future there, but I want to get back to the field.

His expression suddenly becomes serious. 'How do you feel about what happened?'

Without pausing for thought, I say, 'I chose to be there. It's still not clear exactly what happened, but there's no point in being bitter about it. Life's too short.'

He talks about the possibility of lobbying for funds for mine clearance and working towards a ban, then leaves me his card and says that if he can help at all I just need to call him. He also says that because his secretary lives nearby and I'm going to be in isolation for a while she'll pop in during the week to see if there's anything I need.

After he's gone I do my leg exercises and some sit-ups. I'm keeping my shorts and T-shirt on. After two and a half weeks in bed in South Africa I could barely do five half-sit-ups. A week later, after trying like hell, I can do a hundred. At the end I lie back exhausted and go to sleep.

I sit up suddenly when I hear the door. Where am I? I recognize the hospital room. Through the window I see someone in a white coat.

The doctor introduces herself. I explain where I've been and what happened. She asks if I had any problems on the flight and checks my heartbeat, blood pressure and breathing. As she reads my medical file she says, 'You're very lucky to be alive.' She's not wrong.

Before leaving she explains about the MRSA precautions, does my admission paperwork and tells me that the rehabilitation centre works Monday to Friday. She returns to take swabs for MRSA tests. The giant cotton-buds are rubbed on virtually every surface that might have bacteria, including up my nose and on my scabs.

When I'm alone I try to read, but I'm too tired. I doze for a while and then finish unpacking. I put my clock on the table by the bed and wait for my old school friend John, who's due to visit.

There's a knock on the door and I see his cheerful bearded face through the window. As he enters he says, 'Hello skinny! Have you been on some revolutionary new diet?'

I grin. 'I'm going to call it the Blast Plan. I lost a stone and a half in a split second.'

His wife has sent sweets and he presents me with a plastic bag containing paper, envelopes and cards. I must start to teach myself to write properly.

It's good to catch up. After we left school he qualified in osteopathy and has run his own highly successful practice in Warminster for fifteen years. I make an advance booking at a very reduced rate just in case I have back trouble when I get out of hospital. He promises to give me half price on any limb treatment.

When he sees me getting tired he goes. I say, 'I'll be down to see you within a month.'

This is goal number two and I intend to achieve it.

Later on my sister and parents visit. I can see them through the door window. They wave and help each other put on the white plastic aprons and surgical gloves. There's a notice on the door saying I'm in quarantine and that anyone entering has to wear protective clothing.

They all come in together. Dad is still tall, in defiance of his years, and still has a strong, muscular frame. His hair looks greyer than the last time I saw him, but he is in his early seventies. He has strong craftsman's hands with long fingers and intense grey-blue eyes. His voice is loud and jovial. He usually greets me with a laugh or a joke. This time he just holds out his left hand and says, 'I was sorry to hear the news.'

None of us is going to wibble.

Mum is small and wiry. Her slight figure does not reveal the strength she has developed in a lifetime of gardening. She also has a few more grey hairs than the last time I saw her. Perhaps that's my fault. The threat of an uneasy silence lurking in the air is broken when she says, 'We've brought the things you asked for, and I can take any washing back.' I'm pleased she didn't say 'your' washing. It would have made me feel like I couldn't do it.

I phoned them from South Africa and asked them to bring me a few clothes and the spare watch that I'd left with them for safe keeping. It's a second-hand diving watch that I bought a long time ago in Cambodia. My very efficient mother unwraps it from the tissue paper it was preserved in and hands it to me. It feels so heavy that I doubt I'll be strong enough to wear it any more.

I spotted it when I walked past a small market stall. I remember the unforgiving sun, the heat and the dust. The thing that caught my eye was that unlike the cheap battery-operated fakes, the hands were not moving. I asked to look at it. The vendor was pleased. It felt heavy; I shook it next to my ear and heard the rattle of an automatic winding mechanism. I asked him how much, he said, 'Good watch. Only you buy, forty dollar.'

I gave him what he asked. He said he was selling it for a poor woman, his cousin, who had been given it by a man in UNTAC. Now she needed money to feed her children because her husband was an amputee who'd left her to beg and drink himself to death.

I keep trying to put the watch on. I try using my teeth, the stump and resting it on the table. They all know me well enough not to offer to do it for me.

Kate, my sister, looks at me and says, 'You look very pale and your face is so thin all the bones are standing out. It's as shocking to see you so painfully thin and unhealthy as it is to see you with missing limbs.'

I'm relieved she's says what she thinks. 'Don't worry,' I say. 'I'll soon put it back on. I think the reason I look so pale is because of the blood loss. I'm a bit anaemic.'

We're not an over-emotional family, but we've always been close. They hang up my spare clothes in the cupboard. We're all practical so we sort out the stuff before getting down to chatter.

Mum talks about the effect on the grandchildren. Alex is the oldest. She's nearly five. I'm her Godfather. They've explained that I've been hurt. Mum thinks when I get out of hospital it would help if I tell her what happened and let her know that it's all right.

It's nearly the end of March and beyond the window I see the afternoon fading into night. The drizzle is still hanging in the air and the clouds of condensation from car exhausts as they start in the car park tells me that spring has not yet displaced winter, but I know that it soon will.

Ian, my brother-in-law, is looking after the children. He says he'll be in later in the week. I give them my driving licence to pass on with a message asking him to find out my legal position.

My Dad and sister produce a family album from a carrier

bag and pass it over. My Dad says, 'We were looking through this last week and thought you'd like to see it.'

On the first page there is a photograph of us in the garden. Dad and I are planting some ground-cover shrubs near the tree where I shot the pigeon. The next photograph is my vegetable garden. The broad beans and carrots look excellent. The two long rows of potatoes were also very good, but the greens were a disaster that year because I didn't shoot enough pigeons. I tried netting and scarecrows, but it never worked.

The next one is of Roger and me on his farm. It's harvest time and we're standing by a field of barley stubble. We'd just cleared the straw bales before it rained. I remember the simple pleasure of drinking pints of orange squash to quench the thirst of labour in the summer sun.

Now I'm on to my early days in the army. There's my platoon doing the assault course, and there's one of us wearing virtually every item of kit we'd been issued, smiling in the snow. We were on the exercise in Thetford.

I turn the page and see a photo of my parents and me next to their roses. I'm sweating and in my sports kit because I'd just got back from running my favourite circuit on the Downs. I remember the smell of the fresh air and wild flowers.

The next shot is of a friend who lives near them. David retired from the army a few years ago. We became friends when I left the army and joined the legion of the lost. He served more than forty years, most of which he spent in the Parachute Regiment. We're standing in our climbing gear with the Dorset coast behind us, then on the top of Snowdon with a few small clouds passing below. We always took two days' kit and food in our rucksacks.

It's getting late. I'm tired and they need to go. I give them a roll of film that I took in Mozambique and ask them to develop it. As they leave I reassure them that I'm fine and that although I have a few challenges ahead they don't need to worry.

When they've gone I think through the photographs again and remember all those good and happy times. As I massage my stumps I realize that at the moment I couldn't do any one of the activities in the photos. Maybe it would have been simpler to slip away. What have I got left?

The answer is simple. I've got the future.

The nurse comes in with the drugs trolley. She checks my records, reads what the doctor has written in my file, and checks through the folder again. She says, 'The only medication you're on is iron tablets. Is that right?'

'They gave me these for the plane journey, but I didn't need them.' I pass her the plastic bag containing the shiny red and yellow capsules. Just one of them looks powerful enough to relieve a serious neck disorder in a giraffe. I never took one and I'm proud of it.

As the evening progresses I try not to doze because I want a good night's sleep. In spite of the journey, I can't sleep for long. The stumps are giving me a bit of gyp and I can't find a comfortable position to lie in. I find that putting my stump on a pillow helps.

The next morning I watch the breakfast news. I've never really watched it before; I've either been abroad or working. Someone brings me some cereal and a cup of tea. Later a man pops his head round the door and asks if I would like a newspaper.

I immediately get excited. I love reading the papers. When I have time I read two or three. I've got a whole day ahead of me. I ask for several.

He puts a stack on the bed. For a few minutes I sit trying to balance the papers on my lap, wondering where I can put the change. Unfortunately I don't have any pockets. Now the money is in my hand I can't use it to move anything and I don't want to put it down because it'll be difficult to pick up again. I turn to the bedside cupboard. Shit. I've just knocked the table and spilt my tea. Oh well, look on the bright side; at least it's cooled down enough not to scald my goolies.

I rearrange things carefully then reach across and put the change on the top of the cabinet. I restack the papers and finish breakfast. I try to read while I eat, but end up with a trail of cornflakes and spilt milk across the bedclothes.

I wait for them to take the trolley away. I scan all the headlines and the front pages first. I put the broadsheet on the bed table and open it. I try to steady it with what's left of my right arm, but I don't do a very good job. The pages are getting ruffled and soon the whole thing's a crumpled mess.

I can manage a tabloid on the trolley, but after a few minutes I lose concentration and become tired. The ward administrator knocks on the door. She says there's a call for me and the sister says I can go to the phone in my wheelchair if I'd like to. I throw my pile of papers on the floor as I get into the chair. I swivel myself round in circles, banging the bed and door several times before I eventually escape the room. I discover that by using my left leg to push the chair I can move in an almost straight line. The trouble is that I keep hitting the flash burn on my left ankle against the footrest.

It's my brother-in-law. He's spoken to the DVLC, and I have to surrender my driving licence so that they can put my change of circumstance on it and get the requisite medical reports. They're sending me a temporary form, which my doctor can sign to authorize me to drive if he believes I'm safe. I hope he hasn't just witnessed my performance with the wheelchair.

The doctor visits at ten thirty. They will be monitoring my haemoglobin levels carefully to see if I need another blood transfusion. He checks the chart at the end of the bed and tells me they'll need to take a blood sample later. The physiotherapists, prosthetists and medical staff work closely together and later today I'll get a visit from a physio who will discuss rehabilitation and learning to walk again. He warns that it will be a while before I can expect to get a false leg fitted, but the physio will be able to give me more accurate information.

'Is there anything you'd like to know?'

'At the moment I'm finding it difficult to concentrate when I read long articles and my memory isn't quite as sharp as it was. What's causing that?'

He looks at the file again. 'It's a combination of things. Shock, exhaustion, trauma and a large number of general anaesthetics. You'll find it's only temporary. Within six months you'll be back to normal.'

Being in isolation is no problem at all. I think of the time when I was a prisoner in Cambodia. I coped with that and I'll cope with this. As I look at my arm and leg I realize that no matter what I do, I'll never escape from disability, but I'm always going to fight it.

A woman in her late twenties wearing blue trousers and a white jacket introduces herself as Maggie, one of the physiotherapists. There's not a lot they can do until they get the MRSA test results back. Once the oedema, the swelling in the stump, has been sufficiently reduced they can take a cast for the false leg socket and start to manufacture it. Learning to use the leg takes place in the walking school, and it's something you can't really hurry.

Maggie checks the timing of my last operation. 'I'll need to talk to the doctor and prosthetist, but I think we can look at starting an arm prosthesis soon.'

'I need to get back to things as soon as I can. How long is all this going to take?' I ask.

'Between four and six weeks once you're out of quarantine or from when the last operation has healed. It also depends on how young and fit you are.'

I immediately try and look young and fit. 'I want to recover as quickly as possible. What can I do?'

'Stick to the wheelchair and keep the stump on the resting pad because that will take the swelling out of it. As soon as possible we'll get you on to the PAM aid, which is an inflatable bag inside a metal frame. You walk on it and the pressure exerted on the stump starts to reduce the swelling and gets you used to using a false limb. I'll speak to OT and see if they can start you with an arm as soon as possible.'

I wait in quarantine to get the all clear on the MRSA tests, which I keep telling myself will be fine. I'm tired and my writing is slow, but I still have to make the best of things so I tell myself I must be grateful for the chance to watch television. At least I'll be able to answer a lot of Trivial Pursuit questions.

Maggie is as good as her word. With the aid of the inflatable leg bag, foot pump and metal frame I prepare to take my first step. I put what's left of my leg in the grey bag inside the frame and hold it steady as the foot pump inflates the bag. Maggie checks it thoroughly and says, 'That looks right. How does it feel?'

'Fine,' I reply.

'Good. When you've got your crutches you can try standing up.'

I fold the strap over my right forearm and stick it to the Velcro pad. I stand up and slowly put the weight on the stump. It's not too bad. I take small, cautious steps and gradually become more confident.

After what seems like only a few minutes Maggie says, 'That's a good start. If you're getting tired you should rest.'

'No, I'm fine thanks. I'd like to keep going.'

After a few more minutes she says, 'That'll do to begin with. The idea is we start gradually and build up.'

'Yes, I understand. That's very sensible, of course. I guess it's like any sort of physical activity; hill walking or running for example, which I hope to get back to one day. Did I ever tell you . . .' I feel like a naughty child, trying to buy extra time by talking.

'That's enough,' she says.

I realize I'm pushing things too far, but there's a battle here that I have to win.

I sit down. We deflate the bag and look at the stump. She tells me you have to watch it very carefully in the early stages. I listen to every word. If I injure myself it's going to set me back. There's no sense in that. I'm going to push myself to the limit, but not to the point where it's counterproductive.

I explain the exercises I did in South Africa and ask if there are any more she can suggest.

Maggie introduces me to the prosthetist. After examining what's left of my arm he checks the records and says, 'The scar has healed well. Let's take the initial cast and get things started.'

My arm is wrapped carefully in thin plastic to stop the cast sticking. He gets a bowl of water and prepares the plaster bandages. As he moulds them around the stump he says, 'This will feel warm as it sets.'

It does, but it's not unpleasant. He waits for it to set and taps it with his pen several times to make sure it's gone off. Carefully he pulls the cast away. I watch as he does so and think how strange it is to see my hand missing. I still feel it, and remember exactly what it looked like.

Last night I woke suddenly with a spasm of pain in my leg. I realized I could feel my hand. I tried to move my fingers and I could feel them all. I nearly convinced myself there had been some miracle and it had grown back.

In that moment I understood how easy it would be to live my life trying to pretend the accident hadn't happened. I rubbed my stump with my left hand and said to myself, 'Tough shit, Moon. Get used to it, and don't let it get you down.'

I'm able to wash myself in the sink in my room. I take washing drills very seriously. I always try to do them before breakfast. Afterwards I force myself to write, although it's awkward and slow. I know that if I don't practise I'll never improve. But I'm just so tired. I put the pen down. My left hand is aching. Even a five-year-old child can do more than I can at the moment.

I'm going to have visitors. They telephoned before to check it would be convenient. I haven't seen Martin and Huw since we were in Cambodia a year ago. Their cheerful faces peep through the window in the door. Martin sticks his tongue out. Huw holds his face against the glass as he knocks on the door. I laugh.

Huw is a charming, articulate lawyer, but when people try to push him about they bite off more than they can chew. He's a man who doesn't compromise on what he thinks is right. On one occasion I remember him saying, 'If somebody threatened me like that when I was at school, I'd get a wet, rolled-up towel and flick their worthless backside all the way round the gym until they behaved themselves.'

When we were in Cambodia someone, rather uncharitably, nicknamed Martin 'Doctor Death'. It had nothing to do with him or his professional skill; we all trusted him implicitly and relied on him for our own health care. It was simply because so many of his Cambodian patients were dying from malaria or TB when their families took them to the hospital that it was too late for them to respond to treatment.

Dr Death smiles and says, 'We've bought you this.' He opens a green container to reveal a combined backgammon, chess and draughts set, then puts it on the shelf of the bedside cabinet where I can reach it.

They've only been back a few months. Martin is a locum, and he's considering giving up more of his time to travel to distant places to practise medicine where there are few medical services available.

School Bully is returning to commercial law after working in human rights in Cambodia. 'They say you're making an amazing recovery,' he says. 'But we're not at all surprised. Do you know if your todger still works?'

'For a moment I really thought it had been blown off,' I say. 'I just told myself it didn't matter, I'd still be the same person inside.' I paused. 'Thank God I never had to put that theory to the test. I get electric shocks in the stumps when I pee though, particularly the leg.'

'That's the nerves,' says Dr Death.

'Is there anything I can do about it?'

'No, it goes away in time.'

I reach over to have a look at the games box.

'Do you want to come out on Saturday?' School Bully asks. 'Martin's asked the doctors, and as long as your tests come back all right they say it's fine. We'll go and see a film maybe, get something to eat.'

'I'd love to, thanks.'

'How's your writing coming along?' Death asks as he slides my writing paper and pen over on the bed table.

'Slowly. I'd always been strongly right-handed. I can write neatly, but it takes a hell of a long time.'

'It'll come with time. Keep practising. Hopefully we'll see you Saturday.'

On the way out School Bully says, 'Don't worry lad; I'll get Mart to tell the nurses you're a great bloke.'

I pick up my pen and write laboriously to a friend who's running a mine-clearance programme on one of Russia's distant former borders. Now the fighting's stopped, he's training a local team. In his last letter he told me he's training a group of ten demobilized soldiers from the same combat engineer unit. Before the fighting started three years ago, there had been nearly a hundred of them; they'd suffered an 80 per cent casualty rate, and, not surprisingly, had developed an unusual perception of risk. Perhaps Cambodia was more civilized than I thought.

It's taken me two days to write the first page of my reply.

I take a break and return to the story of my First World War pilot. I'm getting to understand what it was like for him. The jolly japes and tally-ho approach was an attempt to conceal the shakes, the nausea, the never-ending fear; the piss-ups offered temporary oblivion from a world where all your mates had creamed in or got toasted.

I sit back and think about Sir Douglas Bader. Even if he was occasionally a bit awkward, I'm full of admiration for his achievements. I think he was a great British hero. I couldn't fly an aircraft when I had two legs.

I always mean to do more writing, but I keep falling asleep. The days are drifting past. I wake up as my Dad and Roger come in to see me. 'You don't seem at all bothered by it,' Roger says.

'I'll be on a false leg soon, so I'll be able to give you a hand with the harvest this summer,' I reply. 'I'm not sure I'll be able to milk cows though.'

Dad laughs and says, 'The way quotas and beef prices are these days it's just as well. Now then, with your change in circumstances I think you should remember the story about the two bulls. The young one said to the old one, Why don't we run up the hill, jump the hedge and serve some of those heifers in the top field? The old bull replied, Let's walk round through the gate and serve the lot.'

Roger looks surprised and says. 'That's unusual. I haven't heard you tell that one before. I thought you'd tell us about *terra firma*. The more firmer the less terror.'

We spend the afternoon talking about farms and farming and remember some very happy times. In their lifetimes agriculture has changed from muscle power to micro electronics.

I get the good news that my MRSA tests are all negative.

Every day I try to walk a little further on the PAM aid. I keep examining the stump, willing it to go down. I rest on Saturday and charge up my batteries. I'm excited about going out. I try to carry on with my letter. Ouch! I've just caught my left thumb nail again. It had soil blasted under it. Luckily my fingernails were facing away from the blast.

The nurse comes to change the dressings. I'm pleased I don't need any more blood transfusions for the time being. They say that's because I was fit. I say, 'I'm sorry to bother you, but could you cut my thumb nail please?'

She gets out the pruning kit and skilfully chops off the blackened nail, removes the dressings and starts to apply the iodine. 'The burns start at the bottom of your legs,' she looks embarrassed for a moment because of her accidental use of the plural, but I smile to show her it's all right, 'and go up your body. It's the first time I've seen anything like it in this unit.'

'It's flash burns from the explosion,' I say. 'I stepped on a mine. What happened to the others here?'

'Most of them have diabetes or some smoking-related illness. There are also a few traffic accident injuries.'

'Do you think the wound on my left ankle will heal, or will it always be scabby scar tissue?'

'Does it bother you?'

It's a good answer. 'No. When do you think I'll be able to pick it off?'

'When it's ready it'll come off.' She shoots me a sideways glance and says. 'Don't pick it.'

'Okay,' I say sleepily. 'I promise.'

She finishes replacing the bandages and draws up the sheet. Then she gives me the sort of smile that makes my nerve endings tingle. 'All part of the service.'

'Fair enough,' I reply. 'By the way, I've been wondering if my todger still works. Any chance of a shag?'

She says, 'Of course. How could I possibly refuse after hearing what that nice Doctor Martin said about you.'

I say, 'Bless him.' This is going to be great.

Then I wake up and find I've been dreaming. I nodded off just after she cut off my thumbnail. I look at the clock. Shit! I'm supposed to be going out in half an hour.

Major panic. It's the first time I've put long trousers on since the accident. I pull on my jeans carefully and button them up. They're miles too big. I'm as skinny as an anorexic stick insect. I fold the floppy trouser leg under the wheelchair pad and grab my pullover.

Fortunately they're a few minutes late, which leaves me time to try and put my watch on. I've been trying every day and so far I haven't succeeded. I fumble with my teeth, left fingers and what's left of my right arm. I put the watch away as I hear the door open.

'Hi lad! How are you?' School Bully grabs my wheelchair and steers me dextrously down the corridor. 'How about a pub by the river, the cinema and a bite to eat? Can you manage all that?'

'Sounds great.' I'm as excited as a train spotter who's just got a flat near Clapham Junction.

'Bring him back in one piece, won't you,' says the nurse as we leave.

'I think it's a bit late for that,' Death says. 'But I'll see what I can do.'

After wrestling with the chair they eventually get it folded and into the back seat on top of Huw's wife Heather and Death.

We sit in the garden of a pub by the side of the Thames. We only have one drink, but when we leave I need to go to the gent's. I see to my horror that the toilets are downstairs and the steps are wet and crowded with blokes waiting their turn. No way! I know they're strong enough to carry me, but I'd prefer to avoid the performance. I toy with the idea of going back and having a few more beers to make me less self-conscious and then get them to carry me down to the gent's while I shout, 'Excuse me, I'm legless!'

I decide the sensible option is to get the driver to push me down the road to a secluded bush. I feel very relieved to be out of the public gaze.

As we make our way through the streets of Richmond to the cinema, they wrestle and bounce me over the edge of the pavement at each road junction. The edges are lowered so it's not too far to bump the chair down, but with only one hand I couldn't possibly do it on my own.

We try to go into several restaurants, but they have steps in the doorway. I wait outside like a dog as my friends plead with the waiter to let me in and find a table where the wheelchair will fit. I feel bad because I'm making things difficult for everyone. I wouldn't have been able to do this on my own. But I must learn.

Eventually we find somewhere with space. When the food arrives, I realize when I ordered I'd forgotten that I only have one hand. I have to ask School Bully to cut up the food for me. At the end of the meal I go to get up like everyone else. I start to put my right leg down and suddenly remember. I stop myself just in time. It still feels like it's there and I've had it for thirty years, so it's going to take a while for me to get used to its absence.

On the way back we chat about Cambodia. It seems like a lifetime ago that Death and I lived in the same dusty street of a small town near the Thai border. The wooden houses were well spaced and each enclosed by a fence to keep out thieves and other people's animals, and to keep in their pigs and bony chickens. Every day, if we finished work in time, we'd run under the palm trees by the pagoda and then by the side of the muddy river to a rickety foot bridge, then back again. As we went, we would talk through the trials and tribulations of our day. Death worked in a hospital where the medical staff didn't get paid enough to live, so although treatment was supposed to be free, they charged for it when the westerners weren't there. He was worried that poor people got poor treatment and died.

When I get back to Roehampton I think through everything we've done. With planning I should be able to get around on my own. And I'm sure I'll be able to drive an automatic car; I just have to convince the doctor.

I was totally reliant on everyone else when we went out. It's the first time I've ever had to ask people to do things for me. It's quite a lesson in humility. I'm determined to be independent again. If all goes well I'll be out of the wheelchair and using a false leg in a few months.

I wonder what the future holds. What will I do? The answer is actually rather simple. My future will be what I make it.

21

GRIPPING YARNS

APRIL 1995

Have you seen this game at the amusement arcade, the one where the prizes are laid out invitingly in a big Perspex cylinder and you try to clutch them with the little grab crane?

Learning to use the hook is just like that. The false arm fits over the stump. It's a nice, fleshy pink colour with a steel ratchet end fitting where the hook clips in. The hook is held on by straps and operates on a simple lever principle, with a cable linked to a band around my left shoulder. The jaws open when I stretch out my arm, and thick rubber bands force them closed when my body relaxes, taking the tension off the cable.

I shuffle around in the wheelchair, to try and get comfortable. Last night the nurse picked out the blue stitches from the large scabby scar below my knee. Next week the physio thinks they'll be able to take a cast and start making my new leg.

'How are you getting on?' Alison the occupational therapist asks.

'I can manage picking things up. As you pointed out, the temptation is to open it all the way rather than just enough to grip whatever I need to.' Using every ounce of concentration, I clutch a red cylindrical peg and push it into a round hole.

'You've certainly got the hang of that. Would you like to try to make something with the Meccano?' She points to a large box. 'It's a good way to practise using the hook because you need two grips to put it all together.'

She doesn't get the box for me. I decide to make something with as many difficult joints and nuts and bolts as I can. I spend the next hour constructing a lorry.

I pick up the tiny tool kit and remember the last time I had a spanner in my hand. Rupert and I were doing a recce near the Zimbabwe border and we had vehicle trouble. I always carried two spare wheels on the roof. I could climb up, unchain the wheel, drop it, jump down, change the wheel and put the tyre on the roof again in about five minutes. Now I'm struggling to do two bolts on a child's toy in the same time.

I look up at Alison as I'm finishing. 'The thing I've learnt this morning is that I can do things, but I have to do them in a different way.'

'I need to show you how to hold a knife, although you've probably already worked it out.' She puts the knife in the hook and rests the handle on the lever where the cable attaches.

'When can I start riding a bike and weight training?' I ask.

She walks to a display of false arm attachments on a wooden shelf, and picks up a stainless steel C-hook. 'This will probably be best, though the cosmetic hand might be better on a bike. You can go to the Douglas Bader Centre and try an exercise bike in the gym.'

I survey the vast range of clip-on attachments. There is a fishing-rod holder, a snooker-cue rest, a brush, a potato peeler and a pair of pliers. 'Most of them don't get used,' she says. 'At the end of the war they sent people home with a suitcase full of clip-on appliances which everyone left in the case. The myo-electric hand is the most commonly prescribed now. It's battery powered and sensors pick up the electrical impulses from the nerve ends in the stump and convert them into movement. In a few months, when your stump has settled down, that's something we can look at fitting.'

I've heard it looks like a real hand. My mother would appreciate that. I look at the steel hook. There's no getting away from it, I don't look like other people. I still haven't been able to put my watch on yet, so I look at the clock. I must go and do my walking practice.

The inflatable leg is comfortable now. The stump is reducing a bit. They still want me to use the crutches, but at least I am walking. Once the leg is inflated and correctly fitted I stagger around. The walking school is in a gymnasium. There are four sets of double bars at waist height. Some of the other patients grip them and begin to walk. While I'm waiting to get the PAM aid fitted I watch them. Some struggle with the pain, some sit hopelessly and some rest in between bouts.

Many of the older ones are outpatients. Some of them go outside to smoke in their wheelchairs because the walking school is a no-smoking area. The prosthetists in their white coats do fittings and make adjustments to false limbs and the physios give encouragement and advice to people as they take their first painful and uncertain steps.

I'm in a hurry and I've asked all the professionals for advice on how to do things as fast as possible. At this stage I still need to get the swelling down. The wound is healing and it's not bleeding any more. I go round the waiting area outside the walking school. I'm always careful not to overdo it, because that would be counter-productive, but I push myself around the carpet as furiously as I can until I feel the stump getting sore, then I get it checked. They think they'll be able to do a cast and start making the leg in the next few days.

A hospital rule says patients from the LSU have to be pushed down to the walking school by a member of the staff, for insurance purposes. A car being driven in the car park smashed into someone in a wheelchair.

As we emerge into the sunshine and on to the road to the rehab centre the porter pulls the chair back sharply. I can hear a car. He shouts. There is a screech of brakes. It seems to happen in slow motion. The black Granada looks enormous from wheelchair height. The car skids sideways, burning rubber. I can't run. It's going to smack straight into me.

The porter puts his hand on my shoulder. The car stops a few feet from me. My heart's beating like a machine-gun and I'm short of breath. I try not to show it. 'This a hospital!' the porter yells. 'There's a five-mile-an-hour speed limit and big bloody signs saying slow and look out for patients. You weren't looking, and you were going too fast. Slow down and open your bloody eyes!'

The driver sits silently. The porter resumes pushing as if nothing has happened. 'You all right mate? I grabbed your shoulder because I thought you might forget you'd lost your leg and try to run. Everyone does it at some stage. It's a reflex. Have you forgotten, stood up and fallen over yet?'

'Not quite.' I remember my day out with School Bully, and smile.

I spend the afternoon walking round the waiting area quietly saying to myself, 'Left, right, left, right.' I enjoy being able to walk. They're putting an attachment on a stick so that it clips into my false arm. They say you have to use two sticks when you start to walk on a prosthesis.

I'm sharing a room now with a young man who had both legs amputated while on a visit to his family in India. He was waiting for a train and as it came into the station the crowd surged forward and he was pushed on to the track. He doesn't remember much about it, just somebody saying, 'Put his legs on the stretcher too.' Apart from a few weekends at home he's spent the last two years in hospital. He's not even twenty.

He reminds me of Som On, the double amputee I saw in the hospital in Cambodia. Thanks to Kike, Som On and his family now have a future. Kike got my note and sent someone to find him. I keep the letter with the one from Houn. I sent messages to thank them for their good wishes, but I can't write back. I have to go and see them. Maybe next year.

The dark of the night is a good time to think. There are some things that can't be communicated or understood, they can only be experienced. It's better now. I've moved away from the edge of the abyss, where death was near enough to touch. Sometimes I still feel it.

I've lost count of the number of times I thought I was going to die. Every time I think it's going to happen, I say my prayers and hope. Curiously, I don't hope for preservation, I hope for justice.

I don't pretend to have all the answers. I just know it's important to ask the questions.

Sunlight is creeping around the corner of the curtains. I reach over to the bedside cabinet and grab my watch. It's eight fifteen. It must be a beautiful spring morning out there. I can't wait to get out. Simon said he'd be over at about ten. We can go across the road to the park and sit by the lake. I've heard the daffodils and crocuses are beautiful, and there are ducks and geese swimming around and crapping on the grass.

I'll wash and shave before breakfast. I throw off the bed-clothes and sit up. I examine the dressing on my right leg and gently pull back the plaster to reveal the long cross-shaped scar. It's improving. There aren't so many fresh scabby bits and it's stopped oozing. A stab of phantom pain makes me jerk what's left of the leg in spasm. It feels like someone is banging a six-inch nail into my ankle. I massage the stump and give it a slap. The result is uncomfortable, but it cures the phantom pain.

I move to the edge of the bed, hop into the wheelchair, put my stump on the padded rest and manoeuvre round the bed to the sink. I've got my washing and shaving drills well sorted, I've had a few weeks' practice.

I balance precariously on my left leg and push my hips

against the sink as I shave, then I put on my clothes and check my watch. It took me twenty-one minutes. About a minute faster than yesterday. I *can* do everything; it's just that it takes longer.

Simon and I went to primary school together and have always kept in touch. He's now head of year and teaches English at a large London school. Shortly after ten o'clock the nurse shows him in. He smiles and automatically offers me his left hand, as if we'd always shaken hands that way. We haven't seen each other for ages. There are so many things to talk about. Simon has always encouraged my love of books and said I should write. He manages to convince the nurse he's a responsible adult, and is allowed to take me out in the wheelchair to the park.

While he's pushing me along the corridor I suddenly get a flood of phantom pain that makes me grimace and involuntarily lift the stumps. He looks away and without changing his tone of voice carries on telling me why I should read more Graham Greene.

We emerge from the hospital into the April morning. I've put on my jumper and coat. It's good to be outside. Even though I'm being pushed in a wheelchair I feel free. The air is clean and fresh and we follow a path with yellow and purple crocuses to the edge of the lake. Simon parks me next to a wooden seat and sits down. Five large hungry geese join us. I don't need to tell him about the shit, he appears to have found out about it himself.

I admire the ornamental trees and spring flowers. 'I'm told this place was a rehabilitation centre for soldiers in the First World War. What a beautiful place.'

A large grey goose with a bright orange bill waddles towards me. He looks big. Sitting in my wheelchair I feel very vulnerable. I hope he doesn't object to us being on his territory. He stops two metres away, extends his neck and hisses.

I try not to sound nervous, 'What do you think we should do?'

Simon laughs. 'I'm not sure, but if it gets any more aggressive I'm running away. What are you going to do?'

'I'm going to ignore it and hope it goes away.'

We sit and enjoy the early April sunshine. In spite of it I start to shiver. I remind Simon about the time he visited the farm in Devon in the middle of winter. He says, 'It was great, but too chilly for me. Unlike you I feel the cold.'

I have to reply honestly, 'That's changed, I'm afraid. I'm too cold to stay here.'

He gets up, flicks the brake off the wheelchair, smiles and says, 'Glad you said that. I'm freezing.'

On the return trip out of the corner of my eye I see him discreetly unbutton his coat, loosen his scarf and wipe a few beads of sweat from his brow.

When we get back I impose on Simon's good nature and ask him to help me wash my hair. I can't do the shampoo, get my head in the sink and rinse it properly with one hand. I'm also worried that I'll slip over. I didn't want to trouble the nurses this morning because they were busy with two patients who are seriously ill.

When he goes to leave he says, 'You know, I've been thinking about disability this morning. The unfair thing is that the onus is very much on you to put others at their ease, isn't it? But it's your problem and you have to face it. What other people think shouldn't matter.'

I have to think before I reply. 'I suppose you're right. But the thing I've found so far is that other people impose limits on me. The thing that frightens me is that I might be a prisoner, unable to travel or get about without their help.'

The next day is Sunday. Most of the others have gone home for the weekend. After breakfast I turn on the television to watch the start of the London Marathon. The year before I went to Cambodia I couldn't get a place so I helped marshal the course. Watching the start of the race brings back fond memories of standing in the drizzle in a large plastic orange vest wishing I'd got a place to run.

They show a panoramic of the Start shot from a helicopter with a seemingly endless snake of colourful dots, each one a marathoner. I watch the elite lithe runners with intense faces and then they show a fat man gasping for breath and I wonder who's trying hardest and who has the greater achievement.

They show runners in fancy dress, one dressed as a chicken. They show a clip of one of the past runs with the great British runner Dave Bedford throwing up. As they show him bending over with his hands on his knees I say, 'They think it's all up. It is now.'

'Nursey' walks past and gives me a strange look. They play the song 'It's A Long Long Road' and show the magic moments of people of all ages doing their best. Some of them in tears as they finish.

As I watch them pound the streets I think of Som On and others like him with no legs and know that next year I have to do the marathon.

Every day I look at the scar below my knee, think positive thoughts and try to make it heal. They say it's happening. John the prosthetist has taken a cast and started to make the leg.

By coincidence many of the people I knew in Cambodia are back in London. Within pushing distance of the hospital there's an Italian restaurant. As long as it's not long spaghetti, eating pasta with one hand is easy. I have to shuffle down the stairs on my backside to use the toilet and it takes ages, but nobody seems to mind.

At long last I can go home for two days. My brother-in-law picks me up mid-morning. I sit waiting with my bag packed. I did it last night.

Ian arrives and pushes me to the car. I hop in as he folds

up the wheelchair and puts it in the boot. I'm excited about having the chance to see the countryside. When we get to the house I push myself around to the back garden. My father has made a wooden ramp so that I can get in through the larger door at the back of the house. We've spoken on the phone about it. As I push my way to the top and roll down the other side he shouts from the garden. 'How is it?'

'Excellent thanks.'

After he's finished filling the peanut dispenser for the birds he puts the steps in the shed and walks down the garden. He walks deliberately and with economy of movement to control his angina. He holds out his left hand and says, 'Good to have you home son. What do you want to do today?'

'Get driving.'

'When?'

'This afternoon. Ian's bravely volunteered to take me.'

'Okay, the car's by the garage. Let's have a coffee and chat for ten minutes. Then you can see the garden and the garage.'

Since retirement Dad has taught himself cabinet-making. He spends most days in the garage at the front of the house making or mending something for someone. People walking their dogs or going to the shop often stop to talk to him, so he always knows what's happening in the village. Everyone says he's always cheerful and friendly and ready to help.

Mum brings the coffee. Benny the cat bounds in after her and welcomes me with loud squawks and a few bites before dashing off through the patio doors to hunt rabbits. Mum laughs and says, 'Presumably you'll be all right shuffling up the stairs?'

'Yes. No problem I'll sit on them and push myself up using my left foot and hand. I've done it at the hospital up two flights to get to the bank.'

I'm pleased they're not making a big deal of things.

Now all I need to do is drive and I'm independent. Ian's

got the steering wheel adaptation to the car. It's simply a knob fitted to the top of the wheel that makes it easier to steer with one hand. I'm used to using them because they're fitted to most tractors with front-end loaders, so the other hand's free to use the controls.

I've got my licence paperwork and insurance with a company the British Limbless Ex-Servicemen's Association recommended. Their leaflets were on display in the hospital.

After a rest I go for a drive with Ian. We head for a long road that merges with a bridleway. I concentrate much harder than I used to. I'm mega cautious. Disabled people get a heavy loading and I don't ever intend to prove the actuaries right.

I practise three-point turns, emergency stops and sharp turns. Operating the lights, indicators and windscreen wipers isn't a problem. I drive back confidently through the town. I return with a sense of accomplishment.

My friend George, who was in the army for forty years, visits and asks me round to his place for tea on Sunday afternoon. He also offers to drive me back to hospital. I spend the rest of the day resting. Not because I ought to, but because I'm too tired to do anything else.

On Sunday I go to the village church with my parents. I only just manage to resist the temptation to leap up and hop about shouting, 'Look. It's a miracle. I can hop.' I know Dad and David, the vicar, would think it was funny, but I don't think anyone else would appreciate it.

At three thirty on Sunday I prepare to go out alone for the first time. I push myself over the wooden ramp, round the house and through the gate. I want to do this. Everyone knows it's important to me to get round here on my own.

I roll down the drive and along the pavement and as I get to the kerb something happens which I hadn't anticipated. I'm terrified. A surge of panic floods through me. It's only a drop of a few inches, but I haven't had to do anything like this before. Perhaps I should push myself back home and get somebody to help me?

I look round. The street is empty. If the worst happens and I fall out I think I'll be able to get back in on my own, but I don't want anybody to see. I used to be able to run to George's in less than a minute and now I think it's going to take at least seven. I hope everything else doesn't take seven times as long when I get out of hospital. I stick my leg down and let the wheelchair drop. My heart's in my mouth. I make it and get up the other side by turning the wheels backwards.

When I get to George's I wonder suddenly how I am going to get into the house. He ushers me to the conservatory where I see he's made a ramp into the garden.

On the drive back to the hospital we talk about our hill walking and climbing expeditions. He knows I want to get fit again. 'The best exercise to start with would be swimming.' He's right. I must go swimming as soon as I can.

When I get back to the hospital I go to bed early. I'm still frustratingly weak.

The next day I get a visit from an old friend from the army. Ted now lives in Barnes and is working in an exciting staff job in the Ministry of Defence in central London. Although not Scottish he resembles Sean Connery, but his hairline hasn't receded quite as much. 'Good to see you back on your feet,' he says as I approach. Then he grins. 'Sorry, I mean foot.'

We arrange my first non-motorized trip to the pub. It's about a ten-minute walk, quicker if you hurry. Ted becomes instantly adept at steering the wheelchair. We have a great evening, putting the world to rights and drinking very moderately.

I've planned everything meticulously. I've got the mini-bar well hidden in my bedside cabinet and we look forward to having a sharpener on return to the hospital. But there is one slight problem. We stop outside and look at the chained metal gates. 'It's all right,' I say. 'We can climb over the wall.'

'It's ten feet high,' Ted says reasonably. 'You probably could climb over it, you daft bugger, but I don't think I can get your wheelchair up there.'

I remember the first time I went climbing in Wales with the army. I struggled to conquer my fear and the wet slippery rock. After that I enjoyed it.

The first principle of climbing is always to have three points of contact. As I look up at the wall I reflect on the fact that I now only have two. I think I could overcome it and create a third by using a combination of my elbow and chin, but now is not a good time. I'll climb it before I leave, though. And I'd prefer to go out rather than in. In the meantime, I decide to head for the other gate by the traffic lights.

In spite of being careful not to drink too much, the next day I have a slight hangover. I realize I have to adjust my alcohol intake to my new size and weight. I'll need to remember this when I drive.

In spite of the headache it's an exciting morning. I'm having the first leg fitting. I slip a sock over the stump and put it into the moulded white foam socket. Then I push it into the false leg and do up the leather strap above the knee.

John the prosthetist, who made my false arm, takes a pen from the pocket of his white coat, makes a mark on the top of the false leg and says, 'How does it feel?'

'Fine. Can I try it?'

Maggie says, 'Yes, but you need to take very slow, small steps between the bars.'

I stand up. John checks the leg is the right length and my hips are level. My heart tells me to try and run. My head tells me to take it easy. When I try to take the first step my body tells me my heart needs to do a reality check.

I grip the bar and follow Maggie's instructions. Carefully I put my weight on the prosthesis. It feels strange, wooden and uncomfortable. Slowly I take a step forward. As I move the limb the nerves tingle as different forces act on the stump. When I put it down I can feel the ankle and the lower leg that are no longer there. Walking now feels the most unnatural activity, it's like balancing on a seesaw.

I do what Maggie says and take slow, small steps and grip the bar with my left hand. I can't understand why I have no sense of balance; after all I've still got one leg. I step forward carefully. When I put the false leg down the pressure feels uncomfortable. I take unsteady steps forward but gradually I gain confidence and improve slightly. I'm soon able to graduate to using the two sticks and get out of the bars. Instead of a handle one of the sticks has a metal attachment that clips into the end of my false arm.

I'm in a hurry and I'm keen. I force myself to follow every piece of advice from the physiotherapists to the letter.

After a few minutes we stop and take the leg off to see how the scar is holding up. It still looks the same. We put it back on again and I shuffle slowly around the walking school for a few more minutes. I'm tired. I stop to rest.

The other patients from the LSU are all doing well. I watch them and try to offer encouragement. They do the same for me.

There are large mirrors against the wall so we can watch our walking. I try hard to walk without a limp but I don't know what I'm doing wrong. The stump starts to feel sore.

'Let's check again,' Maggie says. 'We don't want to overdo it.'

I stop and we take the leg off. There are several blisters appearing on the amputation scar. Everyone gets them to begin with. I have to stop. If I keep going, the scar tissue will break down and I'll have to wait for it to heal.

I sit and wait. I need to go up to the limb-fitting centre for a few adjustments. As I'm waiting Maggie introduces me to a fit-looking bloke who I guess is a soldier.

Bob was serving in Nine Squadron, the Royal Engineers Parachute Unit. He was deployed in Rwanda when he stepped on a mine while working in a cleared area around a bridge. He tells me the first thing he knew about it was seeing his foot smoking. It didn't blow it right off. He trod on a toe blower, probably a VS50, which has a main charge of forty-two grams of TNT. He was taken to a UN medical facility where an Australian surgeon amputated his foot. He was blown up six months ago.

He's accompanying a friend from Headley Court, the Tri-Services Rehabilitation Centre. When he hears I'm waiting to go to the limb-fitting centre he offers to push me. I'm impressed to see how well he walks. I ask him about running and he tells me he wants to do the London Marathon, but he's finding it harder to run than he thought he would.

I mention that I'm going to run, but I have to learn to walk first. I also tell him about a run Huw said I should enter called the Great Sahara Marathon

The most comfortable and fastest way to walk is with an exaggerated limp. They tell me it's the last thing a new amputee should do. I have to take it slowly. If I pick up bad habits now I'll have them for ever. I watch myself in the mirror, ask for advice and attempt to get my technique right. The physios watch and make suggestions. I follow instructions to the letter, and do as much as I can. I must put the work in to get it right now, but the frustrating thing is that no matter how hard I try I can't get it perfect.

It's uncomfortable. I straighten my back, grip my stick until my knuckles whiten. I bang the false arm with the walking-stick attachment on the ground a few times to get it used to taking pressure. The attachment is also useful during rest periods because I can use it to do impersonations of a 'dalek'.

I march slowly up and down. I keep on and on, but I don't seem to get better. They tell me it will take time and that when I leave here I should find a mirror and keep practising.

To begin with I can stay on the false leg for no more than five minutes. Every afternoon we leave our false legs at the walking school because we have to wear them in gradually, under supervision.

I walk a little further each day and religiously practise my gait. I watch in the mirror and see I still have a limp. They say it will take months to get it right, and only then if I keep practising. If the consultant thinks the scar has healed sufficiently and the leg fits I can go home some time in the next few days.

'What about running?' I ask.

'In some cases it's possible; but it will take time. We try to get patients back as near as possible to the level of activity they had before. To maintain future mobility it is vital to protect the residual limb. Without a lower leg you require 30 per cent more energy to walk. When it comes to running the stress and pressure through the stump are enormous. The effect on the back and other parts of the body must also be considered. We'll do what we can, but it will take time.'

At last my discharge day arrives. The paperwork says 28 April. I've done it. I'm out in less than two months. Rupert, who pulled me out of the helicopter in Quelimaine, is back on a long overdue holiday and comes into hospital at lunchtime. He brings cans of cold beer and the first warm spring day. Tom, an old friend who was with Rupert in the Parachute Regiment, joins us and we catch up on the news. I try gripping a beer can in the hook. It's not strong enough. 'I've got some spare elastic bands. Do you think you could put a few more of them on, to give it a bit more grip?'

Rupert sticks another five or six effortlessly around the jaws of the stainless-steel hook. When the nurse comes in he says, 'Hello Nursey. I'm just giving him a hand.' He passes it back to me. I strain to widen the hook enough to get the can in, and once it's in there and I relax the can is crushed. I decide not to tell them I've spent all week trying to get one band and my watch on, and still haven't managed either.

After they've gone I say my goodbyes and thank yous to everyone in the walking school and on the ward. I have an appointment to come back in two weeks to get the false limbs checked. I feel sad now, and curiously guilty. Compared to many of them, I am very lucky.

Sensible Rob comes to pick me up and take me back to Salisbury. When we were at school we all thought he'd be a millionaire business mogul. He majored in business studies and then gave up a promising career in retailing to become a nurse on a specialist burns unit, in North London.

We put my false leg and wheelchair in the boot of the car. When we arrive at my parents we sit and chat. I suddenly realize I need to go to the loo. I get up immediately and as I tumble towards the floor I remember I've only got one leg.

I land on the stump and try hard not to show that it was as painful as having a testicle smashed with a mallet. I don't want anybody to help me. I can't breathe or speak so I hold up my left hand and shake my head.

Rob looks at me, nods and says, 'If you want any help let me know.'

Mum goes into the kitchen to make the tea and Dad lifts up the paper and starts to read.

After regaining my senses I climb back in the wheelchair, pretend nothing has happened and feel thankful for the fact that at least I didn't vomit on the carpet.

Rob says, 'Don't worry. Everybody does that. It can be your party trick.'

Days pass and I take things sensibly, resting and doing as much walking practice as I can. John the prosthetist said I should gradually wear the leg in so that the stump becomes tolerant to wearing it all day. I start to get more confident and arrange to go to London to meet with friends.

Mike was in the Foreign Legion. When we worked in Cambodia he was very popular with the ladies, possibly because of the rumour that he had been endowed with the sort of tackle that would make an elephant feel inadequate. We sit in the early summer sunshine with our companions and then move to a restaurant. I go down the wooden spiral staircase and as I return I realize it only has a right-hand rail. I have nothing to hold on to on the return climb. I step carefully back up the spiral, one step at a time. As I get to the top my false leg slips. Somebody must have spilt something. I thrust my right hand out to grab the rail. It slips, too. No! I don't have a hand any more.

I'm falling. As I tumble back down the staircase I think, Oh dear, this is going to hurt. I land with a thud at the bottom. Everything is still.

Dazed, I look at the blood on the polished wooden boards. My blood. The bright scarlet droplets splash on to the floor like water from a broken tap. I try to move my stumps and realize it's all right; I was able to protect my body from damage by landing on my face.

People continue with their meals, pretending not to notice. Some of them shoot me horrified sideways glances. When I return them they avoid my eyes. At least this situation has taught me something. It's a bummer when your false leg slips on the top of a spiral staircase.

I ask a passing Asian waiter for some napkins so that I

won't bleed on to the floor. As he hands them to me he says, 'No worry. You stay there. I already call ambulance,' and rushes off to deliver plates to the customers before the food gets cold.

'That won't be necessary,' I call after him. 'As soon as I can stand I'll be out of here.' I'm shocked and embarrassed. I've broken my nose, it won't stop bleeding, and I've cut my face open. I know I'll need stitches, but I don't know where.

After a few moments a charming woman asks me if I'm all right and helps me to a chair. She says she's a physiotherapist and asks where my friends are. She goes to get Mike. I sit still, trying to catch the drips of blood and think how bad this would be without my friends. I hope I'm not putting people off their food. I almost feel I need to explain the situation to them.

Mike gets more napkins for me to bleed into. The ambulance men arrive and say that if I don't get stitches I'll have a 'boat race' like Al Pacino in *Scarface*. I say, 'Fine. I don't need to trouble you. I can get a taxi to the hospital.'

At that point I feel a sharp pain in my ribs. Mike gives me a dig and whispers, 'Get in the ambulance. It'll save you a taxi fare.'

The paramedic nods, 'Now we've been called, we have to take you.'

'Thanks very much,' I reply. 'I know this is going to sound strange but I'd like to try to walk up the stairs again.'

After dressing the cut and trying to stop my nose bleeding they agree, as long as the extremely large ex-Legionnaire follows right behind me. I get to my feet. My legs and back are bruised. I take the steps, one at a time. The slippery one isn't a problem now I know it's there.

It's the first time I've been in an ambulance. I thank them for the lift and get taken to wait in Accident and Emergency.

The nurse at Reception is behind a huge glass protective screen. There are only two other people in the waiting room. The nurses say it's going to get really busy later as it's Friday night.

Suddenly ambulances scream past the windows. Blue lights fill the room. The nurse tells us it's a bad road accident. They've got six seriously injured people.

Mike and I sit and chat about what Neil's doing and whether or not he'll marry his latest girlfriend. Suddenly a man in his late twenties walks to the glass barrier with a woman. She has a small piece of white cloth held against her arm. We're behind them and he hasn't seen us. 'This is a fucking disgrace,' he shouts. 'We've been waiting hours. I want something done bloody now.'

Mike suddenly pulls away the bandage I'm holding in front of my nose and starts to pull off my false limbs.

The petite young nurse says, 'I'm really sorry, sir. We're dealing with two very bad road accidents at the moment. We have to treat the most seriously injured first. Somebody will be with you as soon as possible.'

The man swears and bangs his fist against the glass.

Mike completes his task. I can feel the blood running down my face again. He stands up, points at me and his voice booms. 'Excuse me. My friend and I have been here five hours, and we're quite happy to wait. We think you're doing a great job. Don't we?'

I raise my bloody and bandaged face from a heap of distorted and missing limbs and bloody tissues. I smile cheerfully. 'Oh yes. We think you're doing an excellent job. We're quite happy to wait all night. Thank you.' I then collapse back into my chair, Mike sits down and we try not to laugh.

'I bet he did that,' Mike says quietly. 'That's why he's making such a fuss.'

'What do you mean?'

He says darkly, 'I knew a nurse who said people go to hospital with knife wounds inflicted during sadomasochistic sex.'

'You're making this up.'

'I'm not. You go and ask them. I bet they're weirdos.'

'We mustn't jump to conclusions.' I pause. 'You ask.'

The couple start hissing and spitting at each other like two vipers being baited with sticks, so neither of us asks them.

When I go out I know I don't look like everyone else. I feel different standing in a queue, paying for something in a shop or sitting on the tube. Some people notice and then try to pretend they didn't. When they ask what happened I say I was eaten by a crocodile. My immediate reaction is to tell them to mind their own business and leave me in peace to read my book, but I realize I can't be endlessly combative. And besides, they all want to hear the gory details.

The occupational therapist says that now the stump has settled down they are going to try a myo-electric hand. It looks like the real thing, there are no straps, and it opens and closes and grips things.

Barry takes a cast and measures the electrical impulses from my muscles. He shows me how to make the right muscle movements in the stump. It's uncomfortable and they often go into spasm, but the more I practise the easier it gets.

It takes two weeks to construct the hand, which gives me time to build up my strength. He said that because of the way the muscle groups have been connected, one movement gives a very strong impulse and the other is very weak. He warns me that occasionally I'll have the odd spasm, but eventually I should able to control it. He shows me how the emergency grip-release works.

I go to OT and practise opening and closing the hand and picking up various things. Alison shows me that my Meccano creation is still in one piece. Building on my previous training

I'm able to work out how to hold a knife. She notices that I only open it as far as I need to pick things up, and nods her approval. She leaves me with a word of warning, 'Wear it in gradually, and be aware that the muscles will be tired at the end of the day.'

As I walk out of OT I get a cup of coffee from the woman who runs the Friends' shop. When I was in hospital I always spilt my coffee so she would carry it to the table for me. Now with this new hand I think I can do it. Concentrating hard and moving very slowly, I get a result and only spill half of it.

When I emerge into the summer sunshine for the first time I limp to the car and head for Camberwell where I'm meeting School Bully and Death. As we walk into the small wine bar in Brixton I realize what I like about my new hand. For the first time in three months I feel a fully paid-up member of the human race in the company of strangers. More friends join us. My alcohol tolerance has increased slightly now, so on Death's medical advice I'm now allowed two pints during the course of the evening. As the evening rolls on I show everyone proudly how the new hand works. During my demonstration I go for the nearest soft body part. For those of you who might find yourselves in my situation, I suggest you try using someone else's body.

After a while I realize I've been overdoing it because the muscles in the stump go into spasm. Suddenly I'm in agony. Unfortunately I've been resting the hand in my lap, and I now have the most excruciating pain in my left testicle. I writhe and wriggle, as I find one does in these circumstances.

I struggle for breath. My eyes are watering and a wave of nausea rises in my throat. I look down through the tears. The muscle spasm has caused the hand to open and close, and by sheer bad luck it's gripped a gonad.

'Look Martin! Help!' I struggle to release the pained appendage. The more I try to open the hand, the tighter it grips. I can feel the sweat running down my face. I'm starting to panic. It's lucky there's a doctor present.

Death leaps up, slaps his thigh and shouts, 'Great one!' and then rolls around, helpless with laughter.

School Bully is always good in a crisis. I know he'll fix it. He's probably about to leap into action. I shout, 'Huw! Huw! Look! Help!'

Where is he? I can't see him. I fight for composure. If I can control myself I should be able to release it. I think I'm going to be sick.

School Bully returns to the scene and starts a round of applause. Everyone joins in. And I mean everyone. Being a good mate, he's just invited the whole bar to witness the spectacle of the testicle.

I can't reach the thumb to pull back the emergency release, so the only option is to control the spasm. I have to relax my muscles, then gradually move them in the opposite direction to open it. Miraculously it works, the hand loosens and the gonad is released. I stand and take a bow.

School Bully says, 'We always said you've got balls.'

On the way back in the cab my plan to get even nearly goes horribly wrong. Believing the key to success is speed and surprise I wait until they're chatting quietly, then pull off the arm, wave it around and tap their heads. 'Don't ever think you'll be out of my reach.'

The driver is rather surprised and mounts the kerb. He says that I'm the first person to remove body parts in his car, except he doesn't use those exact words.

22

SINK OR SWIM

The sound of laughter and splashing echoes and amplifies around the vast, blue-painted, concrete building. I walk cautiously along the beige ribbed tiles by the side of the pool. Some of them are wet; it would be easy for me to slip.

By the deep end there are some benches. I think that would be the best place to take my leg off. I should be able to hop to the side from there.

I keep looking down at the tiles, watching out for wet bits.

The first time I came to the pool there was a long line of noisy children ahead of me. They went quiet, then whispered and pointed at the silver hook. I found it easier to operate than the hand, and it never grabbed my testicle when I least expected it. I thought, I really don't like this, and went back home.

I returned a few times and there were always too many people waiting or I told myself I was too busy. I do have a lot to do. I walk every day and do my writing practice. I've just got a computer and I need to get the hang of it. But this morning I've decided I *must* get some exercise. I'm so weak and tired, I have to build up my strength again. The false leg doesn't fit any more and it's harder to walk properly. They're making me a new socket because the stump has shrunk. It takes about a month and I can't hide away for ever.

I fold my towel over the stump of my arm and carry on the long walk. As the towel slips off the stump I flick it back over again. The false leg looks nearly normal from a distance, but the bit where the stump fits in is bulbous because it's still new. They say it will shrink a lot in the next four years.

I keep looking at the floor. I don't want to slip. A bather powers up and down the lane nearest me. His crawl strokes cut through the water. I used to be able to swim like that.

The smell of chlorine fills the air and some water splashes on to my leg. I step cautiously back. I don't want a repeat of my spiral staircase experience. I'm vulnerable without the protection of the false arm. The stumps are sore and full of raw nerves.

Out of the corner of my eye I see two women doing breaststroke and bobbing along cheerfully. They stop when they draw level with me.

On my right there is a woman wearing a patterned blue swimming costume and a blue swimming hat. She's taking her daughter swimming. As I go past the woman holds the little girl's hand and says, 'Sshh . . .'

On the other side of the pool, remote on a raised ladder seat, the lifeguard watches like a tennis umpire. Another, dressed in identical white shirt and shorts, patrols the side of the pool. It's large, not far off Olympic size.

Why shouldn't I go swimming?

Out of the corner of my eye I can see they've spotted me, but they're good at their jobs so they keep their eyes on the water.

A large silver clock on the far end wall prolongs my endless humiliation. The seconds tick so slowly it mocks me. I hate it.

I reach the bench and sit down awkwardly. It's too low. I put the towel down. Now they can all see I haven't got a hand either.

I undo the strap and pull the leg off, then I remove the layers of stump socks.

I don't want to risk standing up. I try crawling like an

animal, but the tiles are too hard on the stumps. I edge back
to the wooden bench and raise myself by pushing with my left
hand and driving my left leg up. I jump up the last bit and
wobble like a flamingo in a force ten.

I turn the wobble into forward motion and shuffle and slip
across the tiles. I try not to hop because it always strains my
left leg and that does all the work, so I must look after it. I've
developed the one-legged side shuffle.

It takes all my concentration. When I get close to the edge
I watch for the splashed water. I feel my foot slip slightly. I
stop and decide to crawl the last metre.

I had no idea it was possible to feel more naked than naked.

I get to the edge of the pool and sit with my left leg dangling
in the warm water. I won't be able to stand up. It will be way
over my head. But I want to go in at the deep end. I wonder if
I can still swim?

Of course I can, and even if I can't then I'll be able to tread
water. I could even sink and then push myself up to the surface
from the bottom, take a deep breath, and repeat the process
until I reached the side. I'd only get into difficulty if I panicked.
I've thought it through many times.

How will I get into the water?

I look up and suddenly realize the whole place is silent.
Even the water has gone quiet.

The two ladies are breaststroking towards me. Beneath their
pink bathing caps their eyes are locked on to my stumps with
laser accuracy. The other swimmers paddle and watch. The
pool attendant scans the water and continues to walk non-
chalantly in my direction.

Everyone is frozen except the freestyle swimmer in the near
lane, and each of his strokes is like a lash, reminding me of
something I once had.

I haven't got time to be here. I should be learning to use

my new computer or practising my handwriting. I should be concentrating on my future. It was a mistake coming here. I'd better just cut my losses and go.

I take a last look at the water. It's a question of cowardice. It is easier not to face it, but then I'd be in a prison from which there is no escape.

I think of Som On again. I will not give in. This is a simple test. It doesn't matter what people think. I'm sorry I don't look like everyone else, but there's nothing I can do about it. I want to go swimming.

I try to throw myself into the water. Instead I slip in and sink. Shit, it's deeper than I thought.

The water pressure on the stumps is a bit uncomfortable. It's all right as long as I don't move them too fast. I kick and paddle to the surface and take a deep breath. I hold it as I try treading water.

The stumps move through the water faster because they provide less resistance. Treading water is fine. It feels strange but it's not difficult. Now I'll try my breaststroke. The problem is that I have a tendency to go round in circles.

I adapt my stroke and head down the pool towards the two pink dragons. As I pass them I say, 'Good morning ladies.'

They smile. 'Well done! We think you're doing tremendously.'

They say other nice, encouraging things and I think I may have been slightly uncharitable.

I swim four lengths, resting for a few minutes at each end. I'm panting like a Saint Bernard in a sauna. I keep perfect lane discipline and follow the black tiles.

I swim back to the middle before seeing that I'm under threat. A wayward freestyle swimmer with no sense of direction, arms flailing, eyes closed, has started in the lane to my right and is now suddenly veering towards me. I frantically start swimming to the left. He must be able to see where he's going. No. He's on a collision course.

Whack! For a second the pain numbs me and I breathe water. I start coughing, spluttering and sinking. I'm frightened. I wonder if the bone has come out through the skin? It feels like it.

I thrash around, then gradually force myself to move my limbs slowly and tread water. I keep on coughing, but at least my head is above water now and I can recover my breathing. I look around and see that my assailant has carried on, oblivious. The two ladies stop and swim in the opposite direction to avoid him.

I carry on treading water and look at the stump. The impact was on the end of the bone, which was why it was so painful. He probably had no idea what he swam into, and the impact would have just felt like a slight knock. Next time I'll point my elbow at him if I can't swim out of the way.

After a few minutes I carry on. When I get out of the pool I find the exercise has made me light headed. Very slowly I raise myself and do the one-foot shuffle back to my bits.

I put my leg back on in a daze, and walk back to the changing room. I don't care what people think now. I've done it. I leave exhausted, but with a profound sense of wellbeing.

For the rest of the day I am wiped out. I rest the next day and then go swimming again. I get my ticket and go to the changing room. It takes me a long time to change. Eventually I just cram my false arm and clothes into the cupboard. I can't put the rubber band with the key on my wrist so I have to ask somebody to do it for me. The man looks about fifty. I'm not sure which of us is more embarrassed. Last time nobody was about, but this time the lady at the desk warned me to be on the lookout for thieves. Somebody left their key out yesterday and had their wallet pinched.

I tiptoe very carefully through the footbath trying not to get my false leg wet. I hope they make the new leg soon. My walking is getting worse. It was like this yesterday.

There are more people in the pool than I thought there would be. With each clumsy step, I'm haunted by the things I've lost. I cannot enjoy the countryside, work on a farm, garden, hill walk, soldier with my mates, run, dive, glide or work.

I thought it would be easier today, but it's worse, much worse. I never imagined it could get worse.

What if it never gets any easier?

I stagger to the bench. I keep my head low. It's possible my eyes might leak. I wouldn't want anyone to see. Then I think, stuff them. There's no shame in trying your best.

I force myself back on my foot and hop to the edge of the water. I throw myself in and almost manage a dive. For an instant I'm flying, then I hit the water. It's beautifully cool. I keep my arms outstretched and wriggle my fingers to feel the water. I pull them down to my sides and my body is driven forward. As I glide forward and start swimming, I open my eyes.

23

OPPORTUNITY

SUMMER 1995

Saturday morning in Fulham with the newspapers, orange juice and smell of sizzling bacon. I also have the greatest luxury of all; time to enjoy them with a friend. Through the window I watch the animals in the shopping jungle. There are the antelopes, leaping around, looking for something distracting; there are sheep, shopping because they're supposed to; and there are the anteaters, who know what they want and rummage around until they get it at the right price.

Simon rustles the paper and says, 'What's the definition of stupidity?'

'Shopping in a crowded street on a wet Saturday morning.'

'No. Seriously.'

'Not learning from your mistakes?'

'It's an article about teaching children with learning difficulties,' he says. 'I seem to have several classes full most days.'

'What gives a child learning difficulties?'

'Illness, emotional trauma, congenital defects, poor diet, lack of love, emotional problems, bad parenting, bad teaching, constant change of environment, bad luck, poor discipline and stepping on mines.' He hoovers up bacon, toast and marmalade, and occasionally dabs at his mouth with a napkin in a uniquely English manner.

'What's the hardest thing to deal with?' I ask.

'The bureaucracy. But if you want to know the saddest thing, it's seeing an abused child, or a child who is handicapped in some way and doesn't know how to deal with it.'

We revert to reading and drinking coffee until he says, 'Have you read about Christopher Reeve? He's paralysed from the neck down.'

I nod. 'It makes me feel guilty to think how well off I am in comparison.' I pause. 'Until it happens, you think it'll never happen to you.'

Simon folds the paper closed and pours us more coffee. 'What will you do next?'

'I'm not sure. I'd still like to go back to working in the field, but the stump keeps shrinking so fast I constantly need a new socket for the false leg, so I can't go abroad for any period. The other thing I have to face is that now there are people who can do the job better than me. I've spent some time in the library and found two courses that I like the sound of. One is an LLM in Human Rights and the other is an MSc in Security Management.'

'You should take the chance to study,' he says, folding his paper again. 'Do something new, write more.'

'Growing up in the safety of Middle England, it took me a long time to realize that the fight against ignorance and intimidation is constant. We shouldn't allow the animals to run the zoo.' I start to grab my belongings because I still forget how much longer it takes me to get around.

'Do you still see that girlfriend of yours?' Simon asks.

I shake my head. 'I keep having to disappear for limb fittings, so I can never keep a date. And the last one had never been in a second-hand bookshop, so I realized we just weren't suited. The real problem is, I can't find anyone with a similar sense of humour, therefore a considerable time ago I lost all interest in women and became celibate.'

'Excellent idea,' he says. 'More people should take that

route. It makes life less confusing and gives you more time to read.'

The drive across London is remarkably quick. I'm starting to get my memory back. I don't need to keep stopping to look at the *A to Z*. It's a relief, because even reading the paper is still hard work.

Three o'clock on the dot. It's the first time I've got anywhere on time since I was blown up, and it's because I left an hour earlier than I thought I needed, so I could do some shopping once I'd got here.

'Right let's have a brew. You can drop your kit there,' Pat says. He and I were in the army together.

We get down to the serious business of talking. We don't often discuss the past because the present and future are suddenly much more important. Since leaving the army he's worked in security and frequently travels in Europe and Africa. He's started the MSc in Security Management that I'm interested in but because of his work commitments he's doing the part-time course.

After sitting still for an hour I have to get up and move around because the false leg becomes uncomfortable. I'm still waiting for the new socket to be made. They tell me my stump is shrinking faster than usual because I'm very active.

The South London park is shrouded in a damp, early summer mist that might turn to drizzle or heavy rain. The children's play area is fenced off like a prison camp and locked at night. The buildings and benches are peppered with graffiti. The arcane squiggles look like cries for help from lost souls somehow wanting to leave their mark. I look at them and decide that in some ways we haven't progressed very far since the era of the aboriginal wall painting. The municipal tennis courts stand empty. Apparently, finding out how to book one is harder than the MENSA exam.

As we enter the park Pat glances at my face. 'That cut

healed well, a beautiful stitching job. Been doing any more acrobatics recently?'

'No,' I said. 'But I'm really looking forward to the winter.'

We witness a small suburban mongrel produce a disproportionately large turd. Pat points in admiration. 'Look at that! Have you ever seen anything that large?'

'Not since I was in South Africa.'

'I think they give their pets constipation pills here so they only have to bring them out once a week. When I had my dog I always cleaned up after it. It's like demining really. I never believed in capital punishment, but I'm beginning to rethink.'

The smell fills my nostrils as we walk past the steaming brown heap. 'It's a thought; bit unfair on the dog though.'

'I didn't mean the dogs. It's the owners that are the problem.'

We walk on in silence for a while, with Pat pretending that he always moves this slowly. After a while, he asks me what I'm going to do.

'I haven't decided. I thought I might study for a year. I've narrowed it down to the course you're doing, or an LLM in Human Rights. I still want to go back to fieldwork as soon as I can. That's my first choice.'

'Do the MSc, mate. It's more management orientated and the criminology, law and IT modules are magic. And I know you still want to save the world, but don't forget you've got to earn a living.' He lights a cigar and grins. 'Believe me,' he continues, 'it's a minefield out there.'

He carefully stubs out his cigar, puts it in the bin and says, 'Fancy a beer? When we get back I'll dig out the university forms. Did I tell you about France?'

I was desperate to join them in the mountains. I even got my ticket. The thought of a week's walking was exciting beyond belief, but I found I just couldn't do it. The leg didn't fit so I had to stay and get a new socket. The hospital make them as quickly as they can, but I'm not their only patient, and they've got lots of work on. I still have unrealistic expectations. 'I thought that once I'd got the new leg that would be it, I'd stick it on and off we'd go, but of course it's not that simple.'

'It's bound to take time,' Pat says.

'I know that really. It's a constant process of frustration management. I keep thinking I'm going to be able to do something, then I can't. But there's one thing I'm determined to do – be back at long-distance running in less than a year.' We get to his place just in time to beat the rain.

The next day I head back down the M3 to Salisbury.

When I'm staying with my parents I've established a daily routine. I get up, read the papers and have breakfast, do my handwriting and computer practice, go for a walk, do some editing for various friends who are writing and then fit in a snooze, usually after lunch.

I keep thinking I could do a proper day's work. But I'm kidding myself. It's just not realistic. Things take me so long. Every day I make myself do something I haven't done since the amputation. It might be opening a door using the false hand, carrying a bag on the false arm or walking a little further. I keep telling myself I'll get the running leg in a few months.

It's like being a child again. I'm having to learn to do everything. I even had to teach myself to use a bicycle. I got the man in the shop to raise the gears and put both brakes on the left handle bar. I developed a drill with Steve, another old soldier who lives in the village. Get bike out. Put in low gear. Check no traffic on road. Start pedalling. Stick out false arm. Pray and turn right. Pedal like fury. Veer left towards hill. Keep pedalling like fury. Try to change into lowest gear before going up steep hill. Pedal like fury. If not making it to top, keep trying. Do not give up. Keep pedalling until body hits road. Say loudly, 'Oh dear, that's a bit of bad luck, I've fallen off,' just in case anybody's listening. Then push bike up hill until it's flat enough to get back on again, and repeat.

It took over a month of blood, sweat and tears to get up that hill.

Several years ago my father had a stroke and when he was recovering we'd often go for a slow walk to aid his circulation. He now takes me for walks and has to slow down so I can keep up.

We follow the same short route around the village. Every time I struggle to keep up, we say, 'Left, right, left, right.' I try, but I can't. He waits for me when I fall behind.

My parents and I stop everything to watch the green woodpecker eating ants on the garden path. It sticks its beak between the bricks or flicks out its long, lizard-like tongue. With its brilliant red head and bright green body it's a spectacular sight.

A great spotted woodpecker often flies across the lawn on its way to the bird table where it pecks at the peanuts. I guess they're bigger than ants, and don't wriggle.

Both birds do their best to avoid Benny the cat, who is a magnificent, fluffy, ginger beast. They must know he's a bit schizophrenic; one minute he's a cuddly, friendly chap with a purr like a Spitfire engine, and the next he's a fierce hunter, yomping down the path with a wild rabbit in his mouth. In spite of our many attempts to slow him down with more breakfast he still disappears for hours to catch them. He seems to have got the message about the woodpecker, though. If he scoffs either of them he's on a one-way trip to the vet.

If I could have a pet I'd like a dog, a proper dog, the sort that would be loyal, bark and wag his tail and sniff people's groins. Maybe I will, one day.

Within a week of leaving hospital I negotiated the London Underground stairs and started to walk long distances. It's still uncomfortable, and slower than I'd like, but at least I've now got rid of the walking stick.

One morning I get up shortly after seven. It's a perfect summer morning, bathed in hazy sunshine. Before the accident I'd be dressed and out running in five minutes or less on a day like this. Today I'm going to try a long walk with a short run. I've got to try.

It's taken me thirty minutes to prepare for this and even then I haven't had time to shave. I'm going to do two miles. I set off at a reasonable pace and walk through the village to the track that leads to the Downs. It's secluded and lined with trees. When I reach the wood I look ahead and focus on the gate. I promised myself I'd run to it. I start to move my legs up and down in a running action. When I put the false leg down I get no response and end up fast limping. I keep trying, the stump feels sore and gets sorer. I keep trying, but it's not easy. I think I'm running and it takes everything I've got, but I know I'm really only limping fast. I stop at the gate. That was harder than an eight-mile hill run. I walk back down the hill as fast as I can and the soreness increases.

When I get back home I stagger upstairs, take off the leg, and collapse on my bed. I wake up two and a half hours later. I'm weak and tired. I examine the stump and see a raw welt all down the right side. It takes a long time to heal, but it only hurts when I move. I decide to wait until I have a limb that's designed for running before I try it again, but this has really knocked my confidence. I've been able to do everything else I've set my mind to, even though it's been tough. The thing that worries me about running is that I have done myself so much damage trying. What if I can't ever run again? Does this mean no more long treks in wild places? I know I must never stop trying.

John the prosthetist has researched the best false limb to run on. It's carbon fibre. I have to wait six or seven months from amputation before they can fit it. I have another three months to wait. The running limbs work on a simple principle: they return energy like a spring.

Mike and family have invited a group of friends to America for the week of his wedding. I pack my belongings the day before because I know how much longer it takes me now. I spend hours folding a week's kit and then cramming it into the bag. When I'm in the airport I push my luggage around on a trolley because when I carry a bag I walk like Quasimodo with piles.

I search for the best deal on my flight, which means travelling to Boston via New York. After six hours in the air the stump swells. It's still a relatively recent wound and there's a lot of fluid below the knee. I take off a few stump socks and readjust the fitting in the aircraft toilet.

Mike and his soon-to-be-in-laws live on the New England coast, so as soon as possible I take the chance to swim in the sea. I feel free and invigorated. The other guests are a fun bunch. We all visit a health club and have a competition to see who can stay in the sauna the longest. I win hands down, because I've had more experience of being uncomfortable, and also because when I left my leg outside, somebody moved it back to the changing rooms.

One day before the wedding we are offered the chance to go skeet shooting. I say, 'Are they much of a pest around here?' They laugh and say they like British humour. Mike, whispers, 'Clay pigeons, mate.'

We stand in a clearing in a remote wood. I roll up and insert the foam ear defenders and watch from the area behind the gun. I open the false hand and switch it off at the right distance to make a foregrip rest. When it's my turn I find to my astonishment that my shooting is about the same as it always was, which is not very good.

One of the guests is a merchant banker, and the rest are ex-military. Dave is a Tom Cruise look-alike major in the American Engineers. He introduces me to his friend Mark. They were in the army together until Mark left to become a television star. I thought he was joking until we drove to the local town and stopped at a garage where hoards of screaming girls came and asked for his autograph.

Back at the house where we're staying one of the last guests to arrive is the lovely Alison. She was in the army and now works as contracts and operations manager for a City firm. With beautiful blue eyes, a marvellous sense of humour and a straightforward approach to life I decide immediately she's someone special. She's also unattached. After several conversations and an unusual meeting in which I ensure her my intentions are honourable I feel so relaxed in her presence that I decide to sleep off the jet lag for a few minutes. Before I was injured I was never so weak and easily tired.

The next thing I know my shoulder is being shaken. 'Wake up Chris.'

I emerge from a deep sleep. Mike is shaking my shoulder. 'Well done mate. Think you made a good impression there. We're all getting some sleep. It's nearly breakfast time.'

The next time I speak to Alison is at a barbeque near the sea shore. It's a beautiful moonlit night. I suggest a short walk on the beach. She says, 'All right, but only a short way. I don't want to have to carry you back if you fall asleep.'

From our next few meetings I discover we have a similar attitude to life.

With this unnaturally high concentration of sharply-chiselled males competing for the relatively small number of women present, I'm a bit gloomy about my chances of impressing the lovely Alison, but I decide to try anyway. I can handle rejection and besides that, what have the rest of them got that I haven't?

24

ENDEAVOUR

This is the moment I've been waiting for. I'm going to run again!

The car radio plays 'The Eye of the Tiger'. I think tough and think action. I've put on my old shorts and T-shirt from Cambodia. It reminds me of the times I used to go running in the early evening when we'd finished work. Dan, an ex-commando and all round good bloke, got them made. On the back he got them to print the words: 'If I should die think only this of me; there is some corner of a foreign field that is forever . . . Free of mines.'

I switch off the radio and switch on reality as I put the talcum powder on the outside of the silicon stump sock and roll it on.

The leg is held on by an attachment on the end of a lanyard that screws into a housing on the bottom of the silicon liner. The lanyard is pulled through a hole in the base of the socket. It is then wound round a threaded peg on the side of the socket and held in place by a retaining nut. The manufacturer should call it a piece of string, because that's what it is. I force the stump into the socket and stand up. I tug the cord tight, wrap it round the peg and do up the plastic retaining nut.

I shut the car door, lock it and put the key in the pocket of my shorts. I walk through the recreation ground gate and on to the soft grass. The sky is grey and there's a hint of drizzle. Summer has gone and an autumn chill blows across Salisbury Plain. I bend forward gently and start the stretching exercises.

I can't touch my toes and I can only do the leg exercises on one side.

I planned my start routine six months ago. I'll run twice a week to begin with. I'll fast walk and then jog one length of the football pitch alternately for fifteen minutes and then I'll try to jog all around the outside to finish.

I know it's sensible to start gently, and warm myself up. I haven't run for so long that all my muscles have wasted.

I swing my hips in a circular motion. It's the only warming-up exercise I can do properly now. I walk to the edge of the field and get ready to uncoil like a spring and burst into action. I imagine a leopard poised to accelerate across the veldt.

The reality, sadly, is closer to a three-legged dog with a bad back trying to make it to the nearest lamp-post.

As I take my first steps, the small lump of soft flesh and bone below the knee feels like it's being tapped from underneath with a large wooden mallet. Once it strikes the ground I know I should lift it up again, but I'm not sure how. I thought the running leg would give me more spring. I keep trying hard to move fast enough to be short of breath, but I just can't manage it.

I clump and limp alternate lengths. A man walking his dog looks at me with an air of curious disdain, which seems to say, 'You're a cripple. You shouldn't be trying to run.'

Trying to run again is so hard. I thought I'd get the running leg and be able to just do it. It's not fair. Disappointment engulfs me. Every nerve screams 'it hurts' and my instincts keep telling me to stop, lie on the grass and cry my bloody eyes out.

It's at times like this I can really empathize with ET and the Elephant Man. I must look pathetic, a deluded idiot in pursuit of an unobtainable dream. My leg is held on by a piece of nylon string, for God's sake. It's a good job I don't take myself too seriously and I've learnt not to worry what people think.

Learning to swim again taught me a lot more than how to keep my head above water.

After fifteen minutes it's time to jog around the outside of the recreation ground. Slowly and painfully, I hobble around the field. I slip on the wet mud and fall. Shit, it's the third time I've done that. Time for the falling over drill. 'Gosh, that was bad luck,' I say loudly. 'I slipped.' Then I get up and carry on.

After a few minutes I have to stop and walk. I count to sixty and then force myself on. That vomit-in-the-back-of-the-throat feeling gets worse and I hope I'm not going to throw up. I start to retch and cough.

I've been telling myself I'm running, but I take a reality check when two men about my age sprint past me, doing interval training. They're moving faster than greased amoebic dysentery and disappear into the distance.

They relax to a slow jog as they reach the goal post. Now they're walking. I'm going to try to catch them. I try frantically to sprint, but end up with a more exaggerated wobble.

They start to jog again and pull away from me. Maybe one day I'll get better, perhaps in five years if I train hard and get faster I might be able to overtake them and then I can shout, 'It's all right for you cissies with two legs.'

In the meantime, I have to dream on and try to swallow my vomit.

I glance at my watch. I've been trying for nearly twenty-five minutes. Only five to go. I know I shouldn't see it that way but my back aches, my right leg muscles are ripping, and my stumps have got more phantoms than the United States Air Force flew in 1970.

I'm totally knackered, and to add insult to injury the movement of the stump of my arm has given me screaming phantom pain in the hand. It's a bummer.

I jog on, just a step at a time. I have to get there. I arrive at the gate and check my watch. It's three minutes over the half hour.

I walk back to the car, struggling to control my disappointment. I can't run. There are people who could walk the same distance faster. How will I ever do a marathon?

I sit in the car seat, exhausted. I can't believe I feel so bad after such a short period of exercise. After five minutes I feel all right to drive back home. I came down from Leicester, where I'm now studying, to pick up my desk and some clothes. I made sure the trip coincided with my limb fitting. I'm under serious time pressure for the first time since I was injured.

I drive back carefully to my parents and shower the mud off. I'm so tired I decide to drive back to Leicester in the morning. Mum and Dad help me to load up the car. In the early evening after we've fed the fish in the pond we sit and watch the darkness gather through the patio doors.

I think back over the summer. One of the worst things about staying with my parents was not being able to do anything to help in the garden. I couldn't even mow the lawn. Fortunately Eric, a kind neighbour, came and did it. Dad's angina is so bad he can't do it any more.

Life at the university is a journey of discovery and something of a culture shock. There's a lot to learn, and I frequently feel my brain aching. My handwriting is still untidy and slow. I thought it was fine when I had no pressure, but I've now discovered just how dominantly right-handed I was.

I've tried to plan ahead for every eventuality and I've found a small, one-bedroom flat that's a two-minute walk from the building where our lectures take place. All I have to do is walk up the steps, cross the pelican crossing and walk down the road. If anything goes wrong, I should be within hobbling distance.

I live alone, and do all my cleaning and cooking. The hoovering and ironing are the chores that take the longest. Doing things with one hand doesn't just take twice as long; frequently it's longer. The simplest things, such as chopping vegetables, take three or four times as long. Sometimes it takes eight hours to do the chores, wash and maintain myself and my false limbs.

I soon sort out a daily routine. On weekdays I try to drag myself out of the pit at six forty-five. It's a real effort because I'm always tired. By seven fifteen I'm ready to drive my old car to the pool and swim for forty-five minutes, at least four mornings a week. When I finish I'm light headed, but I know I have to do it if I'm ever going to get strong again.

For three days after the first run in Salisbury I feel like I've had a kicking. My back and legs are the worst. Undeterred, I venture out for a second attempt. It takes me twenty-five minutes to change and put the leg on.

I've measured a mile and a half from a road junction near my flat. It takes a few minutes to run to it. This is the warm up. Then I follow the main road out of Leicester for a mile and a half to the first garage on the right. That's a mile and a half. Then I turn around and come back.

I do my first run under the cover of darkness. It takes over nineteen minutes. Before, I would have done it under nine. When I complete the course and look at my stopwatch I'm tempted to tell myself there's no point, but decide instead that I'll take five minutes off that time by next year.

In spite of my best efforts I run even more slowly on the way back and when I get back to the flat I fall on the bed and go straight to sleep.

I think I've strained all the muscles in my back, so I rest for a few days and then decide I have to stop whimping and have another go. As I put the leg on I notice the stump has shrunk and so I put on several more socks to stop it rattling around. I tie up the lanyard tightly and screw the retaining plastic nut around the string. I give it a few stamps and steam off down the road, determined to do better.

With great joy I find I'm twenty-five seconds faster than last time and it feels as if the mallet blows to the base of the stump are becoming less hard.

I turn round and head for home, determined to improve on the last time. After five minutes the leg slips suddenly and I fall forward. I'm not going fast enough to fall over, so I can hop to recover.

The lanyard cord has broken and the leg has shot off into the road. I can see a bus speeding towards me, close to the kerb. Shit, this looks like the end of the road for my false leg. There's only one thing for it. I'll wave and say my prayers. 'Please God don't let that bus run over my false leg. I don't want to hop a mile home.'

It works. The bus misses my leg so I'm able to pick it up and hop to a wall. I sit down and examine the lanyard fitting. I can't fix it so I put my stump back in the socket and hold it on with my good hand as I walk, very slowly, home.

I'm not sorry I have to go to London to get the leg repaired. It gives me a chance to see Alison. We became friends after Mike's wedding and whenever I get the chance I catch up with her in London.

I travel on the train most weekends, now that I'm a student again. I study on the journey, so it's time well spent. I keep expecting the conductor to say, 'You're a bit of an old git to have a student card, aren't you?' But he never does.

Alison and I get on well with each other's friends and start to see more of one another. I try to see her most weekends if I have time to go to London. She spends Saturdays helping at a club for children with special needs. She understands my attitude to life and never tells me I can't do things. Our lives gel and I study like mad, attempt to learn to jog, have frequent limb fittings and try to be involved with a number of charities. We've decided we'd like to spend more time together in the future.

I keep telling her that I'm the perfect man for her because she lives in a studio flat and she can take bits off me so I fit in nicely.

On Sunday afternoons we usually go for a walk. I'm looking forward to the time when I can run. Today we're driving out to Forestry Commission woodland to see the autumn leaves. As we walk between the beech trees, listen to the birds sing and enjoy the fresh air, clear skies and sunshine, I think how good it is to be alive.

We hold hands and I struggle to keep up, but she knows I don't want her to slow down. As we turn a corner she smiles at the chocolate box view of a village complete with church spire. The wind blows her fair hair and as I look into her blue eyes I think a scary thought. Maybe I'd like to grow old with her. For some time I've been seriously reconsidering my celibacy decision. Help! I can feel the leg socket catching so I have to stop. The stump is constantly reducing so I have to keep dropping my trousers to adjust the leg fitting.*

We emerge from the wood near some converted farm buildings. The red brick stables have been beautifully converted and we join the twenty or so people in the tea shop. They look a respectable crowd, mostly in their sixties. The last table is free and as we sit and wait for our tea and lemon cake, I rest my false arm on the table. It's held on partly by suction, and as I move it, it makes a sound that can only be described as a rippingly loud fart.

The whole place goes quiet. There is not even the chink of

---

* For those readers who think the next bit is going to be about shagging, you're going to be disappointed. However it is definitely worth continuing if you like rude noises.

a spoon on saucer, or denture on cup. The woman on the next table whispers to her husband. 'Disgusting.'

I feel rather embarrassed. What on earth will my beloved think of me now? I look at Alison and say, 'I'm terribly sorry. I must apologize. I'm afraid it does that all the time.'

The man on the next table suddenly spits out his mouthful of tea and starts giggling uncontrollably. Several of the other chaps in the room join in and get stony stares from their wives.

I feel the need to explain further so I pull it off slightly and press it on the arm of the chair quite hard. The noise is even louder, this time. 'You see?'

I glance across at the chap on the next table, and realize he hasn't noticed I have a false hand. I turn back to Alison. The only thing I can think to say is, 'I'm sorry. Would you prefer it if I sat in the car?'

At this point the bloke on the next table spits out another mouthful of tea and starts everyone laughing. Fortunately Alison thinks the whole thing's funny and is laughing too. She's definitely the girl for me.

When bones break, calcium deposits knit them together again. At first I was told I would need to have the bone growth cut off. I find that prospect depressing because I didn't want more surgery, because I'd have to go through the whole ghastly process of constantly needing a new socket again. I still need to, from time to time, and will do for years, but at least it's slowed down a bit.

I also have what the doctor thinks is recurring malaria and a strange blood infection, which manifests itself in the form of large pustular boils, for which there is no treatment. So when the painful red blobs emerge I know that in a few days time they'll burst. To my great relief this has only lasted a week. It's taught me to have a lot of sympathy for lepers, particularly when I had a great throbbing spot the size of a cherry on my face that suddenly popped in the supermarket.

By the end of the year my thinking and writing speed improves enough for me to successfully sit the exams. Slowly, very slowly, I start to run again, and work furiously to raise money for the centre where Som On is now living. I do it in conjunction with Oxfam, and I find out for the first time just how hard and heartbreaking fundraising is.

As autumn merges into winter I wait for an appointment to find out whether or not I have to have an operation to remove the bone spur. Professional opinions are divided. John the prosthetist says he can stick a false leg on the stump and the consultant says as long as the bone doesn't stick out the end I don't need it trimmed. However, the problem with bone spurs is that they're painful.

I was only able to do five slow runs before the stump shrunk so much the leg socket didn't fit any more. It will take until mid-January to make a new one.

I've lost any hope of doing the Great Sahara Marathon before 1997, but I'm still determined to do the London Marathon within a year of leaving hospital. The clock's ticking.

The weeks fly past and the build-up to Christmas is hectic. I spend my time with my parents and frantically write management and criminology papers. I leave my favourite, on law, until last. I produce something that is far from a best effort because it takes me so long to do everything with one hand. I still pass, but now the pressure is really on I find I have to put in two or three times as much effort as everyone else because things take me so much longer to do.

From the end of January I start to run again. Every Sunday I run with Alison. She slows down so I can keep up. When I get back from a run I'm too exhausted to do anything except sleep.

I develop an infection on the stump and for a short while limp around smelling of rotting flesh. By the end of March the furthest I've run is seven miles. When I finished I was shredded. I begin to wonder if I will be able to cover twenty-six-point-two miles. If only I had another month.

A few people have told me I'll look stupid when I fail. In the dark moments of the night I'm haunted by doubts. But I can only do my best.

25

LIMITS

14 APRIL 1996

Alison leans over the barrier, kisses me and says, 'Good luck.'

I look into her beautiful blue eyes and kiss her back. 'Thanks. I'd better get going.'

I move into the crowd before she sees my fear. No one else could notice, but she might.

Behind and in front of me there is an endless wall of runners, nearly 40,000 of them, in myriad running togs, all wearing a London Marathon race number.

A few people behind are pushing. My balance is not as good as it used to be. I start to fall, so I put my forearm on the back of the person in front of me. 'I'm sorry. Please excuse me. I stumbled.' I try to avoid pouring water down the back of his bright green running vest.

The man turns around. He's wearing matching shorts and well-worn trainers and looks a fit fifty. He has a well-trimmed grey beard and short-cropped hair. He laughs and moves sideways to make room for me and says, 'Not to worry. It's all a bit of a bundle to begin with.'

I force myself to drink more water. I need to take on as much as I can. The sun is warm already; it's going to be one of the hottest London Marathons ever. I swallow the last mouthful and feel bloated, but I know I'll soon run it off.

We're near Greenwich, but I'm not sure exactly where. The

place looks different with all the people. The road is lined with metal barriers. Behind them people wave to their loved ones and charity supporters shout encouragement to their runners. Huge trees line the road. They're just coming into leaf. I think they're London plane.

I wonder if I'll make the distance in five and a half hours? Alison is the only person who has any idea what my target time is. Where is she? I look around. As I've moved forward so has she. I wave and shout, 'Can't wait to go!'

The runners behind me surge on again. This time I go with the flow, but the man in front doesn't. He brings his elbow back and bashes the end of my severed arm. A bolt of pain hammers through the stump and nausea grips my guts.

I pull the stump to my chest and cradle it with my left hand. It reminds me of the first time I went swimming. The man in the green vest says, 'Ouch! That looked painful. Are you all right?'

I smile and try not to show that on a pain rating it's up there with a mighty blow to the bollocks with a rubber truncheon. 'I'm fine thanks.'

He makes a bit more space for me and says, 'I admire you for doing this. It must be a lot harder for you. It must affect your balance. If you don't mind me asking, what happened?'

I don't mind him asking at all. As a result of my conversation with Simon after we'd visited the park when I was in hospital I decided the onus is on me to put people at their ease, not the other way round. I explain and finish more frankly than I intended. 'I'm running for a good cause. I hope I finish.'

He puts his hand on my shoulder. 'I'm sure you will.'

The man on my left is wearing a white running vest and looks about forty, although his jet-black hair and athletic body may make him look younger than he is. He gives me a thumbs up and says, 'Go for it mate. Don't worry, you'll do it. The important thing is to start slowly, keep a steady pace and drink early.'

I nod and smile. He's right. The first five miles should be at a pace that allows normal conversation. I bend and tighten the leather strap holding my leg on. I'm terribly worried that it will fly off like it did the night I was training when the lanyard broke.

I'm ready. After spending the last two months travelling the country fundraising, studying frantically for my final Masters Degree exams, and trying to train, it's a relief to be here at last. I turn to the man in the white vest. 'Have you done many of these?'

'About fifteen, but London is my favourite. It's definitely the dog's bollocks. When you finish you'll see what I mean. Have you done much training?'

'I've been eating a lot of pasta.'

There is another surge. The man in the green vest looks at his watch. 'Not long now.'

Way ahead the starting gun booms and a cheer ripples back through the runners like a Mexican wave.

He presses the timer on his watch. 'We're off. When we cross the start I'll tell you how many minutes to take off your finishing time. You'll be able to see it on the clock anyway; I think it'll be six or seven.'

I wave one last time to Alison and the group from Oxfam; then wind myself up. I'm ready to run. I shout 'Good luck' to the people around me.

We walk forward and gradually accelerate to a jog. Even by my standards this is slow. The pace builds and I try to steady my rhythm.

'Who are you running for?' I ask the man in the green vest, trying to make it look as if I'm not trying.

He stretches his arms. 'The roof.'

'Are they a charity for the homeless?'

'The church roof. I'm a vicar. The parishioners have kindly agreed to splash cash if I can run this in four hours. I did it several years ago and that chap was right.' He smiles in response to my unspoken question. 'It really is the dog's bollocks.'

A helicopter circles in the distance.

As we pass the start the vicar looks at his watch. 'Take six and a half minutes off your finish time. What are you hoping for?'

I speak slowly, trying not to let it show that I'm panting. 'I just want to finish.'

The vicar runs alongside me. 'Relax your style and slow down. Keep it nice and steady.'

I know what he's saying is true, but I've only got two running speeds, lumbering and falling over.

A runner in a white charity T-shirt shoots past, then slows and taps me on the shoulder. 'Well done mate. I didn't realize you were doing it on a false leg. Good effort.'

I don't get a chance to thank him. He waves and bounds off.

I lose the vicar in the throng. I'm working hard to maintain the pace. Fellow marathoners run alongside, chat and provide encouragement. They understand why I'm economical with my words.

As we leave Greenwich and head for Woolwich the road slopes downhill. I decide to make use of the incline; I increase my pace to try to catch the vicar. Once we've looped round and back towards Greenwich I try not to think that I've only been five miles. Instead I tell myself I've only got to do that again five times and add a little bit to finish.

Someone hands me a bottle of water at the first stop and I force myself to take gulps even though I'm not thirsty. I carry on running and try to drink. I spill water down my face and running vest.

People along the pavement shout encouragement to us all. I don't seem to have as much breath as everyone else to send my best wishes back.

I'm already covered in sweat and I've only been five miles. I must keep drinking.

A live rhythm and blues band plays outside a pub. I wave and say 'thanks' as I pass them. I run down the street and turn the corner. People line the road. This is the biggest street party I've ever seen.

A woman in her late twenties runs alongside me. 'Hi Chris. Saw you on the local news and read those bits about you in the paper. Well done.' She points to her T-shirt. 'I'm running for Oxfam too.'

The woman runs on and I watch a few more marathoners zoom past. I must be slowing down. I concentrate on keeping my breathing right and maintaining the pace. I grab an isotonic sports drink from the stand and squeeze it into my mouth.

I keep looking round me for the big man in the kilt.

The magnificent stone towers of the naval college loom on my left. Ali is by the pavement with four or five people from Oxfam. As I approach they wave. I get a new lease of life and bounce forward, waving too. 'How far?'

'Seven miles. You're doing well. Keep going.' She smiles her encouragement.

I must slow down. I won't be able to keep this up.

I put all my effort into running and trying to keep a reasonable balance. People around me shout their support. It gives me a lump in my throat.

I focus on running. All my energy goes into putting one foot in front of the other. I step into a time warp. I already feel sick. One foot in front of the other; ignore the discomfort. I'm doing well. This is the fastest I've ever done nine miles. I'm going well; I'm flying!

I look to my right. A fat bloke dressed as a chicken waddles past me and waves.

There's a big sign up ahead that says ten miles. I take more water. The phantom pain has started. I try to ignore it. I can't feel the stump now. I must check it.

I stop, lean against a lamp-post and undo the leather strap holding on the leg. I take it out of the socket and massage the stump. After a few seconds the phantom pain subsides and I can feel it when I tap the stump. I think it's starting to swell up.

A slim runner in a red charity T-shirt stops beside me. He looks about sixty. He puts his hand on my shoulder and says, 'You all right mate? Want a hand?'

I look up. I'm tempted to say, 'Yes please, a right one would be bloody useful.' Instead, I reply, 'No thanks. I'm just making a few adjustments. Thanks for stopping though.'

I try to put the stump back in the socket, but it won't fit. I take off a sock and try again. I just squeeze it in and do up the strap as a pretty girl in her mid-twenties stops and says, 'Can I help?'

'No thanks, I'm fine.'

I stick the false leg down. I think I've got normal sensation again but I'm not sure. I try to run again, but I'm low on energy.

I put one foot in front of the other. 'Left, right, left, right.' I force myself to jog on. I look around. I can see the Thames. Tower Bridge must be close. Behind me there is a huge, pristine office building and around me the ground is planted with low shrubs. Several runners stop to water them.

Up until this point I've really enjoyed the run. Now I'm as knackered as a stretcher bearer at the Somme. I wonder if Captain Wiltshire felt like this before he died at Lindley?

I'm not giving up.

I repeat my marching orders like a mantra. 'Left, right, left, right.'

Nothing else matters.

I think I'm on Jamaica Road.

I can see Tower Bridge. As I cross I can hear Alison and the Oxfam crowd. 'Go on Chris. You're doing a good time! Go for it!'

It lifts me up, I increase the pace as I see them and trundle across the magnificent bridge. I'm doing well. I heard them say so. I look at the Oxfam team. There are loads of my friends there. Wow, they've made the effort to come and cheer me on. I wave and just manage to gasp, 'Thanks guys.'

On the other side of the bridge the road narrows and the crowd thins. We're heading for Canary Wharf. This is the long, lonely road. I keep on jogging. 'Left, right, left, right.' I rub my eyes. I am so tired I could just lie down in the road and go to sleep.

I keep up the mantra. This is the hardest stretch so far. I must keep going.

I hear familiar voices. It's Ken and Jim, my old mates from the Royal Military Police. 'Come on Chris. Doing well. Go for it!'

I wave and shout, 'No wibbling!'

I remember the first day I arrived at the training centre when one of them pretended to be the adjutant and the other a young subaltern sobbing after being given thirty-one extra duties. I seem to remember the real adjutant made a very convincing mess waiter.

As I pass them I shout, 'Have you seen a huge six foot six Scotsman in a kilt?'

They reply in unison. 'No. Keep going.'

For another mile or so I try.

'Left, right.' I'm worried I'm getting slower.

A fat lady passes me and shouts encouragement.

Suddenly, behind me, a man shouts, 'Chris. Chris.'

I stop and scan the runners. I see a tall, athletic man in his twenties. His hair is cut short and he has a slightly awkward running style. Maybe he's got bad blisters or an injury. I look again. His running style is a bit like mine. I recognize the face. It's Bob.

We run towards each other and shake hands. I haven't seen him since Roehampton, when he pushed me about in my wheelchair.

We shake hands. Mine's a bit sweaty and sticky. I've spilt isotonic drink on it.

I say, 'You're doing really well mate.'

'So are you!'

We look at each other and realize that in the excitement we've stopped running. Simultaneously we start again.

Bob is running with Gary Girling and Nanette Arnott. Gary is the public relations manager for Blatchford's, a large prosthetics company, and Nanette is married to Peter Arnott, the Para Olympic sprinter coach. I've spoken to Peter several times on the phone and got some great training advice

We run on.

Bob's old unit Nine Squadron have a reputation for having exceptional standards of fitness and endurance. I know that Bob won't give up. He was a member of an elite unit. I only hope I can keep up.

I ache all over, the residual limb is battered and blistered and I'm so tired I could just lie down and sleep in the road. My armpits have been rubbed raw by the running vest. I usually wear something with sleeves and I'm not used to the distance. I've lost all the fitness I'd ever had in the last year.

We run silently together. My head is spinning. I struggle for breath. 'Bob, how are you really feeling?'

He looks at me sideways, smiles and says, 'Shit. My stump's in tatters.'

I laugh. 'So's mine, and my head's spinning.'

'Let's take it slowly for a bit then, or we won't get there.'

We walk. I struggle through the cramps and whisper my mantra: 'Failure is not an option.'

For the last few miles I've been jogging along with a tall man in a blue running vest. He's in his fifties and has a grey beard. He's a veteran of many marathons and has decided to take it easy on this one. We met when he passed me a bottle of water at a drink stop. It was kind of him because there was a big crush to get the water. It's much hotter than anticipated.

We pass a first-aid point and I see a pasty-faced runner on a stretcher with a drip in his arm, a victim of the heat. Bob and I point. 'Somebody stopped for a rest.'

I pause at the St John's Ambulance line as a volunteer wearing rubber gloves rubs Vaseline under my armpits.

'You haven't had water for three miles,' says the man in the blue vest with the grey beard.

I try to remember his name. I've asked him several times, but I keep forgetting it.

I take a small swig. I feel too sick to drink. We start running again. I stumble.

In the distance I can hear a helicopter. I remember being with Houn and Mr Clever in the jungle clearing watching as the helicopter flew over. I can see his house. And the cruel, hard faces of the Khmer Rouge as they swept the sky with automatic fire.

I see the moment we were waiting by the side of the road for the whispy bearded devil to pass sentence. I remember Houn's face, full of the certainty of death.

Now I'm on fire. Through the burning and stinging I fight to focus my mind. I'm going to be lucky to get out of this alive. I think I'm going to die. I'm back in the minefield. I can see the yellow bone and blasted pink flesh and feel the flames in my throat. I hear the helicopter and now I'm flying. My throat is burning. I have to drink.

I know I'm having flashbacks. I'm on a treadmill, but I don't know how to get off. I pour the water bottle over my head. It's cold. I inhale the water and cough and splutter.

'All right?' asks my mate with the beard. 'You were really pushing it then.'

I stop. He hands me his water bottle. I take a swig and pour it over my head.

Bob comes over. 'You're going a bit faster than me. Go on ahead. I'm going to stop and adjust my leg.'

'We're going the same speed, and I need a breather.' I stagger about for a moment, then go to the side of the road and take deep breaths.

I tell my mate with the grey beard to go ahead. He doesn't want to so I ask him to keep a look out for an enormous man in a kilt.

After a few minutes Bob hobbles back on to the road with Nanette and Gary. The rest gave me time to sort my brain and breathing out; but unfortunately my body has locked up.

Bob and I laugh as we stagger on.

'That was close. I only just got my leg on again,' he says.

'I'm too scared to take mine off; I don't think I'll get it back on.'

We trundle on, with our awkward, jarring run. As we turn into St Catherine's Dock someone shouts, 'This is mile twenty-one. Only five to go.'

Bob and I look at each other and laugh. 'Great. *Only* five to go.'

Suddenly from the side of the road someone else yells, 'Go faster, you one-legged git.'

Bob's expression changes to one of confusion. 'That's Alison,' I explain. 'My girlfriend, giving me some encouragement. Let's go and say hello.'

We say, 'Hello,' and start running again.

As we turn back towards the Thames there's a group of five or six Oxfam supporters. Bob hangs back so I can run past them alone.

In the distance I hear loud music. It must be the Capital Radio Road Show near the Tower of London.

We slow down to hobble over the cobbles. Neither of us want to practise our falling-over drills.

I turn the corner and head for the Embankment. Suddenly I hear the sound of a phone ringing. I look around. Bob undoes his small runner's pouch and pulls out a mobile. 'I must just get that,' he says. 'Hello Granddad. Yes, fine thanks. I'm getting round all right.'

I'm relieved we've slowed down. I'm finding it harder and harder to put one foot in front of the other.

I'm moving in a kind of limbo, where all I want to do is lie down and sleep in the road. I move on as if I'm running through thick treacle. Sometimes I hear Bob say, 'Go on Chris you're doing well.' I know he's lying.

Sometimes I say the same to him.

I still keep my eyes open for the big man in the kilt and I'm finally rewarded near the Embankment underpass. He's there in the full kit, and he's even carrying a broadsword. 'Excuse me,' I say. 'Is your name Alex?'

He nods.

'Guy from the HALO Trust told me to look out for you.'

He smiles. 'Yes he told me about you. Do you want a piggy back?'

'No thanks. I'd rather have my head boiled.'

'He said you'd say something like that. He also said you'd probably beat me. So you'd better get going.'

'I'm not sure I will. This is my mate Bob. He's running for the British Limbless Ex-Servicemen's Association.'

'Well done. You'd better go. Don't let me slow you down. Bloody long way isn't it?'

We run on through the thick porridge of fatigue. Morale suddenly takes a boost as we see the Houses of Parliament. Someone shouts, 'Not far, just around the corner.'

We start to laugh hysterically.

It feels strange to run through the red traffic lights by Big Ben. As we go down Birdcage Walk there are people cheering either side of the route.

We're nearly there. I can push with everything I've got now. I'll soon be able to stop.

I force my tired legs onwards. I lurch from side to side and twist my back to try to go a bit faster. I take deep breaths and try not to hyperventilate.

We turn past Buckingham Palace into The Mall where there is a sea of people. I try to shout encouragement to the other runners. 'Go for it, we're nearly there.'

People are shouting and cheering. I can feel their warmth. The sun's shining and the bright blue sky is cloudless. It reminds me of Cambodia, of going into Rhum with Houn and Sok. Everyone was smiling and no one was afraid. The local people thought we'd been killed and were pleased we were alive.

Bob says, 'I'm going to snog the girlfriend. You go on ahead if you want. I don't want to slow you down.' He somehow manages to sprint across the road.

We're a team, we should do this together. And I don't mean the snogging.

As Bob dashes back, I look into the crowd on my right and see Simon waving and shouting. 'Well done. Keep going. Go on.'

We run with everything we've got towards the Finish. For a moment the pain vanishes. I grab Bob's hand and make a dash for the Finish. We go through the gate together. Five hours, thirty-nine minutes. We've done it. People cheer.

The marshals congratulate us and give us our medals.

I feel dizzy.

We walk back, laughing, to get our kit from the pick-up point. Now we're struggling even to walk. Every step hurts. How could we have been running just a few moments ago? I don't think I can take another step, but I force myself forward, we can all go one step beyond our limits.

We hobble to the meeting point. I can see Alison. She puts her arms round me, kisses me and says, 'Well done. That's one of this year's goals achieved. What's next?'

I lean on her; glad to take some of the weight off my false leg. 'How do you feel about getting married in August?'

She smiles and says, 'Yes.'

26

EPILOGUE

SAHARA DESERT, 4 APRIL 1996

The sound of crashing cymbals, Arab drums and chanting fills my ears. The warm wind strokes my face and I squint to keep out the fine sand. I check my rucksack and put my torch in the outside pocket. It will be dark in a few hours.

I leave my kit beside a large stone and walk towards the nomad musicians. They are dressed in traditional blue cotton robes; some have a curved dagger protruding from a fold of cloth around the waist. Their dark brown leathery faces frown in frantic concentration as they try to make a noise that might fill a small pocket of the empty Sahara. Their task is futile. Behind them the flat ochre desert is punctuated with odd rocks. I see dust clouds on the distant horizon.

'Four army trucks, one o'clock. Better get ready to leap on. There's going to be a scramble for tents the other end. We want to get in and bag a decent one because they're numbered and you have to stay in the same one all week. If you want a hand on the truck let me know,' says Roraigh, a Royal Engineers major.

The speeding dust clouds advance. We amble back to the others and grab our kit. We automatically move to the front edge of the group where we think the lorries will turn and stop for loading.

There is a low murmur and the crowd gravitates towards

the heap of bags. Nick, a well-built six-foot-four accountant of Greek origin, walks over with Chris, a charming entrepreneur who was asked to volunteer to look after the British runners.

Nick narrows his steely eyes, flicks his hand through his hair and booms, 'Welcome to the real Morocco and kiss goodbye to civilization, nothing here except sand and the occasional camel turd. The Marathon des Sables, or, as we Brits would say, Marathon of the Sands, is the toughest foot race on earth. A week of hell served for breakfast. I've seen it make grown men cry.'

The roar of powerful diesel engines drowns out the Bedouin musicians. The four trucks sweep around and come to an abrupt halt before backing towards us. People throw their bags over the tall sides, jump up and start to climb on almost immediately.

Nick and Roraigh move to the back of one of the trucks and start to pass bags to a sapper from Roraigh's team who was first on. They take my bags. I move to the rear wheel. I can just bend my false leg enough to put it on the hub. I throw myself up and try to grab the top rail. I miss and slip back down.

'Let me know if you want a leg up,' says Roraigh as he continues to load everyone else's bags.

'I'm fine thanks,' I say as I land on my chin.

I quickly get up and try again. I jam my hook between the wooden rails on the side of the truck, reach up and sweep my good leg to stand on the tyre. I gradually manoeuvre the false leg to join it and grab the top rail. As I try to pull myself up I meet firm resistance. I quietly mutter, 'Shit my hook's stuck in the side of the truck,' and consider the first principle of climbing, which is to have three points of contact. Problem is I have only two conventional ones. I need a third point, so I stick my bruised chin in between the rails to take some body weight and lever out the hook.

As I pull myself over the top the debonair and moustached Chris says, 'Even if you don't run a step you've already impressed me.'

Roraigh vaults effortlessly on to the front of the lorry and bangs the roof. The Moroccan soldier leans out of the cab door, looks behind, checks the mirrors and accelerates towards the infinite orange horizon.

The lorry lurches over rocks. I grip the cab roof and try to jam the hook in the top rail. You can never do it when you try. Roraigh and I stand at the front of the truck, keen to see the desert. There are no plants here, just gravel and sand.

'Chris said it was just under twenty clicks to the campsite. Should take less than half an hour at this speed,' Roraigh shouts over the roar of the engine.

Eventually black and white dots on the skyline turn into a tented camp. The truck stops five hundred metres short to avoid showering everyone in sand. Nick the accountant from London says, 'We're in the black crappy tents on the left and the nice white ones on the right are for the organizers and media. Let's go and grab a tent.'

Chris, Nick and Roraigh have met before. They did the Great Sahara Run in 1995. We walk to the centre of the camp where they check over the ground to avoid stony areas and choose a dark black tent with strong rough-hewn poles.

The flat desert floor stretching all around us ends on the north-east side of the camp, where a ridge of amorphous red rocky hills extends left and right like a huge sleeping beast.

I scan the yellow-grey valley floor and see a small group of palm trees and a low rocky wall enclosing a few tiny green plants. Roraigh catches my glance and says, 'Hard to believe anybody could live out here, but somehow they do. Last year we couldn't believe how many people found us in remote places and tried to sell us carpets.'

Nick shakes a tent pole and says, 'What about this one, Roraigh?'

They poke the hessian, kick the pegs and examine the poles like doctors examining an Ebola patient before Roraigh announces, 'We think they make these Berber tents out of sugar sacks dyed black and sewn together. They just stick the poles inside, rope round them and tie off on the pegs. Simple and effective, but when the hessian gets old, if there's a strong gust of wind it can break the cloth and the tent falls down. This one's all right though.'

Nick thrusts out his groin and says, 'Okay, baby, then let's do our thing on the carpet.'

Roraigh says, 'Now there's an offer I can't refuse.'

They enter the tent, grab the corners of the carpet, roll it up and clear the stones underneath it. On the basis that I don't want to sleep or sit on jagged stones either, I join them.

We put the Moroccan carpet down again and start to unpack. We're joined by Simon the computer consultant, David the teacher (both wiry-looking runners in their thirties), Simon the student, and Steph and Leo (part of a team from Ireland running to help children in Chernobyl).

All nine of us keep our kit at the back of the tent and have a space just over a metre wide to lie out our sleeping bags.

Chris returns from a meeting with the organizers. He ducks into the tent, squats down, brushes the sand from his moustache and says, 'Race meeting for all runners at seven. Food tonight is at eight, it'll probably be boiled camel and carrot stew like we had last time, the bread's all right, but stand by for a long queue to get served. Tomorrow we get our race numbers when we've seen the doctor, handed in our ECGs and medical certificates, and had all the safety kit checked. They will feed us until Sunday night, then we have to feed ourselves until the race ends next Sunday morning.'

I look at my huge plastic bag of dehydrated spaghetti,

porridge, curry and special rehydration and nutrient drinks. Jeremy Barkworth-Edwards, another runner and ex-military man, kindly arranged my food through Taunton Leisure. It looks more than enough for a week but I decide not to take all the drinks because it'll take too long to mix them when I'm running. I've got all day tomorrow to pack and repack my rucksack. The secret is to take only essential items and make it as light as possible.

At dusk I walk around the camp with Roraigh and Nick. Two Arabs sit quietly with their camels. They smile and tell us in broken English the camels are friendly.

Roraigh says, 'These guys walk the race route. Orange posts every kilometre mark the route; it's easy to follow. They pick up the fallen runners in places where they can't get vehicles.'

I say, 'Being put on the camel and not finishing is my worst nightmare, but they are remarkable animals, they can spit, kick, bite, headbutt and break wind at the same time.'

I walk forward and gently stroke the nearest camel. He tilts his head, blinks and makes a grunting noise. His hair is thick and his bones well covered by flesh.

I arrange a camel ride for the next afternoon before walking a short distance from the camp to watch the stars emerge. The only interruption to the blue night light of the desert is the flickering of a few torches. No one speaks. We gaze at the millions of pinprick stars that are never seen where cities light the sky.

We return to the camp and I spend the evening talking to runners of all nationalities. People look astonished to see I have a false leg. It seems to take them a while to notice, even when I'm wearing shorts.

I climb into my sleeping bag and exchange initial desert observations with Leo, the bearded Irish gentleman. He's about five foot eight and built like an ox; I have no doubt he'll go the distance.

The night is warmer than I'd anticipated. I've heard stories of night temperatures near freezing.

In the morning, like most others in the tent, I rest as long as possible; it's important to conserve energy. I doze and wake with a sudden fright. A terrifying vision confronts me. Nick the large accountant appears to have gone native and is now sporting a small blue loincloth.

I spend the morning packing and repacking my kit. In the afternoon I join the queue. Our spare luggage is handed in and numbered; it will be returned in a week when we complete the two hundred and forty kilometre Marathon des Sables. All race organizers and officials are volunteers. They wear khaki sleeveless jackets with 'official' or 'medic' printed on the back in large black letters.

I walk into the shade of the open-fronted frame tent and show them the items as they call them out: 'Torch, spare batteries, food for week, sleeping bag, spare clothing, whistle, mirror, snake-bite treatment kit, first-aid kit, water bottles, map, compass and knife.'

I try to pack my kit as quickly as I can, but it's slow with one hand. I accept offers of help because I know I'm holding up the next person and people behind me are queuing in the scorching sun.

In a neighbouring tent an athletic, silver-haired fifty-something French doctor is sitting behind a folding table. He gestures to the chair. 'Please take a seat.'

I hand him the ECG and medical form showing I have no heart or breathing condition that would make it dangerous for me to undertake rigorous exercise in a hot climate. He studies the heartbeat graph and says, 'The race rules are that you also have to declare any past injuries so that if there is a problem, we are aware of it and can treat it. Do you have any past injuries that might affect you?'

I take off my leg and put it on the table next to my false arm.

He drops his pen and stares for a moment before smiling and saying, 'This is fantastic, what makes you want to do the toughest race in the world?'

I reply, 'To raise about £100,000 for a Red Cross prosthetics centre, to campaign for money to clear mines and provide assistance for the disabled, and to challenge the concept of limitation. I think that often the biggest limits in life are the ones we put on ourselves.'

He smiles again and says, 'Excellent, we'll do everything we can to help. You must come and ask us to treat your blisters and any other problems. It will be almost impossible for you to do them with one hand. Bonne chance!'

I collect my race number and drop my rucksack off at the tent before going for a short camel ride. The friendly Arab makes throat- and sinus-clearing noises at the camel to make it kneel down so I can sit on its back. The camel grunts and slowly rises and we head towards the round rock hills. It looks a long way from the camel's back to the ground. For several minutes I happily wobble around like a sack of potatoes in the camel saddle, then I pat the camel and nod towards the camp whilst making throat-clearing noises. With a bit of help from the friendly Arab who's not far away, the camel gets the message and heads for home.

All around the camp I see runners resting or packing and repacking their kit or stretching nervously.

At six-thirty the next morning I slide out of my sleeping bag. The sun is already up and it's warm; it's going to be a Sahara scorcher. Roraigh announces that we need to put all our kit outside because they're taking the tents down and if anyone is still inside they'll just take it down on top of them and fold it up. I frantically put on my false leg and running kit. The Moroccans are taking down the tent next to ours. I glance back to see Simon the student frantically chucking his belongings outside the tent.

By eight-thirty all three hundred and fifty-five of us are lined up on the start line. People are drinking water, wishing each other luck, jostling for position and adjusting their shorts. The start signal blasts, we all cheer and start to jog forward. I check my compass bearing and take a gulp of water. The first checkpoint is in eleven kilometres.

Photographers, race officials and cameramen cheer and wish us luck as we pass. In spite of my intention to start slowly I can't help running with everyone else. A helicopter zooms over us, the cameraman leaning out precariously.

I started running with Nick, but we were separated in the crowd. I suspect he and Chris decided to run behind me for a while to make sure I didn't get knocked over. Someone on my right shouts, 'Well done, Moon, you're further up the field than I thought you'd be! Don't forget to take it easy for the first day; you'll get increasingly tired during the week and that can compound injuries. Pig Pen and Jeremy are going to do a steady one today, if you want to stick with them.'

It's Seb Rich, a well-known news cameraman. He was shot in the face in Bosnia a few years ago, but made a rapid recovery. He's running with Jeremy and an ex-Guards officer nicknamed Pig Pen to raise money for a centre helping people deal with addictions. If I had more breath I'd ask him how Pig Pen got his nickname.

I can feel the stump starting to rub raw. I stop and take off a stump sock. Several runners pass and ask if I want help. I politely decline. I have to do this on my own. I check my watch. The map book says today is twenty-six kilometres over reasonable desert tracks.

As I get to the top of a hill I see runners spread out over

several kilometres. Most people are running alone or in pairs. It's hot. I'm drenched in sweat and I feel slightly sick. I force myself to drink and mutter, 'Left, right, left, right.'

The important thing is to keep putting one foot in front of the other. I try to run the downhill and flat stretches and walk all the ups and the soft sand areas.

It's difficult to grasp the time. I keep glancing at my watch to make sure I'm drinking every few minutes. I'm well into my third water bottle. On the horizon there is a shimmering heat mirage with two Land Rovers and a runners' entrance marked with white tape.

I force myself to run into the checkpoint. They take my number and punch the plastic card that's tied round my neck with string. I collect my water bottle. They write my race number on the bottle and its top. If anyone drops litter on the route they are either given a serious time penalty or disqualified.

I've lost all sensation in the stump because phantom pain has taken over, so I lean against the Land Rover and take the false leg off to see how the stump is. I put it back on again, fill my water bottles, gulp as much water as I can and throw the empty bottle in the plastic rubbish sack. With one hand I need to be careful, it would be easy to drop a bottle top. I put the leg back on, tell myself 'I'm lucky to have a false leg,' and stiffly jog on. I glance in the medical tent as I pass. There are five or six people already getting blister treatment and one or two with heatstroke.

I pour precious water into my hat to dampen the cloth covering the back of my neck and stride on telling myself, 'I'll just keep going 'til I fall over.'

I keep passing a huge American who resembles Muhammad Ali. When we reach a rocky area I stop, take out my false arm and put it on. I don't want to risk falling and landing on my arm stump. The rocky track drops into a steep boulder-strewn gorge; there are parts of it where I'll need to scramble with my hands, I've watched the runners in front doing it.

The American points at the distant red-rock hills and says, 'Man, this place is beautiful. If you want any help just let me know.'

I reply, 'Thank you, it's a very kind offer and I really appreciate it, but I'd rather have my head boiled.'

He takes off his white sun hat, fans his face and laughs, saying, 'Hey in these temperatures it's happening to me already!'

We stomp on. I fight nausea.

I manage to get through without falling over and struggle on towards the end of day one. I wipe the sweat from my eyes and can see the white start/finish gate in the distance. A large banner saying 'Marathon des Sables' is suspended between two scaffold gantries supported by steel guy ropes. I can see a group of people around the finish point. As I get closer they start to cheer the runners on. It gives me the strength to jog a little faster.

A cameraman runs towards me and says, 'This is great, amazing, we didn't think you'd make the first checkpoint. Well done!'

As I get nearer I see Seb, Jeremy, Pig Pen and the people I share a tent with. They've come to give moral support.

I cross the day-one finish line; my head is spinning. The official records my number and time. I ask how everyone else got on. They're all in. Nick offers to carry my rucksack, but I can't let him. He understands and takes it very well, calling me 'an independent git'.

We wander back to the tent. At the end of each day the runners are given a can of Coke and two bottles of water. They punch the plastic card every time you take your water. I check the knot on the nylon string round my neck is still strong.

I walk back to the tent with my mates, take off my rucksack and leg and lie on the carpet. It's bliss to be able to stop moving. After a few moments I defy the urge to go to sleep and quickly drink the warm Coca-Cola.

The next 'must' is to get some food down my neck. Roraigh returns to his corner with large cupped handfuls of dry donkey and camel dung. The rest of the tent watch incredulously. To reduce weight he isn't carrying fuel and is burning what he can find. As he prepares the fire under his mess tin he says, 'The last time I was here one of the sappers brought only the absolute minimum of food because he thought the other runners would be throwing their surplus away on days two and three. He went through the bin bags and did very well. Not a risk I'd take though, I like my scoff too much.'

He lights his fire and a pall of white smoke drifts through the tent. Chris says, 'I'd forgotten that burning donkey dung smells exactly how I imagined burning donkey dung smells.'

I sort out my sleeping bag and cook my dehydrated scoff. It's good. I mix up the dessert, which is pink powdered blancmange called Anabolagen. It contains essential nutrients, which restore the natural balance of the body after extreme exercise. I manage two spoonfuls before I start retching. I'm obviously not ready for it yet so I offer the rest of it to Nick, who says 'It's lovely' and offers some to Simon the student who has a slightly more violent reaction to it than I did.

As night falls I compare desert observations with Leo who says, 'One of the funny things about the desert is there's an awful lot of sand.'

The second morning is another mad scramble to get packed and prepared. To save time I don't use my cooker to make my porridge. I mix it with a lot of water in a plastic water bottle, drink it down and frantically pack my kit. All I'm doing is sitting down, but I can still feel myself sweating. It's a lot hotter today.

Day two is twenty-eight kilometres. The first half is over similar desert tracks to day one, but the last fifteen kilometres are on the scorching bed of a dry lake. It looks like it was thousands of years since there was water in the lake. The fine reddy-brown powder flows through every hole in my training shoe. I can feel it rubbing blisters on my taped toes. I stop, take off the training shoe, empty it out and tighten the improvised white cotton gaiter. As runners pass me I tell them how lucky I am because I only get blisters on one foot.

I start moving again and my left foot and stump scream soreness. I focus on what lies ahead. I can see several orange posts marking the route. These orange dots then disappear into a shimmering mirage on the horizon. I focus on it and keep on. I feel like I'm in a dream, in detached reality. I keep walking but the horizon doesn't get any closer. Most of the time I am alone. Sometimes I pass another runner, sometimes they pass me. I shout encouragement to them.

On my left I can see Pig Pen. I want to ask him why he's called that but conversational powers fade after 'Well done, keep it up', and I concentrate on putting one foot in front of the other.

I notice many of the other runners are starting to limp and stagger. Like me they're getting blisters from the abrasion of fine sand inside the training shoe.

I stare at the horizon, sweat stings my eyes. Finally I see shimmering white and black dots that I know must be the camp. I don't believe it was only fifteen kilometres across the lake bed, it must have been at least twenty.

All thoughts vanish as I reach the end of day two. Drinking water, eating and resting are all that matter now. I collect my Coke and two water bottles and slowly limp to find our tent.

Most people are attending to their feet. Roraigh tapes his with zinc oxide in the morning, takes it off in the afternoon when he finishes and re-tapes them the next morning. Most people leave the tape on because pulling it off is a painful business particularly when it's just raw skin underneath.

We compare notes on our adventures at various stages of the course. I'm sorry to learn that Simon the computer man was so dehydrated he had to have two drips and has been pulled from the race on medical grounds. We've already got plenty to talk about, but what's important is what's next.

I sit quietly, sort out my scoff and think. It takes me twice as long to do things with one hand, but I'm still doing my own kit. Tomorrow, twenty-four kilometres through the sand dunes is going to be tougher than anything we've done so far and the blisters are starting to sting and I'm not allowing myself to think about aches and pains; it's all mind over matter – 'You don't mind and it doesn't matter.'

If I can survive the dunes, then the eighty-kilometre day five is going to be tougher, because of the sheer distance and compounding injuries. Then there's the forty-two kilometre marathon on day six, followed by a short twenty kilometre race to finish on Sunday morning. The other factors that will make things harder are fatigue and diet. I don't feel like eating, and although I'm getting my meals down my neck I'm struggling with the high-energy drinks and the pink blancmange. I can already feel I've lost weight.

I think again. Attitude is everything. It would be easy to psyche yourself out by thinking of the total distance still left, the uncertainty of how the prosthesis will work in the sand dunes and the niggling sores and aches, but that would be incorrect and stupid. I need to break it down into stages and steps. I have to take one day at a time and then make maximum use of the rest time in the evening and night to recover.

Nick interrupts my thoughts with a general announcement: 'Tomorrow is gonna be a real toughie. The dunes! It's the one we're all dreading. Whatever you do, take it slowly. Trying to run up that soft sand is impossible. Even the Russian and the Moroccans in the lead walk up them and jog down the other side.'

'How do you know? When have you ever been near the front?' asks Roraigh quizzically.

'The race officials and the media told me, nerd brain,' replies Nick. After a brief pause he readjusts his loin cloth and sniffs his armpit before saying, 'I think desert odour syndrome has arrived.' He continues, 'By the way it would be good if we could reduce the farmyard noises at night. Simon the student tells me he can't sleep because of the coughing, scratching, belching and farting.'

'He obviously hasn't been married or he'd be used to it,' mutters a lone female voice.

The sand dunes are a kilometre or two from the camp. We know the direction we're running because they can't get vehicles into the dunes. All the water is being helicoptered into the checkpoint in the middle.

As we start day three I notice many of the runners are more subdued. I guess like me they're wondering, 'Will I survive the dunes?'

To begin with they rise gently and the sand is fairly firm, but then they become more rounded and the soft sand slips underfoot. I struggle to go up the steep sand hills and stumble down the other side. Already I can feel my training shoe is full of sand. I try different techniques up the dunes. Going diagonally left to right is easier. If I move right to left I can't extend the prosthesis.

At the top of a steep dune I pause to look around. There are endless moguls of golden sand as far as I can see in any direction. They stretch forever.

Sometimes a few small scrubby bushes cling to shady areas of the dunes. Around them I've seen a few dung beetles scurry away from piles of dried dung. I passed the skeleton of a camel earlier. I wonder if they roam wild? How can anything survive here?

I check my compass bearing again as I see the footprints in the sand separate into different paths around a tall dune. I drink with no thirst, just sustained nausea. I have to keep drinking. I must reach the checkpoint soon.

Several runners pass me and I pass a few others. Most people are moving at their own pace, with little spare breath for conversation. The helicopters soar overhead. They're flying the route to make sure nobody drops with heat exhaustion or gets too lost.

Eventually I reach the checkpoint. I get my race card stamped and grab my water. I need to sort myself out. I sit down at the base of the nearest dune. I know I'm getting dehydrated. The whole of the ball of my left foot is becoming a hot spot. It'll start to blister soon, if it hasn't already. I need to tape it.

'How are you? It's amazing you've got this far. You're surprising a lot of people,' says a voice from the direction of the checkpoint.

I look up to see the French doctor.

'I'm doing fine thanks. I can't believe how beautiful it is out here. Even though there are three hundred and sixty runners, most of the time I'm alone in this amazing place,' I reply.

'I like the desert too. You know, there is a saying: "God made the desert so that man could find his soul."'

He pauses and glances at my left foot. 'What's the trouble?'

'Hot spot on the whole of the ball of the foot. I think I should tape it before it blisters. What do you think?'

He says, 'That's one of the most sensible things I've heard. Prevention is always better than cure.'

He opens his bag and produces a thick sticky tape that he expertly attaches to the ball of my foot. A few minutes later I'm back in the dunes feeling better.

I decide to follow my compass rather than the footprints. *Always trust the compass.* I check I'm still on the right bearing. I plod on as if on an endless treadmill. 'Left, right, left, right.'

Hours fade past. I can see a few more spiky bushes now and up ahead a few trees dot the dunes. The trees become more frequent and I can hear a donkey. I pass a small nomad camp. How can they survive here?

Up ahead I can hear a Land Rover engine. I check my bearing again. In the distance I can make out Matthew Benns the journalist and Nigel and Naurelle the photographers. They're a welcome sight – it can't be that far. As I pass them I shout, 'How far?'

'About five kilometres.'

I think, Shit, that's a long way, and stumble on. It's a lot hotter than it was yesterday.

The five K feels more like ten K and seems to be taking hours.

I smile and nod to a group of four or five Japanese runners. They don't speak any English and the only thing I can do to cheer them up is to point in the direction of the camp and say 'Coca-Cola.'

My heart leaps with excitement as I emerge from a group of trees to see the finish gate and camp. Matthew and the photographers shout encouragement as they pass in the Land Rover.

I summon all my strength and try to jog towards the finish. It ends up as a fast limp, but I still keep trying. I can see a figure in blue running towards me. It's Roraigh.

He soon reaches me and says, 'Well done. I thought you might like to borrow my flag.'

He fixes the Union Jack to my rucksack and says, 'Do you mind if I take a photo?'

We jog together and enjoy some politically incorrect military banter, which gives me the oomph to limp at maximum speed and beat the five runners behind me. My fellow runners give me great support. I later try to repay it by shouting congratulations and encouragement to the few finishing behind me. As Roraigh says, 'The longer you're out in the sun, the longer you suffer.'

Although it's not sensible, because I should be resting, I have to go and ring Ali. I retrieve my credit card from a deep corner of my rucksack and join the long queue for the satellite phone tent. Although I'm only away for a short time I miss her and want to give her an update on the run and see how she is.

The sense of relief at surviving the dunes is short-lived. All thoughts are now focused on tomorrow's eighty-kilometre double marathon.

On the way back to the tent I meet the *National Geographic* reporter who's running the event to give a first-hand report. He's limping back from the medical tent with bags covering his blistered feet. He recognizes me and says in an outraged tone, 'You'll never guess what? The bad news is that the medics have said I'm actually fit enough to go on and try the eighty kilometres tomorrow.'

The day starts with hot sun and gets hotter. To the runners' astonishment the first six kilometres are over sand dunes. I steadily plug away, aware that I'll need to keep going all day and all night. I drink constantly. My aim is to get there before day break, but I'm not telling anybody. I know the rucksack should be getting lighter because I've eaten half my food, but it doesn't feel any lighter.

When I get to the first checkpoint I see a line of casualties sitting under the awning of the medical tent. A Japanese girl screams and cries as they treat her blisters. I take my water and plod on, surprised to hear that several runners were psyched out by having to go through sand dunes and jacked at the first checkpoint.

Once you've walked on your blisters for the first half hour they don't hurt as much. I constantly need to stop and adjust the false leg, and the stump's a bit sore, but I have to keep on. When I feel like lying down in the sand and sleeping I remember people I've seen in places like Cambodia who need false limbs. I know from personal experience that it's a bummer when you have to crawl everywhere. I hope I manage to raise a reasonable amount for the Red Cross limb centre.

In the early afternoon I reach a checkpoint beside two solar-powered boreholes. The race organizers paid to have them fitted for the local nomads. I stop and adjust my leg and force down a high-energy bar. Each small mouthful feels like I'm chewing a bale of hay. I decide that fast walking is more pleasant than trying to eat, which means I'm in a bad way and need to be careful. The ground is soft sandy gravel with occasional rocky outcrops.

I step onwards in a time warp. I'm really tired now. I glance behind and see a team of long-legged French Foreign Legionnaires yomping along. They are singing loud, droning French marching songs. The three in front are marching fast like machines. They nod as they pass me. Shortly afterwards another lean and mean Legionnaire with short cropped hair comes alongside, points at the other three and says with a nasal French accent, 'Oh zese bloody Franche! Why is it zey neveer stop singing? I 'ave to listen to zem all zee way across zee bloody desert!'

I try to keep up with them, but can't. Later, as darkness falls, I realize I've spent the last few hours alone. The directions for this stage of the race are to follow the track and the lumo sticks they tie to the trees every few hundred metres. I get my torch out and fit the band over my head. I need my hand free to keep drinking. I don't want to switch the torch on and ruin my night vision, but I need it ready just in case. I break my lumo stick and tie it to the back of my rucksack as the race rules require. I'm surprised it gives enough light to see my feet.

An hour later with a huge sigh of relief I see the first lumo stick marking the route. I'm on the right road. My guts are full of wind, so I breathe deeply and try to expel it. It passes in a continual flow.

I turn a corner and am surprised to see a group of French runners sitting down drinking. I immediately restrain from breaking wind. I'll pass them and then I'll be all right. As I reach them I see it's a group of four, one of them is a woman. To make matters worse they get up and join me.

The next twenty minutes are agony. Just when I thought it couldn't possibly get worse it has. I feel like my insides are going to explode. The woman is right in front of me. Suddenly she stops in the middle of the track lifts her hand and says, 'Attendez.'

I pause and in the blue desert night light we watch her lift her left leg off the ground and let rip with a long, loud fart.

The other three applaud and shout, 'Bravo,' 'Magnifique,' 'Excellent.'

With much relief I break wind and shout the same thing hoping they think she's done another.

We march at the same speed 'til nine-thirty when we reach the third checkpoint. They stop for a sleep and I stop to force myself to rehydrate. I don't ever remember being this tired.

I slowly stomp on in a soporific haze. I keep checking my compass and drinking. The track is getting sandier.

'Left, right, left,' I mutter and stomp.

Just after midnight, when I've been through the last checkpoint, I see two familiar figures ahead. It's Steph and Leo. I catch them up and we march on together. In the far distance in line with the bearing I can see the glow of an electric light. That must be the camp. There's only going to be one light out here.

Hours pass and we step out, but it doesn't seem to get any closer. I rub my eyes and try to work out if the few green lumo sticks I can see glowing in distance are heading towards the light. They're all over the place.

My heart sinks as I reach a huge sand dune. All I can do is keep following the compass bearing. After a few hours I begin to wonder how much further.

I stumble on in an endless dream. The light never gets any closer. 'Left, right, left. Failure is not an option,' I mutter.

The sand dunes are getting steeper and there are no footprints. Leo thinks the wind covered them with sand. He and Steph have started to crawl up the steep ones. Unfortunately I can't because I only have one hand and it fills my false leg with sand. I use my back and hips and think, 'The great thing is to keep on keeping on. We can all go one step beyond our limits.'

Another runner behind me shouts, 'There must be an easier way without going up all the dunes.'

I check my compass and say, 'You'd get lost for a long time trying to contour through the dunes. The only thing is to keep right on the bearing. What do you think, Leo?'

'I'm with you on that one. Not far now,' says the stocky Irishman as he grunts up another dune.

'The dunes will be over soon,' I say confidently, but with nothing to prove it except my belief that my senses are not lying to me and reason and mathematics tell me even allowing for errors I have travelled nearly ninety kilometres and we have to reach the finish point soon. I think they've measured the distance using Global Positioning System and that it's eighty nautical kilometres. On the ground, allowing for ups and downs, it's nearer ninety.

We struggle over two more dunes. Suddenly a bright white light blinds me. My heart leaps. It must be a camera. I slide down the loose sand. I recognize the Italian cameraman.

We run down the last dune and jog with all the strength we can muster towards the finish. It's a race now.

As I cross the line the race official lets off a flare and a red rocket whooshes to the sky and explodes in a pink starburst. 'Well done, faster than everyone thought.'

Behind me there is a loud 'whoop' of delight that could wake the dead as a runner takes off his rucksack and throws it in the air as he crosses the finish line.

It's just before dawn and the first grey light of day is beginning to emerge. I get my water and find our tent. I drink my Coke and know I should sleep but I can't. I have to find out how everyone else got on. Who's here and who's still out there?

Twelve hours later the last runners come in. The only thing on everyone's mind is tomorrow's marathon.

My stomach feels bad and as we start the race I know I'll have to stop a few times. I waste a lot of time and then have to keep stopping to adjust the leg while everyone steams past me.

I have no reason to hold back. I moved up the field a lot yesterday, now I have to try to improve it. I force myself to jog and drink. I know I'll be doing a slow marathon; most people add an hour or more to their times according to Roraigh.

Once I've sorted my leg and stomach out, I start to move up the field. I keep looking at the ground and putting one foot in front of the other. Eventually I catch up with Nick and Seb. They cheer me on and give great encouragement, but I can't keep up. I start to fall behind. I'm dizzy and feel sick. Jeremy is still by my side. After serious sickness on the third day he pulled through and has been going a storm. He keeps asking me if I'm all right. I think it's because I'm stumbling a lot, but I have to keep running.

'Where's Pig Pen?' I ask.

'Not far away,' he says.

A bout of nausea stops me asking how he got his nickname.

My head is spinning and it's getting harder to go in a straight line. I'm not sure which way I should be going. I have to follow the tyre tracks, but there are so many of them.

I'm worried I'm holding Jeremy up, but he says I'm not.

I can see the finish now. I'm surprised we got here so quickly.

My marathon time is around six hours. Just the twenty kilometres now and that's it.

We limp back to our tents.

Later on a party atmosphere envelops the camp. Tomorrow it's the last twenty kilometres. A Spanish runner expresses his delight by borrowing a donkey from a local and riding it around the camp singing 'Arriva Espania'.

I spend the evening talking to Lawrence Williams, another major in the Royal Engineers. Lawrence has done quite well. He's in twentieth place, which is reasonable considering the top thirty or forty runners are all professional.

We're on the edge of the desert and children from the local village stand around the edge of the camp in small groups. The race organizers have said we should put valuable items in the middle of the tent just in case mischievous children try to steal things. I decide to play it safe and stow my leg in the middle next to Nick. I'd rather lose my credit card and passport than my false leg.

For the last time Simon the student endures the farmyard noises of our slumbering tent.

I wake up with a start. My head aches. Unless I'm much mistaken I've been hit on the head by a wooden pole. I try to sit up, but I'm restrained. A gale howls around me.

From the corner of the tent Roraigh says, 'That's bad luck, the tent's just blown down.'

'Well spotted,' says Nick the Greek.

I offer to help put the tent back up, but Nick refuses to pass me my leg.

After a few minutes Roraigh, Leo and Nick successfully re-pitch the tent while Simon the student makes farmyard noises.

The next morning it's cold. Food is short and we just want to get running. I've moved up the field in the last two days, I might even advance a few more places on the last day.

There is a huge cheer as we begin running. I've decided to run with Chris and Nick to start with and let them go ahead when I slow them down.

We run through irrigated green fields and villages with cement houses and date palms. I stare at the trees and vivid green vegetation. As we pass a large stone house I see Jeremy and Pig Pen stopped in the road smiling. 'Listen, it's running water.'

I have to stop and listen to the trickle of the fresh water.

I lose the urge to move up the field. That's not what this event has taught me.

I have been dreaming of completing the Sahara Marathon for two years. Huw and Martin gave me constant encouragement. When I told people I was going to do it some of them laughed and a few said, 'You'll look stupid when you fail.'

What they didn't understand was that for me failure was never an option and the only real failure is not trying.

Putting one foot in front of the other has been tough, but I've had a good reason to do it. This hasn't been about me; it's about something more important and that is raising money for a Red Cross centre providing false limbs for the poor in Vietnam. My target is £100,000. It's also about pushing forward the bounds of prosthetics and challenging the concept of limitation, because often the biggest limits in life are the ones we put on ourselves.

As we run through the oasis into the small town we turn a corner and the finish line comes into view. It's packed with people.

Pain vanishes and Jeremy and the others tell me to run ahead, but I can't, that's not what this is about.

'No chance. Let's link arms and finish together.'

We link arms and Leo says, 'Come on, Pig Pen, get next to me with your Union Jack. Let's have the Irish flag and the British next to each other. It'll show that we've no problems getting on. It's a shame a few others can't learn to get along together.'

As we cross the line I turn to Pig Pen and say, 'Why is it they call you that?'

I'm interrupted by a French journalist who shoves a microphone under my nose and says, 'What did you learn on zis great marathon?'

I reply, 'That we can all go one step beyond our limits and the truth about human relationships is that they should be about interdependence.'